Modernizing Public Administration With New Digital Advancements

Elvettin Akman
Suleyman Demirel University, Turkey

Çiğdem Akman
https://orcid.org/0000-0002-1936-6884
Suleyman Demirel University, Turkey

IGI Global
Scientific Publishing
Publishing Tomorrow's Research Today

Vice President of Editorial Melissa Wagner
Director of Acquisitions Mikaela Felty
Director of Book Development Jocelynn Hessler
Production Manager Mike Brehm
Cover Design Jose Rosado

Published in the United States of America by
IGI Global Scientific Publishing
701 East Chocolate Avenue
Hershey, PA, 17033, USA
Tel: 717-533-8845 | Fax: 717-533-7115
Website: https://www.igi-global.com E-mail: cust@igi-global.com

Library of Congress Cataloging-in-Publication Data

Names: Akman, Elvettin, 1985- editor | Akman, Çiğdem editor
Title: Modernizing public administration with new digital advancements / edited by Elvettin Akman, Çigdem Akman.
Description: Hershey, PA : IGI Global Scientific Publishing, [2026] | Includes bibliographical references and index. | Summary: "This book aims to put forth different best practices of various countries in public administration and technology applications/ digital developments"-- Provided by publisher.
Identifiers: LCCN 2025018910 (print) | LCCN 2025018911 (ebook) | ISBN 9798337314846 h/c | ISBN 9798337314853 s/c | ISBN 9798337314860 ebook
Subjects: LCSH: Public administration--Technological innovations | Public administration--Data processing--Management
Classification: LCC JF1525.A8 M64 2025 (print) | LCC JF1525.A8 (ebook) | DDC 351.0285--dc23/eng/20250708
LC record available at https://lccn.loc.gov/2025018910
LC ebook record available at https://lccn.loc.gov/2025018911
British Cataloguing in Publication Data
A Cataloguing in Publication record for this book is available from the British Library.

Table of Contents

Preface xi

Chapter 1
Digital Public Administration Research, Bibliometric Trends, and Future Directions 1
Beyza Güdek, Karadeniz Technical University, Turkey
Mustafa Kocaoğlu, Necmettin Erbakan University, Turkey

Chapter 2
The Impact of Digital Technologies on Public Administration: Opportunities and Challenges 35
Veysel Eren, Hatay Mustafa Kemal University, Turkey
Hasret Duman, Hatay Mustafa Kemal University, Turkey

Chapter 3
From e-Government to Digital Government: A New Era in Public Administration 65
Andi Asrifan, Universitas Negeri Makassar, Indonesia
Rismawati Rismawati, Universitas Muhammadiyah Palopo, Indonesia

Chapter 4
Examining Open Government Data in Public Administration: Past, Present, and Future 93
Ali Roziqin, Universitas Muhammadiyah Malang, Indonesia
Ahmad Luthfi, Universitas Merdeka Malang, Indonesia
M. Husni Tamrin, Universitas Hang Tuah, Indonesia
Tangguh Okta Wibowo, Universitas Multimedia Nusantara, Indonesia
Azaria E. Pradana, Universitas Diponegoro, Indonesia
M. Ihwan Salsabila, Universitas Muhammadiyah Malang, Indonesia

Chapter 5
Promoting Public Value Creation Through the Use of Digital Technologies ... 123
Yakup Karaca, Aydin Adnan Menderes University, Turkey
Namık Kemal Öztürk, Mugla Sıtkı Koçman University, Turkey

Chapter 6
AI in Public Administration: Transforming Governance and Public Services .. 153
Mustafa Kayyali, Maaref University of Applied Sciences, Syria

Chapter 7
Artificial Intelligence-Induced Algorithmic Bias in Public Services: A Framework for Fair and Transparent Governance 181
Gamze Sinem Özer, Akdeniz Üniversitesi, Turkey

Chapter 8
AI-Based Chatbots in Public Service Delivery: The Case of BAGBI in Türkiye 207
Sebiha Düz, Süleyman Demirel University, Turkey

Chapter 9
Artificial Intelligence (AI) Policies in Public Administration: The Case of Estonia 235
Aysun Öcal, Aksaray University, Turkey
Mustafa Zihni Tunca, Suleyman Demirel University, Turkey

Chapter 10
Organizational Dynamics of AI Integration in Italian Public Administration: A Case Study of INPS 269
Davide de Gennaro, University "Parthenope" of Naples, Italy
Ludovica Del Barone, University of Salento, Italy
Filomena Buonocore, University "Parthenope" of Naples, Italy

Chapter 11
The Artificial Intelligence Policy of Italy 301
Çiğdem Pank Yildirim, Muğla Sıtkı Koçman University, Turkey

Compilation of References 329

About the Contributors 385

Index 393

Detailed Table of Contents

Preface xi

Chapter 1
Digital Public Administration Research, Bibliometric Trends, and Future Directions 1
Beyza Güdek, Karadeniz Technical University, Turkey
Mustafa Kocaoğlu, Necmettin Erbakan University, Turkey

The rapid development of digital technologies offers significant opportunities for modernization and increased efficiency in public administration. Tools such as artificial intelligence, big data, blockchain, the internet of things, and cloud computing support decision-making processes and increase service quality while encouraging citizen participation. This study examines how the issues of digitalization and digital transformation in public administration are addressed in academic literature using the bibliometric method. The findings show that publications in this field have increased rapidly, especially in the last five years, and concepts such as "e-government," "digital transformation," and "artificial intelligence" have come to the fore. It is emphasized that digital transformation includes not only technological but also ethical, administrative, and citizen-oriented dimensions; the study provides a guiding framework for future research and policy development.

Chapter 2
The Impact of Digital Technologies on Public Administration: Opportunities and Challenges 35
Veysel Eren, Hatay Mustafa Kemal University, Turkey
Hasret Duman, Hatay Mustafa Kemal University, Turkey

This study aims to comprehensively examine the impact of digital technologies on public administration. The process of digital transformation has led to profound changes in various areas, from the delivery of public services to decision-making mechanisms. Framed around the concepts of e-government and digital government, this transformation strengthens governance principles such as transparency, accountability, efficiency, and citizen participation. However, along with these opportunities, digitalization also presents new risks such as data security, digital inequality, and ethical concerns. By evaluating the integration of next-generation technologies (artificial intelligence, big data, blockchain, Internet of Things) into public services, the study offers a comparative analysis of the benefits and challenges of digital transformation.

Chapter 3
From e-Government to Digital Government: A New Era in Public Administration 65
Andi Asrifan, Universitas Negeri Makassar, Indonesia
Rismawati Rismawati, Universitas Muhammadiyah Palopo, Indonesia

This chapter explores the transformation from e-Government to digital government, highlighting the shift from service digitization to systemic innovation in public administration. Drawing on international best practices and theoretical frameworks, the text examines the integration of artificial intelligence, blockchain, cloud computing, and citizen-centric design in reshaping governance. The discussion encompasses the ethical and operational implications of algorithmic bias, data privacy, and the digital divide, while presenting policy innovations and adaptive strategies to ensure future-ready governance. Emphasizing inclusion, transparency, and responsiveness, the chapter presents digital government not as a mere technological evolution, but as a strategic reimagining of statecraft in the 21st century. The narrative concludes with future-oriented reflections on policy design, participatory frameworks, and institutional agility that align digital transformation with the creation of sustainable public value.

Chapter 4
Examining Open Government Data in Public Administration: Past, Present, and Future 93
Ali Roziqin, Universitas Muhammadiyah Malang, Indonesia
Ahmad Luthfi, Universitas Merdeka Malang, Indonesia
M. Husni Tamrin, Universitas Hang Tuah, Indonesia
Tangguh Okta Wibowo, Universitas Multimedia Nusantara, Indonesia
Azaria E. Pradana, Universitas Diponegoro, Indonesia
M. Ihwan Salsabila, Universitas Muhammadiyah Malang, Indonesia

Open Government Data (OGD) has an enormous chance to improve public administration by increasing openness, accountability, and citizen involvement. This study explores the evolution of OGD research in the field of Public Administration. This research employed a bibliometric analysis approach which conducted using VOS Viewer and Biblioshiny R Package based on the Scopus database. This study found that the themes that emerged in OGD in the context of public administration included information management, interoperability, Link Open Data (LOD), big data, transparency, and data portals. In addition, the trending topics and word frequencies show that more literature focuses on information management and government data processing, rather than integration and interoperability. Therefore, future research is needed to examine the integration and interoperability of OGD practices in promoting more accessible data governance.

Chapter 5
Promoting Public Value Creation Through the Use of Digital Technologies ... 123
Yakup Karaca, Aydin Adnan Menderes University, Turkey
Namık Kemal Öztürk, Mugla Sıtkı Koçman University, Turkey

Today, digital technologies are not only transforming the delivery of public services but also reshaping how public value is defined and produced. This study examines the strategic use of technologies such as artificial intelligence, big data, machine learning and the internet of things in the public sector to strengthen public value through transparency, accountability, citizen satisfaction and social justice. The study covers four key dimensions: the relationship between digital governance and public value, case studies from developed and developing countries, ethical and institutional challenges posed by digitalization, and strategic policy recommendations. Through a comparative analysis of Estonia, Singapore, the United States, and Turkey, a multidimensional framework of digital transformation is presented and strategic directions that are particularly applicable to developing countries are suggested.

Chapter 6
AI in Public Administration: Transforming Governance and Public Services .. 153
Mustafa Kayyali, Maaref University of Applied Sciences, Syria

Artificial Intelligence is no longer the distant future of public administration—it is the pressing present. This chapter examines how AI is reshaping the machinery of governance, offering unprecedented opportunities for smarter service delivery, predictive policymaking, and real-time responsiveness. It investigates both the technical and human dimensions of this transformation, exploring how automation, data analytics, and machine learning are redefining the roles of public servants, the expectations of citizens, and the core principles of transparency and accountability. At the same time, the chapter does not romanticize technological change. It critically addresses the challenges posed by AI systems—algorithmic opacity, systemic bias, privacy concerns, and the ethical dilemmas inherent in delegating public decisions to machines. Ultimately, this chapter offers a nuanced portrait of AI's role in public administration—not as a neutral tool, but as a transformative force that demands foresight, vigilance, and deep ethical grounding.

Chapter 7
Artificial Intelligence-Induced Algorithmic Bias in Public Services: A Framework for Fair and Transparent Governance 181
Gamze Sinem Özer, Akdeniz Üniversitesi, Turkey

With the rapid advancement of technology, AI-supported chatbots are increasingly used in public administration to enhance efficiency, provide 24/7 service, reduce costs, and streamline bureaucratic processes. However, these systems may suffer from algorithmic bias—systematic errors in AI models that result in unfair or discriminatory outcomes for certain groups, often due to biased training data or design flaws. Such biases challenge the presumed neutrality of AI and risk reinforcing existing social inequalities, raising ethical and governance concerns. This study examines algorithmic bias in the context of public administration, aiming to explore its sources, impacts on public services, and implications for social justice. By reviewing academic literature, the research proposes a conceptual framework to support the development of more transparent, accountable, and fair AI systems in the public sector.

Chapter 8
AI-Based Chatbots in Public Service Delivery: The Case of BAGBI in Türkiye 207
Sebiha Düz, Süleyman Demirel University, Turkey

This study examines the chatbot application named BAGBI of Bağcılar Municipality, which is an important example of artificial intelligence-supported service delivery in local governments in Türkiye. The role played by chatbot technologies in the digital transformation process of public services is discussed in the contexts of public value production, accessibility, participatory governance and data-based decision-making. In-depth interview technique, which is one of the qualitative research methods, was used in the study; interviews were conducted with experts from the IT Department who took a crucial part in the design and implementation processes of BAGBI. The interview data were analyzed with thematic analysis method, and findings were obtained especially in the project's design process, service quality, institutional capacity, citizen interaction and ethical dimensions. The obtained data reveal that BAGBI is not only a technical innovation, but also a transformation tool that reshapes the administrative and conceptual boundaries of digitalized public services at the local level.

Chapter 9
Artificial Intelligence (AI) Policies in Public Administration: The Case of Estonia 235
Aysun Öcal, Aksaray University, Turkey
Mustafa Zihni Tunca, Suleyman Demirel University, Turkey

As a pioneer in digital governance, Estonia exemplifies how AI can revolutionize public service delivery, with 99% of services accessible online, including AI-driven platforms like the federated virtual assistant network Bürokratt. Estonia's success stems from its phased infrastructure development, multi-stakeholder collaboration, and regulatory frameworks that balance efficiency with fundamental rights. However, challenges such as algorithmic bias risks, legacy system integration, and bureaucratic resistance persist. The study provides a conceptual framework for understanding Estonia's milestones while offering actionable recommendations for policymakers.

By analyzing Estonia's model, this research highlights transferable lessons for nations pursuing digital sovereignty, particularly in harmonizing AI innovation with democratic values. Future research should explore longitudinal societal impacts and comparative governance models, especially in the context of the EU's evolving AI policies.

Chapter 10
Organizational Dynamics of AI Integration in Italian Public Administration: A Case Study of INPS 269
Davide de Gennaro, University "Parthenope" of Naples, Italy
Ludovica Del Barone, University of Salento, Italy
Filomena Buonocore, University "Parthenope" of Naples, Italy

The integration of Artificial Intelligence (AI) in public administration is reshaping governance, improving efficiency, and transforming service delivery. This chapter examines the case of Italy's National Institute for Social Security (INPS), which has adopted AI to enhance administrative processes, fraud detection, and citizen engagement. While AI implementation presents significant opportunities—such as increased efficiency, predictive analytics, and data-driven decision-making—it also poses organizational challenges related to bureaucratic inertia, workforce adaptation, regulatory compliance, and ethical concerns. By analysing the INPS case, this study highlights the organizational barriers to AI adoption, the need for digital upskilling, the importance of transparent governance, and the broader benefits AI can bring to public administration. The findings contribute to the broader discourse on digital transformation in the public sector, emphasizing the balance between technological innovation and institutional constraints.

Chapter 11
The Artificial Intelligence Policy of Italy 301
Çiğdem Pank Yildirim, Muğla Sıtkı Koçman University, Turkey

Artificial intelligence is known as systems that imitate human intelligence in order to perform certain tasks and can improve themselves by renewing the information they obtain. The ability to imitate human intelligence distinguishes artificial intelligence from today's technologies. Increasing the economic volumes of countries has made artificial intelligence a strategic value in international competition. Italy is also among the countries that see dealing with artificial intelligence as a strategic need, as it is among the countries that want to show their claim in technology. The aim of the study is to reveal the change that Italy's artificial intelligence policies have created on Italy and to evaluate its impact. In line with this purpose, the study examines the regulations regarding the use of artificial intelligence systems in Italy and evaluates the artificial intelligence strategy developed by Italy in the processes of creating public policy and providing public services. The document analysis method is used in the study.

Compilation of References 329

About the Contributors 385

Index 393

Preface

Modernizing Public Administration With New Digital Advancements brings together cutting-edge scholarship on how emerging technologies are redefining the principles, structures, and practices of governance in the 21st century. As the pace of technological innovation accelerates, public administration systems worldwide face a critical imperative: to modernize in ways that enhance efficiency and transparency while upholding democratic values, social equity, and ethical responsibility.

This edited volume explores the multifaceted dimensions of digital transformation in public administration through theoretical, empirical, and comparative perspectives. By examining artificial intelligence, big data, open government data, algorithmic governance, and citizen-centric digital services across diverse national and institutional contexts—including Türkiye, Indonesia, Estonia, Italy, and more—this book offers a panoramic understanding of the promises and complexities shaping the future of public governance.

Collectively, the chapters highlight a shared message: digital transformation is not only a technological upgrade; it is an administrative, ethical, institutional, and societal evolution. Through this comprehensive compilation, we aim to provide researchers, practitioners, and policymakers with conceptual tools, case-based insights, and strategic pathways for navigating the ongoing digital revolution in public administration.

CHAPTER OVERVIEW

Chapter 1 – Digital Public Administration Research, Bibliometric Trends and Future Directions

Güdek and Kocaoğlu map the academic evolution of digital public administration through a bibliometric analysis of global literature. Their findings show a rapid rise in scholarship on digital transformation, especially in the last five years, with major themes including e-government, AI, and data-driven governance. The chapter emphasizes the need to view digital transformation as both a technological and socio-ethical process and establishes an agenda for future research and policy development.

Chapter 2 – The Impact of Digital Technologies on Public Administration: Opportunities and Challenges

Duman and Eren explore how next-generation technologies such as AI, IoT, big data, and blockchain reshape public administration by enhancing efficiency, transparency, accountability, and participation. The chapter also highlights the challenges that accompany digitalization, including cyber risks, ethical concerns, and widening digital inequalities, offering a balanced assessment of both its transformative potential and inherent risks.

Chapter 3 – From e-Government to Digital Government: A New Era in Public Administration

Asrifan and Rismawati examine the shift from traditional e-government systems to holistic digital government ecosystems. They analyze international best practices and advanced technological integrations while addressing critical issues such as algorithmic bias, privacy, and inclusivity. The chapter positions digital government as a strategic reimagining of governance centered on sustainability, participation, and adaptability.

Chapter 4 – Examining Open Government Data in Public Administration: Past, Present and Future

Roziqin and co-authors provide a bibliometric review of Open Government Data (OGD) research, identifying key themes like interoperability, linked open data, transparency, and information management. Their findings reveal a growing emphasis on data processing rather than integration. The chapter calls for future research that deepens understanding of interoperability challenges and enhances accessible, integrated data governance frameworks.

Chapter 5 – Promoting Public Value Creation Through the Use of Digital Technologies

Karaca and Öztürk investigate how digital technologies can strengthen public value by improving transparency, accountability, satisfaction, and social justice.

Through comparative case studies from Estonia, Singapore, the U.S., and Turkey, the chapter develops a multidimensional framework for digital public value creation and offers strategic guidance for developing countries seeking to implement meaningful digital reforms.

Chapter 6 – AI in Public Administration: Transforming Governance and Public Services

Kayyali explores AI's transformative influence on governance, focusing on automation, predictive analytics, and real-time decision-making. The chapter discusses the evolving roles of public servants and the shifting expectations of citizens while addressing ethical concerns such as algorithmic opacity and bias. It presents AI as a powerful but non-neutral force that requires responsible, ethically grounded governance.

Chapter 7 – Artificial Intelligence-Induced Algorithmic Bias in Public Services: A Framework for Fair and Transparent Governance

Özer examines the sources and impacts of algorithmic bias in AI-powered public services, particularly in systems like chatbots. She critiques the assumption of algorithmic neutrality and highlights how biased models can exacerbate social inequalities. The chapter proposes a conceptual framework for building transparent, fair, and accountable AI systems that safeguard justice and equity within public administration.

Chapter 8 – AI-Based Chatbots in Public Service Delivery: The Case of BAGBI in Türkiye

Düz offers an in-depth case study of BAGBI, a municipal AI chatbot in Türkiye. Through expert interviews and thematic analysis, the chapter explores BAGBI's role in local digital transformation, focusing on accessibility, public value, citizen engagement, service quality, and ethical concerns. The findings illustrate how chatbots can reshape not only administrative procedures but also the conceptual boundaries of local governance.

Chapter 9 – Artificial Intelligence (AI) Policies in Public Administration: The Case of Estonia

Öcal and Tunca analyze Estonia's globally recognized digital leadership and its strategic AI-driven public administration model. Highlighting key platforms such as Bürokratt, the chapter explores how Estonia balances innovation with fundamental rights. It also outlines challenges such as algorithmic risks, legacy systems, and bureaucratic resistance while offering policy recommendations relevant to countries pursuing digital sovereignty.

Chapter 10 – Organizational Dynamics of AI Integration in Italian Public Administration: A Case Study of INPS

De Gennaro, Del Barone, and Buonocore examine AI integration within Italy's National Institute for Social Security (INPS). Their analysis reveals both the benefits—fraud detection, streamlined processes, data-driven services—and the organizational barriers to AI adoption, including resistance to change and skill gaps. The chapter emphasizes the need for workforce development, ethical oversight, and transparent governance to ensure successful AI integration.

Chapter 11 – The Artificial Intelligence Policy of Italy

Pank Yıldırım analyzes Italy's national strategy for artificial intelligence, focusing on its regulatory frameworks, policy design processes, and public sector applications. The chapter underscores AI's strategic importance for international competitiveness and explores how Italy seeks to balance innovation with legal, ethical, and institutional considerations. Through document analysis, it evaluates the impact of Italy's AI policies on governance and public service delivery.

Together, these chapters provide a comprehensive, forward-looking examination of how digital technologies are reshaping the foundations of public administration. This volume not only maps current advancements but also offers critical insights and future directions for building ethical, inclusive, and efficient digital governance systems worldwide.

Chapter 1

Digital Public Administration Research, Bibliometric Trends, and Future Directions

Beyza Güdek
https://orcid.org/0000-0002-7432-9234
Karadeniz Technical University, Turkey

Mustafa Kocaoğlu
https://orcid.org/0000-0002-9341-6341
Necmettin Erbakan University, Turkey

ABSTRACT

The rapid development of digital technologies offers significant opportunities for modernization and increased efficiency in public administration. Tools such as artificial intelligence, big data, blockchain, the internet of things, and cloud computing support decision-making processes and increase service quality while encouraging citizen participation. This study examines how the issues of digitalization and digital transformation in public administration are addressed in academic literature using the bibliometric method. The findings show that publications in this field have increased rapidly, especially in the last five years, and concepts such as "e-government," "digital transformation," and "artificial intelligence" have come to the fore. It is emphasized that digital transformation includes not only technological but also ethical, administrative, and citizen-oriented dimensions; the study provides a guiding framework for future research and policy development.

DOI: 10.4018/979-8-3373-1484-6.ch001

1. INTRODUCTION

The rapid and widespread development of digital technologies has brought about not only operational but also structural and paradigmatic transformations in public administration systems. Innovative technologies such as artificial intelligence (AI), big data analytics, blockchain, cloud computing and the internet of things (IoT) have triggered radical changes in many areas, from the delivery methods of public services to decision-making processes, from forms of interaction with citizens to governance models (Datta et al., 2020; Rohoza, 2024). This process not only increases the efficiency of public services but also transforms their administrative innovation, institutional learning, and policy-making capacities (Casalino et al., 2017; Mergel, 2019).

Digital transformation in public administration is considered not only as a technological modernization, but also as a strategic, institutional, and cultural restructuring. In this context, it is aimed to strengthen basic governance principles such as transparency, accountability, citizen participation, data-based decision-making, and open government practices (Bonomi Savignon et al., 2024; Galetta, 2018) (Chatfield & Reddick, 2018). In addition, the digital transformation process redefines policy-making processes by enabling public policies to be developed in a more flexible, faster, and data-based manner (Desouza & Jacob, 2017; Di Giulio & Vecchi, 2023).

This study aims to analyze the phenomenon of digital transformation in public administration in a multidimensional manner in the light of academic literature. In this context, scientific production on digital public administration will be systematically mapped using the bibliometric analysis method, and prominent themes, leading researchers, collaborations, and methodological approaches will be evaluated. In addition, it is aimed to establish a strategic framework that can guide future research by identifying gaps in the literature. In this way, it will be revealed more comprehensively how digital transformation is institutionalized in public administration, in which areas it is effective, and what kind of managerial vision it creates.

To anchor the analysis conceptually, we frame the chapter with two complementary lenses: Digital Era Governance (DEG) and Public Value Theory (PVT). DEG highlights the shift from siloed e-government projects to integrated, platform-based, and networked governance, emphasizing interoperability, data sharing, and co-production across organizations. PVT, in turn, reorients success criteria from process efficiency alone to the creation of public value trust, accountability, inclusiveness, and citizen-centred outcomes. These perspectives provide an analytic scaffold for interpreting our bibliometric findings on AI, blockchain, and big data in relation to institutional capacities and governance arrangements.

2. THE EVOLUTION OF DIGITAL TRANSFORMATION AND ITS INTEGRATION INTO PUBLIC ADMINISTRATION

2.1. Digitalization and Digital Transformation

The concept of digital transformation refers to the deep and holistic change that digital technologies create in social, economic, and institutional structures. This concept does not only mean the application of digital tools, but also a process that restructures the ways organizations operate, service delivery models, and value production mechanisms. Shevchenko & Mihaylov (2021) emphasize that the strategic goal of digital transformation is to reshape the value production logic of the enterprise by creating a completely new digital business model by distinguishing digitalization from automation. In this context, digital transformation has not been limited to the private sector; it has been the harbinger of radical changes in many sectors such as education, health, finance, and production (Patwari et al., 2024).

Public administration has also undergone significant transformation; it has transitioned from conventional bureaucratic approaches to an evidence-based, adaptive, and citizen-driven model of governance. The process of digital transformation enhances the efficiency of operations through reengineering the business processes of public organizations and consolidates democratic principles such as accountability and transparency through the utilization of digital technologies (Kaivo-oja et al., 2022). In this regard, advanced digital technologies such as artificial intelligence, big data analytics, the Internet of Things (IoT), blockchain technology, and cloud computing enable public service delivery in a way that is ever more effective, accurate, and inclusive (Aryanto et al., 2023; Ricart et al., 2020).

Besides, digital transformation is not only a technology-focused modernization program; it is also a holistic transformation tool facilitating data-driven decision-making processes, consolidating participatory democracy, and advancing sustainable development goals in the framework of public policy making (Ghani, 2024). Thus, the effective realization of digital transformation in public administration also demands not just the creation of the appropriate technical infrastructure but a full-fledged transformation of institutional culture, leadership practices, ethical norms, and regulatory frameworks (Kyrychenko & Kyrychenko, 2025).

2.2. Beyond Digitization: Citizen-Centric and Data-Driven Transformation in Public Administration

This tendency has reached the public sector in a very brief period; it has transformed various fields, such as the operational methods of public institutions and their interaction with the citizenry. For Matnenko, (2020), the digitalization occurring in the public sector is an unavoidable transformation and has significantly enhanced the quality of public service delivery. The growth of the public sector is more than just a transfer of services to a digital platform; it has also rearranged how citizens engage with government institutions. Ciancarini et al. (2023) sustain that digital transformation in the public sector not only entails technological advancement but also significant organizational and cultural transformation; the transformation is founded upon four main elements: data, digital competences, information and communications technologies (ICT), and service development agile methodologies. Digital transformation in public administration has commonly started with the implementation of e-government programs. In the course of this transformation, public services have been made available via digital portals, which have ushered in greater transparency, speed, and efficiency in administrative processes. However, over time, this innovation has caused evolution not just in the methods of service delivery but also in the management strategies employed. Based on a systematic review of the literature, Mountasser & Abdellatif (2023) describe that digital transformation yields enormous transformational impacts on areas that include efficiency, accountability, as well as public administration's involvement of citizens.

Mkrtchyan & Melkumyan (2023) state that digital transformation in public administration is not only a tool but also a strategic component for a citizen-centered governance model, while Obolonsky, (2022) emphasizes the contribution of digitalization to data-based decision-making processes. This transformation also aims to make public administration more participatory, accessible, and accountable.

The concept of digital transformation has evolved from its origins in the private sector to the public sector and has transformed from a technological tool in public administration to an administrative vision. This process both increases the efficiency of service delivery and redefines the understanding of governance by transforming the citizen-state relationship. Therefore, digital transformation in public administration is not only a technical innovation but also the reconstruction of public value. Viewed through the DEG lens, the observed move towards data-driven, agile, and cross-organizational practices signals a systemic transition from digitizing services to redesigning the state's operating model. From a PVT perspective, this transition is meaningful insofar as it demonstrably enhances public value, improving transparency, equity of access, and participatory mechanisms rather than merely introducing new technologies.

2.3. Use of Advanced Digital Technologies in Public Administration

Digital transformation in public administration includes not only the modernization of digital service delivery, but also the integration of advanced digital technologies such as artificial intelligence (AI), blockchain, cloud computing, big data, the internet of things (IoT), augmented reality (AR), data analytics and cybersecurity into all structural and functional processes of the state. These technologies enable public institutions to become more efficient, transparent, and participatory. This multi-layered dimension of digital transformation leads to paradigmatic changes both in internal administrative processes and in interaction with citizens (Aryanto et al., 2023; Huang, 2021). Lutsenko (2024) emphasizes that the widespread use of these technologies in public administration makes the relationship between citizens and the state more transparent, reliable, and effective; he also states that processes such as decision-making, document management, and service monitoring have changed radically.

While the integration of artificial intelligence with automation and decision support systems increases the speed and accuracy of public services, big data and cloud computing solutions strengthen data management and analysis processes (Onabanjo A., 2024; Erhueh et al., 2024) Similarly, blockchain technology provides reliability and immutable record systems in public services; augmented reality applications are used in education, emergency planning, and professional development of public employees (Radziwill, 2018).

Internet of Things (IoT) and cybersecurity systems play a critical role, especially in smart city projects, by providing integrated solutions for monitoring and protecting public infrastructures (Shaikh et al., 2022; Shao et al., 2023). This comprehensive digital transformation process supports the evolution of public administration into a more transparent, accountable, and effective structure (Ricart et al., 2020).

2.3.1. Artificial Intelligence Applications

Artificial intelligence (AI) has become an increasingly strategic tool in the context of the digitalization of processes in public administration. This technology provides significant contributions to public institutions in the automation of administrative work, more effective management of resources, performance of predictive analyses, and evidence-based policy development processes. AI systems enable decision-makers to make sense of large data sets, predict trends, and proactively manage service demands (Showkat Ahmad Dar, 2024). In particular, operational benefits such as simplifying administrative processes through automation, shortening service times, and reducing error rates come to the fore (Saprudin, 2024).

In addition, AI applications are not limited to internal processes only but also transform public communication with digital solutions that increase citizens' participation and interaction (Gesk & Leyer, 2022). AI-based chatbots, feedback systems, and interactive platforms facilitate citizens' access to public services and promote processes of participation in governance (Cholyshkina et al., 2024; Storozhenko, 2023).

However, the use of AI-supported predictive analysis is increasing in complex areas such as policy development and crisis management, allowing data-based strategic planning and preventive public policies to be developed (Aust & Harmash, 2024; Loukis et al., 2019). However, it is emphasized that these developments should also be evaluated in areas such as ethics, accountability, and data security (Söker, 2024).

2.3.2. Blockchain Based Solutions

Blockchain technology is not only a technical innovation in the context of public administration, but also a structural transformation tool in terms of transparency, accountability, and reliable data management. It stands out as an effective tool in the fight against corruption, especially thanks to its functions such as monitoring public expenditures, digitally recording contract processes, and securing documents against forgery (Ibrahimy et al., 2022). Thanks to the distributed ledger structure of blockchain, it becomes possible to store transaction records carried out in public tenders in an unchangeable manner; this increases accountability and establishes trust in the citizen-state relationship (Weingärtner et al., 2021).

Blockchain applications in public administration go beyond tenders. There is more interest in applying this technology to essential public services like verification of identity, digital registry management, and most importantly land registration. For example, a combination of land registration systems and blockchain technology in many countries renders transactions of title deeds secure and cancels out any conflicts related to land ownership (Sah & Chandavarkar, 2023; Verma et al., 2024). Given that blockchain technology is irreversible and easy to trace, every transaction on property documents leaves an indelible mark that can be traced, greatly improving the credibility of public record systems (Bhole et al., 2021; Mansoor et al., 2023; Rizal Batubara et al., 2019).

In the European context, we see blockchain technology being used as a tool of digitalization in government systems. In Estonia, Georgia, and Spain, examples of effective use of this technology in digital identification, digital land registries, and official record systems are worth mentioning (Lazuashvili et al., 2019). In this case, blockchain is not just a technical fix; it is considered a useful tool for the construction of a more accountable, transparent, and citizen-focused public administration (Mezquita et al., 2021).

2.3.3. Cloud Computing and Data Access

Cloud computing technologies are today one of the fundamental building blocks of public administration digital transformation processes. Cloud solutions for public institutions are not only strategically relevant for data storage and management, but also for the provision of uninterrupted access to services on a 24/7 basis and cost savings (Jha & Jha, 2024). In particular, 24/7 availability of public services depends on the configuration of in-house software and services on flexible infrastructures. This flexibility improves the operational efficiency of institutions and facilitates the provision of services based on citizen satisfaction (Brzozowska-Rup et al., 2024).

In addition to that, cloud technologies offer a lot of operational advantages such as reducing maintenance costs, easing data backup processes, and ensuring business continuity (Gladkov, 2024). However, the implementation of these technologies within the public administration has to be duly planned not only on the technical level but also on the governance, security, and legislative levels. Cloud strategies, especially carried out in European Union institutions, have made the development of reliable and regulatory-compliant service models a priority (Ducatel et al., 2020).

In this context, cloud-based digital transformation is not only a technological transition process in public administration but also a critical transformation tool for restructuring service delivery and increasing digital capacity for the public good (Nanos et al., 2019).

2.3.4. Big Data and IoT Integration

Among the advanced digital technologies, Big Data and the Internet of Things (IoT) enable more accurate design of public policies and data-based restructuring of public services. While sensor data collected through IoT devices provides real-time data in areas such as transportation, environmental management, and urban planning, meaningful conclusions are drawn from this information thanks to big data analytics, and the effectiveness of public decisions is increased. Karpa et al. (2023) state that the combination of artificial intelligence and IoT technologies, especially in smart city infrastructures, directly contributes to the quality of social services.

Big data stands out as not only a supporting tool of public administration today, but also as one of the fundamental components of Public Administration 5.0, a new governance paradigm. This paradigm represents the adoption of faster, accountable, and data-based processes in public institutions, along with the integration of digital tools into the state structure (Kocaoğlu & Şahnagil, 2022).

In terms of application areas, big data plays a critical role in many sectors, especially health, education, security, transportation, disaster management, and public service delivery. In the field of health, by keeping records of citizens in digital systems and analyzing these data, both regional distribution balance in service delivery is ensured and early detection of epidemics and chronic diseases becomes possible (Çeliksoy, 2021; Wang et al., 2018).

Similarly, in the education system, deficiencies are determined and education policies are updated by analyzing student and teacher data; this contributes to the establishment of a contemporary and inclusive education structure. In the field of security, findings obtained from unstructured data are used in crime prevention and risk analysis at individual and societal levels.

In transportation policies, smart transportation systems supported by big data and IoT optimize traffic flow while enabling citizens to travel more safely and economically. Disaster and emergency management is one of the most strategic application areas of big data. Pre-disaster risk estimation, resource coordination during disasters, and post-disaster recovery processes are supported by multi-source data sets such as IoT sensors, satellite data, and social media content.

The service delivery methods of public institutions are also transforming under the influence of these technologies. Electronic government (e-government) systems provide faster, more transparent, and accessible services with the support of IoT and cloud technologies (Çeliksoy, 2021). While citizens can access services such as tax, education, and social security from a digital environment, public institutions are also developing analytics-based decision support systems to manage the increasing data volume.

Public administration applications based on big data around the world vary according to the digital maturity levels of countries. Estonia, one of the leading countries in this field, offers a pioneering model that addresses the use of big data in public administration with a systematic and holistic approach. Estonia, which built its post-independence state structure on digital solutions, sets an example for many countries with its e-government applications and digital identity infrastructures (Koç, 2021).

Indeed, big data and IoT technologies offer a strong potential for strategic decision-making in public administration, increasing service quality, and developing a citizen-focused governance model. The effective use of these technologies necessitates not only technical infrastructure but also multidimensional reforms such as institutional capacity, legal regulations, and data ethics.

2.3.5. Cyber Security Approaches

Digital transformation processes in public administration necessitate not only technological integration in service delivery but also the development of infrastructures that ensure the security of these services. In this context, cybersecurity technologies have become an integral component of digital transformation. The proliferation of digital services has brought about new security needs, especially in critical areas such as the security of identity verification systems, the protection of public data, and the provision of digital service continuity (Mijwil et al., 2023). At this point, the success of digital transformation initiatives directly depends on how strong and comprehensive cybersecurity policies are (Sandhu, 2021).

Systematic reviews in the literature reveal that the sustainability of digital transformation depends on the capacity to adapt to changing cyber threats and the establishment of digital governance structures that can manage these threats (Belkhamza, 2023). The transition to advanced digital governance models, especially GovTech, is possible not only with technological adaptation but also with the operation of these systems in a secure and reliable digital environment (Kocharian, 2023).

In this context, the effective and secure maintenance of digital public services is possible with the integration of cybersecurity technologies and strategies that need to be constantly updated. Indeed, digital transformation should be considered not only as a technological change but also as a security-based structural transformation process (SERAC, 2023).

2.3.6. Managerial Capacity and Ethical Issues

In the literature, advanced digital technologies are understood not merely to digitize services but to reconfigure the state's operating logic, citizen state interactions, and the production of public value. When effectively integrated AI, blockchain, cloud computing, IoT, big data, and cybersecurity these technologies can support more transparent, rapid, inclusive, and accountable public administration, yet the transformation enables presupposes holistic reform across technical and administrative capacity, ethical frameworks, and human resources. Complementing this technology-centric view, scholarship also foregrounds the social and institutional preconditions of digital government: the digital divide conditions who benefits from e-services; organizational research highlights resistance and the need for structured change management; and legal-ethical work stresses that privacy, data protection, cybersecurity, and algorithmic accountability are prerequisites for public trust and digital legitimacy Mkrtchyan & Melkumyan (2023).

3. DIGITALIZATION IN PUBLIC ADMINISTRATION: THE ESTONIAN EXAMPLE

Estonia, which facilitates the daily transactions of its citizens by offering electronic solutions, is a good example of digital applications. Estonia, which gained its independence from the Soviet Union in 1990, has risen again and taken great steps to become a center of attraction for international capital by playing an active role in the world economy. It has been seen as an investment and trade center by many international organizations (KOÇ, 2021). To reach its current status and create an environment of trust, Estonia has transformed its management approach into governance and laid a technological foundation. The new order that has been established has been shaped as an e-governance system. Thanks to this system, it has risen to an ambitious position by offering all its services to the public, including individuals and the private sector. It offers its services with both public and private sector partnerships (Koç, 2021; Nielsen, 2017). Although Estonia gained independence from the Soviet occupation, it had nothing left and had to restructure everything. It has nothing of its own, neither in terms of infrastructure, management, or law. Estonia, which fell into great chaos, has made radical decisions and made serious progress by trusting its citizens. These advances have turned Estonia into a digital society. The country has been able to file online taxes since 2001, use digital identity and digital signatures since 2002, and vote online since 2005 (Kalvet, 2012). While communication and technology tools have only just begun to take hold in many homes and have not yet fully felt the impact of the internet and its tools, Estonia has established its technological infrastructure, collected, processed, and provided its data with a data infrastructure that many countries are still struggling to cope with. It has come to a remarkable position with rational decisions in an environment of uncertainty, emerging from a great war. It can provide all kinds of social services that come to mind online, such as education, justice, police, or establishing a company. Many situations that you may encounter in daily life, such as looking at health records, applying for assistance, or objecting to a parking ticket, are being carried out online (Koç, 2021). It would be easier to talk about the services that Estonia does not offer online. Moreover, their number is not much more than five fingers. For example, they still need to be present to get married or divorced, to obtain ID cards, and to sell real estate.

Of course, it was not easy for Estonia to provide a fast and profitable service by creating a completely paperless environment, and this caused them to make different decisions. Because as a state that has digitalized itself, Estonia has almost gotten rid of the bureaucratic labyrinth. In other words, a different management approach has been adopted than known. For example, the council of ministers is carried out completely electronically and operates with 0 paper. This change and transformation is a very difficult event. Because all citizens can receive services online only if they participate in the online environment and share all their information. In this sense, the changing state role and the provision of a digitalized environment of trust come to the fore. It has established an efficient and, of course, user-centered system that responds to the expectations of citizens, responds to their needs instantly. However, he suggested that technology could be the solution to the problem of citizens not trusting the government and the government not trusting the citizens (Nielsen, 2017).

In this context, Estonia has not digitized the bureaucracy as it is, but has redesigned the rules and procedures by determining common and effective decisions. Although this is a very courageous move for a state that emerged victorious from the war, it is also a risky situation. For Estonia to transform into E-Estonia, the strict hierarchical structure brought by bureaucracy has been abandoned, unnecessary information collection and multiplication of work have been avoided, and open and transparent behavior has been achieved. For example, when we look at the key elements of the design principle of electronic Estonia, data and information privacy are guaranteed. This is provided by a reliable digital identity that is compatible with everything given by the state. Again, this identity is found in every Estonian citizen and is legally binding not only in Estonia but also in the European Union, and it becomes two identities with a digital signature. The working principle of the ID card in question is as follows. After identifying the person who will use the card suitably and securely and logging in to the system, it allows the citizen to access their data and all community services from a single place and to perform any transaction with their digital signature. The citizen's data is located in a single location and is always recorded and retrieved from there. Moreover, they do this with other important principles that the state determined during the transformation, which they call "only once" (Anthes, 2015). With this principle, the state can ask the same information from its citizens only once and store it only in one place. This situation can be explained as follows. If a birth or marriage certificate is given to the population office only once, this data is stored only by the population office and no other institution or organization requests this information again. The only once rule, which comes to the fore here with great power and perhaps plays the most effective role in the digitalization of the country, establishes the data community structure in the country such as which information is defined where and whose responsibility it is, and ensures its up-to-dateness by preventing the collection and copying of information in many places. Since the data and information are not duplicated or copied to different places, it allows the data and information in the system to be accessed safely and securely at all times. Public institutions can provide services in this way. The X-Road data exchange program, which has been used in the Estonian government since 2001, undertakes this task. It carries out the data exchange between institutions and organizations, such as all public institutions, local governments, and private businesses, in real time, in accordance with the rules and in a reliable manner (Björklund, 2016; Kalvet, 2012; Martinson, 2019). After each transaction, it leaves an auditable trace and creates the control mechanism.

The importance of the data in every service provided is quite great. Mechanisms become operational thanks to the data that is found in every area of life, just like cells, and gain meaning as they combine. This data highlights both personal and public privacy. Especially in the digital world, the importance of information integrity and reliability is vital for operational activities. For this reason, the Estonian state uses blockchain technology, designed in 2007, to ensure log records, software components, data exchange rules, and data integrity simultaneously. With this technology, Estonia guarantees data control, data access, and recording of data transactions by monitoring them. If there is data and information, the issue of data ownership comes to the fore. Although some laws and decrees limit the sharing of data with third parties after it is shared with public institutions or private companies, data traceability is not possible. However, another important principle of Estonia is the issue of data ownership, which is created with the principle of confidentiality and transparency. In the Estonian state, the individual is the owner of the data taken from them, and everyone has the right to know who uses their information. For this, the person can track their data transparently with log records (Martinson, 2019).

Although Estonia provides data at the highest level, access was restricted in 2007, some networks were completely closed, and a major cyber attack was launched. After this attack, they considered different security measures and decided to stop recording data. Inviolable embassy areas are being established outside of their territory throughout the country. They have established data embassies that protect their sovereignty to maintain both the protection and continuity of the most important digitalization. They have also received a security certificate even in physical attacks on cyber parts that should not be fragmented. Estonia can perform business and transactions stored electronically by getting rid of papers, and they have made it possible to store them anywhere in the world. It has developed an e-citizenship application, a start-up that has the government in its hands, which has taken this to a further level. With e-citizenship, a wide-ranging digital business can be established in the European Union, online banking transactions can be carried out, and it can be managed in E-Estonia through only an identity card (Anthes, 2015; Koç, 2021).

4. METHODOLOGY

The main purpose of this study is to systematically examine how the concepts of digitalization and digital transformation in public administration are addressed in academic literature. By identifying the main trends in the field, concentrations in the field of research, influential publications, and collaboration patterns through bibliometric analysis, the academic development of digital transformation in public administration will be mapped. The findings obtained in this direction aim to guide future research and provide strategic insights for policymakers.

Bibliometric analysis is a method that allows quantitative examination of scientific publications. This analysis method is used to reveal the development of academic production over time, research trends, collaboration networks, the most influential studies, authors, and publications. Bibliometric analysis provides researchers with a comprehensive framework to determine the structure, direction, and potential gaps of a field (Donthu et al., 2021). Unlike traditional literature reviews, it stands out with its ability to be applied systematically on large data sets and its reliance on objective indicators (Aria & Cuccurullo, 2017).

In this study, data were obtained from the Scopus database. The determined research query was:

TITLE-ABS-KEY ("public administration" AND "digitalization" OR "digital transformation") AND (LIMIT-TO (LANGUAGE, "English"))

The query was limited to publications in English only; in order to obtain a wider range of literature on the subject, a search was conducted in the fields of title, abstract, and keywords. A total of 910 academic publications were identified in the time period between 2010-2025 (all years) without any document type or disciplinary limitation.

This bibliographic dataset was analyzed using the open-source R-based program "Bibliometrix". Bibliometrix provided scientific mapping and display capabilities, allowing various types of analysis to be performed, such as frequency analysis, citation analysis, co-author/network analysis, and thematic mapping (Aria & Cuccurullo, 2017). The findings obtained in this process quantitatively revealed the evolution of the subject of digital transformation in public administration in academic literature.

5. FINDINGS

In this study, which was conducted within the scope of bibliometric analysis, the academic literature in the field of public administration and digital transformation was evaluated in the light of quantitative indicators. In line with the obtained data, the basic trends of the literature, production volume, prominent researchers, institutions, and countries were examined in detail; in addition, its conceptual structure was revealed through keyword analysis and thematic mapping. The findings presented below systematically explain the current status of the digital public administration literature and make the academic development in the field visible in its different dimensions.

Figure 1. Managerial Capacity and Ethical Issues

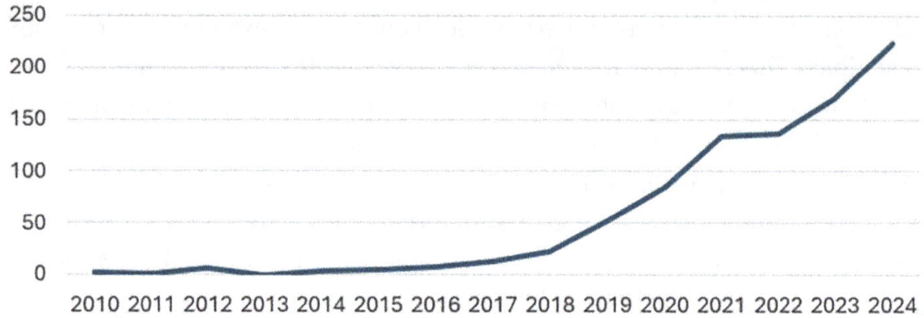

Figure 1 shows the annual production of academic publications on the theme of public administration and digital transformation. The production process, which started with a very limited number of publications since 2010, has entered a significant increasing trend, especially after 2018. The momentum has increased even more in 2020, and a remarkable increase has occurred between 2021 and 2024. As of 2024, the number of publications has reached approximately 230.

This increase is related to the more effective use of digital technologies in the public sector. The necessity of digitalization in the post-COVID-19 pandemic period has rapidly increased academic interest in the field of public administration. In addition, the integration of technologies such as artificial intelligence, blockchain, IoT, and big data into public policies has found a wide place in the research agenda. This trend shows that the subject of digital public administration is studied comprehensively not only in its technical but also in its administrative, ethical, and strategic dimensions.

Figure 2. Most Relevant Source

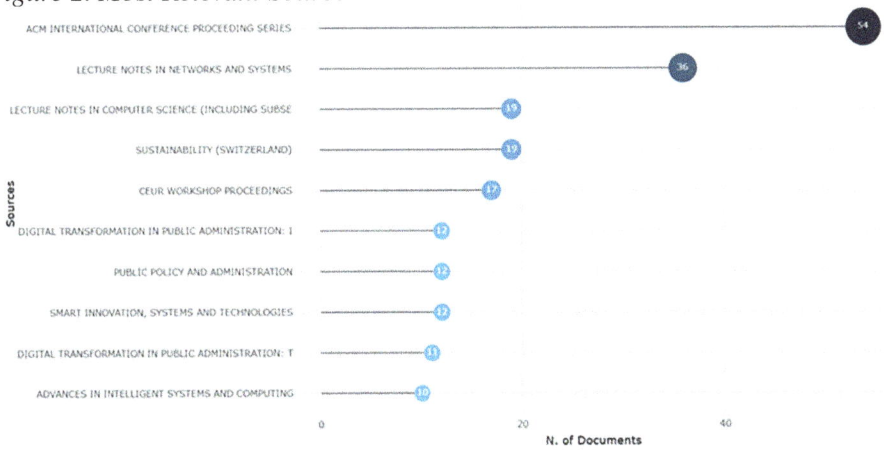

Figure 2 shows the academic resources with the most publications in the field of public administration and digital transformation. The source that published the most documents was by far the ACM International Conference Proceeding Series. This compilation is followed by Lecture Notes in Networks and Systems and Lecture Notes in Computer Science, which generally include content based on information technologies and engineering.

When the resources in the list are examined, an interdisciplinary publication trend based on both public administration and computer science is noticeable. The fact that multidisciplinary open-access journals such as Sustainability (Switzerland) are also at the top shows that digital public administration studies cover a wide perspective that includes not only technical but also sustainability and societal dimensions.

In addition, the fact that thematic conference series such as Digital Transformation in Public Administration are among the top 10 resources shows that the subject is also intensively discussed in international scientific meetings. This finding reveals that digital transformation-themed research has a high representation rate not only in academic journals but also in conference literature, where current developments are discussed.

Figure 3. Most Relevant Authors

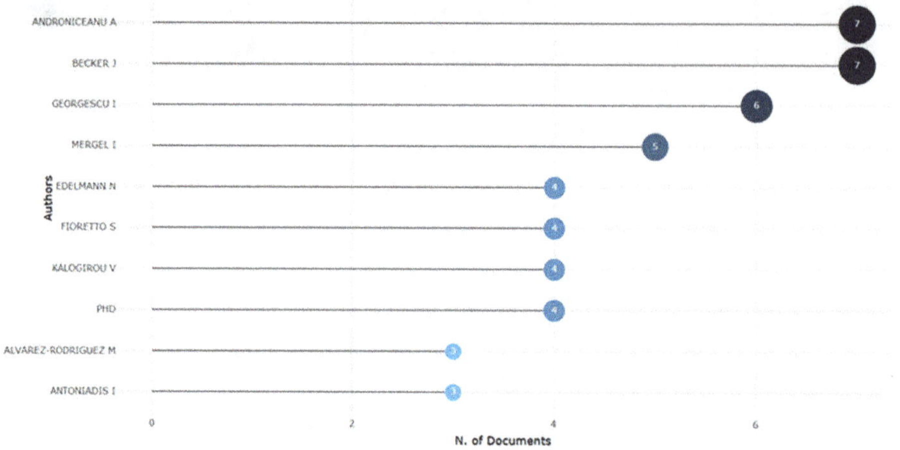

Figure 3 lists the authors with the most publications in studies on the theme of public administration and digital transformation. Androniceanu A and Becker J are at the top of the list with seven publications each, indicating that both authors are prominent researchers in the field of digital public administration. They are followed by influential authors such as Georgescu I and Mergel I.

This table shows that the subject of digital transformation is being studied sustainably by many academics and that certain authors are pioneers in the field. The presence of internationally recognized names in public sector innovation and digital governance, such as Mergel I, on the list reveals that the literature on digital public administration is based on an interactive academic ground at a global level.

In addition, authors at the bottom of the list, but with three or four publications, stand out as researchers who contribute to the development of the field. This shows that the subject has received academic attention in various geographical and institutional contexts, confirming the diversity of collaboration and research in the field.

Figure 4. Most Relevant Affilitions

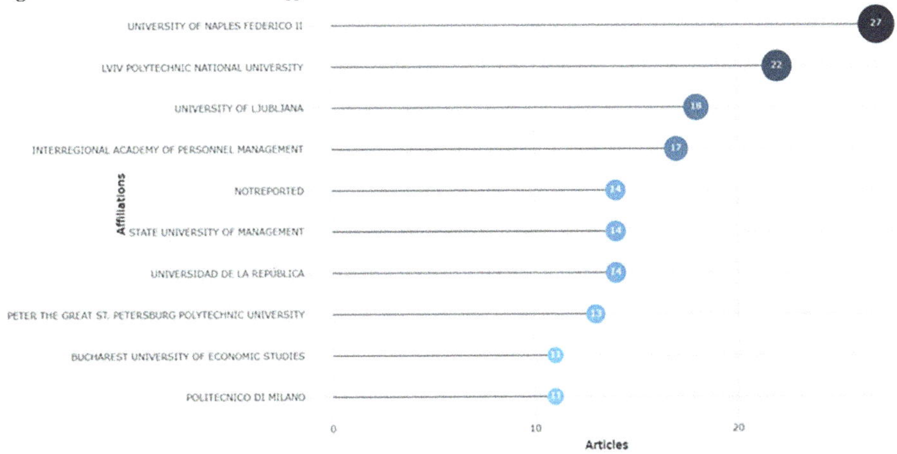

Figure 4 shows the academic institutions with the most publications on public administration and digital transformation. The University of Naples Federico II is clearly at the top of the list with 27 articles. This institution is followed by Lviv Polytechnic National University and the University of Ljubljana. The top 10 institutions are mostly of European origin.

It is understood that universities based in Italy, Ukraine, Slovenia, and Russia are particularly active in this field. This shows that digital transformation is at the center of the public administration research agenda, not only in the Anglo-Saxon world but also in Central and Eastern European countries.

The number of institutions listed as Not Reported is also significant, indicating that the author's institution information in some articles is incomplete. However, the fact that institutions specialized in technical and economic fields, such as Politecnico di Milano and Bucharest University of Economic Studies, are also in the top 10 reinforces the multidisciplinary nature of the subject of digital public administration.

Figure 5. Countries' Scientific Production

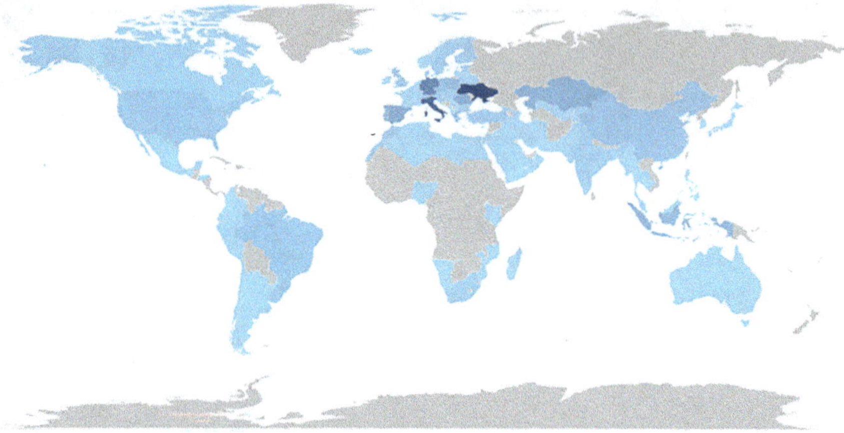

Figure 5 shows the distribution of academic publications on the theme of public administration and digital transformation by country. Countries highlighted in dark blue on the map have produced more publications, while light blue countries have contributed less. In this context, Ukraine stands out as the country with the highest publication production.

While the European continent is particularly central to scientific production in this field, the contribution of Central and Eastern European countries is striking. The intensive production of countries such as Ukraine, Italy, Romania, Slovenia, and Russia in this field also coincides with the institutional contributions highlighted in Figure 4. Similarly, countries with high scientific research capacity, such as the United States, Canada, China, India, Australia, and Brazil, also play an important role in publication production.

On the African continent and in the Middle East, scientific production is more limited. This situation can be closely associated with regional digitalization levels, access to academic resources, and the technological transformation process of the public sector.

In general, the map shows that the subject of digital public administration has attracted global attention, but publication production is concentrated in some regions. This distribution also points to opportunities for international cooperation and reveals that some countries have become leaders in this field.

Figure 6. Most Frequent Words

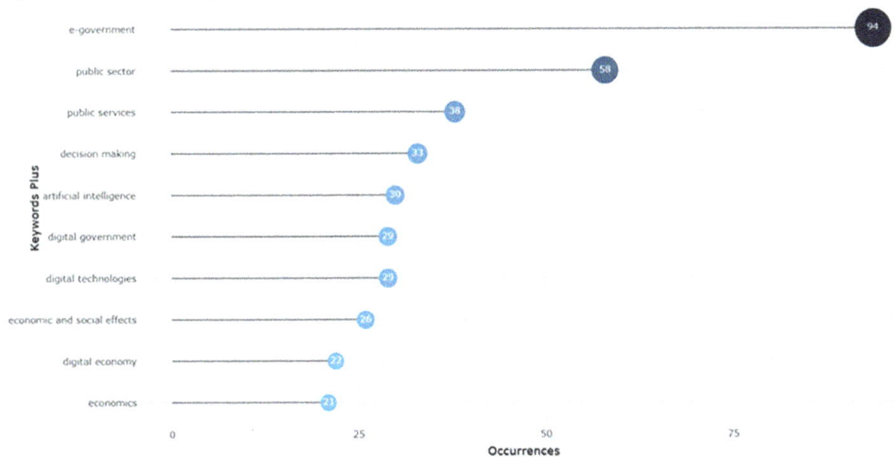

Figure 6 shows the terms labeled with the expression "Keywords Plus" most frequently used in the publications examined within the scope of bibliometric analysis. The most prominent keyword by far is "e-government", which reveals that digital transformation is the theme most associated with public administration.

"Public sector" and "Public services" come in second place, and this shows that the studies focus directly on public structures and service delivery systems. Keywords such as "Decision making" and "Artificial intelligence" reveal that the integration of data-based management approaches and technological applications into public decision-making processes is emphasized.

"Digital government" and "digital technologies" (both n=29) show that digitalization is addressed in public administration with its technical and structural dimensions. Keywords such as "economic and social effects", "digital economy", and "economics", which are in the last places, reflect that digital transformation is not limited to governance but is also analyzed in terms of socio-economic effects. These findings show that digital public administration studies have a multi-dimensional structure and show that there is a rich literature base shaped around technology, management, and social effects.

Figure 7. Trend Topics

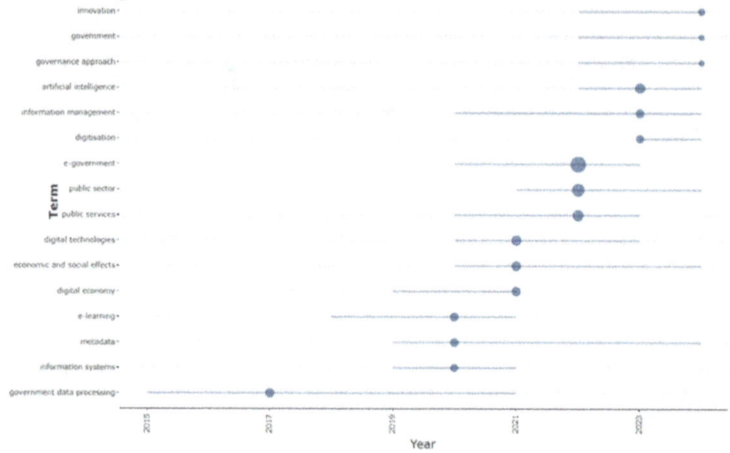

Figure 7 shows the trends of key concepts that have emerged over time in the public administration and digital transformation literature. The horizontal axis represents the years, while the time period and intensity in which each term is active are expressed by the size of the bubbles.

The first topics that emerged in the 2015–2018 period include "government data processing", "information systems", "metadata", and "e-learning". These themes reflect the first research focused on the establishment of digital infrastructures and data management. After 2020, the focus has gradually expanded; themes such as "e-government", "public sector", "public services", "digital technologies", and "economic and social effects" have become more discussed. In this period, the topic of "e-government" in particular has had the greatest impact both in terms of duration and volume. In the post-2022 period, more strategic and structural topics such as "artificial intelligence", "governance approach", "government", and "innovation" have become more prevalent. This situation shows that digital transformation is now being analyzed not only at the service delivery level but also at the governance and strategy level.

Therefore, the figure reveals that the literature has evolved from technical infrastructure to governance dimensions; digital transformation has settled on a more holistic and strategic discussion axis in public administration.

Figure 8. Thematic Map

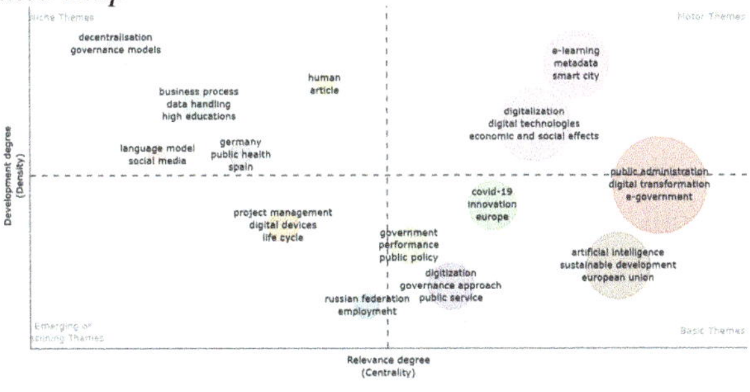

Figure 8 shows the thematic map where themes in the public administration and digital transformation literature are classified according to their centrality (relevance degree) and development degree. The motor themes in the upper right quadrant constitute the driving force of the research field as topics with high centrality and high development level. In this quadrant, themes such as e-learning, metadata, and smart city, as well as digitalization, digital technologies, and economic and social effects, are particularly noteworthy. These topics are intensively studied and expand the scope of digital public administration with both technical and social effects. The largest thematic cluster, public administration, digital transformation, and e-government, constitutes the basic building blocks of this literature and indicates a multi-centered structure.

The basic themes in the lower right quadrant are concepts with high centrality but relatively low development level. Artificial intelligence, sustainable development, and the European Union are in this quadrant; this situation shows that these concepts are important in terms of the research field, but still have the potential to be deepened in the literature. In particular, the integration of artificial intelligence and sustainability themes with digital public administration is still in its infancy. However, studies conducted in the context of the European Union offer remarkable opportunities in terms of regional regulation and governance dimensions.

The upper left quadrant shows niche themes that have a high level of development but are considered less central in the literature. Topics such as decentralization, governance models, business process, data handling, and higher education are included in this group; although they have been studied in depth, they show limited interaction with the general structure in the literature. This suggests that the themes in question appeal to more specialized subfields and focus on specific subtopics in the literature.

The lower left quadrant includes themes that are both low in centrality and development, developing, or losing their importance. Titles such as project management, digital devices, and life cycle are positioned here and represent topics that have not yet become established in the literature or have lost their appeal. The fact that themes such as Covid-19, innovation, and Europe are located close to this region shows that the temporary effects of the pandemic have created a short-term research wave and that these topics have not yet become a central structure.

In general, the thematic map reveals that the digital public administration literature is highly developed, structured, and shaped around central themes; however, new research areas with strategic potential are also developing. This situation shows that both the existing structures are consolidating, and the discipline is open to enrichment with new concepts in the coming period.

6. RESULTS

The bibliometric analysis conducted within the scope of this study has comprehensively revealed the quantitative structure of the academic literature on the theme of digital transformation in public administration. The analysis results reveal that the publication production in this field has increased rapidly, especially in the last five years, and that digital technologies are addressed in a multidimensional manner in the context of public administration.

First of all, when the publication trends are examined by year, it is seen that the academic production, which started with a limited number of publications in 2010, gained rapid momentum after 2018, and reached approximately 230 publications by 2024. This increase is directly related to the fact that digital technologies have become mandatory in the public sector, especially after the COVID-19 pandemic. This situation shows that digital transformation is discussed intensively not only as a technical but also as a managerial and strategic issue.

It was observed that interdisciplinary publications such as ACM International Conference Proceeding Series, Lecture Notes in Networks and Systems, and Sustainability (Switzerland) stand out among the analyzed sources. This situation reveals that digital public administration studies exhibit a multi-disciplinary structure between information technologies, engineering, and social sciences.

In the author analyses, Androniceanu A and Becker J stand out as the most productive names, while internationally renowned academics such as Mergel I have also contributed to the field. This situation shows that the field is nourished by a global academic interaction network. In terms of institutional contributions, the University of Naples Federico II, Lviv Polytechnic National University, and the University of Ljubljana are prominent institutions. In country-based production, Central and Eastern European countries such as Ukraine, Italy, Romania, and Slovenia show clear leadership.

In the keyword analysis, it was seen that terms such as "e-government", "public sector", "public services", and "artificial intelligence" were at the forefront, and digitalization was studied especially through public services, decision processes, and technology integration. In time series analyses, while themes focused on data infrastructure and information systems were prominent between 2015-2018, themes focused on e-government, artificial intelligence, innovation, and governance were prominent in the period after 2020.

According to the thematic map analysis, topics such as "digital transformation", "e-government", and "public administration" have a high level of centrality and development and constitute the building blocks of the literature. On the other hand, it is understood that strategic topics such as "artificial intelligence" and "sustainable development" are still in the development phase and that in-depth studies are needed in these areas. In addition, it has been observed that niche themes such as "governance models" and "data handling" are addressed in a more limited but detailed manner in the literature.

In general, these findings show that academic production in the field of digital public administration is increasing, thematic diversity is expanding, and governance dimensions are coming to the fore. The literature is enriched in terms of both technical infrastructures and political and social effects; this confirms that digital transformation brings with it a multi-dimensional paradigm shift.

To broaden the chapter's global representativeness beyond Europe, we briefly note experiences from other regions. In Africa, Rwanda's one-stop Irembo portal and Kenya's mobile-first e-service ecosystem show how coordinated platforms can expand access under capacity constraints. In Latin America, Brazil's gov.br and long-standing electronic invoicing illustrate how national digital identity and transactional services scale across ministries. In Asia, India's digital public infrastructure demonstrates how interoperability can drive inclusion and service uptake.

7. CONCLUSION AND RECOMMENDATION

The bibliometric analyses show that the theme of digital transformation in public administration has gradually become a mature, multi-layered, and strategic research area. The increase in the volume of publications, especially after 2018, shows that digital technologies have become not only a technical tool in the public sector but also a decisive element in reshaping the governance vision. This situation coincides with Matnenko's (2020) findings that digital transformation provides an increase in the quality of public services. Overall, the results align with DEG's assumption that digital technologies reconfigure coordination and accountability across government layers, while PVT urges that future reforms be assessed against public value metrics (e.g., trust, inclusiveness, legitimacy). Accordingly, we recommend that subsequent empirical sections report not only technological uptake but also value outcomes and distributional effects.

E-government, one of the concepts frequently emphasized in the literature, stood out as the most dominant term in the keyword analyses obtained in the study. This finding is directly related to Obolonsky's (2022) emphasis on the centrality of data-based decision-making processes in public administration. At the same time, Mergel's contributions on digital innovation and public sector reform represent the intersection of the literature and the findings, as they are among the most frequently cited authors in the analysis.

The thematic map findings of the study revealed that the clusters of "public administration", "digital transformation", and "e-government" have a high level of centrality and development. This situation is directly consistent with the four basic building blocks (data, skills, technology, agility) approach of Ciancarini et al. (2023) that digital transformation necessitates not only technological but also organizational and cultural change. Similarly, the views of Kaivo-oja et al. (2022) that public administration redefines the principles of transparency and accountability with digital tools are consistent with the concept clusters highlighted in the study.

Another element frequently mentioned in the literature, regional differences and administrative capacities, was confirmed by the analysis conducted at the country level in the study. While countries such as Ukraine, Italy, and Slovenia stand out, it is seen that digital public administration can be institutionalized with a holistic, trust-oriented, and efficiency-oriented approach, as in the case of Estonia (Kalvet, 2012; Koç, 2021). Estonia's practices, such as the X-Road and the "only once" principle, can be associated with concepts such as "artificial intelligence", "metadata", and "governance models" that are not yet mature but have strategic importance on the thematic map. In this context, the views of (Kyrychenko & Kyrychenko, 2025) that digital transformation should include not only technical but also ethical and administrative restructuring are supported.

Technologies such as blockchain, cloud computing, and big data came to the forefront in the study, both in technical themes and among trending topics. In particular, a strong relationship was observed between literature findings that blockchain technology contributes to transparency and trust in public services (Weingärtner et al., 2021) and titles such as "digital technologies" and "economic and social effects" in the upper right quadrant of the thematic map. Similarly, Lutsenko's (2024) study that blockchain and AI-based applications make public-citizen interactions transparent, is also supported by analytical findings.

In this context, the findings obtained reveal the contributions of the study at three levels: conceptual, methodological, and policy-oriented. Conceptually, the study mapped how the themes of digital transformation are positioned in the public administration literature, revealing that digitalization is not only a service modernization in the public sector; it is also a part of an administrative, ethical, and strategic transformation. The weight of themes such as e-government, digital technologies, artificial intelligence, and big data, which are the basic building blocks of digital public administration, in the academic literature was systematically analyzed, and the structural development of the field was demonstrated.

Methodologically, the study identified the trends in the literature in the light of objective indicators with the Bibliometrix-based systematic analysis approach and presented a multi-dimensional data-based assessment of the digital public administration literature. The most frequently studied themes, influential authors, institutions, and countries were determined, and the academic production capacity and regional concentrations of the digitalization field were revealed. In particular, the systematic visibility of the topics that are still developing in the field of digital public administration has high potential, but has not been sufficiently deepened with the help of the thematic map is an important contribution of this method.

When evaluated from the perspective of policymakers, the study points to a multidimensional transformation process in which digital transformation redefines the basic elements of public administration, such as administrative capacity, institutional culture, ethical infrastructure, and citizen participation. In this context, the study directly contributes not only to academic research but also to the shaping of public policies.

In line with the findings obtained, some suggestions can be made for future research in the field of digital public administration Future research should systematically report value outcomes and distributional effects trust, inclusiveness, and perceived legitimacy alongside technological uptake, to strengthen cross-country comparability and policy relevance.. First of all, it is necessary to focus more on topics that have a high thematic centrality level but are not yet sufficiently mature in the literature, such as artificial intelligence, sustainable development, and governance models. Qualitative and applied studies to be conducted in these areas will fill the gaps in the literature and shed light on practical policy development processes.

Beyond Europe, experiences in Kenya, Brazil, and India one-stop portals, national service platforms, and interoperable digital public infrastructure reinforce the generalizability of our findings. It is seen that digital transformation practices are still concentrated in certain regions; academic contribution remains limited in regions such as Africa, the Middle East, and South Asia. This situation reduces the representativeness of the global literature and limits regional diversity. Therefore, increasing regional comparative analyses will contribute to the development of a more holistic understanding of how digital public administration evolves in different social, economic, and administrative contexts.

In addition, interdisciplinary studies are needed to bridge the technical, social, and administrative dimensions of digital public administration research. Frameworks to be developed jointly by engineering, public policy, sociology, law, and information sciences will facilitate the multi-faceted analysis of digital transformation processes.

Finally, in digitalization processes, research focusing not only on technology but also on normative values such as data security, individual rights, ethical governance, and transparency should be increased. The digitalization of public services also necessitates the re-establishment of trust and legitimacy in citizen-state relations in the digital environment. Therefore, for digital public administration to progress healthily, it needs to be redesigned not only technically but also with an ethical, inclusive, and trust-based understanding.

This study not only provides a systematic framework for the digital public administration literature but also serves as a resource that can guide future research in terms of thematic orientations, regional expansions, and methodological contributions. However, the study has some limitations. The analysis was conducted only with the Scopus database; literature that could be obtained from different databases was excluded. In addition, certain themes were prioritized while selecting keywords, which caused some potential studies to be excluded. Therefore, future research can be designed to include larger databases and more comprehensive keyword sets.

REFERENCES

Anthes, G. (2015). Estonia. *Communications of the ACM, 58*(6), 18–20. DOI: 10.1145/2754951

Aria, M., & Cuccurullo, C. (2017). bibliometrix : An R-tool for comprehensive science mapping analysis. *Journal of Informetrics, 11*(4), 959–975. DOI: 10.1016/j.joi.2017.08.007

Aryanto, E., Mabruk, H., & Narendroputro, W. (2023). Artificial Intelligence Implementation Strategy to Make It Happen Smart Government Indonesia Gold 2045. *The International Journal of Science in Society, 5*(5), 172–197. DOI: 10.54783/ijsoc.v5i5.877

Aust, K., & Harmash, O. (2024). Predictive Analytics, Emerging Trends and Future of State Governance. *Science of Law, 2024*(2), 16–27. DOI: 10.55284/sol.v2024i2.129

Belkhamza, Z. (2023). Cybersecurity in Digital Transformation applications: Analysis of Past Research and Future Directions. *International Conference on Cyber Warfare and Security, 18*(1), 19–24. DOI: 10.34190/iccws.18.1.1005

Bhole, K., Galphat, Y., Bathija, K., Saini, T., & Bhosale, A. (2021). Allocation and Tracking of Public Funds using Blockchain. *2021 4th Biennial International Conference on Nascent Technologies in Engineering (ICNTE)*, 1–4. DOI: 10.1109/ICNTE51185.2021.9487782

Björklund, F. (2016). E-government and moral citizenship: The case of Estonia. *Citizenship Studies, 20*(6–7), 914–931. DOI: 10.1080/13621025.2016.1213222

Bonomi Savignon, A., Zecchinelli, R., Costumato, L., & Scalabrini, F. (2024). Automation in public sector jobs and services: a framework to analyze public digital transformation's impact in a data-constrained environment. *Transforming Government: People. Transforming Government, 18*(1), 49–70. DOI: 10.1108/TG-04-2023-0044

Brzozowska-Rup, K., Nowakowska, M., & Zdradzisz, M. (2024). Cloud computing in the Polish public administration: Current state and development prospects. *Technological Forecasting and Social Change, 205*, 123500. DOI: 10.1016/j.techfore.2024.123500

Casalino, N., Rubichi, V., Gasparri, C., & Pizzolo, G. (2017). Organization of Processes Digitization and E-Invoicing Services for an Effective Digital Transformation of Public Sector. *DigitCult – Scientific Journal on Digital Cultures, 2*(1), 53–62.

Çeliksoy, E. (2021). Kurumsal Bilgi Yönetimi: Teknolojik Eğitilmler. In Kocaoğlu, M., & Usta, S. (Eds.), *Kamuda Büyük Veri* (Vol. 1, pp. 119–135). Eğitim Yayınevi.

Chatfield, A. T., & Reddick, C. G. (2018). All hands on deck to tweet #sandy: Networked governance of citizen coproduction in turbulent times. *Government Information Quarterly, 35*(2), 259–272. DOI: 10.1016/j.giq.2017.09.004

Cholyshkina, O., Karnaukh, A., Volianiuk, O., Ostapenko, M., & Holishevska, A. (2024). Public participation and innovative technologies: the role of artificial intelligence in public administration and sustainable development. *Salud, Ciencia y Tecnología - Serie de Conferencias, 3*, 974. DOI: 10.56294/sctconf2024974

Ciancarini, P., Giancarlo, R., & Grimaudo, G. (2023). Digital Transformation in the Public Administrations: A Guided Tour For Computer Scientists. *ArXiv. Abs, 2305*, 05551. DOI: 10.1109/ACCESS.2024.3363075

Datta, P., Walker, L., & Amarilli, F. (2020). Digital transformation: Learning from Italy's public administration. *Journal of Information Technology Teaching Cases, 10*(2), 54–71. DOI: 10.1177/2043886920910437

Desouza, K. C., & Jacob, B. (2017). Big Data in the Public Sector: Lessons for Practitioners and Scholars. *Administration & Society, 49*(7), 1043–1064. DOI: 10.1177/0095399714555751

Di Giulio, M., & Vecchi, G. (2023). Implementing digitalization in the public sector. Technologies, agency, and governance. *Public Policy and Administration, 38*(2), 133–158. DOI: 10.1177/09520767211023283

Donthu, N., Kumar, S., Mukherjee, D., Pandey, N., & Lim, W. M. (2021). How to conduct a bibliometric analysis: An overview and guidelines. *Journal of Business Research, 133*, 285–296. DOI: 10.1016/j.jbusres.2021.04.070

Ducatel, K., Michlmayr, T., Merle, P., Baskovc, D., & Mestre, F. (2020). The European Commission goes 'cloud first': A roadmap towards trusted cloud adoption to seize the opportunities of digital transformation for EU institutions and agencies. *Cyber Security: A Peer-Reviewed Journal, 3*(3), 220. DOI: 10.69554/YDMP5350

Erhueh, O. V., Nwakile, C., Akano, O. A., Esiri, A. E., & Hanson, E. (2024). Digital transformation in energy asset management: Lessons for building the future of energy infrastructure. *Global Journal of Research in Science and Technology, 2*(2), 010–037. DOI: 10.58175/gjrst.2024.2.2.0071

Galetta, D.-U. (2018). Access to Administrative Documents and to Public Sector Information in Italy. In *The Right of Access to Public Information* (pp. 343–367). Springer Berlin Heidelberg., DOI: 10.1007/978-3-662-55554-5_8

Gesk, T. S., & Leyer, M. (2022). Artificial intelligence in public services: When and why citizens accept its usage. *Government Information Quarterly*, *39*(3), 101704. DOI: 10.1016/j.giq.2022.101704

Ghani, A. S. (2024). Revolutionizing Supply Chains: A Comprehensive Study of Industry 4.0 Technologies (IoT, Big Data, AI, etc.). *International Journal of Scientific Research in Engineering and Management*, *08*(04), 1–5. DOI: 10.55041/IJSREM30037

Gladkov, M. Yu. (2024). Features of the Cloud Governance as Part of the Digital Transformation of the Public Administration SECTOR. *Science and Art of Management / Bulletin of the Institute of Economics. Management and Law of the Russian State University for the Humanities*, *3*(3), 10–23. DOI: 10.28995/2782-2222-2024-3-10-23

Huang, J. (2021). Leveraging Big Data and Machine Learning for Digital Transformation. *Journal of Integrated Design & Process Science*, *23*(3), 1–3. DOI: 10.3233/JID190020

Ibrahimy, M. M., Norta, A., & Normak, P. (2022). *Achieving Corruption-Transparency in Service Governance Processes with Blockchain-Technology Based e-Participation.*, DOI: 10.1007/978-3-031-09917-5_29

Jha, M., & Jha, R. K. (2024). Exploring the Influence of Cloud Computing on Workflow Efficiency in Public Administration. *Recent Research Reviews Journal*, *3*(1), 148–168. DOI: 10.36548/rrrj.2024.1.011

Kaivo-oja, J., Santonen, T., Lauraëus, T., & Knudsen, M. S. (2022). *Google Big Data Trend Index Analysis of Industry 4.0 Technologies: Technology and Key Concept Trends of Global Landscape in 2004–2021* (pp. 193–206). DOI: 10.1007/978-3-031-07920-7_15

Kalvet, T. (2012). Innovation: a factor explaining e-government success in Estonia. *Electronic Government, an International Journal, 9*(2), 142. DOI: 10.1504/EG.2012.046266

Karpa, M., Kitsak, T., Domsha, O., Zhuk, O., Akimova, L., & Akimov, O. (2023). Artificial Intelligence as a Tool of Public Management of Socio-Economic Development: Economic Systems, Smart Infrastructure, Digital Systems of Business Analytics and Transfers. *Ad Alta: Journal of Interdisciplinary Research, 13*(1), 13–20. DOI: 10.33543/1301341320

KOÇ, H. (2021). Dijital Dünyada Yeni Vatandaşlık Konsepti: Estonya'da E-Vatandaşlık Örneği. *OPUS Uluslararası Toplum Araştırmaları Dergisi, 17*(35), 2254–2289. DOI: 10.26466/opus.869773

Kocaoğlu, M., & Şahnagil, S. (2022). *Veriye Dayalı Kamu Politikası - Yerel Düzeydeki Yansımaları; Kuram, Kavram & Ülke Örnekleri*. Necmettin Erbakan Üniversitesi Yayınları.

Kocharian, M. (2023). TRENDS OF THE DIGITAL TECHNOLOGIES APPLICATION IN PUBLIC ADMINISTRATION. *Modern Scientific Journal*, 91–96. DOI: 10.36994/2786-9008-2023-1-12

Kyrychenko, O., & Kyrychenko, M. (2025). THE IMPACT OF DIGITALISATION ON THE EFFICIENCY OF BUSINESS PROCESSES IN THE MODERN ECONOMY. *Економіка Розвитку Систем*, *6*(2), 117–122. DOI: 10.32782/2707-8019/2024-2-16

Lazuashvili, N., Norta, A., & Draheim, D. (2019). *Integration of Blockchain Technology into a Land Registration System for Immutable Traceability: A Casestudy of Georgia.*, DOI: 10.1007/978-3-030-30429-4_15

Loukis, E., Maragoudakis, M., & Kyriakou, N. (2019). *Economic Crisis Policy Analytics Based on Artificial Intelligence.*, DOI: 10.1007/978-3-030-27325-5_20

Lutsenko, K. (2024). Digitalisation of public administration: Challenges and prospects. *Health Leadership and Quality of Life*, *3*. Advance online publication. DOI: 10.56294/hl2024.434

Mansoor, M. A., Ali, M., Mateen, A., Kaleem, M., & Nazir, S. (2023). Blockchain Technology for Land Registry Management in Developing Countries. *2023 2nd International Conference on Emerging Trends in Electrical, Control, and Telecommunication Engineering (ETECTE)*, 1–6. DOI: 10.1109/ETECTE59617.2023.10396736

Martinson, P. (2019). *Estonia – the Digital Republic Secured by Blockchain.*

Matnenko, N. N. (2020). Digital Transformation of the Public Sector off the Economy. *Scientific Journal Economic Systems*, *13*(3), 32–44. DOI: 10.29030/2309-2076-2020-13-3-32-44

Mergel, I. (2019). Digital service teams in government. *Government Information Quarterly*, *36*(4), 101389. DOI: 10.1016/j.giq.2019.07.001

Mezquita, Y., Parra, J., Perez, E., Prieto, J., & Corchado, J. M. (2021). *Blockchain-Based Systems in Land Registry, A Survey of Their Use and Economic Implications* (pp. 13–22). DOI: 10.1007/978-3-030-57805-3_2

Mijwil, M., Youssef Filali, , Mohammad Aljanabi, , Mariem Bounabi, , & Humam Al-Shahwani, . (2023). The Purpose of Cybersecurity Governance in the Digital Transformation of Public Services and Protecting the Digital Environment. *Mesopotamian Journal of CyberSecurity*, *2023*, 1–6. DOI: 10.58496/MJCS/2023/001

Mkrtchyan, T., & Melkumyan, N. (2023). The Foundations of Digital Transformation of the Public Administration System. *Alternative*, •••, 118–127. DOI: 10.55528/18292828-2023.2-118

Mountasser, T., & Abdellatif, M. (2023). Digital Transformation in Public Administration: A Systematic Literature Review. *International Journal of Professional Business Review*, *8*(10), e02372. DOI: 10.26668/businessreview/2023.v8i10.2372

Nanos, I., Manthou, V., & Androutsou, E. (2019). *Cloud Computing Adoption Decision in E-government.*, DOI: 10.1007/978-3-319-95666-4_9

Nielsen, M. M. (2017). eGovernance and Online Service Delivery in Estonia. *Proceedings of the 18th Annual International Conference on Digital Government Research*, 300–309. DOI: 10.1145/3085228.3085284

Obolonsky, Y. V. (2022). Digital Transformation of Public Administration. *Ekonomika I Upravlenie: Problemy, Resheniya, 10/1*(130), 103–109. DOI: 10.36871/ek.up.p.r.2022.10.01.014

Onabanjo A., E. (2024). Digital Transformation: The impact of AI on Cloud Transformation. *Journal of Artificial Intelligence General Science (JAIGS) ISSN:3006-4023, 5*(1), 174–183. DOI: 10.60087/jaigs.v5i1.188

Patwari, S., Ashish, S. S., Vashisht, A., Rajpurohit, E., & K, V. (2024). Digital Transformation in Various Sectors of the Indian Economy. *2024 8th International Conference on Computational System and Information Technology for Sustainable Solutions (CSITSS)*, 1–6. DOI: 10.1109/CSITSS64042.2024.10816887

Radziwill, N. (2018). *Quality 4.0: Let's Get Digital - The many ways the fourth industrial revolution is reshaping the way we think about quality.*

Ricart, G., Gonzalez, J., Papanikolaou, V., Santer, H., Clari, F., Sarris, N., Van Daele, P., & Tavernier, W. (2020). The Next Generation Internet Initiative. In *ICT Policy, Research, and Innovation* (pp. 217–253). Wiley. DOI: 10.1002/9781119632481.ch9

Rizal Batubara, F., Ubacht, J., & Janssen, M. (2019). Unraveling Transparency and Accountability in Blockchain. *Proceedings of the 20th Annual International Conference on Digital Government Research*, 204–213. DOI: 10.1145/3325112.3325262

Rohoza, A. (2024). Directions of digital transformation of analytical activities in public administration. *Actual Problems of Innovative Economy and Law, 2024*(1), 41–45. DOI: 10.36887/2524-0455-2024-1-9

Sah, C. K., & Chandavarkar, B. R. (2023). Adoption of Blockchain Technology in Land Registry Systems. *2023 Third International Conference on Secure Cyber Computing and Communication (ICSCCC)*, 548–553. DOI: 10.1109/ICSCCC58608.2023.10176550

Sandhu, K. (2021). *Advancing Cybersecurity for Digital Transformation.*, DOI: 10.4018/978-1-7998-6975-7.ch001

Saprudin, S. (2024). Artificial Intelligence Function Management in Supporting the Process of Government Implementation and Public Services in Indonesia. *Journal of Management and Administration Provision, 4*(1), 88–96. DOI: 10.55885/jmap.v4i1.352

Serac, C. A. (2023). Digital Transformation Vulnerabilities: Assessing The Risks and Strengthening Cyber Security. *The Annals of The University of Oradea. Economic Sciences, 3*(1), 771–781. Https://Doi.Org/10.47535/1991auoes32(1)059

Shaikh, F. K., Karim, S., Zeadally, S., & Nebhen, J. (2022). Recent Trends in Internet-of-Things-Enabled Sensor Technologies for Smart Agriculture. *IEEE Internet of Things Journal, 9*(23), 23583–23598. DOI: 10.1109/JIOT.2022.3210154

Shao, D., Ishengoma, F. R., Alexopoulos, C., Saxena, S., Nikiforova, A., & Matheus, R. (2023). Integration of IoT into e-government. *Foresight, 25*(5), 734–750. DOI: 10.1108/FS-04-2022-0048

Shevchenko, D., & Mihaylov, V. (2021). Digital Transformation of the Service Sector. *Scientific Research and Development. Economics of the Firm, 10*(3), 41–54. DOI: 10.12737/2306-627X-2021-10-3-41-54

Showkat Ahmad Dar. (2024). Unleashing the Power of Artificial Intelligence and Automation in Public Administration. *Journal of Public Administration Research, 1*(1), 01–13. DOI: 10.32996/jpar.2024.1.1.1

Söker, B. (2024). Leveraging Artificial Intelligence for Public Sector Decision-Making: Balancing Accountability and Efficiency in Digital Public Services. *Human-Computer Interaction, 8*(1), 105. DOI: 10.62802/ejr09s21

Storozhenko, L. (2023). Using Artificial Intelligence in Public Management: Aspects of Integration. *Krakowskie Studia Małopolskie, 40*(4), 37–49. DOI: 10.15804/ksm20230403

Verma, S., Kumar Pathak, S., Chaudhary, P., Yadav, P., & Yousuf, S. (2024). Land Registry System Using Blockchain Technology. *2024 International Conference on Emerging Innovations and Advanced Computing (INNOCOMP)*, 170–177. DOI: 10.1109/INNOCOMP63224.2024.00035

Wang, X., Liu, Y., Zhang, H., Ma, Q., & Cao, Z. (2018). Public Health Emergency Management and Multi-Source Data Technology in China. *Intelligent Automation & Soft Computing*, *24*(1), 89–96. DOI: 10.1080/10798587.2016.1267246

Weingärtner, T., Batista, D., Köchli, S., & Voutat, G. (2021). Prototyping a Smart Contract Based Public Procurement to Fight Corruption. *Computers*, *10*(7), 85. DOI: 10.3390/computers10070085

Chapter 2

The Impact of Digital Technologies on Public Administration:

Opportunities and Challenges

Veysel Eren
https://orcid.org/0000-0003-3607-1583
Hatay Mustafa Kemal University, Turkey

Hasret Duman
https://orcid.org/0000-0002-7187-7729
Hatay Mustafa Kemal University, Turkey

ABSTRACT

This study aims to comprehensively examine the impact of digital technologies on public administration. The process of digital transformation has led to profound changes in various areas, from the delivery of public services to decision-making mechanisms. Framed around the concepts of e-government and digital government, this transformation strengthens governance principles such as transparency, accountability, efficiency, and citizen participation. However, along with these opportunities, digitalization also presents new risks such as data security, digital inequality, and ethical concerns. By evaluating the integration of next-generation technologies (artificial intelligence, big data, blockchain, Internet of Things) into public services, the study offers a comparative analysis of the benefits and challenges of digital transformation.

DOI: 10.4018/979-8-3373-1484-6.ch002

INTRODUCTION

The evolution of civilization began with the transition from hunting and gathering to agriculture and was later shaped by industrial revolutions. The First Industrial Revolution enabled mechanized production through the construction of railways and the use of steam engines. The Second Industrial Revolution radically transformed production processes through mass production enabled by electricity and the assembly line. The Third Industrial Revolution laid the groundwork for digital transformation, driven by the advent of computers and the internet. Today, advancements such as artificial intelligence, machine learning, quantum computing, and nanotechnology signal the onset of the Fourth Industrial Revolution (Schwab, 2023: 15–17).

Today, billions of devices such as smartphones, tablets, and computers are increasingly connected to the internet, with both their numbers and users growing steadily. The rapid advancement of technology is driving profound transformations across numerous sectors, giving rise to new business models while disrupting existing organizations and altering patterns of production, consumption, and service delivery. Simultaneously, it is reshaping how governments, institutions, and citizens work, communicate, access information, and engage in leisure activities. For instance, contemporary governments are abandoning traditional policy-making approaches to keep pace with the speed of digital technologies, adopting more flexible and agile governance models. Centralized, top-down decision-making processes are being replaced by more adaptable, participatory, and decentralized management approaches. This transformation is redefining public service delivery, decision-making processes, and citizen engagement, while enhancing transparency and accountability. In this context, digital transformation has evolved beyond a mere technical innovation in public administration to become a fundamental dynamic that reshapes service delivery processes and transforms the functioning of public institutions.

On the other hand, digital transformation in public administration presents both significant opportunities and critical challenges. Emerging technologies such as big data analytics, artificial intelligence, blockchain, the Internet of Things, and quantum computing are enhancing public services, accelerating decision-making processes, and strengthening citizen engagement. However, issues such as data security, cyber threats, and digital inequality pose substantial risks to the sustainability of digital governance. Accordingly, this study examines the impact of digital technologies on public administration, assessing both the benefits and risks of digitalization in the public sector. To this end, the concepts of e-government and digital government are first defined, followed by an exploration of global trends. Subsequently, the integration of new digital technologies into public administration and their effects on public services are analyzed. This analysis draws upon relevant literature and practical case studies. Within this scope, the study aims to contribute to a deeper understanding of how digital transformation is shaping governance processes in the 21st century.

BACKGROUND

Public administration has undergone transformation throughout history in response to social, economic, political, and technological changes. While the traditional model of public administration was characterized by a centralized, hierarchical, and rule-based structure, the societal and technological developments that emerged in the second half of the 20th century led to a reconfiguration of public administration paradigms. More specifically, in addition to the domestic issues faced by the United States in the late 1960s -such as the Vietnam War, campus movements, minority rights, and uneven development- global challenges including poverty, African independence movements, the Soviet Union's intercontinental missile capabilities, population explosion, environmental pollution, feminist and anti-nuclear protests brought forth criticism that traditional public administration methods were insufficient to address contemporary social demands. Within this context, the reform proposals led by Dwight Waldo and his colleagues, as well as the 1968 Minnowbrook Conference, played a pivotal role in the emergence of the New Public Administration Movement. This movement advocated for a model of public administration that is responsive to social change, prioritizes citizen participation, and places social justice and equality at the core alongside effectiveness and efficiency (Waldo, 1948; Marini, 1971; Üstüner, 1995; Özgür, 2014).

Following the oil crises of the 1970s, the severe post–World War II economic downturn and the rise of liberal-conservative political movements questioning the welfare state model reignited debates over the role of the state. Particularly in developed Western countries, public administration underwent significant transformations, shifting from rigid, hierarchical, and bureaucratic structures toward more flexible, market-oriented, efficient, and performance-driven approaches. Within this context, the New Public Management (NPM) model gained prominence in the field of public administration. NPM advocated the adoption of private sector techniques in public governance, emphasized customer-oriented service delivery, and sought to enhance efficiency. As a result, concepts such as flat, horizontal, and network-based organizational structures; decentralization and delegation of authority; transparency and openness; accountability; dynamic administration; citizen-as-customer approaches; output and performance measurement; and interorganizational collaboration began to gain importance in public administration (Ömürgönülşen, 2014).

The shift in the balance of power between the state and the market in favor of the market -particularly from the final quarter of the 20th century onward- led to a transformation in the state's monopolistic status and the integration of non-state actors into governance processes. In this context, alongside New Public Management (NPM), the governance theory -formulated by international organizations- began to take shape. The concept of governance, frequently featured in the official discourse of institutions such as the IMF, the World Bank, the World Trade Organization, the Organisation for Economic Co-operation and Development (OECD), and the European Union, essentially refers to the inclusion of institutions and individuals outside of the government in the socio-political system. By the 1990s, public institutions had moved away from being the sole actors in public service delivery and began to operate in collaboration with other public agencies, civil society organizations, and the private sector (Orhan & Yalçın, 2015: 179). In this framework, cooperative organizational structures based on principles such as collaboration, transparency, accountability, participation, effectiveness, and responsibility emerged. Moreover, the transnational nature of issues such as terrorism, poverty, sustainability, migration, and global warming -as well as criticisms regarding the inadequacy of managerial, short-term output-focused approaches and the treatment of citizens merely as service recipients- have emphasized the need to explore governance opportunities in the digital age, thus bringing new approaches to the forefront. Among these are New Public Governance, Public Value Management, Digital Era Governance, and the Neo-Weberian State (Köseoğlu & Sobacı, 2015).

Since the early 2000s, the significant advancement and widespread adoption of information and communication technologies have marked the beginning of the digitalization process in the public sector. Digitalization in the public sector has enabled the delivery of public services efficiently and swiftly, without the constraints of time and place, while also paving the way for the emergence of new approaches in public administration (Yavuz, 2015). In this context, the theory of Digital Era Governance has developed, focusing on the use of digital technologies in public administration (Dunleavy, Margetts, Bastow & Tinkler, 2006). Digital Era Governance is shaped around principles such as reintegration in public administration, need-based holism, and digitization, and from the 2010s onward, it has incorporated new technologies such as Web 2.0, social media, and cloud computing (Margetts & Dunleavy, 2013).

The rapid digitalization of the state has led to a significant shift in communication and interaction between the state and non-state actors, moving largely to the electronic domain. This transformation has been shaped not only by the public administration reforms mentioned above but also by environmental, managerial, and political factors. First, the global economy's shift from a production-based model to an information-based model has accelerated the digital transformation process of governments. The rise of the information society has highlighted the need for governments to effectively utilize information and communication technologies. Secondly, citizens' expectations for speed, transparency, convenience, and affordability from -public institutions- shaped by their experiences with online services in the private sector have been a major driving force behind the widespread adoption of e-government initiatives. Lastly, the need for governments to increase political participation and regain citizens' trust has amplified the importance of concepts such as e-democracy and e-participation. This process has been supported by the goals of strengthening democratic governance and making public policy decisions more participatory (Yıldız, 2014).

All these developments have shaped the evolution of e-government theory and practices, opening the door to a new era in state-citizen interaction and leading to the emergence and widespread adoption of concepts such as e-governance, e-democracy, and e-participation. E-government refers to the use of the internet and other information and communication technologies in public administration. At this point, citizens can access public services easily, quickly, and with high quality, without the constraints of time and place. E-governance, which represents the electronic dimension of governance, refers to the use of information and communication technologies in the interaction between the state and non-state actors (Bannister & Connolly, 2012). With the development of technology, citizens' ability to obtain information and communicate has improved, and the participation of non-state actors in the policy-making process has become easier. Providing non-state actors, especially citizens, with information and responsibilities in the policy-making and implementation processes has brought e-participation to the forefront. In this context, e-government and e-participation practices have encouraged greater citizen involvement in public administration, enhancing the transparency and accountability of public services. Digitalized public administration, by utilizing innovative technologies such as AI-supported management systems and big data analytics, has made public services more effective and efficient (Meijer, 2015).

In conclusion, the transition from the traditional public administration model to a flexible, market-based, digitalized, and participatory form of governance has formed the foundation of public administration reforms. The integration of information and communication technologies into management processes to respond more effectively to changing societal needs has brought about a profound transformation in public administration.

1. CONCEPTUAL FRAMEWORK

1.1. E-Government

The digital transformation process has led to profound changes across a wide spectrum, from individuals' daily lives and working conditions to their habits and value systems, and this transformation has become noticeable in every area of life. With the rapid advancement of technology, the public sector has also been deeply influenced by this change, with public institutions starting to deliver many services through digital platforms. The most prominent example of this process is e-Government applications.

The idea of producing and delivering public services through information technology applications was incorporated into government reform through the 1993 National Performance Review Report (Yıldız, 2007). In fact, even before the invention of the Internet and the World Wide Web, information technology was used for internal communication within institutions, but from the 1990s onwards, information technologies began to be utilized for outward communication and to directly deliver public services to citizens. This change in public administration has led to a shift from traditional bureaucratic governance to a citizen-centered service delivery model based on the e-Government paradigm (Ho, 2002; King, 1982; Norris & Kraemer, 1996; Sobacı, 2012).

There is no universally accepted definition of the concept of e-Government (Halchin, 2004). In the Benchmarking E-Government: A Global Perspective report, e-Government is defined as ''*utilizing the Internet and the World-Wide-Web for delivering government information and services to citizens.*'' According to the OECD (2003), e-Government is the use of information and communication technologies and the internet to contribute to better governance practices. Similarly, Duffy (2000) describes e-Government as the use of technology to ensure the uninterrupted delivery of public services. Brown and Brudney (2001) define it as a process that increases access to public services through web-based applications and aims to improve efficiency in service delivery. Moon (2002) defines it as providing online services to simplify and improve transactions between governments, citizens, businesses, and other state institutions for more effective governance.

The concept of e-Government has a multifaceted structure and gains various meanings within different contexts and relationships. It is essentially defined through dimensions such as e-service, e-governance, and e-democracy (Yıldız, 2007; Harfouche & Robbin, 2015). E-service refers to the process of delivering online services to citizens, businesses, and institutions via digital platforms, while e-governance emphasizes transparency, accountability, citizen participation, and open data sharing in public administration. E-democracy, on the other hand, involves the use of digital tools, social media, online surveys, and other digital platforms to ensure active citizen participation in decision-making processes. In this context, processes such as e-information, e-consultation, and e-decision-making form significant components of e-Government, supporting e-participation and contributing to the development of democratic processes.

On the other hand, e-government applications involve various interaction models to facilitate the flow of information and services between different stakeholders in public administration. These interactions are categorized into subgroups, including Government-to-Government (G2G), Government-to-Citizen (G2C), Government-to-Business (G2B), Government-to-Civil Society Organizations (G2CS), and Citizen-to-Citizen (C2C) (Yıldız, 2014). Harfouche & Robbin (2015) have added additional relationships, such as Government-to-Supplier (G2S), Government-to-Government Employees (G2GE), and Government-to-Non-Governmental Organizations (G2N-GO). Each of these subcategories represents different aspects of the e-government phenomenon, which occurs through information and communication technologies between stakeholders.

The Government-to-Government (G2G) model facilitates the sharing of information, documents, and services between public institutions, while the Government-to-Citizen (G2C) model encompasses public services directed at citizens, such as tax payments, identity processing, and healthcare services. The Government-to-Business (G2B) model refers to services aimed at businesses, such as tax declarations and trade documents. The Government-to-Civil Society Organizations (G2CS) model involves the sharing of information and services with civil society organizations. The Citizen-to-Citizen (C2C) model refers to platforms that facilitate the sharing of information and services between individuals. The Government-to-Supplier (G2S) model defines the relationship between the state and suppliers in public procurement and supply processes. The Government-to-Government Employees (G2GE) model covers topics such as internal communication, personnel management, and the digitization of institutional processes. The Government-to-Non-Governmental Organizations (G2NGO) model refers to interactions involving the sharing of information and services between the government and non-profit organizations.

The intense competitive environment brought about by globalization, the changing and increasing demands of citizens, and the need to improve government processes, reduce costs, and manage performance have accelerated the differentiation and spread of e-government applications (Sobacı, 2012). Consequently, the scope of e-government has expanded to not only include the provision of public services through online platforms but also to encompass the use of ICT to enable open government data.

E-government applications are a continuous process, and most governments initially begin with the basic phase of providing online information and gradually develop these services over time (Almarabeh & AbuAli, 2010). In this process, the stages a country or institution reaches in its digital transformation journey and the development levels of e-government services reveal the maturity level of e-government applications. In the e-government literature, there are various development models for e-government, based on different research and studies. Layne and Lee (2001) proposed a four-stage e-government development model that progresses from simple to complex. This model demonstrates how e-government services evolved from a basic online information provision phase to fully integrated and complex systems. The model includes the stages of 'Cataloguing,' 'Transaction,' 'Vertical Integration,' and 'Horizontal Integration.' In the Cataloguing stage, basic information is provided online, and citizens and other stakeholders can access the information provided by public institutions. This is the most basic and initial stage of e-government. In the Transaction stage, users can perform online transactions, such as paying taxes, applying for documents, or completing official procedures. This stage represents a period when e-government services became more interactive and functional. In the Vertical Integration stage, local systems are integrated with higher-level systems. For example, when local governments connect with central government systems, it enhances data sharing and collaboration. This is a phase where e-government services become more consistent and coordinated. In the Horizontal Integration stage, integrated systems are created between different functions and institutions. This stage provides the "one-stop shop" experience, where citizens can access multiple services from a single point (e.g., an e-government portal). This stage represents the most advanced level of e-government services, where they are fully integrated and user-centered.

The development model introduced by the United Nations Division for Public Economics and Public Administration (UNDPEPA) and the American Society for Public Administration (ASPA) presents five stages: 'Emerging,' 'Enhanced,' 'Interactive,' 'Transactional,' and 'Seamless.' In the Emerging stage, the government establishes an online presence through several independent official websites, offering limited, basic, and static information. In the Enhanced stage, content is updated more frequently, and the amount of information provided increases. In the Interactive stage, users can download forms, communicate with officials, make appointments, or submit requests. In the Transactional stage, users can pay for services or carry out financial transactions online. In the Seamless stage, all e-services are integrated across government institutions (UN & ASPA, 2002).

In the relevant literature, there are models that guide governments in their digital transformation journey and demonstrate how e-government services can be made more effective and efficient. Although these models may have different names and stages, they generally range from creating a website to provide public services to the development of integrated service delivery mechanisms.

1.2. Digital Government

The concept of digital government refers to a more comprehensive structure than e-government (Bakar, Ibrahim & Yunus, 2020). While e-government focuses on the digitization of public services, digital government centers on the digital transformation of all public administration processes. Reports published by the United Nations and the OECD indicate that e-government primarily considers the delivery of services via the internet, infrastructure, and education levels, whereas digital government is based on more advanced criteria such as data management, artificial intelligence use, and integrated service delivery (UN, 2024; OECD, 2024). In this context, digital government is built on new technologies and the new mindset they bring, with its development occurring in three stages: E-Government (online services in the 2000s), Open Government (transparency, participation, and collaboration in the 2010s), and Digital Government (sustainability from 2015 onwards) (Viana, 2021). However, there are differing views in the literature regarding the distinction between digital government and e-government. While some scholars do not accept a clear separation between the two concepts, others argue that technological advancements since the 2000s have transformed e-government. In this regard, the literature presents various perspectives, including considering e-government as part of the digital government development model, viewing digital government and e-government as outputs of public administration approaches, perceiving e-government as an immature field that encompasses digital government, and interpreting it as a paradigm shift (Sağlam, 2022: 2133-2134).

The concept of digital government has long been a part of the public administration literature; however, the rapid development of next-generation technologies, such as artificial intelligence, has led to a more dynamic and complex structure in this field. Today, as citizens increasingly demand easy, fast, and efficient access to public services, the digitalization process has become not just an option but a fundamental necessity in governance. In this context, digital transformation is regarded not only as a technological innovation but also as a strategic tool that enhances the efficiency of public services and strengthens democratic participation. Additionally, in light of global challenges such as economic fluctuations, climate change, health crises, and cybersecurity threats, strengthening the digital government infrastructure has become a critical element (UN, 2024). On the other hand, while leveraging the opportunities brought by digitalization, issues such as data security, ethical use, and digital inequality must be carefully addressed. Therefore, the development of digital government should not be limited to technological investments but should also be supported by legal and governance mechanisms (OECD, 2024: 1).

The United Nations' E-Government 2024 Report provides a comprehensive framework for integrating digital government transformation with sustainable development goals. This framework emphasizes that digital government is not merely a technological issue but requires a holistic approach that also encompasses societal, economic, and environmental dimensions (UN, 2024).

Figure 1. United Nations Digital Government Model Framework

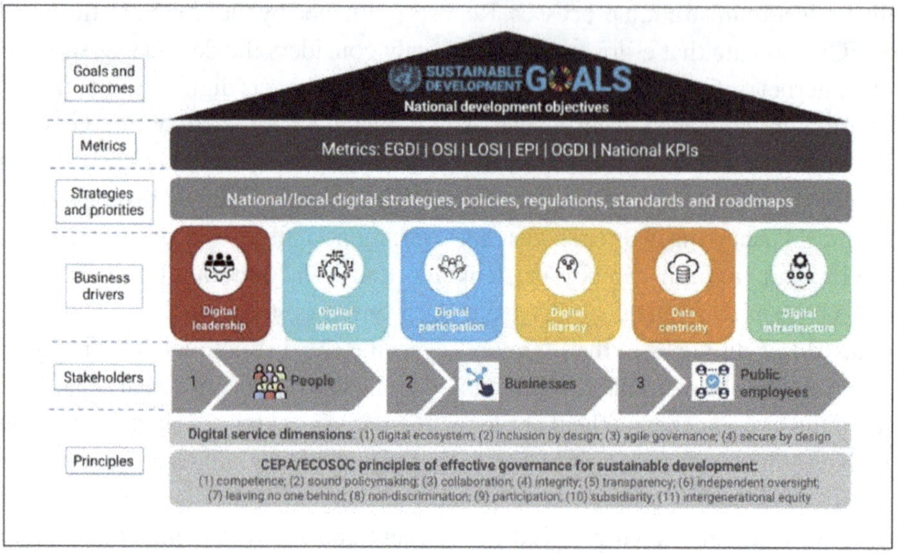

As presented in Figure 1, the ultimate goals of digital government transformation are defined as sustainable development and citizen-centric service delivery. The metrics used to achieve these goals include international standards such as the E-Government Development Index (EGDI), Online Service Index (OSI), Local Online Service Index (LOSI), E-Participation Index (EPI), and Open Government Data Index (OGDI), along with national Key Performance Indicators (KPIs). Since digital government transformation is linked to the United Nations Sustainable Development Goals (SDGs), the integration of national development goals with digital strategies is of great importance. In this context, digital leadership, digital identity, digital participation, digital literacy, data centrality, and digital infrastructure are the building blocks that enable the system to reach its strategic objectives. The government, citizens, private sector, civil society organizations, and other stakeholders form the relevant parties in the process.

Additionally, according to the model, a successful digital government should include four fundamental dimensions of digital services: 1) Digital Ecosystem, 2) Inclusion by Design, 3) Agile Governance, and 4) Secure by Design, along with the CEPA/ECOSOC Effective Governance Principles. The Digital Ecosystem refers to an integrated system where different stakeholders work together; Inclusion by Design refers to services that are designed to be accessible to everyone; Agile Governance represents fast and flexible decision-making processes; and Secure by Design refers to integrating security as a core element in the design.

The CEPA/ECOSOC Effective Governance Principles outline the fundamental guidelines for how public administration can be conducted more effectively, transparently, and participatively in order to achieve sustainable development goals. These principles include: 1) The Competence Principle, which requires public institutions and administrators to possess the necessary knowledge, skills, and capacity to perform their duties. This necessitates establishing an effective management structure with trained and experienced personnel. 2) Sound Policymaking, which emphasizes the creation of policies based on evidence and data. 3) Collaboration, which calls for strong cooperation and coordination between public institutions, the private sector, civil society, and other stakeholders to ensure the efficient use of resources and the development of inclusive solutions. 4) Integrity, which highlights the importance of transparency, accountability, and ethical behavior in management processes. 5) Transparency, which ensures that public institutions provide open and accessible information to citizens about their activities and decision-making processes. 6) Independent Oversight, which requires regular independent audits of the activities of public institutions. 7) Leaving No One Behind, which ensures that sustainable development goals encompass all segments of society, with equal opportunities, especially for disadvantaged groups (e.g., the poor, people with disabilities, women, children). 8) Non-Discrimination, which ensures the equitable and fair delivery of public services and policies. 9) Participation, which aims to strengthen social participation mechanisms and ensures active citizen involvement in decision-making processes. 10) Subsidiarity, which stipulates that decisions should be made at the most appropriate level (local, regional, or national). 11) Intergenerational Equity, which includes environmental sustainability and the fair use of natural resources to protect the rights and resources of future generations.

2. GLOBAL TRENDS IN E-GOVERNMENT AND DIGITAL GOVERNMENT

With the rapid acceleration of technological developments, e-government systems are constantly evolving and gaining new dimensions. Today, various indexes are being developed to measure the sustainability, effectiveness, and efficiency of citizen-centered e-services in e-government systems. The most well-known of these is the E-Government Development Index (EGDI) presented by the United Nations (UN). The E-Government Development Index is a critical tool for measuring the effectiveness and development level of digital government applications, as it not only includes the provision of online services but also considers digital infrastructure and digital literacy levels that facilitate citizens' access to these services. In this context, EGDI consists of three main components: the Online Services Index (OSI), the Telecommunications Infrastructure Index (TII), and the Human Capital Index (HCI) (United Nations, 2024: 1-4). The Online Services Index (OSI) evaluates the level of public services provided in digital environments. The Telecommunications Infrastructure Index (TII) consists of elements that determine the development of digital infrastructure in a country, while the Human Capital Index (HCI) measures individuals' digital skills and their capacity to use e-services. The components and sub-indexes are presented in Figure 2.

Figure 2. Components and Subindices of the EGDI

Components	Subindices
Online Services Index	☐ Institutional Framework ☐ Service Provision ☐ Content Provision ☐ Technology ☐ E-Participation Index *-E-Information* *-E-Consultation* *-E-Decision Making*
Telecommunication Infrastructure Index	☐ Percentage of individuals using the internet. ☐ Mobile phone subscriptions. ☐ Wireless broadband subscriptions. ☐ Internet access cost.
Human Capital Index	☐ Adult literacy rate. ☐ Gross school enrollment rate. ☐ Expected and average years of schooling. ☐ E-government literacy.

The success of e-government applications is dependent on a strong IT infrastructure and technological capacity. Technological elements such as telecommunications infrastructure, internet access, mobile services, cloud computing, and artificial intelligence are among the factors that determine the effectiveness of e-government. On the other hand, overcoming the issue of digital inequality (digital divide) is critical to ensuring that e-government services are accessible to all citizens (Norris, 2001). Furthermore, due to the large amount of personal and public data contained in e-government systems, cybersecurity measures, data privacy policies, and strategies for ensuring user security are of paramount importance. Therefore, e-government can be considered a comprehensive transformation process.

Figure 3 presents the composite and component values of the 2024 EGDI for 18 countries that are leading in e-government development globally. Countries in this category are considered to be the top performers in e-government applications. Their success in EGDI reflects their commitment to effectively managing digital transformation processes and providing citizen-centered services (UN, 2024). Figure

4 shows the geographical distribution of the 2024 EGDI groups. The map categorizes countries worldwide into four main groups (Very High, High, Middle, Low) based on their EGDI values. Additionally, regions with missing data are indicated on the map. Notably, countries in North America, Europe, and East Asia predominantly fall into the 'Very High' and 'High' categories, while much of Africa, as well as some countries in the Middle East and South Asia, are categorized as 'Middle' and 'Low' (UN, 2024).

Figure 3. Countries Leading E-Government Development in 2024 (Index Values)

Country	Rating class	Region	OSI	HCI	TII	EGDI (2024)	EGDI (2022)
Denmark	VH	Europe	0.9992	0.9584	0.9966	0.9847	0.9717
Estonia	VH	Europe	0.9954	0.9497	0.9731	0.9727	0.9393
Singapore	VH	Asia	0.9831	0.9362	0.9881	0.9691	0.9133
Republic of Korea	VH	Asia	1.0000	0.9120	0.9917	0.9679	0.9529
Iceland	VH	Europe	0.9076	0.9953	0.9983	0.9671	0.9410
Saudi Arabia	VH	Asia	0.9899	0.9067	0.9841	0.9602	0.8539
United Kingdom of Great Britain and Northern Ireland	VH	Europe	0.9535	0.9450	0.9747	0.9577	0.9138
Australia	VH	Oceania	0.9222	1.0000	0.9509	0.9577	0.9405
Finland	VH	Europe	0.9097	0.9836	0.9791	0.9575	0.9533
Netherlands (Kingdom of the)	VH	Europe	0.9212	0.9688	0.9715	0.9538	0.9384
United Arab Emirates	VH	Asia	0.9163	0.9436	1.0000	0.9533	0.9010
Germany	VH	Europe	0.9238	0.9672	0.9236	0.9382	0.8770
Japan	VH	Asia	0.9427	0.9117	0.9509	0.9351	0.9002
Sweden	VH	Europe	0.8836	0.9275	0.9868	0.9326	0.9410
Norway	VH	Europe	0.9117	0.9175	0.9654	0.9315	0.8879
New Zealand	VH	Oceania	0.9453	0.9615	0.8728	0.9265	0.9432
Spain	VH	Europe	0.9054	0.8961	0.9603	0.9206	0.8842
Bahrain	VH	Asia	0.9030	0.8680	0.9877	0.9196	0.7707

Sources: 2022 and 2024 United Nations E-Government Surveys.

Figure 4. Geographical Distribution of the Four EGDI Groups, 2024

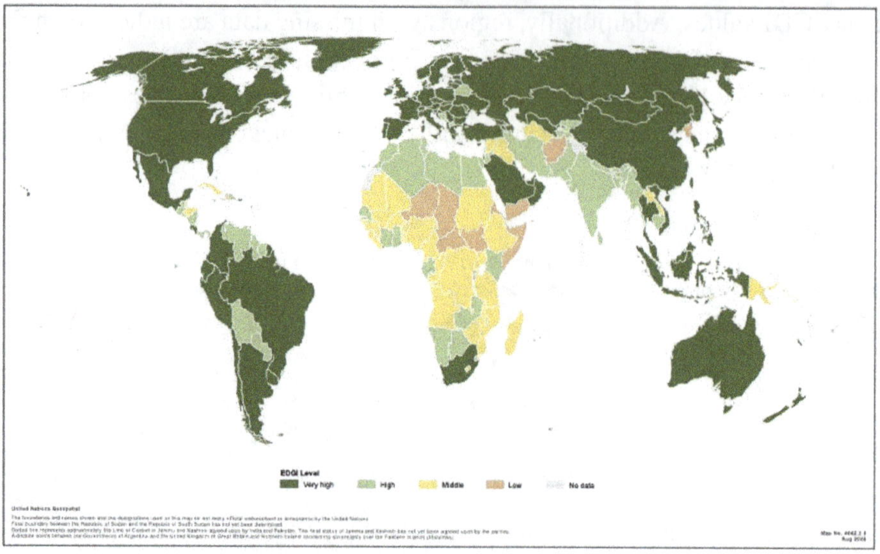

Source: 2024 United Nations E-Government Survey.

In addition to the E-Government Development Index (EGDI), digital government measurement parameters also address different criteria. For instance, according to the OECD Digital Government Policy Framework, the maturity of digital governments is evaluated based on six dimensions (OECD, 2020): 1) Digital by Design: Government policies are developed with a focus on digitalization. 2) Data-Driven Public Sector: Decisions are made based on data analysis. 3) Government as a Platform: The creation of interoperable platforms for public service delivery. 4) Open by Default: The adoption of transparency and data-sharing policies. 5) User-Driven: Services are designed with a citizen-centered approach. 6) Proactiveness: Public services are provided to citizens proactively, in anticipation of their needs.

The OECD Digital Government Index 2023 report examines the public sector digital transformation processes that took place between January 1, 2020, and October 31, 2022. This report evaluates countries' capacities to carry out a human-centered digital transformation by effectively utilizing data and technology in their digital government practices. The top 10 performing countries in the 2023 Digital Government Index are as follows: 1. South Korea (0.935), 2. Denmark (0.811), 3. United Kingdom (0.775), 4. Norway (0.770), 5. Australia (0.753), 6. Estonia (0.742), 7. Colombia (0.736), 8. Ireland (0.714), 9. France (0.665), and 10. Canada (0.655). These countries have demonstrated effective performance across the six key dimensions outlined above. Furthermore, according to the report, almost all countries have achieved a performance score of above 0.5 on a scale from 0 to 1, positioning themselves above the OECD average of 0.605. This result highlights that governments have made significant strides in the digitalization of the public sector, with most countries coming very close to achieving this goal (OECD, 2024).

3. THE IMPACT OF DIGITAL TRANSFORMATION ON PUBLIC ADMINISTRATION

Digital technologies are making the relationship between the state and citizens more interactive and transparent, while modernizing the operations of public institutions. Especially web-based technologies are enhancing transparency, accountability, and citizen participation in public administration, making governance processes more effective (Cordella & Bonina, 2012). However, digitalization weakens the dominance of traditional centralized government structures, fostering decentralization and increasing competition. This process accelerates the transition from top-down decision-making mechanisms to more participatory and flexible governance models. In policy-making, the focus is no longer on speed or quantity, but on creating inclusive and adaptable management frameworks that can respond to changing socio-economic conditions (Schwab, 2023).

While digital transformation presents significant opportunities for public administration, there are various challenges that need to be addressed to effectively manage this process. According to the World Bank's 'Digital Progress and Trends Report 2023', the benefits and risks of digitalization are interconnected (Figure 5).

Figure 5. Conceptual Framework of Digital Transformation: Balancing Benefits and Risks

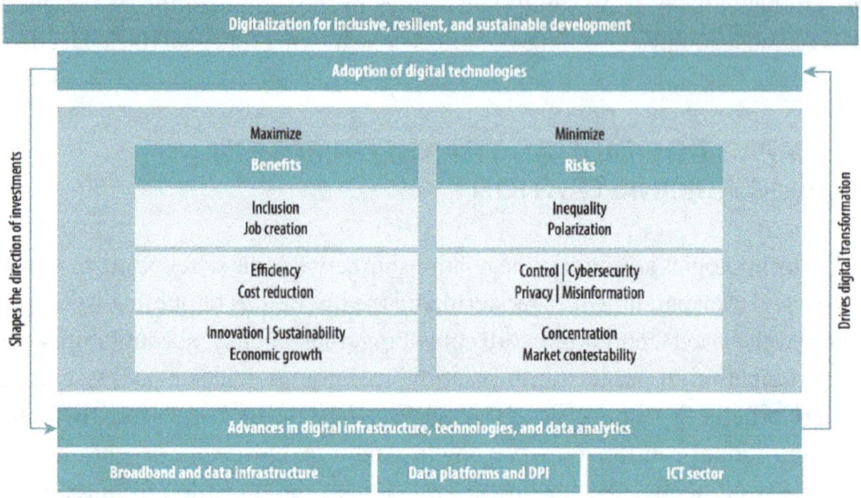

Source: Based on World Bank 2016.
Note: DPI = digital public infrastructure; ICT = information and communication technology.

Figure 5 highlights that 'broadband and data infrastructure', 'data platforms and digital public infrastructure', and 'information and communication technology sectors' are the fundamental elements of digitalization. Within this context, digital transformation offers benefits in areas such as inclusivity, job creation, efficiency, cost reduction, innovation, and economic growth. However, it also presents risks related to inequality, polarization, control, cybersecurity, privacy, misinformation, concentration, and reduced market competition.

According to the World Bank report, digitalization can create jobs, increase inclusivity, and provide large businesses with greater efficiency and lower costs. However, this can also lead to higher inequality, polarization, and power asymmetry, and make it easier for governments and companies to monitor and control individuals. In this context, issues like cybersecurity, privacy, and misinformation come to the forefront, creating significant risks that could undermine the benefits of digitalization (World Bank, 2024).

3.1. Opportunities of Using Digital Technologies in the Public Sector

Emerging digital technologies such as Big Data, the Internet of Things (IoT), Artificial Intelligence (AI), cloud computing, and blockchain are driving profound transformations in public administration by reshaping the delivery of public services and administrative processes (Viana, 2021: 39–40). Big Data refers to complex and rapidly expanding datasets. By enabling the collection and analysis of vast amounts of information, it allows for more accurate predictions, integrates data from diverse sources, generates knowledge, and facilitates the provision of improved and more efficient services (Yan, 2018). According to Sarker, Wu, and Hossin (2018), the application of Big Data in the public sector enhances efficiency, transparency, and the speed of service delivery. The authors argue that Big Data increases the productivity of public institutions, contributes to cost and financial savings, and facilitates collaboration with various internal and external stakeholders. Additionally, it empowers governments with data-driven decision-making capabilities and can be used for policy development, system planning, resource allocation, and performance monitoring. Maciejewski (2017) highlights several areas of Big Data application in the public sector, including public auditing, regulation, and service delivery. In the context of public oversight, Big Data enables the detection of irregularities. In regulatory processes, it allows for monitoring operational performance, improving existing regulations, and making more effective regulatory decisions. Furthermore, it helps policymakers better understand the societal impacts of their decisions and achieve higher-quality outcomes through feedback. In public service delivery, Big Data serves as a crucial tool for enhancing current services and designing new ones (2017: 124). Similarly, Yan (2018) argues that Big Data is generally used in public administration for macro-level control decisions, risk alerts, and surveillance purposes. Therefore, by leveraging Big Data, public managers can reduce costs and promote sustainable development. Moreover, Big Data supports administrative performance by enhancing government transparency and credibility.

According to Fredriksson, Mubarak, Tuohimaa, and Zhan (2017), the use of Big Data in the public sector offers significant benefits such as increased efficiency, enhanced transparency, and the promotion of citizen participation. In this context, Big Data has been successfully utilized in various areas including the management of health records, monitoring of epidemic outbreaks, assessment of air quality, optimization of transportation systems through real-time data in urban management, analysis of citizen feedback, and the development of urban governance strategies.

The Internet of Things (IoT) constitutes the backbone of smart city architecture. Equipping a city with IoT technology enables comprehensive monitoring and rapid response across all dimensions of urban life (Shin, 2009). Examples of IoT use in public administration include urban traffic optimization measures, car-sharing systems, smart bus stops and parking facilities, monitoring air and water pollution levels, real-time river level measurement, municipal waste management, smart lighting systems, real-time consumption tracking for fault detection, crime and threat identification, acceleration of emergency response services, and automation-based smart buildings (Polkowski and Jozwiak, 2021). Velsberg, Westergren, and Jonsson (2020) also emphasize that IoT is a critical technology for implementing smart public services and enabling public sector innovation.

Although the adoption of blockchain applications in public administration is still relatively recent, it has been growing steadily. Blockchain technology generally enhances the transparency and security of public transactions. For instance, the California Department of Motor Vehicles utilizes blockchain to ensure transparent and immutable property records, thereby preventing fraud and streamlining title transfer processes (Reuters, 2024). Similarly, China has developed a national-level digital identity system called RealDID, which uses blockchain to authenticate citizens and facilitate access to online services (Shen & Haldane, 2023). Blockchain also contributes to improved efficiency and citizen engagement in the public sector. According to Aliti, Leka, Luma, and Trpkovska (2022), blockchain technology can strengthen trust, transparency, and accessibility in public services while reinforcing the relationship between citizens and governments. In the same vein, Jalakas (2018) evaluated blockchain in the context of public administration through the case of Estonia and found that the technology has the potential to reduce transaction costs, enhance data security, increase transparency, and support citizen participation in the long term.

The use of Artificial Intelligence (AI) in public administration enables both increased efficiency and improved service delivery (Valle-Cruz et al., 2019). Van Noordt and Misuraca (2022) examined 250 case studies across the European Union on the application of AI in the public sector. Their findings indicate that AI technologies are primarily used to improve service delivery, followed by enhancements in internal management, with limited but notable influence in policymaking. Benkirane and Benazzi (2024) argue that the integration of AI technologies into public services brings advantages such as increased efficiency, cost savings, and transparency. Similarly, Mishra, Tyagi, Dananjayan, Rajavat, Rawat, and Rawat (2024) contend that incorporating AI into public administration can lead to significant improvements in efficiency, transparency, and accountability. Depending on how it is used, AI can provide substantial benefits and public value to citizens (Van Noordt & Misuraca, 2022: 1). For example, Singapore's GovTech office offers 24/7 services to citizens through AI-powered chatbots. Additionally, Duman (2024) highlights that AI applications have reduced costs and increased efficiency in the management of migration processes. For more effective disaster and emergency management, AI can utilize a wide array of digital technologies and data sources, including satellite imagery, drones, aerial videos, sensor networks, IoT devices, LiDAR from air and ground, simulations, spatial data, crowdsourcing, social media, mobile GPS, and Call Detail Records (Eren & Duman, 2025; Yu, Yang & Li, 2018; Babaoğlu & Duman, 2025).

In summary, the digitalization process in public administration emerges as a strategic transformation tool that enhances the quality of public service delivery, supports data-driven decision-making processes, and strengthens citizen participation. This transformation not only increases the efficiency and effectiveness of public institutions but also reinforces transparency, accountability, and traceability in governance. Furthermore, the automation, integration, and analytical capabilities offered by digital technologies facilitate cost reduction, improved service quality, process optimization, and the achievement of sustainable public administration goals.

3.2. Challenges of Using Digital Technology in the Public Sector

While digitalization in public administration offers numerous advantages, it also presents several structural and managerial challenges. Key issues such as safeguarding the privacy of personal data, ensuring the accuracy and effective use of digital information, inadequacy of current regulatory frameworks, limited public budgets, and a shortage of qualified personnel pose significant risks to the sustainability of digital public administration.

With the ongoing process of digitalization, digital technologies have become central to social, economic, and administrative life. In this context, a structure heavily dependent on energy flow has emerged in almost every domain—from public services and the financial sector to education and healthcare systems. However, this dependency has also rendered societies increasingly vulnerable. Issues such as personal data breaches, data leaks, cyberattacks, and digital inequality reveal that such vulnerabilities are not only technical but also encompass social and ethical dimensions. For instance, the rapid development of emerging technologies often outpaces existing legal frameworks, leading to legal inadequacies and ethical dilemmas. Moreover, the adoption of automated technologies such as artificial intelligence, big data analytics, and algorithmic decision-support systems can render decision-making processes less transparent and harder to audit (Danaher et al., 2017).

Data breaches and cyberattacks may severely damage the reputation of public institutions and erode citizens' trust in government. According to Hamid & Huda (2025), unlike violations in other sectors, such incidents in the public domain not only have far-reaching consequences but also hold the potential to significantly undermine governance and national security. Today, public institutions are among the primary targets of cyberattacks due to the sensitive data they possess. These institutions hold critical information such as citizens' identity details, health records, tax data, and manage critical infrastructure systems—making them highly attractive targets for cybercriminals. For example, in the United States, between 2004 and 2019, approximately 1.1% of state and local governments experienced data breaches originating from external sources; the most frequently targeted entities included state governments, counties, and school districts (Curti, Ivanov, Macchiavelli & Zimmermann, 2024).

Cybersecurity has become a critical prerequisite for sustaining trust, resilience, and operational continuity in digital public administration. As governments digitize their services, they inevitably become custodians of vast amounts of sensitive personal and institutional data, making them high-value targets for malicious actors (ENISA, 2023). Cyber threats—ranging from Distributed Denial-of-Service (DDoS) attacks to ransomware and phishing—can disrupt essential services, undermine public trust, and compromise national security. To address these risks, international best practices emphasize, mandating strong identity verification, and implementing encryption and continuous monitoring systems (NIST, 2020). Strengthening inter-agency coordination, investing in workforce cybersecurity skills, and establishing independent oversight bodies are essential to ensure that digital transformation does not come at the expense of security and privacy.

Public institutions collect and process citizens' personal data including identity, health, and financial information. Inadequate protection of digital systems against cyberattacks can result in this sensitive data falling into the hands of malicious actors. Cybercriminals employ various techniques to gain unauthorized access to information systems. Li & Liu (2021) identify some of these methods as follows: Denial of Service (DoS) attacks aim to exhaust system resources, preventing legitimate users from accessing public services. These attacks pose a significant threat to the continuity of public service delivery. Man-in-the-Middle (MitM) attacks involve an attacker intercepting communication between a user and a network gateway to eavesdrop or manipulate data packets, thereby seriously compromising data confidentiality and integrity. Malware -viruses or worms infiltrating users' devices- can grant unauthorized control of systems and lead to data leakage. Phishing attacks, in turn, deceive users into sharing confidential information such as passwords or identification numbers by imitating legitimate communication. Each of these techniques exploits vulnerabilities in public institutions' cybersecurity infrastructure, posing significant threats to both institutional reputation and citizen safety.

Alongside technical safeguards, ethical considerations must be integrated into the governance of digital systems. The ethical dimensions of digital governance particularly concerning artificial intelligence, big data, and automated decision-making are increasingly under scrutiny. Key concerns include algorithmic bias, surveillance, and the opaque nature of AI-driven processes (EU, 2024). The OECD AI Principles and the EU AI Act stress the importance of transparency, explainability, fairness, and human oversight in the deployment of digital technologies.

Embedding ethical guidelines into public sector ICT procurement, mandating algorithmic impact assessments, and ensuring citizens' rights to contest automated decisions are vital safeguards. Moreover, public administrations must engage in open dialogue with stakeholders to co-create ethical standards that reflect societal values and enhance public trust.

The increased reliance on digital technologies in public service delivery also brings the continuity and reliability of physical and digital infrastructures into sharp focus. In other words, natural disasters, technical malfunctions, cyberattacks, or power outages can severely disrupt digital infrastructures, leading to service interruptions, restricted access to essential services, and diminished public trust. A dramatic example of this fragility was the widespread power outage that occurred in Spain and Portugal in 2025. Beginning at 12:33 PM on April 28 and lasting approximately ten hours, the blackout significantly disrupted public service operations affecting sectors such as healthcare, education, transportation, and communication. This incident underscored the risks associated with the public sector's growing dependence on digital infrastructures.

Furthermore, the use of digital technologies in public services often reproduces existing social and economic inequalities in the digital realm a phenomenon discussed in the literature under the concept of the *digital divide*. The digital divide refers to disparities in individuals' access to, use of, and benefit from information and communication technologies. In particular, elderly populations, residents of rural areas, low-income groups, and individuals with limited digital literacy are often unable to fully benefit from digitalized public services. This results in structural inequities in access to essential public services (Warschauer, 2004). Thus, it is crucial not only to develop digital service infrastructures but also to enhance citizens' capacity to access and use these services effectively. In this regard, addressing digital inequality is a strategic necessity for ensuring that digital government initiatives are inclusive and equitable.

Digital transformation in public administration must be grounded in the principle of equitable access to ensure that no social group is left behind. The digital divide remains a persistent challenge, particularly among rural populations, low-income households, elderly citizens, and individuals with disabilities (OECD, 2021). To bridge this divide, governments are implementing multi-faceted strategies, including subsidized broadband programs, public internet access points, and targeted digital literacy training (ITU, 2022). The concept of "Inclusion by Design", endorsed by the United Nations E-Government Survey (2024), requires that digital services be designed with accessibility features, multilingual interfaces, and low-bandwidth compatibility from the outset. By prioritizing inclusivity, public administrations can not only enhance social cohesion but also ensure the legitimacy and uptake of digital services.

CONCLUSION

This study systematically examines the transformative impact of digital technologies on public administration. In today's context, digitalization has triggered profound changes across a wide spectrum from the delivery of public services to decision-making mechanisms. Shaped within the frameworks of e-government and digital government, this transformation has significantly contributed to the development of public administration, while also introducing a variety of new challenges.

Digital technologies offer critical opportunities to enhance service quality, strengthen decision-making processes, and encourage citizen participation in public administration. E-government initiatives reinforce governance principles such as transparency, accountability, and efficiency, while also yielding structural benefits such as cost reduction, shorter service delivery times, and improved interagency coordination. Similarly, emerging digital innovations -such as artificial intelligence, the Internet of Things (IoT), blockchain, and cloud computing- support the automation of public services and simplify operational processes. Through these technologies, data sharing among public institutions becomes more seamless, integrated service models can be developed, and nationwide digital alignment can be achieved.

Public trust is both a driver and an outcome of successful digital transformation. Citizens' willingness to adopt digital public services is influenced by perceptions of security, reliability, and fairness. Negative experiences—such as service outages, data breaches, or inaccessible platforms—can erode trust and slow adoption rates. To cultivate trust, governments must ensure consistent service quality, transparent communication about risks and safeguards, and mechanisms for user feedback and redress. Participatory design processes, where citizens are involved in the co-creation of services, have been shown to enhance legitimacy and user satisfaction (UN, 2024).

The digital transformation process also brings along various structural and administrative challenges. Issues such as data security, personal privacy, and ethical decision-making mechanisms render the use of digital technologies in public administration a more delicate matter. On the other hand, inequalities in access to digital services may lead to the exclusion of certain social groups. Moreover, the lack of digital competencies among public employees, deficiencies in technical infrastructure, and institutional resistance can hinder the comprehensive and sustainable implementation of the transformation.

To ensure continuous improvement and accountability, systematic evaluation mechanisms must be institutionalized. Robust evaluation frameworks are essential for assessing the effectiveness, efficiency, and equity of digital public services. Traditional performance metrics such as service uptake rates should be complemented with qualitative indicators of user experience, trust, and social impact. Global tools such as the E-Participation Index, the Open Government Data Index, and the Balanced Scorecard for Digital Government provide multidimensional benchmarks. Embedding real-time monitoring dashboards and open data portals enables continuous performance tracking, while independent audits strengthen accountability. By institutionalizing evaluation, public administrations can iteratively refine their strategies and ensure alignment with evolving societal needs.

For digital transformation to be implemented sustainably within public administration, comprehensive strategies must be developed. These strategies should include robust cybersecurity measures, digital literacy programs, and well-defined ethical frameworks. Furthermore, reducing digital inequality through international cooperation and aligning technological innovations with democratic values are essential for ensuring inclusive and responsible governance.

REFERENCES

Aliti, A., Leka, E., Luma, A., & Trpkovska, M. A. (2022). A Systematic Literature Review on Using Blockchain Technology in Public Administration. In *2022 45th Jubilee International Convention on Information, Communication and Electronic Technology (MIPRO)* (pp. 1031-1036). IEEE. DOI: 10.23919/MIPRO55190.2022.9803797

Almarabeh, T., & AbuAli, A. (2010). A general framework for e-government: Definition maturity challenges, opportunities, and success. *European Journal of Scientific Research*, *39*(1), 29–42.

Babaoğlu, C., & Duman, H. (2025). Afet Yönetimi Açısından Sosyal Medya: Fırsatlar ve Riskler. *Türk Deprem Araştırma Dergisi*, *7*(1), 25–35. DOI: 10.46464/tdad.1538677

Bakar, K. A., Ibrahim, R., & Yunus, Y. (2020). Digital government evolution and maturity models: A review. *Open International Journal of Informatics*, *8*(2), 70–87.

Bannister, F., & Connolly, R. (2012). Defining e-governance. *E-government*, *29*(1), 1–12.

Brown, M. M., & Brudney, J. L. (2001). Achieving advanced electronic government services: An examination of obstacles and implications from an international perspective. *Journal of Public Administration: Research and Theory*, *11*(1), 1–11. DOI: 10.22259/2642-8318.0101001

Cordella, A., & Bonina, C. M. (2012). A public value perspective for ICT enabled public sector reforms: A theoretical reflection. *Government Information Quarterly*, *29*(4), 512–520. DOI: 10.1016/j.giq.2012.03.004

Curti, F., Ivanov, I. T., Macchiavelli, M., & Zimmermann, T. (2024). Exposure to Cyber Risk and Inadequate Cybersecurity Regulations: Evidence from Municipalities. *Chicago Fed Letter, 501*.

Danaher, J., Hogan, M. J., Noone, C., Kennedy, R., Behan, A., de Paor, A., Felzmann, H., Haklay, M., Khoo, S.-M., Morison, J., Murphy, M. H., O'Brolchain, N., Schafer, B., & Shankar, K. (2017). Algorithmic governance: Developing a research agenda through the power of collective intelligence. *Big Data & Society*, *4*(2), 1–21. DOI: 10.1177/2053951717726554

Duffy, D. (2000). The internet as a research and dissemination resource. *Health Promotion International*, *15*(4), 349–353. DOI: 10.1093/heapro/15.4.349

Duman, H. (2024). Use of Digital Technologies in Migration and Asylum Management. In *Media representation of migrants and refugees* (pp. 169–188). IGI Global. DOI: 10.4018/979-8-3693-3459-1.ch011

Dunleavy, P., Margetts, H., Bastow, S., & Tinkler, J. (2006). New public management is dead—Long live digital-era governance. *Journal of Public Administration: Research and Theory, 16*(3), 467–494. DOI: 10.1093/jopart/mui057

ENISA. (2023). *European Cybersecurity Threat Landscape 2023*. European Union Agency for Cybersecurity.

Eren, V., & Duman, H. (2025). Artificial intelligence support in disaster management. *Kamu Yönetimi ve Teknoloji Dergisi, 7*(1), 13–36. DOI: 10.58307/kaytek.1580460

EU. (2024). *Artificial Intelligence Act*. Official Journal of the European Union.

Fredriksson, C., Mubarak, F., Tuohimaa, M., & Zhan, M. (2017). Big data in the public sector: A systematic literature review. *Scandinavian Journal of Public Administration, 21*(3), 39–61. DOI: 10.58235/sjpa.v21i3.11563

Halchin, L. E. (2004). Electronic government: Government capability and terrorist resource. *Government Information Quarterly, 21*(4), 406–419. DOI: 10.1016/j.giq.2004.08.002

Hamid, S., & Huda, M. N. (2025). Mapping the landscape of government data breaches: A bibliometric analysis of literature from 2006 to 2023. *Social Sciences & Humanities Open, 11*, 101234. DOI: 10.1016/j.ssaho.2024.101234

Harfouche, A., & Robbin, A. (2015). E-Government. In book: Wiley Encyclopedia of Management. DOI:DOI: 10.1002/9781118785317.weom070001

Ho, A. T. K. (2002). Reinventing Local Governments and the E-Government Initiative. *Public Administration Review, 62*(4), 434–444. DOI: 10.1111/0033-3352.00197

ITU. (2022). *Measuring digital development: Facts and figures*. International Telecommunication Union.

Jalakas, P. (2018). *Blockchain from public administration perspective: Case of Estonia*. Tallinn University of Technology.

King, J. L. (1982). Local government use of information technology: A survey of recent research. *Public Administration Review, 42*(1), 25–36. DOI: 10.2307/976089

Köseoğlu, Ö., & Sobacı, M. Z. (2015). Kamu yönetimi kuramının geleceği: yeni kamu işletmeciliğinden hibritleşmeye doğru. In Köseoğlu, Ö., & Sobacı, M. Z. (Eds.), *Kamu Yönetiminde Paradigma Arayışları: Yeni Kamu İşletmeciliği ve Ötesi* (pp. 297–314). Dora Yayıncılık.

Layne, K., & Lee, J. (2001). Developing fully functional e-government: A four stage model. *Government Information Quarterly*, *18*(2), 122–136. DOI: 10.1016/S0740-624X(01)00066-1

Li, Y., & Liu, Q. (2021). A comprehensive review study of cyber-attacks and cyber security; Emerging trends and recent developments. *Energy Reports*, *7*, 8176–8186. DOI: 10.1016/j.egyr.2021.08.126

Maciejewski, M. (2017). To do more, better, faster and more cheaply: Using big data in public administration. *International Review of Administrative Sciences*, *83*(1, suppl), 120–135. DOI: 10.1177/0020852316640058

Margetts, H., & Dunleavy, P. (2013). The second wave of digital-era governance: A quasi-paradigm for government on the Web. *Philosophical Transactions of the Royal Society A: Mathematical, Physical and Engineering Sciences, 371*(1987), 20120382.

Marini, F. (1971). *Toward a new public administration: The Minnowbrook perspective*. Chandler Publishing.

Meijer, A. (2015). E-governance innovation: Barriers and strategies. *Government Information Quarterly*, *32*(2), 198–206. DOI: 10.1016/j.giq.2015.01.001

Mishra, A. K., Tyagi, A. K., Dananjayan, S., Rajavat, A., Rawat, H., & Rawat, A. (2024). Revolutionizing government operations: The impact of artificial intelligence in public administration. *Conversational Artificial Intelligence*, 607-634.

Moon, M. J. (2002). The evolution of e-government among municipalities: Rhetoric or reality? *Public Administration Review*, *62*(4), 424–433. DOI: 10.1111/0033-3352.00196

NIST. (2020). *Zero Trust Architecture*. National Institute of Standards and Technology, Special Publication 800–207.

Norris, D. F., & Kraemer, K. L. (1996). Mainframe and PC Computing in American Local Governments: Myths and Realities. *Public Administration Review*, *56*(6), 568–576. DOI: 10.2307/977255

Norris, P. (2001). *Digital divide: Civic engagement, information poverty, and the Internet worldwide*. Cambridge University Press. DOI: 10.1017/CBO9781139164887

OECD. (2003). *The e-government imperative*. Organisation for Economic Co-operation and Development.

OECD. (2020). The OECD Digital Government Policy Framework: Six dimensions of a Digital Government. In *OECD Public Governance Policy Papers, No. 02*. OECD Publishing., DOI: 10.1787/f64fed2a-

OECD. (2021). *Bridging the Digital Divide*. OECD Publishing.

Ömürgönülşen, U. (2014). Kamu sektörünün yönetimi sorununa yeni bir yaklaşım: Yeni kamu işletmeciliği. In Acar, M., & Özgür, H. (Eds.), *Çağdaş kamu yönetimi I: Konular, kuramlar, kavramlar* (pp. 1–35). Nobel Yayıncılık.

Orhan, G., & Yalçın, S. (2015). Yönetişim ve kamu yönetimi. *Kamu Yönetimi Dergisi, 47*(1), 175–190.

Özgür, H. (2014). Yeni Kamu Yönetimi Hareketi. Çağdaş Kamu Yönetimi 1. Nobel yayınları, Ankara.

Polkowski, Z., & Jozwiak, M. (2021). Internet of things in public administration. In *2021 Fourth International Conference on Computational Intelligence and Communication Technologies (CCICT)* (pp. 343-349). IEEE.

Reuters. (2024). *California DMV puts 42 million car titles on blockchain to fight fraud*. https://www.reuters.com/technology/california-dmv-puts-42-million-car-titles-blockchain-fight-fraud-2024-07-30/

Sarker, M. N. I., Wu, M., & Hossin, M. A. (2018). Smart governance through bigdata: Digital transformation of public agencies. In *2018 international conference on artificial intelligence and big data (ICAIBD)* (pp. 62-70). IEEE.

Schwab, K. (2023). *Dördüncü Sanayi Devrimi* (Çev. Zülfü Dicleli). Dünya Ekonomik Forumu. İstanbul: Optimist Yayınları.

Shen, X., & Haldane, M. (2023). Blockchain-managed IDs arrive in China with new government-backed scheme aiming to reduce data leaks. *South China Morning Post*. https://www.scmp.com/tech/policy/article/3245028/blockchain-managed-ids-arrive-china-new-government-backed-scheme-aiming-reduce-data-leaks

Shin, D. H. (2009). Ubiquitous city: Urban technologies, urban infrastructure and urban informatics. *Journal of Information Science, 35*(5), 515–526. DOI: 10.1177/0165551509100832

Sobacı, M. Z. (2012). E-devlet: Kuramsal bir bakış. In Sobacı, M. Z., & Yıldız, M. (Eds.), *E-Devlet: Kamu Yönetimi ve Teknoloji İlişkisinde Güncel Gelişmeler* (pp. 3–37). Nobel Yayınları.

United Nations. (2020). *E-Government Survey 2020: Digital Government in the Decade of Action for Sustainable Development*. United Nations.

United Nations. (2022). E-Government Development Index: Trends and Analysis.

United Nations. (2024). E-Government Survey 2024: Accelerating Digital Transformation for Sustainable Development with the addendum on Artificial Intelligence

Üstüner, M. (1995). Kamu Yönetiminde Kimlik Arayışı ve Yeni Kamu Yönetimi Hareketi. *Ankara Üniversitesi Siyasal Bilgiler Fakültesi Dergisi, 50*(3), 89–103.

Valle-Cruz, D., Alejandro Ruvalcaba-Gomez, E., Sandoval-Almazan, R., & Ignacio Criado, J. (2019). A review of artificial intelligence in government and its potential from a public policy perspective. In *Proceedings of the 20th annual international conference on digital government research* (pp. 91-99). DOI: 10.1145/3325112.3325242

Van Noordt, C., & Misuraca, G. (2022). Artificial intelligence for the public sector: Results of landscaping the use of AI in government across the European Union. *Government Information Quarterly, 39*(3), 101714. DOI: 10.1016/j.giq.2022.101714

Velsberg, O., Westergren, U. H., & Jonsson, K. (2020). Exploring smartness in public sector innovation-creating smart public services with the Internet of Things. *European Journal of Information Systems, 29*(4), 350–368. DOI: 10.1080/0960085X.2020.1761272

Viana, A. C. A. (2021). Digital transformation in public administration: from e-Government to digital government. *International Journal of digital law, 1*(1), 29-44.

Waldo, D. (1948). *The administrative state: A study of the political theory of American public administration*. Ronald Press.

Warschauer, M. (2004). *Technology and social inclusion: Rethinking the digital divide*. MIT press.

World Bank. (2024). Digital Progress and Trends Report 2023. Washington, DC: World Bank. . https://openknowledge.worldbank.org/server/api/core/bitstreams/95fe55e9-f110-4ba8-933f-e65572e05395/contentDOI: 10.1596/978-1-4648-2049-6

Yan, Z. (2018). Big data and government governance. In *2018 International Conference on Information Management and Processing (ICIMP)* (pp. 111-114). IEEE. DOI: 10.1109/ICIMP1.2018.8325850

Yavuz, N. (2015). Dijital çağda kamu yönetimi ve e-devlet. *Kamu Yönetimi Dergisi, 50*(2), 270–285.

Yıldız, M. (2007). E-government research: Reviewing the literature, limitations, and ways forward. *Government Information Quarterly*, *24*(3), 646–665. DOI: 10.1016/j.giq.2007.01.002

Yıldız, M. (2014). E-devlet teorisi ve pratiğinin genel bir değerlendirmesi. M. Acar ve H. Özgür (Ed.), Çağdaş Kamu Yönetimi-1 (s. 305-328). İstanbul: Nobel Yayınları.

Yu, M., Yang, C., & Li, Y. (2018). Big data in natural disaster management: A review. *Geosciences*, *8*(5), 165. DOI: 10.3390/geosciences8050165

Chapter 3
From e-Government to Digital Government:
A New Era in Public Administration

Andi Asrifan
https://orcid.org/0000-0002-9934-6129
Universitas Negeri Makassar, Indonesia

Rismawati Rismawati
https://orcid.org/0000-0001-8046-6764
Universitas Muhammadiyah Palopo, Indonesia

ABSTRACT

This chapter explores the transformation from e-Government to digital government, highlighting the shift from service digitization to systemic innovation in public administration. Drawing on international best practices and theoretical frameworks, the text examines the integration of artificial intelligence, blockchain, cloud computing, and citizen-centric design in reshaping governance. The discussion encompasses the ethical and operational implications of algorithmic bias, data privacy, and the digital divide, while presenting policy innovations and adaptive strategies to ensure future-ready governance. Emphasizing inclusion, transparency, and responsiveness, the chapter presents digital government not as a mere technological evolution, but as a strategic reimagining of statecraft in the 21st century. The narrative concludes with future-oriented reflections on policy design, participatory frameworks, and institutional agility that align digital transformation with the creation of sustainable public value.

DOI: 10.4018/979-8-3373-1484-6.ch003

1. INTRODUCTION

1.1. Defining e-Government and Digital Government: Shifts in Terminology and Scope

The evolution from e-Government to digital government signifies a profound paradigm shift in public administration, reflecting the increasingly intertwined relationship between technological progress and governance structures. Traditionally, e-Government refers to the application of information and communication technologies (ICTs) to improve the efficiency, accessibility, and responsiveness of government services to citizens, businesses, and intergovernmental entities (Alenezi, 2022). The core focus of e-Government lies in digitizing existing processes without necessarily transforming underlying institutional frameworks.

In contrast, digital government encompasses a broader, more systemic transformation. It implies the strategic integration of digital technologies not only in service delivery but across all dimensions of governance — including policy formulation, inter-agency coordination, stakeholder participation, and data governance (Ciancarini et al., 2023). This reconceptualization marks a shift from automation toward innovation, agility, and inclusion, where government becomes a platform enabling co-creation with society (Tan & Taeihagh, 2020).

Furthermore, the terminological evolution highlights a conceptual reframing: e-Government is often linear and transactional, while digital government is iterative, adaptive, and participatory (Mergel et al., 2020). The adoption of technologies such as artificial intelligence, cloud computing, blockchain, and big data analytics reinforces this redefinition, allowing real-time insights into policymaking and personalized public services. In this landscape, citizen-centricity becomes central, with users no longer treated as passive recipients but as active contributors to service design and governance innovation.

Digital government also introduces new standards of transparency, interoperability, and accountability, requiring public institutions to rethink legacy systems and adopt agile digital infrastructures. These developments necessitate cultural change, workforce re-skilling, and a rebalancing of power between central authorities and local innovation nodes. The underlying assumption is that digital government is not merely a technical evolution but a strategic, societal transformation with ethical, legal, and political implications. In summary, while e-Government initiated the digital journey in public administration, digital government represents its maturation — aiming for a reimagined statecraft that is resilient, anticipatory, and equitable in the face of rapid technological disruption and evolving citizen expectations.

1.2. Theoretical Perspectives: From Technological Determinism to Socio-Technical Systems

The evolution of public administration in the digital age necessitates a critical examination of underlying theoretical frameworks that shape our understanding of technological integration. Two prominent perspectives—technological determinism and socio-technical systems theory—offer contrasting lenses through which to analyze the interplay between technology and organizational structures.

Technological determinism posits that technological development drives societal change, often in a linear and inevitable manner. This perspective suggests that the adoption of digital tools in public administration leads to predefined outcomes, such as increased efficiency and transparency, irrespective of the social context (Smith & Marx, 2020). However, critics argue that this view overlooks the complex socio-political factors influencing technology implementation and may lead to technocratic governance models that marginalize stakeholder input (Wyatt, 2021).

In contrast, the socio-technical systems (STS) approach emphasizes the interdependence between technological artifacts and social structures. STS theory advocates for a holistic view, recognizing that successful digital transformation in public administration requires the alignment of technological capabilities with organizational culture, stakeholder engagement, and policy frameworks (Trist & Emery, 2022). This perspective encourages participatory design processes and iterative development, ensuring that technological solutions are adaptable to the evolving needs of public institutions and citizens alike.

Empirical studies underscore the efficacy of the STS approach in public sector innovation. For instance, research on e-government initiatives in various countries reveals that projects incorporating stakeholder feedback and cross-sector collaboration tend to achieve higher adoption rates and user satisfaction (Bovens & Zouridis, 2023). Moreover, the integration of artificial intelligence and big data analytics in public services has demonstrated that ethical considerations and transparency are paramount, aligning with STS principles that advocate for responsible innovation (Margetts & Dorobantu, 2024). In conclusion, while technological determinism offers insights into the potential impacts of digital tools, the socio-technical systems perspective provides a more nuanced framework for understanding and guiding digital transformation in public administration. Embracing the STS approach facilitates the development of inclusive, adaptable, and ethically grounded digital governance models that resonate with the complex realities of contemporary public service delivery.

1.3. Public Sector Innovation: Drivers and Barriers in the Digital Transformation

The digital transformation of the public sector is propelled by various drivers that aim to enhance efficiency, transparency, and citizen engagement. One significant driver is the advancement of digital technologies, such as artificial intelligence, big data analytics, and cloud computing, which offer new avenues for service delivery and decision-making processes. Additionally, the increasing expectations of citizens for more responsive and accessible public services have compelled governments to adopt innovative approaches.

However, the journey towards digital transformation is fraught with barriers. Organizational resistance to change is a prevalent obstacle, often stemming from entrenched bureaucratic cultures and a lack of digital literacy among public servants. Moreover, legacy IT systems pose significant challenges, as they are often incompatible with new technologies and require substantial investment to upgrade. Budget constraints further exacerbate these issues, limiting the capacity of public institutions to invest in necessary technological infrastructure and training.

Another critical barrier is the lack of a clear strategic vision for digital transformation. Without coherent policies and leadership commitment, digital initiatives may lack direction and fail to achieve their intended outcomes. Furthermore, concerns about data privacy and security can hinder the adoption of digital solutions, as public trust is paramount in the deployment of new technologies.

To overcome these barriers, a multifaceted approach is required. This includes fostering a culture of innovation within public institutions, investing in capacity building, and developing comprehensive digital strategies that align with organizational goals. Engaging stakeholders, including citizens, in the design and implementation of digital initiatives can also enhance their relevance and acceptance. Moreover, establishing robust governance frameworks to address data privacy and security concerns is essential to build public trust and ensure the sustainability of digital transformation efforts. In conclusion, while the digital transformation of the public sector presents numerous opportunities for innovation and improved service delivery, it also entails significant challenges. Addressing these barriers requires strategic planning, organizational change, and stakeholder engagement to realize the full potential of digital technologies in public administration.

DIGITAL TRANSFORMATION IN PUBLIC ADMINISTRATION

2.1. Reconfiguring Bureaucracy: Agile Structures and Adaptive Governance

The digital transformation of public administration has triggered a paradigm shift in how bureaucratic structures are conceptualized and executed. Traditional hierarchical and rigid bureaucracies are increasingly viewed as ill-equipped to respond to the rapid pace of change in contemporary governance. In response, the concepts of agile structures and adaptive governance have emerged as key strategies to enhance public sector responsiveness and operational efficiency.

Agile organizational structures emphasize flexibility, cross-functional collaboration, and rapid decision-making cycles. In the context of the public sector, adopting agile principles enables institutions to respond more effectively to dynamic societal needs and external pressures. Mergel, Edelmann, and Haug (2020) found that integrating agile methodologies into governmental projects led to increased stakeholder satisfaction and organizational efficiency.

Meanwhile, adaptive governance highlights the capacity of institutions to continuously learn and adjust their operations in response to complex and uncertain environments. This approach acknowledges the limitations of linear decision-making models and promotes stakeholder participation, experimentation, and iterative feedback loops. According to Janssen and van der Voort (2020), adaptive governance enhances governmental resilience by embedding flexibility and responsiveness into institutional frameworks.

Successful implementation of agile and adaptive models in public administration necessitates significant shifts in organizational culture, workforce skills, and regulatory frameworks. For instance, the United Kingdom's Government Digital Service (GDS) has embraced agile practices in the development of public digital services, allowing for user-centered design and iterative improvements (Greenway et al., 2021).

However, several challenges must be addressed. Structural rigidity, resistance to change, and limited digital literacy among civil servants often hinder transformation efforts. Moreover, outdated legacy systems and fragmented policy environments may obstruct the seamless integration of agile principles. Thus, leadership commitment, continuous capacity-building, and strategic change management are essential. In conclusion, reconfiguring bureaucracies through agile structures and adaptive governance offers a promising pathway for enhancing public sector effectiveness in the digital age. These approaches enable governments to become more proactive, citizen-centric, and responsive to rapidly evolving socio-technological landscapes.

2.2. Digital Platforms and Service Delivery: Enhancing Responsiveness and Inclusion

The integration of digital platforms into public service delivery has fundamentally transformed the landscape of public administration, offering avenues for increased responsiveness and inclusivity. These platforms facilitate real-time interactions between governments and citizens, streamline service processes, and broaden access to public services.

Digital platforms, encompassing websites, mobile applications, and integrated service portals, enable governments to provide services more efficiently and responsively (Bäckström, 2023). For instance, Estonia's e-government initiatives have demonstrated how digital platforms can streamline administrative processes, reducing bureaucracy and enhancing citizen satisfaction (Wattoo et al., 2025) . Similarly, the implementation of AI-powered tools in e-government systems has improved municipal responsiveness by enabling quicker processing of citizen requests.

Inclusivity is a critical aspect of digital service delivery. Digital platforms have the potential to bridge gaps in service accessibility, particularly for marginalized and remote communities. The United Nations Development Programme emphasizes the importance of inclusive digital public services to ensure equitable access for all citizens (Hofeditz et al., 2025; Wattoo et al., 2025) . However, challenges persist, such as digital literacy barriers and unequal access to technology, which can hinder the effectiveness of digital platforms in reaching all segments of the population.

To address these challenges, governments must implement strategies that promote digital inclusion. This includes investing in digital literacy programs, ensuring affordable internet access, and designing user-friendly platforms that cater to diverse user needs. Moreover, engaging citizens in the development and evaluation of digital services can enhance their relevance and usability. In conclusion, digital platforms hold significant promise for enhancing the responsiveness and inclusivity of public service delivery. By embracing technological innovations and prioritizing digital inclusion, public administrations can better meet the evolving needs of their constituents.

2.3. Citizen-Centricity and Participatory Models in the Digital Era

The digital era has ushered in a transformative shift in public administration, moving from authority-driven governance to citizen-centric and participatory models. This evolution reflects a fundamental redefinition of the citizen–state relationship, where individuals are no longer passive recipients of services but active collaborators in shaping policies, services, and governance outcomes.

Citizen-centric governance places the needs, preferences, and rights of citizens at the heart of public service design and delivery. This approach challenges traditional bureaucratic models by fostering personalized services, responsive feedback mechanisms, and empathetic public engagement. In digital contexts, citizen-centricity is operationalized through the deployment of digital identity systems, integrated service platforms, and real-time feedback channels that adapt dynamically to users' needs (Wibowo, 2025).

Participatory models further extend this paradigm by enabling collective input, deliberation, and co-creation. Through digital platforms such as e-consultation tools, civic technology (civic tech) applications, online town halls, and crowdsourcing portals, governments can harness distributed public knowledge, enhance policy legitimacy, and cultivate democratic inclusivity. These tools provide avenues for marginalized voices to be heard and can serve as mechanisms to rebuild public trust.

However, the implementation of digital participatory governance is not without challenges. Significant barriers include the digital divide, disparities in digital literacy, and the risk of excluding vulnerable populations. Moreover, the legitimacy of digital participation may be questioned when public input does not translate into tangible policy impact or when processes lack transparency and accountability. Ensuring meaningful engagement requires thoughtful design, moderation, and integration of public feedback into decision-making processes.

To address these concerns, governments must embed participatory values into institutional frameworks, prioritize inclusive design, and commit to transparent governance. Capacity-building programs, multilingual interfaces, and mobile-friendly applications can expand access, while secure and anonymized platforms can foster trust among participants (Olanipekun, 2025; Shi & Sun, 2024; Singh et al., 2024). In conclusion, citizen-centric and participatory models—when empowered by digital technologies—hold the potential to transform governance into a more responsive, equitable, and accountable system. By embracing inclusive innovation, public administrations can not only meet the evolving expectations of the digital citizen but also revitalize the democratic fabric of society.

TECHNOLOGIES SHAPING DIGITAL GOVERNMENT

3.1 Artificial Intelligence and Big Data Analytics in Public Sector Decision-Making

The integration of Artificial Intelligence (AI) and Big Data Analytics (BDA) into public sector decision-making represents a critical leap forward in the evolution of digital government. These technologies are transforming the ways in which governments analyze complex data, forecast societal trends, and allocate public resources with greater precision and responsiveness.

AI enables the automation of routine administrative tasks, such as document processing, fraud detection, and predictive maintenance in public infrastructure. Machine learning algorithms, in particular, are capable of identifying patterns in large, unstructured datasets, which enhances the capacity of public agencies to detect anomalies, anticipate service demands, and respond proactively to emerging issues (Bello et al., 2024; Hadjidemetriou et al., 2021; Hofeditz et al., 2025). In areas such as health surveillance, transportation, and public safety, AI systems have already demonstrated measurable improvements in efficiency and service accuracy.

Big Data Analytics complements AI by processing high-volume, high-velocity, and high-variety data collected from diverse sources, including sensor networks, social media, open government platforms, and citizen feedback systems. With the rise of real-time data flows, public administrators are increasingly able to shift from reactive policy models to anticipatory governance (Choi & Park, 2023; Muiderman et al., 2023; Olanipekun, 2025). For instance, predictive analytics can inform urban planning decisions by analyzing traffic flows, pollution levels, and demographic shifts in real-time, enabling more targeted interventions.

However, the adoption of AI and BDA in the public sector also raises critical concerns. Algorithmic bias, data privacy, and lack of transparency in decision-making processes can undermine public trust if not managed ethically. Furthermore, the absence of digital skills among public servants may hinder effective implementation and oversight of these systems. Ethical governance frameworks and robust accountability mechanisms are therefore essential to ensure that these technologies align with democratic values and human rights.

Moreover, institutional readiness remains a significant challenge. Public agencies must build internal capacities for data stewardship, establish interoperable data infrastructures, and invest in long-term digital innovation strategies. Cross-sector collaboration with academia, civil society, and private technology firms is also necessary to promote inclusive and responsible AI development in the public domain (Abujaber & Nashwan, 2024; Naik et al., 2023). In summary, AI and Big Data Analytics are not just tools for operational efficiency—they are catalysts for evidence-based, responsive, and citizen-centric governance. When strategically integrated, these technologies can empower governments to make smarter decisions, optimize service delivery, and ultimately advance public value in the digital era.

3.2 Blockchain for Transparency and Trust in Governance

In the quest for more transparent, accountable, and citizen-trusting governments, blockchain technology has emerged as a transformative instrument. Characterized by its decentralized architecture, immutability, and cryptographic security, blockchain offers a new foundation for reimagining governance structures and rebuilding public confidence in institutional processes.

At its core, blockchain is a distributed ledger system that allows for the recording of transactions in a secure, chronological, and tamper-proof manner. In the context of public administration, this ensures that every governmental action—be it financial disbursement, policy approval, or asset registration—can be traced and verified without the need for centralized control. This level of verifiability significantly reduces opportunities for corruption, fraud, and bureaucratic opacity (Akaba et al., 2020).

Several governments have already begun integrating blockchain into public sector operations. For instance, blockchain-enabled land registry systems in countries like Georgia and Sweden have enhanced data integrity, reduced property disputes, and increased administrative efficiency. Similarly, blockchain applications in procurement processes allow for transparent bidding, contract execution, and fund tracking, thereby improving fairness and accountability in public spending (Saha, 2025; Sund et al., 2020).

Moreover, blockchain fosters a paradigm shift toward citizen empowerment. Through smart contracts and decentralized applications (dApps), citizens can securely interact with public services, submit documentation, or verify credentials without intermediary intervention. This not only enhances service accessibility but also strengthens the legitimacy of digital interactions between the state and its constituents.

However, the deployment of blockchain in governance is not without challenges. Issues such as scalability, energy consumption, interoperability with legacy systems, and legal uncertainty pose significant barriers to widespread adoption. Furthermore, the governance of blockchain itself—who controls the code, updates the protocol, or resolves disputes—remains a contentious topic that public institutions must navigate with caution (Saha, 2025; Toufaily et al., 2021).

To fully harness blockchain's potential, governments need to establish clear regulatory frameworks, promote inter-agency collaboration, and invest in technical capacity building. Equally important is fostering public awareness and trust in the technology itself, as its value lies not only in technical integrity but in its perceived fairness and inclusivity. In conclusion, blockchain represents more than a technological innovation; it is a governance innovation. By embedding transparency and trust into the architecture of digital government, blockchain paves the way for a more resilient, participatory, and accountable public sector in the digital age.

3.3 Cloud Computing, IoT, and Interoperability Across Government Agencies

As governments advance from isolated digital initiatives toward fully integrated digital governance, technologies such as cloud computing, the Internet of Things (IoT), and interoperability frameworks have become essential components of public sector transformation (Tangi et al., 2021). These technologies underpin the digital infrastructure needed to deliver responsive, scalable, and citizen-centric services while enabling seamless collaboration across institutional boundaries.

Cloud computing offers governments unprecedented flexibility and cost-efficiency in managing digital services. By shifting from on-premise data centers to cloud-based platforms, public agencies can store, process, and retrieve vast amounts of data in real time. Cloud infrastructure enables elastic scaling of services, disaster recovery capabilities, and reduced IT overhead, thereby supporting more agile and resilient public administration systems. Moreover, cloud environments facilitate cross-agency collaboration by providing (Ahmadi, 2024; Demartini et al., 2024; Nandini et al., 2024) centralized, accessible platforms for data sharing and digital service deployment.

Complementing this, the Internet of Things (IoT) enhances situational awareness and real-time decision-making in various domains of public governance. IoT devices embedded in urban infrastructure—such as traffic sensors, air quality monitors, and smart waste management systems—generate continuous data streams that can be analyzed to optimize public service delivery. In sectors like transportation, energy, and environmental protection, IoT empowers governments to transition (Hadjiefthymiades, 2020; Megahed & Abdel-Kader, 2022; Sompie et al., 2024) from reactive service models to predictive and preventative governance.

However, the true value of cloud and IoT technologies is unlocked when government systems are interoperable—able to communicate, exchange, and interpret data seamlessly across departments and jurisdictions. Interoperability reduces information silos, enhances service integration, and promotes cohesive policy implementation. For example, interoperable health and social service systems allow for holistic responses to community needs, particularly in crisis management or cross-cutting social programs (Headrick et al., 2022).

Despite these advantages, significant challenges remain. Data standardization, cybersecurity, privacy protection, and digital sovereignty are persistent concerns.

Moreover, legacy systems often lack the compatibility needed for integration with modern platforms. Addressing these barriers requires not only technological investments but also regulatory reform, strategic governance frameworks, and capacity building within public institutions. In conclusion, the convergence of cloud computing, IoT, and interoperability constitutes the backbone of digital government infrastructure. These technologies enable governments to move beyond fragmented digital efforts and toward unified, data-driven, and citizen-focused governance models fit for the complexities of the 21st century.

CHALLENGES AND ETHICAL CONSIDERATIONS IN DIGITAL GOVERNMENT

4.1 Data Privacy, Cybersecurity, and Algorithmic Bias

As governments transition from e-Government to full-scale digital government, the ethical landscape becomes increasingly complex. Among the most pressing concerns are data privacy, cybersecurity, and algorithmic bias—three interconnected challenges that, if unaddressed, can erode public trust, compromise democratic accountability, and obstruct the equitable delivery of digital services.

Data privacy is a foundational principle in digital governance. With public institutions increasingly collecting, storing, and analyzing vast volumes of personal information—ranging from biometric identifiers to behavioral patterns—there is a heightened risk of misuse or unauthorized exposure. Transparent data governance frameworks, data minimization principles, and informed consent mechanisms must therefore be embedded in every digital public service to uphold citizens' fundamental rights and maintain institutional legitimacy (Rossi & Lenzini, 2020; Xu et al., 2024).

Alongside privacy, cybersecurity is a critical concern. As governments migrate sensitive functions to cloud-based platforms and interconnected networks, they become more vulnerable to cyberattacks, data breaches, and digital sabotage. Public sector systems have been targets of ransomware attacks, phishing schemes, and political interference, highlighting the urgent need for robust cybersecurity protocols. These include real-time threat monitoring, multi-factor authentication, public-private cybersecurity partnerships, and ongoing staff training to build cyber resilience across the entire governance ecosystem (Binhammad et al., 2024; Hossain et al., 2025).

A subtler yet equally serious issue is algorithmic bias, particularly in systems powered by artificial intelligence. Algorithms used in decision-making—such as welfare eligibility, predictive policing, or loan approvals—can inadvertently perpetuate existing social inequalities if trained on biased datasets or designed without adequate oversight (Cossette-Lefebvre & Maclure, 2022; Jeganathan et al., 2024;

Olanipekun, 2025). When opacity clouds algorithmic logic, affected individuals may have no means to understand, challenge, or appeal decisions that significantly affect their lives. Hence, algorithmic transparency, explainability, and fairness must be institutionalized as ethical safeguards in digital government initiatives.

Moreover, these ethical risks are often magnified in vulnerable populations, such as marginalized communities, migrants, or individuals with low digital literacy. Without deliberate inclusion strategies, digital government risks becoming exclusionary and unjust. Thus, ethical design must be proactive, not reactive. In conclusion, the success of digital government depends not only on technological capability but also on ethical integrity. Upholding data privacy, ensuring cybersecurity, and mitigating algorithmic bias are not ancillary tasks—they are central obligations. Only through principled governance can digital transformation truly serve the public good and foster inclusive, trustworthy state–citizen relationships.

4.2 Digital Divide and Access Inequality in Policy Implementation

The promise of digital government lies in its potential to democratize access to public services, improve efficiency, and enhance participatory governance. However, this vision remains unrealized for many, as the digital divide continues to exacerbate existing social inequalities. Digital exclusion is not merely a technological issue—it is a policy failure that risks deepening socioeconomic divides and undermining inclusive governance (Heeks, 2022; Manoharan et al., 2022).

The digital divide refers to disparities in access to digital infrastructure, connectivity, digital literacy, and usage capabilities. These gaps are particularly pronounced in rural areas, low-income households, and marginalized communities. While urban centers may benefit from high-speed internet and smart services, peripheral regions often struggle with unreliable networks and limited device availability. This asymmetry restricts meaningful access to digital government services and alienates those most in need of public assistance (Adamopoulos et al., 2024; Kiviaho & Einolander, 2023; Torabi et al., 2023).

Moreover, digital literacy plays a crucial role in shaping access. Even when infrastructure exists, a lack of skills to navigate online platforms or understand e-government tools renders citizens functionally excluded. Elderly populations, persons with disabilities, and linguistically diverse groups often face additional layers of exclusion unless inclusive design principles are prioritized in policy implementation.

Policy efforts that do not account for these disparities risk reinforcing a form of digital elitism—where only the digitally fluent benefit from innovation, while others are left behind. This challenges the core public value principle of equity, which is fundamental to ethical public administration. Without targeted interventions, digital transformation can inadvertently marginalize the very groups it claims to empower.

To mitigate these risks, governments must adopt equity-centered policy frameworks. This includes expanding broadband infrastructure in underserved areas, subsidizing access to digital devices, and integrating digital skills training into public education and community outreach. Moreover, digital government services must be co-designed with users, ensuring that platforms are multilingual, mobile-responsive, accessible to people with disabilities, and culturally sensitive (Manoharan et al., 2022; Nogueira et al., 2021; Owens et al., 2023). In addition, offline alternatives must remain available as part of an inclusive service delivery model. True digital transformation does not mandate uniformity—it embraces flexibility and responsiveness to diverse needs. In conclusion, closing the digital divide is not a peripheral concern but a central ethical imperative in digital governance. Equity in access must underpin all efforts to ensure that digital government serves as a bridge, not a barrier, to public participation and justice.

4.3. Ethics of Automation: Accountability and Human Oversight in AI-Driven Governance

The integration of artificial intelligence (AI) into public administration has introduced unprecedented opportunities for efficiency, scalability, and predictive governance. However, as governments increasingly delegate decision-making functions to automated systems, ethical considerations surrounding accountability, transparency, and human oversight have become critical in preserving democratic legitimacy and public trust (Elliott et al., 2021; Henman, 2020; Kuziemski & Misuraca, 2020; Sholola et al., 2024).

AI systems deployed in public governance—ranging from algorithmic risk assessments in welfare allocation to automated surveillance in law enforcement—often operate with a level of opacity that challenges traditional norms of public accountability. When decisions affecting individuals' rights or access to public services are made by non-transparent algorithms, it becomes difficult for citizens to understand, question, or appeal outcomes. This undermines core principles of due process and administrative fairness.

Moreover, automation in governance risks reinforcing existing biases if AI models are trained on historical data imbued with social and institutional prejudices. Without intentional auditing and ethical design, algorithmic decision-making may perpetuate discrimination, disproportionately impacting marginalized communities. These systems, while efficient, must not become tools of exclusion or unaccountable authority.

The ethical governance of automation requires that human oversight remains an integral component of AI deployment. Public administrators must be able to interpret, contest, and override automated recommendations when necessary. This involves designing human-in-the-loop frameworks where algorithmic suggestions are subject to review and contextual judgment by trained professionals. Furthermore, ethical impact assessments and algorithmic transparency reports should be standardized across public sector AI initiatives (Green, 2022; Morgan et al., 2023; Olanipekun, 2025).

Another key dimension is explainability—the ability of automated systems to provide understandable justifications for their decisions. This is vital for both institutional learning and citizen empowerment. Citizens must know not only what decisions are being made, but also how and why those decisions are derived. To uphold ethical standards, governments must adopt comprehensive AI governance policies that emphasize fairness, accountability, and inclusivity. These policies should be shaped in consultation with ethicists, technologists, civil society, and affected communities. Ethical automation is not a technical add-on; it is a foundational principle in designing just and trustworthy digital government. In conclusion, as automation reshapes the public sector, it must be grounded in a commitment to human dignity, democratic accountability, and institutional transparency. Technology should serve society—not the other way around.

POLICY INNOVATIONS AND FUTURE DIRECTIONS

5.1. Best Practices from Smart Nations: Estonia, Singapore, and the UAE

The global transition from e-Government to digital government is best exemplified by the strategic innovations and policy frameworks implemented in leading "smart nations." Countries such as Estonia, Singapore, and the United Arab Emirates (UAE) have pioneered comprehensive digital governance models that serve as benchmarks for other nations seeking to modernize their public sectors. These case studies offer invaluable insights into the key drivers of successful digital transformation: infrastructure, integration, inclusion, and innovation (Gil-García & Flores-Zúñiga, 2020).

Estonia is often hailed as the world's most digitally advanced state. Its *X-Road* interoperability platform connects over 900 public and private sector institutions, enabling seamless data exchange across agencies. Nearly all government services—from tax filing to voting—are conducted online, underpinned by robust digital identity (e-ID) infrastructure. Estonia's proactive legal framework and emphasis on transparency, cybersecurity, and data ownership have positioned it as a model for citizen-centric digital governance (Deni et al., 2020; Ekarini & Wibowo, 2022).

Singapore adopts a centralised, data-driven approach through its *Smart Nation* initiative. Government services are unified under platforms like *SingPass*, enabling residents to access over 2,000 digital services securely. The use of real-time data analytics for urban planning, traffic management, and public health demonstrates how AI and IoT can be harnessed for anticipatory governance. Importantly, Singapore invests heavily in digital literacy and inclusion, ensuring no citizen is left behind in its transformation journey (Bibri et al., 2024; Luo et al., 2024).

The UAE, through its *Digital Government Strategy 2025*, emphasizes innovation, artificial intelligence, and proactive service delivery. The Emirates ID system integrates biometric verification for secure access to digital services, while blockchain has been institutionalized for document authentication. The UAE's *Happiness Meter* and other feedback-driven tools illustrate its commitment to user experience and continuous service improvement. Strategic leadership and regulatory agility have enabled the UAE to implement disruptive technologies while maintaining institutional trust (Alteneiji et al., 2020; Benuyenah & Pandya, 2020; Mansour & Bick, 2024).

Despite differences in governance style and socioeconomic context, these nations share common success factors: strong political will, cross-sectoral collaboration, inclusive digital policy design, and sustained investment in digital infrastructure. Their experiences highlight the importance of aligning technology with public value and citizen empowerment. In conclusion, the experiences of Estonia, Singapore, and the UAE illuminate the pathways toward holistic, resilient, and ethically grounded digital government. Their models offer not blueprints for replication, but adaptable lessons for innovation anchored in context and purpose.

5.2. Frameworks for Digital Policy Governance and Public Value Creation

In the digital era, effective governance is no longer defined solely by institutional control or service efficiency. Rather, it is increasingly measured by a government's capacity to generate public value—outcomes that improve societal well-being, democratic engagement, and institutional trust. To achieve this, governments must adopt robust digital policy governance frameworks that align technological innovation with the core principles of inclusivity, transparency, and responsiveness (Manny et al., 2021; Manoharan et al., 2022; Tuebou, 2024).

Digital policy governance refers to the structured process by which public institutions design, implement, and evaluate digital strategies within legal, ethical, and participatory boundaries. These frameworks are essential in ensuring that digital transformation does not become a technocratic exercise but remains accountable to the citizens it aims to serve. Effective frameworks embed clear objectives, stakeholder engagement protocols, data governance standards, and performance measurement mechanisms.

One widely cited model is the Public Value Framework, which emphasizes outcome-driven governance by measuring digital investments in terms of social impact, trust, and equity—not merely financial returns. This approach encourages governments to design digital services that address real citizen needs, foster co-creation, and enable inclusive access, especially for vulnerable populations. Public value thus becomes a guiding compass for evaluating the legitimacy and effectiveness of digital policies (Virtanen & Jalonen, 2023; Weigl et al., 2024).

Equally important is the adoption of agile governance principles in digital policymaking. Given the rapid pace of technological change, traditional bureaucratic cycles often lag behind emerging challenges. Agile frameworks promote iterative development, policy experimentation, and adaptive regulation. For example, regulatory sandboxes allow policymakers to test digital innovations in controlled environments, minimizing risks while accelerating public sector learning (Ahern, 2021; Moe & Mikalsen, 2020).

Moreover, data stewardship and ethical AI governance must be institutionalized to manage risks related to data privacy, algorithmic discrimination, and digital exclusion. Interdisciplinary policy labs, ethics boards, and citizen review panels are increasingly used to scrutinize the societal implications of digital technologies, ensuring alignment with democratic values. In conclusion, frameworks for digital policy governance are not just managerial instruments—they are expressions of public purpose in a digital age. When designed with foresight and integrity, these frameworks enable governments to transform digital tools into catalysts for public value, social justice, and sustainable innovation.

5.3. Future-Proofing Digital Governance: Trends, Risks, and Opportunities

As digital technologies continue to evolve at an unprecedented pace, governments must proactively prepare for a future in which governance is increasingly mediated by algorithms, platforms, and data ecosystems. Future-proofing digital governance entails anticipating disruptions, building institutional agility, and embedding resilience into public sector systems. It is a forward-looking imperative that blends strategic foresight with ethical commitment and technological adaptability (Adie et al., 2024; Choi & Park, 2023).

One major trend shaping the future of digital governance is the rise of artificial intelligence and autonomous systems in policy implementation and service delivery. From real-time traffic management to predictive social interventions, AI promises substantial gains in efficiency and responsiveness. However, it also raises concerns about oversight, algorithmic bias, and democratic control. Another trend is the growing influence of platform-based governance, where governments rely on integrated digital platforms to manage citizen interactions, data flows, and inter-agency collaboration (Eom & Lee, 2022; Lewis, 2023; Manoharan et al., 2022).

At the same time, data sovereignty and digital geopolitics are emerging as pivotal issues. As public institutions increasingly depend on cloud services and transnational infrastructures, questions of national control, cybersecurity, and digital ethics gain urgency. Future-proof governance requires robust legal frameworks that protect (Fratini et al., 2024) digital autonomy while fostering cross-border cooperation and interoperability.

Nevertheless, this transformative potential is accompanied by significant risks. Technological obsolescence, cybersecurity breaches, and systemic exclusion of digitally marginalized communities can undermine the credibility and inclusiveness of digital governance. Additionally, the commodification of public data and surveillance capitalism pose long-term threats to citizen trust and civil liberties (Calzada, 2023).

To address these challenges and seize emerging opportunities, governments must invest in adaptive capacities. This includes developing future literacy within public institutions, enabling foresight analysis, scenario planning, and digital ethics training for civil servants. Governments should also embrace multi-stakeholder ecosystems, where academia, civil society, and the private sector collaboratively shape digital governance agendas (Wilner & Roy, 2020; Yadav & Banerji, 2024).

Moreover, digital governance must be grounded in values-driven innovation—anchored in transparency, human rights, and public accountability. As emerging technologies redefine governance boundaries, the public sector must lead not just in adopting tools, but in setting the moral and civic terms of their use. In conclusion, future-proofing digital governance is not about predicting a fixed future—it is about preparing for multiplicity, complexity, and uncertainty. It is a commitment to designing public institutions that remain relevant, responsive, and resilient in the face of accelerating change.

CONCLUSION

The transition from e-Government to digital government signifies not only technological progress but also a profound transformation in governance, citizenship, and public value. This chapter demonstrates that digital transformation alters the manner in which states formulate policies, provide services, and interact with their populations. The amalgamation of artificial intelligence, big data analytics, blockchain, cloud computing, and the Internet of Things signifies a pivotal transition from transactional frameworks to anticipatory, adaptive, and participative governance structures. This shift, however, is fraught with conflict, as it prompts essential inquiries regarding ethics, equity, and institutional preparedness.

The future of digital government hinges on the equilibrium between efficiency and inclusivity. Although digital platforms can enhance service efficiency and broaden accessibility, they may also exacerbate digital gaps if infrastructure, affordability, and digital literacy are not routinely addressed. While algorithmic decision-making provides efficiency and predictive ability, it requires accountability, openness, and human monitoring to mitigate prejudice and maintain democratic legitimacy. These dualities underscore that technology should function as a tool to benefit society, rather than an objective in its own right.

Case studies from technologically sophisticated countries like Estonia, Singapore, and the United Arab Emirates illustrate that success depends not alone on technological investment but also on robust political will, legal clarity, and inclusive design. Their experiences underscore the significance of developing interoperable systems, fostering digital trust, and ensuring that innovation is grounded in the needs of citizens. However, these models highlight the peril of presuming that uniform strategies can be applied universally across varied socio-political environments. Local adaptation and cultural sensitivity are essential for sustained digital change.

To ensure its longevity, digital government must be fortified with foresight, resilience, and ethical reflexivity. This entails equipping institutions for ongoing transformation, integrating participatory frameworks, and promoting interdisciplinary cooperation. It necessitates a commitment to uphold human rights, ensure data sovereignty, and foster public trust.

Ultimately, digital government must be perceived as more than a technology initiative; it constitutes a civic commitment. By harmonizing innovation with democratic principles, inclusivity, and social justice, governments may guarantee that digital transformation serves as a conduit for enhanced transparency, accountability, and citizen-focused governance in a progressively intricate world.

REFERENCES

Abujaber, A. A., & Nashwan, A. J. (2024). Ethical framework for artificial intelligence in healthcare research: A path to integrity. In World Journal of Methodology (Vol. 14, Issue 3). DOI: 10.5662/wjm.v14.i3.94071

Adamopoulos, T., Brandt, L., Chen, C., Restuccia, D., & Wei, X. (2024). Land Security and Mobility Frictions. *The Quarterly Journal of Economics*, *139*(3), 1941–1987. DOI: 10.1093/qje/qjae010

Adie, B. U., Tate, M., & Valentine, E. (2024). Digital leadership in the public sector: a scoping review and outlook [Review of Digital leadership in the public sector: a scoping review and outlook]. International Review of Public Administration, 29(1), 42. Taylor & Francis. DOI: 10.1080/12294659.2024.2323847

Ahern, D. (2021). Regulatory Lag, Regulatory Friction and Regulatory Transition as FinTech Disenablers: Calibrating an EU Response to the Regulatory Sandbox Phenomenon. *European Business Organization Law Review*, *22*(3), 395–432. DOI: 10.1007/s40804-021-00217-z

Ahmadi, S. (2024). Systematic Literature Review on Cloud Computing Security: Threats and Mitigation Strategies. *Journal of Information Security*, *15*(2), 148–167. DOI: 10.4236/jis.2024.152010

Akaba, T. I., Norta, A., Udokwu, C., & Draheim, D. (2020). A Framework for the Adoption of Blockchain-Based e-Procurement Systems in the Public Sector. In Lecture notes in computer science (p. 3). Springer Science+Business Media. DOI: 10.1007/978-3-030-44999-5_1

Alenezi, M. (2022). Understanding digital government transformation. *arXiv preprint arXiv:2202.01797*. https://doi.org//arXiv.2202.01797DOI: 10.48550

Alteneiji, H. R., Ahmed, V., & Saboor, S. (2020). A qualitative approach to investigate emergency preparedness state for the built environment in the UAE. *Engineering, Construction, and Architectural Management*, *28*(7), 2005–2022. DOI: 10.1108/ECAM-05-2020-0296

Bäckström, K. (2023). New technology and in-store service encounters: An analysis of coping practices and work experiences among frontline employees. *International Review of Retail, Distribution and Consumer Research*, *33*(5), 494–518. DOI: 10.1080/09593969.2023.2271191

Bello, S. A., Wada, I., Ige, O. B., Chianumba, E. C., & Adebayo, S. A.Sakiru Folarin BelloIfeoluwa Uchechukwu WadaOlukayode B IgeErnest C ChianumbaSamod Adetunji Adebayo. (2024). AI-driven predictive maintenance and optimization of renewable energy systems for enhanced operational efficiency and longevity. *International Journal of Science and Research Archive, 13*(1), 2823–2837. DOI: 10.30574/ijsra.2024.13.1.1992

Benuyenah, V., & Pandya, B. (2020). Meaning of "employee happiness" within the context of complex organisations? An explanatory review on the UAE labour force. *Rajagiri Management Journal, 14*(2), 169–180. DOI: 10.1108/RAMJ-04-2020-0012

Bibri, S. E., Huang, J., Jagatheesaperumal, S. K., & Krogstie, J. (2024). The synergistic interplay of artificial intelligence and digital twin in environmentally planning sustainable smart cities: A comprehensive systematic review. *Environmental Science and Ecotechnology, 20*, 100433. DOI: 10.1016/j.ese.2024.100433 PMID: 38831974

Binhammad, M. H. Y., Alqaydi, S., Othman, A., & Abuljadayel, L. H. (2024). The Role of AI in Cyber Security: Safeguarding Digital Identity. *Journal of Information Security, 15*(2), 245–278. DOI: 10.4236/jis.2024.152015

Bovens, M., & Zouridis, S. (2023). From street-level to system-level bureaucracies: How information and communication technology is transforming administrative discretion and constitutional control. *Public Administration Review, 83*(2), 234–245. DOI: 10.1111/puar.13345

Calzada, I. (2023). Disruptive Technologies for e-Diasporas: Blockchain, DAOs, Data Cooperatives, Metaverse, and ChatGPT. *Futures, 154*, 103258. DOI: 10.1016/j.futures.2023.103258

Choi, S., & Park, S. (2023). Governmental Transformation in the Era of the Post Pandemic: Analyzing the Impacts of the Pandemic on Organizational Cultural Change in Government. *Public Organization Review, 23*(2), 451–467. DOI: 10.1007/s11115-023-00703-7

Ciancarini, P., Giancarlo, R., & Grimaudo, G. (2023). Digital transformation in the public administrations: A guided tour for computer scientists. *arXiv preprint arXiv:2305.05551*. https://doi.org//arXiv.2305.05551DOI: 10.48550

Cossette-Lefebvre, H., & Maclure, J. (2022). AI's fairness problem: Understanding wrongful discrimination in the context of automated decision-making. *AI and Ethics, 3*(4), 1255–1269. DOI: 10.1007/s43681-022-00233-w

Demartini, C. G., Sciascia, L., Bosso, A., & Manuri, F. (2024). Artificial Intelligence Bringing Improvements to Adaptive Learning in Education: A Case Study. *Sustainability (Basel)*, *16*(3), 1347. DOI: 10.3390/su16031347

Deni, S., Husain, T., & Deni, A. (2020). Bureaucracy and Challenges in Digital Era: A New Concept of Information Technology Integration in the Archipelagic Country. *Journal of Public Policy and Administration*, *4*(4), 71. DOI: 10.11648/j.jppa.20200404.12

Ekarini, M. I., & Wibowo, L. A. (2022). *The Implementation of Digital Transformation on Improving Public Services. Advances in Economics*. Business and Management Research/Advances in Economics, Business and Management Research., DOI: 10.2991/aebmr.k.220701.096

Elliott, K., Price, R., Shaw, P., Spiliotopoulos, T., Ng, M., Coopamootoo, K., & van Moorsel, A. (2021). Towards an Equitable Digital Society: Artificial Intelligence (AI) and Corporate Digital Responsibility (CDR). *Society*, *58*(3), 179–188. DOI: 10.1007/s12115-021-00594-8 PMID: 34149122

Eom, S.-J., & Lee, J. (2022). Digital government transformation in turbulent times: Responses, challenges, and future direction. *Government Information Quarterly*, *39*(2), 101690. DOI: 10.1016/j.giq.2022.101690 PMID: 35291492

Fratini, S., Hine, E., Novelli, C., Roberts, H., & Floridi, L. (2024). Digital Sovereignty: A Descriptive Analysis and a Critical Evaluation of Existing Models. *Digital Society : Ethics, Socio-Legal and Governance of Digital Technology*, *3*(3), 59. Advance online publication. DOI: 10.1007/s44206-024-00146-7

Gil-García, J. R., & Flores-Zúñiga, M. Á. (2020). Towards a comprehensive understanding of digital government success: Integrating implementation and adoption factors. *Government Information Quarterly*, *37*(4), 101518. DOI: 10.1016/j.giq.2020.101518

Green, B. (2022). The flaws of policies requiring human oversight of government algorithms. *Computer Law & Security Review*, *45*, 105681. DOI: 10.1016/j.clsr.2022.105681

Greenway, A., Terrett, B., Bracken, M., & Loosemore, T. (2021). *Digital transformation at scale: Why the strategy is delivery*. London Publishing Partnership.

Hadjidemetriou, G. M., Herrera, M., & Parlikad, A. K. (2021). Condition and criticality-based predictive maintenance prioritisation for networks of bridges. *Structure and Infrastructure Engineering*, *18*(8), 1207–1221. DOI: 10.1080/15732479.2021.1897146

Hadjiefthymiades, S. (2020). Internet of Things in E-Government: Applications and Challenges. https://www.igi-global.com/gateway/article/257274

Headrick, G., Ruth, A., White, S., Ellison, C., Seligman, H. K., Bleich, S. N., & Moran, A. J. (2022). Integration and coordination across public benefit programs: Insights from state and local government leaders in the United States. *Preventive Medicine Reports, 31*, 102077. DOI: 10.1016/j.pmedr.2022.102077 PMID: 36483579

Heeks, R. (2022). Digital inequality beyond the digital divide: Conceptualizing adverse digital incorporation in the global South. *Information Technology for Development, 28*(4), 688–704. DOI: 10.1080/02681102.2022.2068492

Henman, P. (2020). Improving public services using artificial intelligence: Possibilities, pitfalls, governance. *Asia Pacific Journal of Public Administration, 42*(4), 209–221. DOI: 10.1080/23276665.2020.1816188

Hofeditz, L., Jung, A.-K., Mirbabaie, M., & Stieglitz, S. (2025). Ethical Guidelines for the Application of Generative AI in German Journalism. *Digital Society : Ethics, Socio-Legal and Governance of Digital Technology, 4*(1), 4. Advance online publication. DOI: 10.1007/s44206-024-00151-w

Hossain, S. T., Yiğitcanlar, T., Nguyen, K., & Xu, Y. (2025). Cybersecurity in Local Governments: A Systematic Review and Framework of Key Challenges [Review of Cybersecurity in Local Governments: A Systematic Review and Framework of Key Challenges]. Urban Governance. Elsevier BV. DOI: 10.1016/j.ugj.2024.12.010

Janssen, M., & van der Voort, H. (2020). Agile and adaptive governance in crisis response: Lessons from the COVID-19 pandemic. *International Journal of Information Management, 55*, 102180. DOI: 10.1016/j.ijinfomgt.2020.102180 PMID: 32836637

Jeganathan, S., Raj, L. A., Parthasarathy, S., Khan, A. A. A., & Sathick, K. J. (2024). OptCatB: Optuna Hyperparameter Optimization Model to Forecast the Educational Proficiency of Immigrant Students based on CatBoost Regression. *Journal of Internet Services and Information Security, 14*(3), 111–132. DOI: 10.58346/JISIS.2024.I2.008

Kiviaho, A., & Einolander, J. (2023). Digital transformation, well-being and shrinking communities: Narrowing the divides between urban and rural. *Heliyon, 9*(8), e18801. Advance online publication. DOI: 10.1016/j.heliyon.2023.e18801 PMID: 37600410

Kuziemski, M., & Misuraca, G. (2020). AI governance in the public sector: Three tales from the frontiers of automated decision-making in democratic settings. *Telecommunications Policy, 44*(6), 101976. DOI: 10.1016/j.telpol.2020.101976 PMID: 32313360

Lewis, K. (2023). Colonising the narrative space: Unliveable lives, unseeable struggles and the necropolitical governance of digital populations. *Information Communication and Society*, *26*(12), 2398–2418. DOI: 10.1080/1369118X.2023.2230260

Luo, J., Liu, P., Xu, W., Zhao, T., & Biljecki, F. (2024). A perception-powered urban digital twin to support human-centered urban planning and sustainable city development. *Cities (London, England)*, *156*, 105473. DOI: 10.1016/j.cities.2024.105473

Manny, L., Duygan, M., Fischer, M., & Rieckermann, J. (2021). Barriers to the digital transformation of infrastructure sectors. *Policy Sciences*, *54*(4), 943–983. DOI: 10.1007/s11077-021-09438-y PMID: 34751195

Manoharan, A., Melitski, J., & Holzer, M. (2022). Digital Governance: An Assessment of Performance and Best Practices. *Public Organization Review*, *23*(1), 265–283. DOI: 10.1007/s11115-021-00584-8

Mansour, T., & Bick, M. (2024). How can physicians adopt AI-based applications in the United Arab Emirates to improve patient outcomes? *Digital Health*, *10*, 20552076241284936. Advance online publication. DOI: 10.1177/20552076241284936 PMID: 39351313

Margetts, H., & Dorobantu, C. (2024). Rethinking public policy in the age of AI: A socio-technical perspective. *Policy and Internet*, *16*(1), 5–20. DOI: 10.1002/poi3.234

Megahed, N. A., & Abdel-Kader, R. F. (2022). Smart Cities after COVID-19: Building a conceptual framework through a multidisciplinary perspective. *Scientific African*, *17*, e01374. Advance online publication. DOI: 10.1016/j.sciaf.2022.e01374 PMID: 36128003

Mergel, I., Edelmann, N., & Haug, N. (2020). Defining digital transformation: Results from expert interviews. *Government Information Quarterly*, *37*(4), 101385. DOI: 10.1016/j.giq.2019.06.002

Moe, N. B., & Mikalsen, M. (2020). Large-Scale Agile Transformation: A Case Study of Transforming Business, Development and Operations. In Lecture notes in business information processing (p. 115). Springer Science+Business Media. DOI: 10.1007/978-3-030-49392-9_8

Morgan, D., Hashem, Y., Straub, V. J., & Bright, J. (2023). "Team-in-the-loop" organisational oversight of high-stakes AI. arXiv (Cornell University). https://doi .org//arxiv.2303.14007DOI: 10.48550

Muiderman, K., Vervoort, J., Gupta, A., Norbert-Munns, R. P., Veeger, M., Muzammil, M., & Driessen, P. (2023). Is anticipatory governance opening up or closing down future possibilities? Findings from diverse contexts in the Global South. *Global Environmental Change*, *81*, 102694. DOI: 10.1016/j.gloenvcha.2023.102694

Naik, K., Goyal, R. K., Foschini, L., Chak, C. M., Thielscher, C., Zhu, H., Lu, J., Lehár, J., Pacanoswki, M. A., Terranova, N., Mehta, N., Korsbo, N., Fakhouri, T., Liu, Q., & Gobburu, J. (2023). Current Status and Future Directions: The Application of Artificial Intelligence/Machine Learning for Precision Medicine. *Clinical Pharmacology and Therapeutics*, *115*(4), 673–686. DOI: 10.1002/cpt.3152 PMID: 38103204

Nandini, N., Indora, P., & Singh, R.R K Singh. (2024). Artificial Intelligence in Journalism: An Overview of its Applications and Uses. *Journal of Communication Management (London)*, *3*(3), 237–242. DOI: 10.58966/JCM2024337

Nogueira, V. B., Teixeira, D. G., de Lima, I. A. C. N., Moreira, M. V. C., de Oliveira, B. S. C., Pedrosa, I. M. B., Queiroz, J. W., & Jerônimo, S. M. B. (2021). Towards an inclusive digital literacy: An experimental intervention study in a rural area of Brazil. *Education and Information Technologies*, *27*(2), 2807–2834. DOI: 10.1007/s10639-021-10711-z PMID: 34493924

Olanipekun, S. O.Samson Olufemi Olanipekun. (2025). Ethical frameworks for AI in journalism: Balancing technological innovation and journalistic integrity. *World Journal of Advanced Research and Reviews*, *25*(1), 1342–1351. DOI: 10.30574/wjarr.2025.25.1.0187

Owens, M. A., Ravi, V., & Hunter, E. J. (2023). Digital Inclusion as a Lens for Equitable Parent Engagement. *TechTrends*. Advance online publication. DOI: 10.1007/s11528-023-00859-5 PMID: 37362590

Rossi, A., & Lenzini, G. (2020). Transparency by design in data-informed research: A collection of information design patterns. *Computer Law & Security Review*, *37*, 105402. DOI: 10.1016/j.clsr.2020.105402

Saha, A. K., & Khan, I. (2025). Disaggregating air, water and renewable energy disclosures in developing economies: The role of regulatory impact and board characteristics. *Journal of Applied Accounting Research*, *26*(2), 498–530. DOI: 10.1108/JAAR-08-2023-0233

Shi, Y., & Sun, L. (2024). How Generative AI Is Transforming Journalism: Development, Application and Ethics. *Journalism and Media*, *5*(2), 582–594. DOI: 10.3390/journalmedia5020039

Sholola, Y. A., Banjo, Y. O., Saliu-Yusuf, M. J., Ogundeyi, T. S., & Ayantunji, K. A.-A. (2024). Perceived effect of Artificial Intelligence on Ethical Journalism among Journalists in Kwara State. *International Journal of Research and Innovation in Social Science, 2051*(II), 2051–2063. Advance online publication. DOI: 10.47772/IJRISS.2024.802145

Singh, N., Misra, R., Quan, W., Radić, A., Lee, S.-M., & Han, H. (2024). An analysis of consumer's trusting beliefs towards the use of e-commerce platforms. *Humanities & Social Sciences Communications, 11*(1), 899. Advance online publication. DOI: 10.1057/s41599-024-03395-6

Smith, J., & Marx, L. (2020). *Does technology drive history? The dilemma of technological determinism*. MIT Press., DOI: 10.7551/mitpress/9780262691673.001.0001

Sompie, S. R. U. A., Sambul, A. M., & Rumpesak, I. C. A. (2024). IoT-Based Monitoring and Control of a Hybrid Renewable Energy System Utilizing Solar and Microhydro Sources. *Journal of Sustainable Engineering Proceedings Series, 2*(1), 23–28. DOI: 10.35793/joseps.v2i1.3942

Sund, T., Lööf, C., Nadjm-Tehrani, S., & Asplund, M. (2020). Blockchain-based event processing in supply chains—A case study at IKEA. *Robotics and Computer-integrated Manufacturing, 65*, 101971. DOI: 10.1016/j.rcim.2020.101971

Tan, S. Y., & Taeihagh, A. (2020). Smart city governance in developing countries: A systematic literature review. *arXiv preprint arXiv:2001.10173.* https://doi.org//arXiv.2001.10173DOI: 10.48550

Tangi, L., Janssen, M., Benedetti, M., & Noci, G. (2021). Digital government transformation: A structural equation modelling analysis of driving and impeding factors. *International Journal of Information Management, 60*, 102356. DOI: 10.1016/j.ijinfomgt.2021.102356

Torabi, Z.-A., Rezvani, M. R., Hall, C. M., & Allam, Z. (2023). On the post-pandemic travel boom: How capacity building and smart tourism technologies in rural areas can help - evidence from Iran. *Technological Forecasting and Social Change, 193*, 122633. DOI: 10.1016/j.techfore.2023.122633 PMID: 37223653

Toufaily, É., Zalan, T., & Dhaou, S. B. (2021). A framework of blockchain technology adoption: An investigation of challenges and expected value. *Information & Management, 58*(3), 103444. DOI: 10.1016/j.im.2021.103444

Trist, E., & Emery, F. (2022). The socio-technical systems perspective. In *Organizational Change and Innovation Processes* (pp. 123–150). Springer., DOI: 10.1007/978-3-030-12345-6_6

Tuebou, B. F. (2024). The Digitization of Public Services and Its Contribution to the Quality of Service in Relation to User Satisfaction. *Open Journal of Applied Sciences*, *14*(9), 2697–2716. DOI: 10.4236/ojapps.2024.149177

United Nations Department of Economic and Social Affairs. (2024). E-Government survey 2024: A digital government model framework for sustainable development. *UN Publications*. https://desapublications.un.org/sites/default/files/publications/2024-09/E-Government_Survey_2024.pdfDESA Publications

Virtanen, P., & Jalonen, H. (2023). Public value creation mechanisms in the context of public service logic: An integrated conceptual framework. *Public Management Review*, *26*(8), 2331–2354. DOI: 10.1080/14719037.2023.2268111

Wattoo, M. U., Du, J., Shahzad, F., & Kousar, S. (2025). Shaping E-commerce Experiences: Unraveling the Impact of Service Quality on Youth Customer Behavior in a Developing Nation. *SAGE Open*, *15*(1), 21582440241311786. Advance online publication. DOI: 10.1177/21582440241311786

Weigl, L., Roth, T., Amard, A., & Zavolokina, L. (2024). When public values and user-centricity in e-government collide – A systematic review [Review of When public values and user-centricity in e-government collide – A systematic review]. Government Information Quarterly, 41(3), 101956. Elsevier BV. DOI: 10.1016/j.giq.2024.101956

Wibowo, H. A. (2025). An Explication Of How Website Design Actually Shapes Online Customer Loyalty: Incorporating Sem And Person-Items Map Analysis. *International Journal of Social Service and Research*, *5*(1), 123–135. DOI: 10.46799/ijssr.v5i1.1190

Wilner, A., & Roy, M. (2020). Canada's emerging foresight landscape: Observations and lessons. *Foresight*, *22*(5/6), 551–562. DOI: 10.1108/FS-03-2020-0027

Wyatt, S. (2021). Technological determinism is dead; long live technological determinism. In *The Handbook of Science and Technology Studies* (pp. 165–180). MIT Press., DOI: 10.7551/mitpress/9780262539487.003.0009

Xu, Y., Gao, W., Wang, Y., Shan, X., & Lin, Y. (2024). Enhancing user experience and trust in advanced LLM-based conversational agents. *Computers and Artificial Intelligence*, *2*(2), 1467. DOI: 10.59400/cai.v2i2.1467

Yadav, M., & Banerji, P. (2024). Systematic literature review on Digital Financial Literacy. *SN Business & Economics*, *4*(11), 142. Advance online publication. DOI: 10.1007/s43546-024-00738-y

ADDITIONAL READING

Ahtiainen, R., Pulkkinen, J., & Jahnukainen, M. (2021). The 21st century reforms (re)shaping the education policy of inclusive and special education in Finland. *Education Sciences, 11*(1), 19. DOI: 10.3390/educsci11110750

Bovens, M., & Zouridis, S. (2023). From street-level to system-level bureaucracies: How information and communication technology is transforming administrative discretion and constitutional control. *Public Administration Review, 83*(2), 234–245. DOI: 10.1111/puar.13345

Calzada, I. (2023). Disruptive technologies for e-diasporas: Blockchain, DAOs, data cooperatives, metaverse, and ChatGPT. *Futures, 154*, 103258. DOI: 10.1016/j.futures.2023.103258

Choi, S., & Park, S. (2023). Governmental transformation in the era of the post pandemic: Analyzing the impacts of the pandemic on organizational cultural change in government. *Public Organization Review, 23*(2), 451–470. DOI: 10.1007/s11115-023-00703-7

Elfert, M., & Ydesen, C. (2023). *Global governance of education: The historical and contemporary entanglements of UNESCO, the OECD and the World Bank.* Springer., DOI: 10.1007/978-3-031-40411-5

Eom, S.-J., & Lee, J. (2022). Digital government transformation in turbulent times: Responses, challenges, and future direction. *Government Information Quarterly, 39*(2), 101690. DOI: 10.1016/j.giq.2022.101690 PMID: 35291492

Hossain, S. T., Yiğitcanlar, T., Nguyen, K., & Xu, Y. (2025). Cybersecurity in local governments: A systematic review and framework of key challenges. *Urban Governance, 5*(1), 50–63. DOI: 10.1016/j.ugj.2024.12.010

Virtanen, P., & Jalonen, H. (2023). Public value creation mechanisms in the context of public service logic: An integrated conceptual framework. *Public Management Review, 26*(8), 2331–2352. DOI: 10.1080/14719037.2023.2268111

Weigl, L., Roth, T., Amard, A., & Zavolokina, L. (2024). When public values and user-centricity in e-government collide: A systematic review. *Government Information Quarterly, 41*(3), 101956. DOI: 10.1016/j.giq.2024.101956

KEY TERMS AND DEFINITIONS

Adaptive Governance: An adaptable methodology in public administration that prioritizes ongoing education, agility, and robustness amid unpredictability and swift technological advancement.

Algorithmic Bias: Systematic and inequitable results in automated decision-making processes occur when algorithms mirror or exacerbate existing societal biases present in their training data.

Blockchain: A decentralized digital ledger system that securely and openly records transactions, minimizing potential for corruption and bolstering faith in public government.

Citizen-Centric Governance: A framework for public service design and delivery that prioritizes citizens' needs, rights, and involvement in decision-making processes.

Cloud Computing: The provision of computing services—comprising data storage, software, and processing power—via the internet, allowing governments to enhance service scalability and cost-efficiency.

Digital Divide: The disparity between persons or groups possessing dependable access to digital technology and abilities, and those lacking such access, resulting in inequities in participation and service availability.

Digital Government: The deliberate application of digital technologies throughout governance to enhance efficiency, transparency, citizen involvement, and the generation of public benefit.

Interoperability: The capacity of various governmental systems, platforms, and agencies to effortlessly communicate, interpret, and utilize data for cohesive and coordinated service provision.

Participatory Governance: A governance model that engages citizens directly in decision-making via mechanisms such as digital consultations, online forums, and crowdsourcing platforms.

Public Value: The societal advantages produced by governmental acts and policies encompass trust, equity, accountability, and enhanced quality of life for citizens.

Chapter 4
Examining Open Government Data in Public Administration:
Past, Present, and Future

Ali Roziqin
https://orcid.org/0000-0001-8336-3103
Universitas Muhammadiyah Malang, Indonesia

Ahmad Luthfi
https://orcid.org/0000-0003-2546-0903
Universitas Merdeka Malang, Indonesia

M. Husni Tamrin
https://orcid.org/0000-0001-9131-9807
Universitas Hang Tuah, Indonesia

Tangguh Okta Wibowo
https://orcid.org/0000-0002-2619-6561
Universitas Multimedia Nusantara, Indonesia

Azaria E. Pradana
https://orcid.org/0009-0002-3839-1310
Universitas Diponegoro, Indonesia

M. Ihwan Salsabila
https://orcid.org/0009-0008-8088-7380
Universitas Muhammadiyah Malang, Indonesia

ABSTRACT

Open Government Data (OGD) has an enormous chance to improve public administration by increasing openness, accountability, and citizen involvement. This study explores the evolution of OGD research in the field of Public Administration. This research employed a bibliometric analysis approach which conducted using VOS Viewer and Biblioshiny R Package based on the Scopus database. This study found that the themes that emerged in OGD in the context of public administration included information management, interoperability, Link Open Data (LOD), big data, transparency, and data portals. In addition, the trending topics and word frequencies show that more literature focuses on information management and

DOI: 10.4018/979-8-3373-1484-6.ch004

government data processing, rather than integration and interoperability. Therefore, future research is needed to examine the integration and interoperability of OGD practices in promoting more accessible data governance.

INTRODUCTION

In recent decades, open government data (OGD) has piqued the interest of researchers and practitioners from a variety of fields, including information systems, management science, political and social science, and law (Charalabidis et al., 2016). In the context of public administration, open government initiatives have become a crucial administrative reform a focus around the world (Ruijer & Meijer, 2020; Safarov, 2020). Open Government Data (OGD) initiatives are increasingly being adopted by public administrations worldwide to enhance transparency, accountability, and citizen participation. Why is this so? Because the government is the main source of data associated with information about citizens, organizations, or transactions in the course of providing public services (Hermanto et al., 2018). OGD refers to the provision of public sector information freely and easily accessible to everyone (Cho, 2023).

The concept of Open Government Data (OGD) has emerged as a cornerstone of modern governance, promising to enhance transparency, accountability, and public participation (Hansson et al., 2015). The development of the internet and information and communication technology requires data that can be accessed by the public based on the principles of transparency and integrity (Almuqrin et al., 2022). These principles are important assets in realizing democratization (Hermanto et al., 2018). As governments worldwide strive to adapt to the demands of the digital era, OGD initiatives have proliferated, opening vast repositories of public data to citizens, researchers, and businesses. In public administration, the adoption of OGD has been seen not only as a tool for democratic renewal but also as an enabler of innovation and more efficient public service delivery. Countries such as the United States, the United Kingdom, and South Korea have led global rankings in open data implementation, inspiring a wave of policy reforms and platform developments across various administrative levels.

Scholars in public administration and e-government have responded to this phenomenon with a growing body of literature that explores OGD from multiple angles (Wirtz & Birkmeyer, 2015). Early studies primarily focused on the technical infrastructure and legal frameworks necessary for data openness (Izdebski et al., 2021; Viscusi et al., 2014). More recent research has expanded into areas such as the socio-political implications of OGD, citizen engagement through open platforms, and the impact of open data on public sector innovation (Mergel et al., 2018; Viscusi et al., 2014). Especially amid the rise of social media, open government data has the potential to be both an opportunity and a challenge as a means of communication between the government and the public (Wirtz et al., 2018). Institutionally, OGD can also be a strategic step during a country's transition of government (Safarov, 2020).

Since its introduction, both the concept and practice of OGD have become emerging issues in the field of public administration. The research field of OGD has been on the rise over the last decade. While the number and heterogeneity of contributions are increasing, comprehensive literature reviews remain scarce in the context of public administration. Previous review articles have been conducted by several scholars, including Hansson et al. (2015), who reviewed OGD from a democratic practice perspective. Furthermore, Wirtz & Birkmeyer (2015) reviewed the scope of OGD based on conceptual perspectives. Tai (2021) reviewed open government research over the past decade and found that the key conceptualizations in OGD are public participation and transparency. Additionally, Wirtz et al. (2022) reviewed the potential of OGD in the digital economy. Most recently, Silva & Silva (2025) reviewed the health sector. Although there have been many reviews of OGD, those using bibliometric reviews and specifically focusing on the field of public administration are still limited.

Given these gaps, this paper seeks to provide a comprehensive examination of OGD in public administration by analyzing its past developments, current state, and future directions. This chapter seeks to evaluate the trends of research subjects on OGD in public administration field, including trends each year, authors, institutions, and nations that are the key contributors, and clustering of research topics in the past, present and future directions. This chapter intends to contribute to a better understanding of how OGD has impacted and will continue to influence public administration study and practice. In addition, this study try to offer a clearer understanding of where the field stands today, identify persistent challenges and underexplored areas, and propose an agenda for future research that can guide both scholars and practitioners in navigating the complex landscape of open government data.

LITERATURE REVIEW

Open Government Data (OGD) has emerged as one of the strategic initiatives aimed at enhancing transparency, accountability, and innovation in public governance. The open government initiative was first voiced by the U.S. government, particularly under President Barack Obama (Grimmelikhuijsen & Feeney, 2017; Mergel, 2015; Nikiforova & Lnenicka, 2021), and then spread to various countries. According to Valli Buttow and Weerts (2022), the OECD plays a significant role in promoting OGD as part of a global reform movement toward data-driven governance. This policy is designed to improve evidence-based decision-making and foster public trust in governmental institutions. However, the implementation of OGD has not always been smooth. Kawashita et al. (2024) highlight challenges in Brazil, such as low digital literacy among the population, limited infrastructure, and a lack of supportive regulations. Hogan et al. (2017) suggest that cross-sector collaboration involving the government, private sector, and civil society can serve as a solution to overcome these obstacles. Linåker & Runeson (2020) further emphasize that such collaborative models need to be complemented with intensive training for stakeholders to optimize the utilization of data.

Advanced technology also plays a significant role in supporting the success of OGD. Kalampokis et al. (2021) highlight how Explainable Artificial Intelligence (XAI) can simplify complex data analysis, enhance transparency, and expand public access. Janssen et al. (2015) support this view by demonstrating that advanced technology can accelerate the decision-making process. Furthermore, Ruijer et al. (2024) emphasize that interactive technologies, such as digital platforms, can enhance public participation in policymaking processes. Local challenges, such as bureaucratic resistance and interagency coordination, remain major obstacles. Katsikas and Gritzalis (2017) note that rigid organizational cultures in Greece hinder the adoption of OGD. Bacchus et al. (2024) suggest the need for a flexible regulatory framework to support data interoperability and security. Bernot et al. (2024) highlight the importance of robust institutional capacity for the successful implementation of OGD. Moreover, Ibrahim et al. (2021) point out that the benefits of OGD are not evenly distributed in developing countries. Most advantages are predominantly enjoyed by academic and business sectors, while the general public often faces access barriers. Charalabidis et al. (2012) emphasize the importance of data interoperability to ensure broader inclusivity. Janssen and van den Hoven (2012) add that the Big and Open Linked Data (BOLD) initiative can serve as a breakthrough for enhancing transparency. However, Bertot et al. (2010) caution that the success of OGD heavily relies on the government's commitment to fostering a supportive culture of transparency.

The OGD initiative promotes transparency by making government data accessible to the public, enabling citizens to monitor government activities and hold officials accountable. Gómez (2017) shows that OGD plays a major role in creating organizational change, software development, applications, and processes that are useful for citizens to access public data. These digital services have led governments around the world to increasingly release non-personal data and data that can be freely used, reused, and distributed to anyone (Çaldağ et al., 2019). OGD principles such as transparency and accountability encourage governments to exploit the distribution and use of data (Roa et al., 2019). Lee & Chu (2018) revealed that OGD is an extraordinary resource for the Taiwanese government because the quantity and centrality of the data collected can be made open and usable by the public. On the other hand, Viscusi et al. (2014) emphasize that OGD must adhere to public principles such as accountability and avoid a one-dimensional system. The purpose of transparency and accountability in OGD is to encourage public participation in decision-making (Hardy & Maurushat, 2017).

By providing access to data, OGD encourages citizen engagement and participation in the governance process, fostering a collaborative environment between government and society (Hardy & Maurushat, 2017). Villegas Tovar & Marcos Recio (2019) also emphasize the need for specific institutions and regulations on public information access to ensure compliance and penalize misuse of information. This aligns with Yang (2017) statement that the benefits of OGD must not violate privacy and national security and that open data should be freely used and redistributed by the public.

In terms of economic and social value, OGD can stimulate economic growth by enabling the development of new products and services through the reuse of public data. OGD also has the potential to create social value by improving public services and policies (Abdullah Alhujaylan, 2021). Public data helps businesses utilize OGD to gain market insights, leading to new product innovations and better services (Bittencourt et al., 2019). Nikiforova et al. (2023) revealed that the availability of high-quality data can drive economic growth by enabling technology actors to create value. Additionally, open data also has the potential to stimulate economic growth through value-added applications developed by the public, including citizens, private companies, and non-profit organizations (Al-Ababneh et al., 2024). In Taiwan, recognizing the importance of open data, the Taiwanese government has begun promoting related initiatives at the central and local government levels (Villegas Tovar & Marcos Recio, 2019).

The push for data openness drives innovation—innovation that supports public services, application development, websites, and even national data collections (Nikiforova et al., 2023). Albano (2013) emphasizes that innovation in OGD must involve generating information, processing information, storing information, offering products/services, distributing, and presenting. Open government data (OGD) innovation transforms how public sector information is used to drive progress in governance, the economy, society, and technology (Almuqrin et al., 2022).

Managing and handling large amounts of data in a government environment is a significant challenge. Ensuring data quality, format consistency, and accessibility are critical technical obstacles that must be overcome. Therefore, understanding these obstacles is crucial in optimizing OGD initiatives and ensuring their potential is realized. Anwa (2022) found that inconsistencies and inaccuracies were the causes of low data quality, which confused users and reduced public trust. In addition, heterogeneity in data formats (such as PDF, Word, and Excel) hindered the integration process (Khadidja Bouchelouche et al., 2024). Nnenna et al. (2024) showed that infrastructure limitations are also a major challenge, particularly in East Africa, where inadequate technological infrastructure limits the use of OGD. Furthermore, open data often has poor navigation, making it difficult for people with disabilities to access (Mexhid Ferati, 2020).

The success of OGD initiatives can also be influenced by political principles, government priorities, and legal frameworks that support technical implementation. These challenges stem from concerns about data privacy, security, and quality. Kellerhals (2018) explains that the principle of 'open by default' has not been widely accepted by governments, thereby limiting the proactive release of data. On the other hand, legal frameworks often prioritize data protection, creating hesitation to disclose information to the public (Khadidja Bouchelouche et al., 2024). This often occurs in regimes with less transparency in data management, leading to public suspicion. Ultimately, government priorities in establishing legal frameworks are key to the success of OGD initiatives.

The successful implementation of Open Government Data (OGD) relies on several key factors that enhance its effectiveness. Firstly, strong political leadership and supportive policy frameworks are essential to drive OGD initiatives and address institutional resistance. These elements reflect an organization's readiness to embrace technology and a commitment to transparency (Sayogo & Yuli, 2018). Secondly, a robust IT infrastructure and effective information management are critical for the smooth execution of OGD programs (Izdebski et al., 2021). Thirdly, providing high-quality, easily accessible data is vital to building public trust and encouraging the use of OGD (Kučera et al., 2013). Institutions are more inclined to adopt OGD when they perceive clear advantages, such as enhanced transparency and better public services. Additionally, incorporating crowdsourcing in OGD initiatives can foster greater public engagement (Ceray Aldemi, 2021). To ensure comprehensive OGD implementation, collaboration among government bodies, academic institutions, communities, and the private sector is necessary to create a supportive data-sharing ecosystem.

METHODS

This chapter was utilized a bibliometric analysis. According to Mukherjee et al. (2022) bibliometric analysis is defined as quantitative analysis that describes scientific topics within a specific time period. Additionally, Donthu et al. (2021) state that the purpose of bibliometric analysis is to analyze performance and map scientific knowledge. This chapter examined the scientific structure of open government data in the field of public administration during a certain time period, beginning with annual output and subject areas, and progressing to top cite articles by the most productive writers, contributing institutions, and countries. Furthermore, bibliometric investigations are carried out using VOS Viewer and Biblioshiny R packages, which we combine to visualize data. Research data was collected from the Scopus database. Scopus was selected as the database because it is the world's largest peer-reviewed document database covering all fields of science, including computer science and social sciences (Vujković et al., 2022). This study used the PRISMA framework by applying inclusion and exclusion to obtain the number of documents reviewed.

Figure 1. Exclusion and inclusion criteria through PRISMA workflow

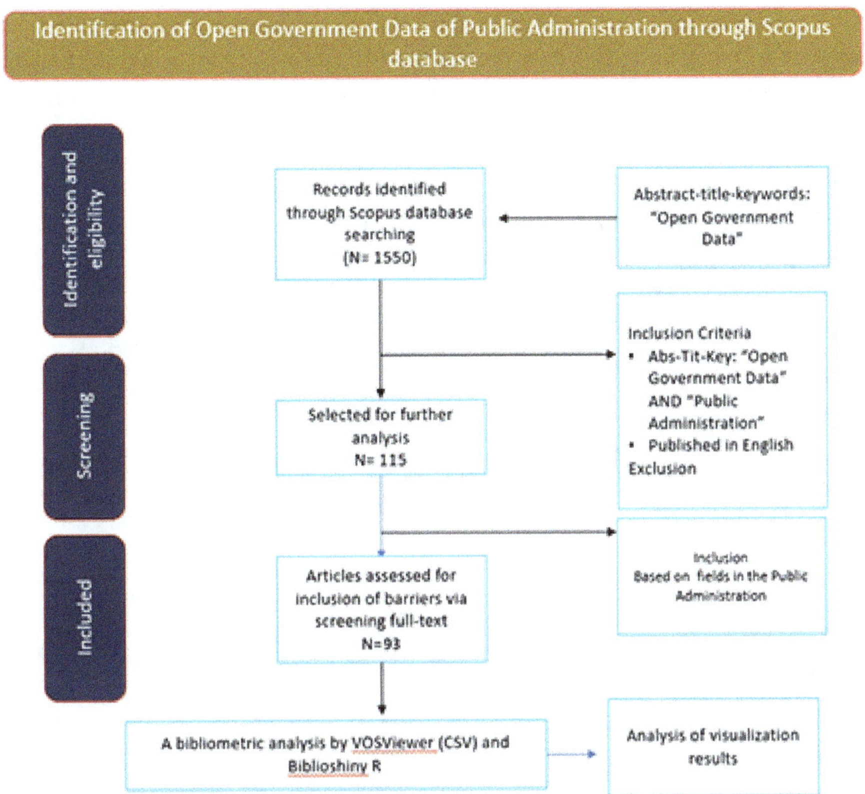

Source: Scopus database gathered 13 January 2025

Figure 1 explains the process of identification and eligibility through search strategies, screening by applying inclusion and exclusion criteria, data analysis using software, and interpretation of data visualization. First, this study began by identifying the keywords "Open Government Data". Abstract-Title-Keywords in the Scopus database. Second, the researchers conducted screening with strict inclusion and exclusion criteria. The aim was to obtain documents relevant to public administration studies. A total of 93 documents were finally included for review. These documents were extracted into a CSV file, which was then processed using VOS Viewer and the Biblioshiny R package. Third, these two software tools were used to visualize the data through their various features. This visualization became a pivotal finding in answering the main question in this chapter.

RESULTS AND DISCUSSION

1. Annual Scientific Publication and Descriptive Analysis

As part of examining the past, present, and future of Open Government Data (OGD) in public administration, the trend in annual scientific publications from 2011 to 2024 reveals a growing academic interest in this field.

Figure 2. Annual publication of scientific papers

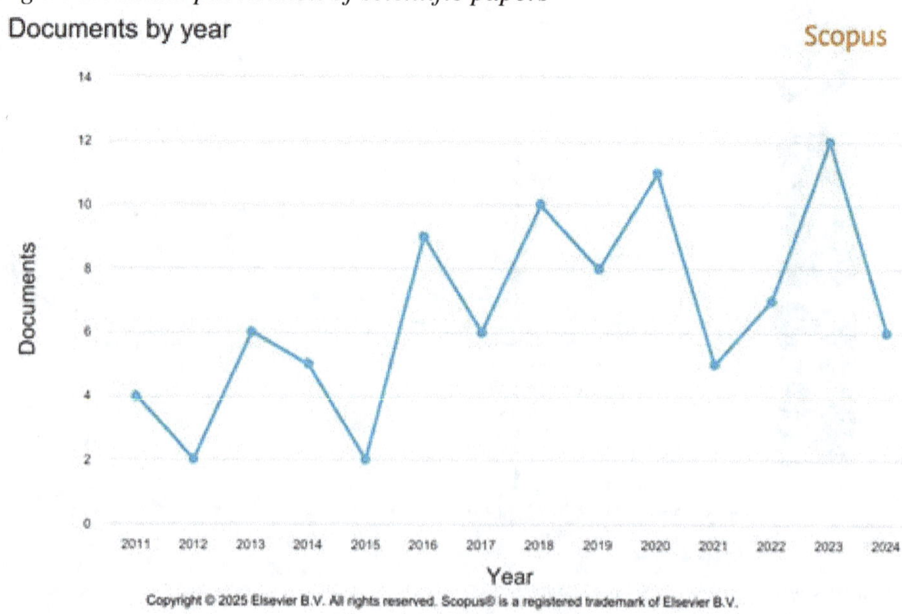

Source: Scopus database

Figure 2 illustrates the annual distribution of 93 scientific documents related to Open Government Data (OGD) in the field of public administration from 2011 to 2024. The trend demonstrates a fluctuating yet generally upward trajectory in research output over the years. Early in the period, between 2011 and 2015, publication numbers remained relatively modest, with annual outputs mostly below seven documents. A significant increase is observed starting in 2016, marking a period of heightened academic interest that continued through the following years. The peak occurred in 2023, with 12 documents published, highlighting the growing recognition of OGD as a vital component in modern governance and administrative reforms. Although a slight decline is visible in 2024 with six documents, the overall trend suggests sustained scholarly engagement with the topic.

This pattern reflects the maturation of OGD research within public administration, moving from exploratory and conceptual discussions in the early 2010s toward more empirical and evaluative studies in recent years. In the early years, such as 2012 and 2015, the low number of publications indicated that OGD was still in its infancy, primarily discussed within technocratic circles. The spikes in publication output around 2016, 2018, 2020, and 2023 suggest that global policy developments and technological advancements may have acted as catalysts for academic inquiry. Over time, however, research themes evolved to address interagency integration, data interoperability, and the use of advanced technologies such as AI and digital platforms. Nevertheless, the inconsistency in yearly outputs indicates that while interest is rising, the field is still evolving and subject to external influences such as policy shifts, advancement ICT and social challenges (Lee et al., 2019).

2. Most Contributing Authors, Institutions and Countries

For more than a decade, OGD studies in public administration have involved many authors from various institutions and countries. This study collected data from 98 articles related to open government data from 2011 to 2024. Figure 3 show details the top ten authors based on productivity. Alexapoulos, C. ranked first as the most productive author with four articles (4.08%), reflecting significant contributions to this field. Two authors ranked second together, each contributing three articles (3.06%) related to the research topic. This analysis considers the total articles to assess the relevance of open government data research. In addition, there is Marijn Janssen, a leading professor in the field of Information and Communication Technology (ICT) and Governance at the Faculty of Technology, Policy, and Management at Delft University of Technology, Netherlands.

Figure 3. 10 most productive authors

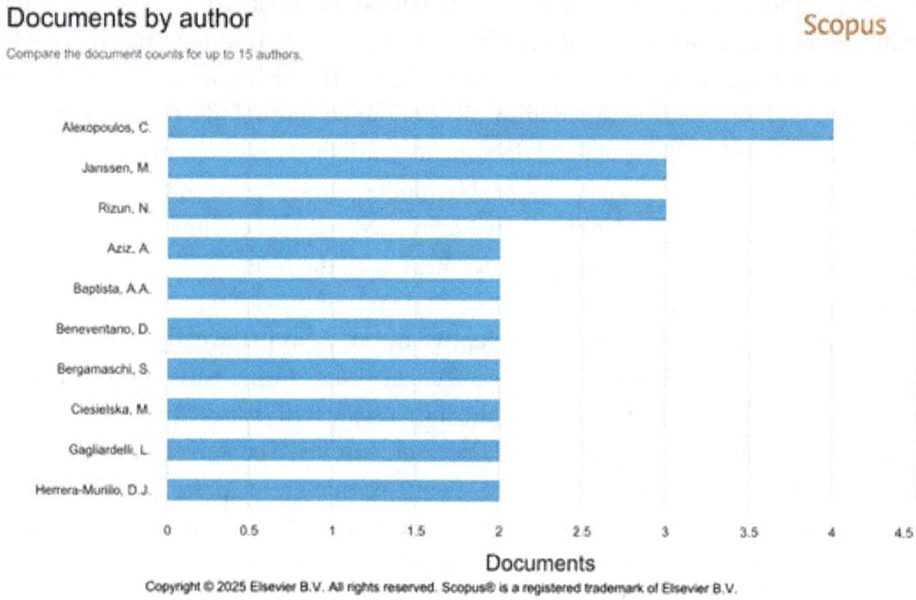

Figure 4. 10 most productive institutions

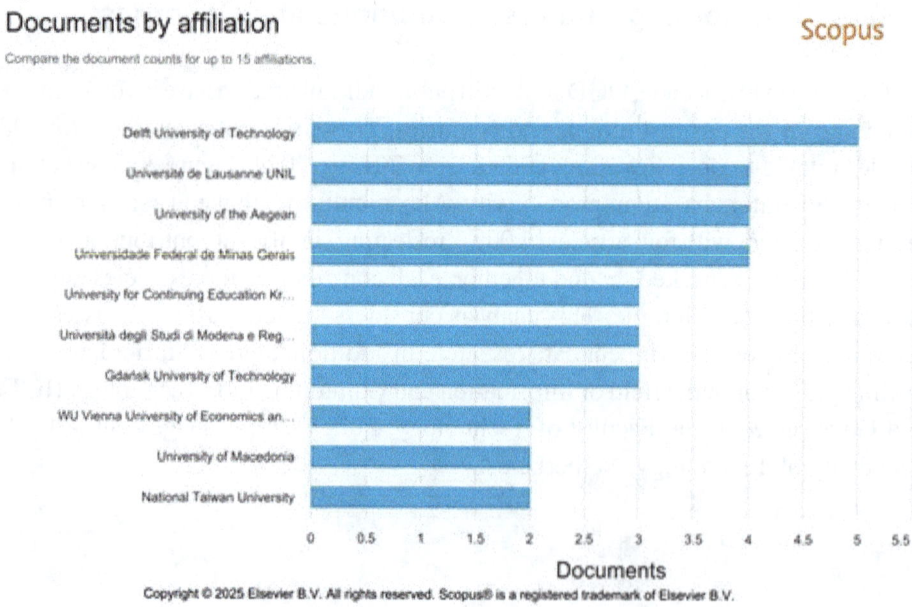

Figure 4 illustrates the research collaboration network involving 150 institutions from 2011 to 2025. The figure 4 identifies 10 pioneering institutions significantly contributing to research output, showing their strategic position in driving innovation. Most of these institutions are from Europe. This region is more advanced in the field of ICT for government than other regions, supported by advanced research institutions and universities. Only one institution is from Asia, namely National Taiwan University. Deft University of Technology stands out as the best institution with five publications. At the same time, Université de Lausanne UNIL (4), University of the Aegean (4), Universidade Federal de Minas Gerais (4), University for Continuing Education Krems (3), Università degli Studi di Modena e Reggio Emilia (3), and Gdańsk University of Technology (3) also recorded high productivity. Austria strengthened its relations with the University for Continuing Education Krems (3) and the WU Vienna University of Economics (2). In addition, Greece also strengthened its position, just like Austria, with two universities, the University of the Aegean (3) and the University of Macedonia (2), in open government data research. In addition, it is influenced by the presence of researchers who consistently conduct research affiliated with research centers and study groups within the public administration department.

Figure 5. 10 most productive countries

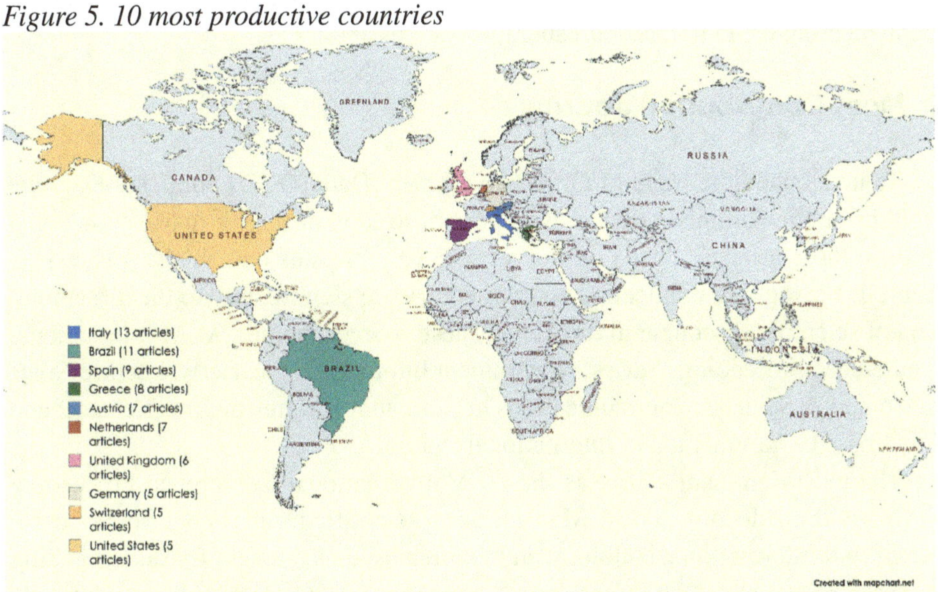

Source: Scopus and analysis author

Figure 5 shows the 10 countries with the highest contribution of articles and citations in open government data research. Italy leads in productivity with 13 publications, taking the top position. Brazil follows in second place with productivity, with 11 publications. Spain ranks third with productivity, with nine publications. The surge in research productivity in Italy and Brazil in the last decade shows an excellent opportunity for these countries to become leaders in the quantity and quality of academic citations on open government data.

Acknowledging that implementing good governance in the public sector is an important prerequisite for managing government is critical. In response to the importance of a sound governance system, the Italian legislature has implemented the Transparency Law (Maramieri, 2014; Palmirani et al., 2014). The Italian implementation is the OpenCoesione initiative, which focuses on providing data on the implementation of cohesion investment projects, in increasing transparency and improving decision-making processes in the public sector (Origlia et al., 2016). In addition, Italy views the implementation of open government data as a tool to increase accountability in providing data services to the public (Viscusi et al., 2014). Thus, Italy is committed to building transparent, accountable, and participatory governance by integrating regulation and technology. These findings show that developed countries continue to dominate the top 10 rankings. However, the emergence of Brazil as part of the list confirms the shifting trend towards inclusivity in global research.

OGD research in the field of public administration is dominated by developed countries, meaning that developed countries have comprehensive instruments for implementing OGD in their bureaucratic systems.

3. Most Contribution Journals

To understand the trend of Open Government Data (OGD) publications in the field of public administration, it is important to look at the journals/sources that publish these articles. Based on the results of the Scopus data analysis shown in Table 1, the top five publication sources contribute significantly to the dissemination of scientific discourse in this field. These sources include ACM International Conference Proceedings Series, Government Information Quarterly, Lecture Notes in Computer Science, Communications in Computer and Information Science, and Electronic Government, and International Journal.

The most dominant source is the ACM International Conference Proceeding Series, with 22 documents. ACM is a leading scientific forum in the field of computers and information technology and is often used as a forum for disseminating research results based on information systems, including Open Government Data applications. Although it is a proceedings series, it is indexed in Scopus with good metrics, namely a Cite Score of around 1.2–1.5 (varying annually), but generally does not have a quartile (as it is a proceedings series, not a regular journal), and the editorial board consists of an international community, predominantly from the United States and Europe.

Second place goes to Government Information Quarterly (GIQ). Published by Elsevier, this journal is a leading publication in the fields of ICT, digital transformation, and e-government. Many scholars around the world publish articles on OGD in this journal, which is ranked Q1 in Scimagojr, with an Impact Factor of 7.8. Next is Lecture Notes in Computer Science (LNCS), published by Springer, with 14 articles. This book series is well-indexed in both Scopus and Web of Science and is widely recognized in the field of computer science and technology applications for presenting ideas in the form of conferences. Subseries such as Lecture Notes in Artificial Intelligence and Lecture Notes in Bioinformatics are also included in this book series. LNCS has a Scientific Journal Ranking (SJR) of 0.352, Quartile 2, and an H-Index of 499. LNCS has editors from various countries, with a dominance of Europe and East Asia.

Other sources, such as CEUR Workshop Proceedings, Communications in Computer and Information Science (CCIS), and four journals in the field of public administration, contributed less, with less than five documents each. Overall, OGD publications were mostly in the form of conferences and book series, which are often understood by scholars as preliminary studies. Meanwhile, empirically, comprehensive studies published in reputable journals remain limited, including Information Polity, International Review of Administrative Sciences, and Public Performance and Management Review. GIQ, on the other hand, is an application that serves as the intersection between public administration and ICT studies. Therefore, these results indicate that research on open government data and public administration is dominated by scientific forums and conferences. This reflects an approach that remains strongly system- and technology-based, rather than purely administrative or classical public policy studies. This could present an opportunity to promote integration between public administration theory and more applied and contemporary technological approaches.

Table 1. Journal Contribution

No	Source	Type	Publisher	Documents
1	ACM International	Conference Proceeding	Association for Computing Machinery	22
2	Government Information Quarterly	Journal	Elsevier	19
3	Lecture Notes in Computer Science Including Subseries Lecture Notes in Artificial Intelligence and Lecture Notes in Bioinformatics	Conference Proceeding	Springer	14
4	Communications in Computer and Information Science	Book Series	Springer	6
5	Electronic Government, an International Journal	Journal	Inderscience	4
6	Ceur Workshop Proceedings	Conference Proceeding	CEUR-WS	4
7	Information Polity	Journal	Sage	4
8	American Review of Public Administration	Journal	Sage	3
9	International Review of Administrative Sciences	Journal	Sage	2
10	Public Performance and Management Review	Journal	Sage	2

Source: author analysis

4. Influential Works

For more than a decade, OGD has been a subject of study supporting digital transformation in government. There are many articles that have been referenced by several scholars in discussing OGD in the field of public administration. Table 2 lists the top 10 most frequently cited studies, indicating that these articles have a significant theoretical influence on another research. The article with the highest number of citations is titled 'A Systematic Literature Study to Unravel Transparency Enabled by Open Government Data: The Window Theory' by Matheus & Janssen (2020), which has been cited 114 times. This article develops a comprehensive model of the factors that can promote or hinder transparency through open government data, along with the expected impacts, by reviewing public administration and information systems literature.

Public administration literature generally highlights aspects of participation and trust, while information systems literature emphasizes user interfaces, user experience, and data quality. Digital government literature seeks to bridge these two perspectives. In this context, this article introduces the Window Theory as an approach to unify existing models by integrating various factors into a single framework. This window theory enables the development of models that are contextual, comprehensive, and simple. This study identifies 42 determinants and 8 effects of transparency, categorized into several clusters. This article provides a comprehensive synthesis of the determinants and effects of transparency, which is highly useful as a foundational reference for interdisciplinary researchers. The topics addressed are highly relevant to contemporary issues such as accountability, citizen participation, and digital governance, attracting attention from various fields such as policy science, information technology, and governance—one of the reasons why this document is widely cited. Additionally, the article introduces the Window Theory, a new conceptual model that integrates approaches from public administration and information systems literature to explain how open government data can generate transparency, and most importantly, the document is openly available, enabling widespread access and distribution (Matheus & Janssen, 2020).

The second article, titled Citizen-centric data services for smarter cities, was written by Aguilera et al. (2017), which has been cited 109 times. This article discusses the development and implementation of the IES Cities platform, a digital architecture that supports the creation of citizen-centric smart city services. The main focus of this platform is to combine data from various sources (government, sensors, and citizens) into a city data ecosystem that can be accessed and utilized uniformly by various stakeholders, especially application developers and citizens. This article validates the platform in four European cities: Zaragoza, Bristol, Rovereto, and Majadahonda, with results showing the platform's effectiveness in accelerating city application development and citizen engagement. This article is widely cited because it combines the Internet of Things, Open Government Data, and citizen-contributed data into a single city service ecosystem and popularizes the idea of citizen integration into smart city digital infrastructure. It offers a real-world model for smart city governance that can be adapted in technology-based public policy research, which is also one of the reasons why this document is widely cited.

The third article, with 106 citations, is titled When Bureaucracy Meets the Crowd: Studying Open Government in the Vienna City Administration, written by Kornberger et al. (2017). This article explores how the principles of open government, which emphasize transparency, public participation, and information distribution, interact and clash with Weberian bureaucratic principles in the administrative context of the Vienna City Government in Austria. The study employs a qualitative approach with in-depth interviews of senior city officials and highlights how open government is practically transformed into open government data (OGD), which tends to be technocratic. Using the metaphor of the city park (Stadtpark), the article illustrates how openness is symbolically interpreted yet remains controlled by bureaucracy. Additionally, it provides a sufficiently comprehensive framework to understand how bureaucracy successfully adapts and maintains itself by translating democratic values into technical practices. The conceptual findings are elaborated by reviving Max Weber's bureaucracy theory in the digital age context, a rare approach. By contextualizing open government within the classical bureaucracy framework, this article fills the theoretical gap between Old Public Administration and digital governance, which is one reason why it has been widely cited by other research.

Based on the 10 articles above, OGD is generally considered an important instrument for improving transparency, accountability, and public participation in public administration. These articles highlight that the benefits of OGD are not automatically achieved simply by opening data. Instead, various factors such as data quality, user interface, citizen participation, and local socio-political context greatly influence the success of OGD implementation. For example, the 'Window Theory' offers a comprehensive model of the determinants that support or hinder OGD-based transparency, encompassing technical and social dimensions such as data reliability, citizen engagement, and the effectiveness of communication among stakeholders (Matheus & Janssen, 2020). Additionally, best practices and real-world challenges emerge from case studies in various countries such as Austria, Switzerland, Italy, and the Netherlands. Empirical evaluations emphasize that OGD requires a supportive institutional framework, incentive mechanisms, and active engagement from both the public and bureaucracy. For instance, a study in Switzerland highlights the need to distinguish between technical data openness and substantive citizen empowerment. Meanwhile, research from the Netherlands uses a "practice lens" approach to highlight the importance of social interaction between government and citizens in meaningfully utilizing OGD. Open data work-under. The success of OGD depends on the integration of technology, organizational culture, and institutional capacity to manage openness strategically and collaboratively.

Table 2. Most influential study and conceptual contributions

No	Authors	Title	Journal	Conceptual Contribution	Year	Citation
1	R. Matheus, M. Janssen	A Systematic Literature Study to Unravel Transparency Enabled by Open Government Data: The Window Theory	Public Performance and Management Review	Presenting a new theory (Window Theory) that integrates Public Administration and Information Systems literature to comprehensively understand OGD-based transparency.	2020	114
2	U. Aguilera, O. Peña, O. Belmonte, D. López-de-Ipiña	Citizen-centric data services for smarter cities	Future Generation Computer Systems	Integrating urban data and promoting the active role of citizens as data prosumers.	2017	109
3	M. Kornberger, R.E. Meyer, C. Brandtner, M.A. Höllerer	When Bureaucracy Meets the Crowd: Studying "Open Government" in the Vienna City Administration	Organization Studies	The city government uses OGD as a symbol of innovation	2017	106
4	P. Parycek, J. Höchtl, M. Ginner	Open government data implementation evaluation	Journal of Theoretical and Applied Electronic Commerce Research	Strategic evaluation of OGD based on organization and public values	2014	80
5	B.W. Wirtz, J.C. Weyerer, M. Rösch	Open government and citizen participation: an empirical analysis of citizen expectancy towards open government data	International Review of Administrative Sciences	TAM transparency model for predicting the use of Open Government Data	2019	75

continued on following page

Table 2. Continued

No	Authors	Title	Journal	Conceptual Contribution	Year	Citation
6	J. Kučera, D. Chlapek, M. Nečaský	Open government data catalogs: Current approaches and quality perspective	Lecture Notes in Computer Science (including subseries Lecture Notes in Artificial Intelligence and Lecture Notes in Bioinformatics)	Mapping the quality of OGD catalogues and techniques for improving them	2013	68
7	E. Ruijer, S. Grimmelikhuijsen, J. van den Berg, A. Meijer	Open data work: understanding open data usage from a practice lens	International Review of Administrative Sciences	OGD is understood as a contextual social practice, not a technical one	2020	63
8	M.E. Cortés-Cediel, A. Segura-Tinoco, I. Cantador, M.P. Rodríguez Bolívar	Trends and challenges of e-government chatbots: Advances in exploring open government data and citizen participation content	Government Information Quarterly	E-government chatbot framework for OGD access and citizen participation	2023	31
9	G. Viscusi, B. Spahiu, A. Maurino, C. Batini	Compliance with open government data policies: An empirical assessment of Italian local public administrations	Information Polity	OGD compliance index based on public data quality dimensions	2014	29
10	T. Cahlikova, V. Mabillard	Open Data and Transparency: Opportunities and Challenges in the Swiss Context	Public Performance and Management Review	Data openness does not automatically result in substantive transparency	2020	27

Source: Scopus database, gathered by May 2025

5. Trend Analysis by Cluster Analysis

Clustering in this section serves to see what topics have been discussed in previous studies on Open Government Data. This clustering aims to provide scholars with information on frequently discussed topics so that they can help identify research gaps. In addition, this clustering can serve as guidance for scholars when conducting research related to each topic in a particular cluster. This will make the explanation process much more comprehensive and in-depth.

Figure 6 shows the clustering obtained from VOS Viewer through the co-occurrence feature. This visualization was obtained from 98 papers extracted into CSV format and then processed by VOS Viewer. There are six clusters in the OGD study.

Figure 6. Cluster analysis by co-occurrence VOS viewer

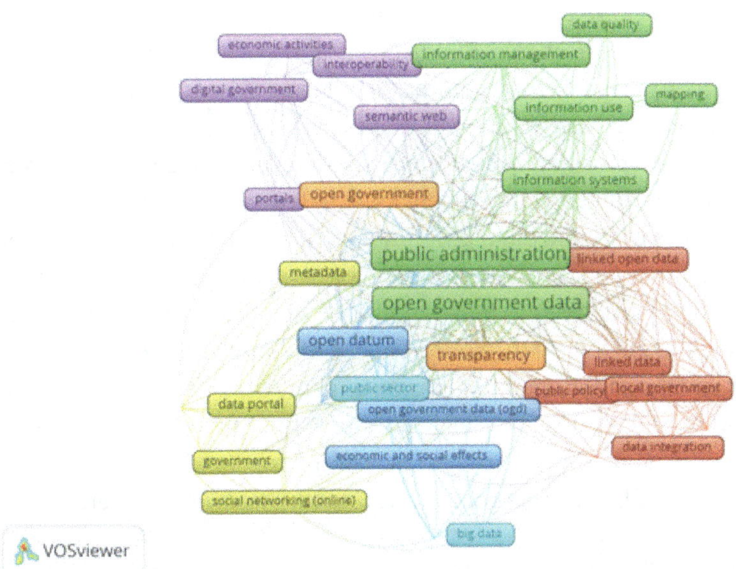

Cluster 1. Information management (green). Information Management is a significant research area within the broader field of information systems, offering concepts, theories, and frameworks that can be adapted and expanded for deeper analysis and exploration of OGD management challenges (Charalabidis et al., 2016). Information management encompasses a series of strategic processes, from the collection, storage, and processing to the distribution of data managed by the government for the public good. Generally, the government builds a management

information system in the form of a website or application to regulate the circulation of services to the community.

In the era of information and technology, the availability of adequate information is needed by the community to ensure the issue of openness in realizing the principles of democratization (Hansson et al., 2015). The use of the website is intended to display information that can be utilized for government communication channels with the public freely (Grimmelikhuijsen & Feeney, 2017; Kučera et al., 2013; Nikiforova & McBride, 2021). These initiatives can also encourage the principles of transparency, accountability, and community participation in social and political issues, such as mitigating corruption or strengthening inclusive decision-making (Lee et al., 2019).

Cluster 2. Interoperability. One of the issues of concern and challenge to date in OGD practice is interoperability (Nikiforova et al., 2023; Wirtz et al., 2022). Many public organizations such as public firms, government, public banks are in need of data networks that are connected to each other (Charalabidis et al., 2016). Interoperability will facilitate user-related synchronization and integration of public services. In the era of governance that requires the role and synergy of many actors, interoperability will be an effective link between the actors involved.

Many OGD initiatives have stagnated because the data that is opened is still fragmented in diverse formats, standards and technical languages. Without interoperability, open data only becomes available data, not useful data. The absence of a common standard hinders the process of cross-sector data integration, both for the purpose of transparency, public participation, and data-driven innovation. Standardization of data formats (such as JSON, XML, CSV), the use of Application Programming Interfaces (APIs), and the adoption of linked data principles are becoming common practice in an effort to bridge silos between institutions. Initiatives such as the Open Data Charter explicitly emphasize the importance of interoperability as a prerequisite for open data to be utilized on a broader scale, including by the private sector, academia, and civil society.

Interoperability is no longer just a matter of technical agreement, but is evolving into a more complex governance issue (Kawabata & Camargo, 2023). Future challenges include aligning global standards, integration with emerging technologies such as blockchain and artificial intelligence, and managing data privacy and security in interconnected systems. In the context of Public Administration, the future of a truly open OGD depends on governments ability to adopt data architectures that are interoperable across jurisdictions, both nationally and internationally. Thus, interoperability can be viewed as a vital pillar that determines OGD's success in realizing its main goals: government transparency, cross-sector collaboration, and data-driven public service innovation. Without interoperability, the OGD's grand vision in public administration risks being caught in counterproductive digital fragmentation.

Cluster 3. Linked open data. Linked Open Data (LOD) is an advanced development in the practice of open government data (OGD) that focuses on the connection between public data semantically. LOD utilizes the principles of linked data to connect various government datasets using open web standards such as RDF (Resource Description Framework) and URIs (Uniform Resource Identifiers) (Nikiforova & Lnenicka, 2021). With this approach, LOD enables easier integration of data across sectors and jurisdictions, thereby increasing the potential added value of government data in public decision-making, transparency and innovation. LOD also opens up new opportunities for collaboration between the public, private and civil society sectors, as the available data is not only open, but can also be interconnected and processed automatically by machines.

In the context of Public Administration, the implementation of LOD carries strategic implications for data governance and the development of the government's digital ecosystem. The implementation of LOD encourages public organizations to build stronger data governance, from metadata standardization to interoperability between digital platforms. In addition, LOD supports the realization of smart government by providing data infrastructure that enables the development of public services based on artificial intelligence and Big data Analytics. However, to achieve optimal benefits from LOD, challenges such as technological readiness, human resource skills, and a supportive regulatory framework must be addressed simultaneously.

Cluster 4. Big data. This cluster shows that OGD is not only viewed as a source of public information, but also as a strategic asset in supporting data-driven policy making (Hardy & Maurushat, 2017; Mergel et al., 2018). The use of big data in the future will increase government transparency and accountability. In addition, the use of big data also predicts public policy trends in the modern era quickly and accurately. Cluster 5. Transparency. Looking at its history, OGD cannot be separated from the vision of government that prioritizes the principle of transparency (Mergel, 2015). The studies in this cluster also highlight the important role of OGD in improving community participation and accountability of public officials, as well as implementation challenges, such as capacity gaps in government agencies, data quality, and limited community digital access (Viscusi et al., 2014). Findings in the Transparency cluster confirmed that the success of OGD is determined not only by the availability of data, but also by the quality of Information Presentation, clarity of metadata, as well as the courage of the government in opening sensitive but relevant data for the public interest (Almuqrin et al., 2022).

Lastly, Cluster 6. Data portals. Concrete evidence of the implementation of open government data is the availability of data portals. In a study (Cho, 2023) in South Korea found that data portals greatly help government work in various ways depending on the level of government, ranging from basic matters such as population administration, education, business, and health to crucial sectors such as security and health. Data portals are indispensable for governments in crisis conditions that demand rapid decision-making processes (Nikiforova, 2020). In addition, data portals can also provide detailed information to the public. The results of this clustering complete the study (Charalabidis et al., 2016) on OGD taxonomies consisting of management and policies, infrastructure, interoperability, usage and value. So it will enrich the discourse on OGD, especially in the context of Public Administration.

6. Future Research Direction

OGD studies in the field of Public Administration are believed to be growing and complex as the demands of transparency in modern society. Therefore, the mapping of research themes will be a guideline in the development of OGD research directions in the future. Based on the figure, motor themes such as linked open data, public administration, open government data, and information systems are in the quadrant with a high level of relevance (centrality) and development (density). This indicates that these themes are key pillars in OGD research and mature public administration and have the potential to become central to the development of theory and practice in the future. Future research is expected to further explore the relationship between these themes, for example, in the context of how linked open data supports transparency and data-driven decision-making in the public sector.

Figure 7. Themes research

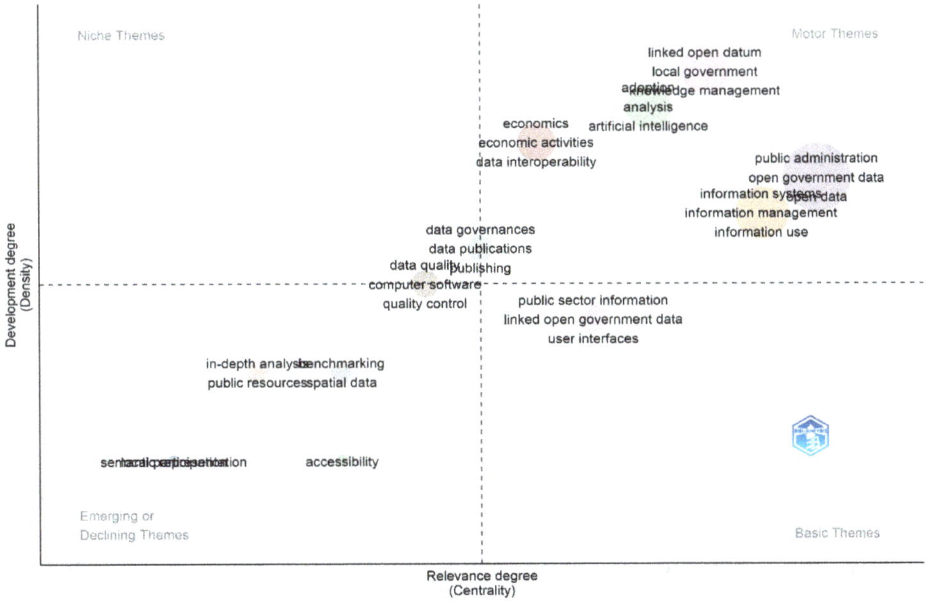

Themes such as public sector information, user interfaces, and accessibility are in the basic themes quadrant with a high level of centrality but low density. These themes are important in the OGD ecosystem but require further deepening and development. Future research will need to explore how these aspects influence the successful implementation of OGD, for example through the study of user experience design in government OGD platforms or how accessibility standards affect the involvement of the wider community in the utilization of government data (Nikiforova & Lnenicka, 2021). In addition, the linkage with issues such as data literacy and digital inclusion can be a strategic development space to enrich OGD discourse in public administration.

Niche themes such as data quality, data interoperability, and data governance also show important potential for further research, although they currently have a lower level of connectedness in OGD research maps. The future of research can focus on how to build an effective data governance framework, integrate various data sources across sectors, and establish reliable data quality standards are an important part of the demand for accessible and integrated government data. In the context of Public Administration, data is the initial input by the government in making decisions accurately (Almuqrin et al., 2022). Credible, transparent, and well-connected Data will make it easier for policy actors. Thus, future research needs to encourage innovation in technology, regulation, and collaboration models in the OGD ecosystem to address new challenges in open and responsive governance (Ruijer & Meijer, 2020).

CONCLUSION

This study has mapped the development of Open Government Data (OGD) in the context of public Administration comprehensively. The results found that OGD has an impact on increasing transparency, accountability, participation, economic, social value to government innovations. This study also shows that the trend of OGD research in the period 2011 to 2015 is still relatively small. OGD trends in research began to increase from the period 2016 to 2024, supported by technological developments and AI. OGD is universally discussed by researchers, institutions, and developed countries in Europe and America.

Open Government Data studies are often discussed on the topics of information management, big data, and transparency. However, there is still little discussed on the topic of interoperability, open data links and data portals. The findings can be a research gap to be completed by researchers in the future. Many OGD initiatives experience constraints on data that is still fragmented in diverse formats, standards, and technical languages. So, the data is only open but has not been able to be used by the public. Therefore, interoperability is very important for the integration of data to the public in the success of open government.

This study has limitations such as, using only a database from Scopus which causes the document to have only one source. Although in fact most of the articles reviewed are also indexed Web of Science, but the main data using Scopus. To be more comprehensive, other studies can add data sources from other indexations such as the Web of Science Core Collection and dimension. In practice, the study confirms that the implementation of OGD is more in the developed countries of Europe and America. There are several studies that explain the practice of OGD in developing countries on other continents such as Asia or Africa. Therefore, future research may address OGD practices in developing countries and the challenges of OGD interoperability in the field of Public Administration.

REFERENCES

Abdullah Alhujaylan, L. C. & M. R. (2021). Towards an Integrated Conceptual Model for Open Government Data in Saudi Arabia. *Intelligent Sustainable Systems, pp 741–764*.

Aguilera, U., Peña, O., Belmonte, O., & López-de-Ipiña, D. (2017). Citizen-centric data services for smarter cities. *Future Generation Computer Systems, 76*, 234–247. https://doi.org/https://doi.org/10.1016/j.future.2016.10.031. DOI: 10.1016/j.future.2016.10.031

Al-Ababneh, H. A., Fedorchuk, Y., Tymchyshyn, A., Pishchenko, G., & Hrytsai, S. (2024). THE USE OF BIG DATA IN THE DETECTION OF ECONOMIC CRIMES IN PUBLIC PROCUREMENTS. *Journal of Theoretical and Applied Information Technology, 102*(24), 8860–8871.

Albano, C. S. (2013). Open government data: A value chain model proposal. *ACM International Conference Proceeding Series,* June 2013, 285–286. DOI: 10.1145/2479724.2479775

Almuqrin, A., Mutambik, I., Alomran, A., Gauthier, J., & Abusharhah, M. (2022). Factors Influencing Public Trust in Open Government Data. *Sustainability (Basel), 14*(15), 9765. Advance online publication. DOI: 10.3390/su14159765

Anwa, S. M. A. A. M. I. N. (2022). *Challenges in Open Government Data Implementation: A Systematic Literature Review*. IEEE.

Bittencourt, C., Estima, J., & Pestana, G. (2019). Open Data Initiatives in Brazil. *2019 14th Iberian Conference on Information Systems and Technologies (CISTI), June*, 1–4. DOI: 10.23919/CISTI.2019.8760592

Bouchelouche, K., Ghomari, A., & Zemmouchi-Ghomari, L. (2024). From Barriers to Boosters: Optimizing Open Government Data through Publishing Guidelines and Data Protection Strategies. *Recent Research Reviews Journal, 3*(1), 56–69. DOI: 10.36548/rrrj.2024.1.004

Çaldağ, M. T., Gokalp, M. O., & Gokalp, E. (2019). Open Government Data: Analysing Benefits and Challenges. *1st International Informatics and Software Engineering Conference: Innovative Technologies for Digital Transformation, IISEC 2019 - Proceedings*. DOI: 10.1109/UBMYK48245.2019.8965581

Ceray Aldemi, E. Ş. (2021). A Model Proposal for Local Governments to Increase Citizen Involvement in the Age of Information Society and E-Government: Crowdsourcing. *Handbook of Research on Global Challenges for Improving Public Services and Government Operations, 19.*

Charalabidis, Y., Alexopoulos, C., & Loukis, E. (2016). A taxonomy of open government data research areas and topics. *Journal of Organizational Computing and Electronic Commerce, 26*(1–2), 41–63. DOI: 10.1080/10919392.2015.1124720

Cho, J. (2023). Comparative analysis of open government data topics and usability. *Quality & Quantity, 57*(6), 5655–5671. DOI: 10.1007/s11135-023-01630-x PMID: 36811111

Donthu, N., Kumar, S., Mukherjee, D., Pandey, N., & Lim, W. M. (2021). How to conduct a bibliometric analysis: An overview and guidelines. *Journal of Business Research, 133*(April), 285–296. DOI: 10.1016/j.jbusres.2021.04.070

Gómez, E. A. R. (2017). Perceptions about the concept and benefits of open government in local governments in Spain. *ACM International Conference Proceeding Series, Part F1280*, 594–597. DOI: 10.1145/3047273.3047338

Grimmelikhuijsen, S. G., & Feeney, M. K. (2017). Developing and Testing an Integrative Framework for Open Government Adoption in Local Governments. *Public Administration Review, 77*(4), 579–590. DOI: 10.1111/puar.12689

Hansson, K., Belkacem, K., & Ekenberg, L. (2015). Open Government and Democracy: A Research Review. *Social Science Computer Review, 33*(5), 540–555. DOI: 10.1177/0894439314560847

Hardy, K., & Maurushat, A. (2017). Opening up government data for Big Data analysis and public benefit. *Computer Law & Security Review, 33*(1), 30–37. DOI: 10.1016/j.clsr.2016.11.003

Hermanto, A., Solimun, S., Fernandes, A. A. R., Wahyono, W., & Zulkarnain, Z. (2018). The importance of open government data for the private sector and NGOs in Indonesia. *Digital Policy. Regulation & Governance, 20*(4), 293–309. DOI: 10.1108/DPRG-09-2017-0047

Izdebski, W., Zwirowicz-Rutkowska, A., & Nowak da Costa, J. (2021). Open data in spatial data infrastructure: The practices and experiences of Poland. *International Journal of Digital Earth, 14*(11), 1547–1560. DOI: 10.1080/17538947.2021.1952323

Kawabata, M. K., & Camargo, A. S.Jr. (2023). E-Government Innovation Initiatives in Public Administration: A Systematic Literature Review and a Research Agenda. *Administration & Society, 55*(9), 1758–1790. DOI: 10.1177/00953997231185847

Kellerhals, A. (2018). Open Government Data – ein Beitrag zur Digitalisierung von Demokratie und öffentlicher Verwaltung. *Yearbook of Swiss Administrative Sciences*, *9*(1), 66. DOI: 10.5334/ssas.120

Kornberger, M., Meyer, R. E., Brandtner, C., & Höllerer, M. A. (2017). When Bureaucracy Meets the Crowd: Studying "Open Government" in the Vienna City Administration. *Organization Studies*, *38*(2), 179–200. DOI: 10.1177/0170840616655496

Kučera, J., Chlapek, D., & Nečaský, M. (2013). Open government data catalogs: Current approaches and quality perspective. *Lecture Notes in Computer Science (Including Subseries Lecture Notes in Artificial Intelligence and Lecture Notes in Bioinformatics), 8061 LNCS*, 152–166. DOI: 10.1007/978-3-642-40160-2_13

Lee, L.-W., & Chu, P.-Y. (2018). A user approach to open government data impact assessment. In R. A.C. & B.-L. R. (Eds.), *Proceedings of the European Conference on e-Government, ECEG* (Vols. 2018-Octob, pp. 111–118). Academic Conferences Limited.

Lee, S. Y., Díaz-Puente, J. M., & Martin, S. (2019). The Contribution of Open Government to Prosperity of Society. *International Journal of Public Administration*, *42*(2), 144–157. DOI: 10.1080/01900692.2017.1405446

Maramieri, J. (2014). Open Government Data: A citizen's right or a concession of public authorities? *Journal of E-Learning and Knowledge Society*, *10*(2). https://doi.org/https://doi.org/10.20368/1971-8829/928

Matheus, R., & Janssen, M. (2020). A Systematic Literature Study to Unravel Transparency Enabled by Open Government Data: The Window Theory. *Public Performance & Management Review*, *43*(3), 503–534. DOI: 10.1080/15309576.2019.1691025

Mergel, I. (2015). Opening Government: Designing Open Innovation Processes to Collaborate With External Problem Solvers. *Social Science Computer Review*, *33*(5), 599–612. DOI: 10.1177/0894439314560851

Mergel, I., Kleibrink, A., & Sörvik, J. (2018). Open data outcomes: U.S. cities between product and process innovation. *Government Information Quarterly*, *35*(4), 622–632. DOI: 10.1016/j.giq.2018.09.004

Mexhid Ferati, F. D. (2020). *Z. K.* Open Government Data Through the Lens of Universal Design. In Universal Access in Human-Computer Interaction. Applications and Practice., DOI: 10.1007/978-3-030-49108-6_24

Mukherjee, D., Lim, W. M., Kumar, S., & Donthu, N. (2022). Guidelines for advancing theory and practice through bibliometric research. *Journal of Business Research*, *148*(May), 101–115. DOI: 10.1016/j.jbusres.2022.04.042

Nascimento Silva, P., & Nascimento Silva, S. (2025). Open government data in health sector: A systematic literature review open government data in health sector. *BMC Public Health, 25*(1), 47. Advance online publication. DOI: 10.1186/s12889-024-21149-6 PMID: 39762782

Nikiforova, A. (2020). Timeliness of Open Data in Open Government Data Portals through Pandemic-related Data: A long data way from the publisher to the user. *2020 4th International Conference on Multimedia Computing, Networking and Applications, MCNA 2020*, 131–138. DOI: 10.1109/MCNA50957.2020.9264298

Nikiforova, A., & Lnenicka, M. (2021). A multi-perspective knowledge-driven approach for analysis of the demand side of the Open Government Data portal. *Government Information Quarterly, 38*(4), 101622. DOI: 10.1016/j.giq.2021.101622

Nikiforova, A., & McBride, K. (2021). Open government data portal usability: A user-centred usability analysis of 41 open government data portals. *Telematics and Informatics, 58*(December 2020), 101539. DOI: 10.1016/j.tele.2020.101539

Nikiforova, A., Rizun, N., Ciesielska, M., Alexopoulos, C., & Miletić, A. (2023). Towards High-Value Datasets Determination for Data-Driven Development: A Systematic Literature Review. In L. I., C. C., K. E., T. E., J. M., Z. A., V. P. G., & V. S. (Eds.), *Lecture Notes in Computer Science (including subseries Lecture Notes in Artificial Intelligence and Lecture Notes in Bioinformatics): Vol. 14130 LNCS* (pp. 211–229). Springer Science and Business Media Deutschland GmbH. DOI: 10.1007/978-3-031-41138-0_14

Ugwu Jovita Nnenna, Ugwuanyi Ifeoma Perpetua, Asuma Mariita Nchaga, Tushabe Hadijah, E. M. and T. O. N. (2024). Challenges and Opportunities in Implementing Open Government Data Initiatives in East Africa. *International Academic Association Journal, 10(2):1-11.*

Origlia, C., Cersosimo, D., Bianchi, T., & Fortunato, A. (2016). Assessing an Open Government Data Initiative. The Case of OpenCoesione. *2016 Conference for E-Democracy and Open Government (CeDEM)*, 164–171. DOI: 10.1109/CeDEM.2016.26

Palmirani, M., Martoni, M., & Girardi, D. (2014). Open Government Data Beyond Transparency. *Electronic Government and the Information Systems Perspective (EGOVIS 2014)*, 275–291. DOI: 10.1007/978-3-319-10178-1_22

Roa, H. N., Loza-Aguirre, E., & Flores, P. (2019). A survey on the problems affecting the development of open government data initiatives. *2019 6th International Conference on EDemocracy and EGovernment, ICEDEG 2019*, 157–163. DOI: 10.1109/ICEDEG.2019.8734452

Ruijer, E., & Meijer, A. (2020). Open Government Data as an Innovation Process: Lessons from a Living Lab Experiment. *Public Performance & Management Review, 43*(3), 613–635. DOI: 10.1080/15309576.2019.1568884

Safarov, I. (2020). Institutional Dimensions of Open Government Data Implementation: Evidence from Transition Countries. *Public Performance & Management Review, 43*(6), 1359–1389. DOI: 10.1080/15309576.2020.1805336

Sayogo, D. S., & Yuli, S. B. C. (2018). Critical success factors of open government and open data at local government level in Indonesia. *International Journal of Electronic Government Research, 14*(2), 28–43. DOI: 10.4018/IJEGR.2018040103

Tai, K. T. (2021). Open government research over a decade: A systematic review. *Government Information Quarterly, 38*(2), 101566. DOI: 10.1016/j.giq.2021.101566

Villegas Tovar, R., & Marcos Recio, J. C. (2019). Information intermediaries within the open government model. *Ibersid, 13*(1), 37–42.

Viscusi, G., Spahiu, B., Maurino, A., & Batini, C. (2014). Compliance with open government data policies: An empirical assessment of Italian local public administrations. *Information Polity, 19*(3–4), 263–275. DOI: 10.3233/IP-140338

Vujković, P., Ravšelj, D., Umek, L., & Aristovnik, A. (2022). Bibliometric Analysis of Smart Public Governance Research: Smart City and Smart Government in Comparative Perspective. *Social Sciences (Basel, Switzerland), 11*(7), 293. Advance online publication. DOI: 10.3390/socsci11070293

Wirtz, B. W., & Birkmeyer, S. (2015). Open Government: Origin, Development, and Conceptual Perspectives. *International Journal of Public Administration, 38*(5), 381–396. DOI: 10.1080/01900692.2014.942735

Wirtz, B. W., Daiser, P., & Mermann, M. (2018). Social Media as a Leverage Strategy for Open Government: An Exploratory Study. *International Journal of Public Administration, 41*(8), 590–603. DOI: 10.1080/01900692.2017.1289388

Wirtz, B. W., Weyerer, J. C., Becker, M., & Müller, W. M. (2022). Open government data: A systematic literature review of empirical research. *Electronic Markets, 32*(4), 2381–2404. DOI: 10.1007/s12525-022-00582-8 PMID: 36158525

Yang, L. (2017). Exploring the factors influencing agencies' engagement in open data: A case study of Taichung city government. *Journal of Educational Media and Library Science, 54*(2), 185. DOI: 10.6120/JoEMLS.2017.542/0026.RS.BM

Chapter 5
Promoting Public Value Creation Through the Use of Digital Technologies

Yakup Karaca
https://orcid.org/0000-0002-6902-4057
Aydin Adnan Menderes University, Turkey

Namık Kemal Öztürk
https://orcid.org/0000-0002-7264-4791
Mugla Sıtkı Koçman University, Turkey

ABSTRACT

Today, digital technologies are not only transforming the delivery of public services but also reshaping how public value is defined and produced. This study examines the strategic use of technologies such as artificial intelligence, big data, machine learning and the internet of things in the public sector to strengthen public value through transparency, accountability, citizen satisfaction and social justice. The study covers four key dimensions: the relationship between digital governance and public value, case studies from developed and developing countries, ethical and institutional challenges posed by digitalization, and strategic policy recommendations. Through a comparative analysis of Estonia, Singapore, the United States, and Turkey, a multidimensional framework of digital transformation is presented and strategic directions that are particularly applicable to developing countries are suggested.

DOI: 10.4018/979-8-3373-1484-6.ch005

INTRODUCTION

The rapid development of digital technologies has led to structural transformations in public administration and policies, replacing the traditional, hierarchical, and bureaucratic approach with data-driven, flexible, and citizen-participation-based management models. This transformation is not limited to the renewal of technical infrastructure; it has created a wide range of impacts, from organizational structures to decision-making processes, accountability to citizen-state relations.

In this context, the concept of "public value" has become a multidimensional concept that needs to be re-examined in light of the dynamics of the digital age. Moore's work, "Creating Public Value," emphasizes that public services should be measured not only by outputs but also by quality of life, democratic participation, ethical governance, and social justice. Today, decision support systems based on big data and artificial intelligence accelerate the production of public value while also bringing new debates to the forefront, such as algorithmic transparency and data security.

In this context, the production of public value now depends not only on managerial skills but also on digital capacity, ethical standards, and relationships with citizens. The aim of this study is to examine the effects of digital technologies on the production of public value at the conceptual and practical levels, to evaluate different country applications comparatively, and to offer strategic recommendations to public administrators and policymakers.

The main research questions sought to be answered in this context are as follows:

- How do digital technologies transform the elements of public value?
- To what extent does digitalization support values such as ethics, transparency and participation as well as the efficiency of public services?
- What are the potential and challenges of digital technologies for public value creation in developing countries?
- How can strategic models be developed that are applicable for decision makers in this transformation process?

In the light of these questions, the study aims to provide both a theoretical contribution to the literature and a guiding framework for policymakers in the digitalizing public administration conjuncture.

1. THEORETICAL BACKGROUND: THE RELATIONSHIP BETWEEN PUBLIC VALUE AND DIGITAL GOVERNANCE

In the digital age, redefining public value requires that this concept be considered not only as a normative ideal but also as central to administrative decision-making processes. A management approach that is responsive to citizen expectations and prioritizes the public interest necessitates a comprehensive assessment of approaches that generate public value today. In this context, Moore's "strategic public triangle," Stoker's governance-based contributions, and Benington's approach emphasizing the social context form the theoretical foundation of the new public service paradigm shaped by digital transformation.

1.1. Theories of Public Value: Moore, Stoker and Benington's Approaches

The concept of public value has been systematically developed in public administration literature, particularly by Mark H. Moore. Moore (1995, p. 28) argues that public administrators should focus not only on output-oriented goals such as efficiency and effectiveness, but also on the public good. His "Strategic Public Value Triangle" provides public administrators with a framework for producing meaningful value for citizens, building the institutional capacity to deliver it, and conducting the process on the basis of democratic legitimacy. This model sees balancing the definition of the public good, the legitimacy of decisions, and the alignment of institutional capacity as the key to sustainable value production.

Expanding on Moore's approach, Gerry Stoker (2006, p. 44) emphasizes that public value should be based not only on individual preferences but also on social values and democratic processes. According to him, public administration operates within the framework of "network governance" shaped by stakeholders rather than centralized structures. In this context, public value emerges through transparent, participatory, and pluralistic interaction processes between managers, citizens, and civil society.

John Benington, on the other hand, states that public value is shaped by historical, social, and political contexts. According to Benington and Moore (2011, p. 34), the criteria for public value are not only service quality but also democratic participation, ethical responsibilities, and social legitimacy. This approach views the effective participation of citizens in decision-making processes as a fundamental element of public value and transforms the concept into a dynamic field that builds "social consensus" and "the common good" beyond administrative efficiency.

1.2. New Public Management (NPM) and New Public Service (NPS) Perspectives

New Public Management (NPM) has advocated the adaptation of private sector management techniques to the public sector since the 1980s, emphasizing performance measurement, competition, customer-focused service, and resource efficiency. This approach has guided public institutions toward performance management models based on transparency, accountability, and fiscal discipline by operating them according to market logic (Hood, 1991, p. 5).

In contrast, the New Public Service (NPS) approach criticizes the "citizen-customer" concept and defines the fundamental role of public administrators as "co-managers" rather than "service providers." According to Denhardt and Denhardt (2000), public service should prioritize democratic participation, ethical values, and the public interest. Within this framework, managers are positioned as facilitators of public discourse rather than technocrats.

NPS requires not only a rethinking of instrumental managerial techniques but also of the fundamental values of public administration. The success of public policies should be evaluated not by performance indicators but by the trust relationship established with citizens, the quality of participation, and contributions to the common good. Thus, public administration evolves from an efficiency-centered approach to a more holistic structure based on the production of social values.

1.3. The Concept of Digital Governance and its Impact on Public Value

Digital governance refers to the integration of information and communication technologies into public administration processes, that is, their effective use in public administration. This concept aims to make public services more transparent, effective and accessible through digital infrastructures and opens the decision-making mechanisms of public institutions to citizen participation through digital platforms (Cordella & Bonina, 2012, p. 514). In this context, digital governance contributes to increasing public value by facilitating citizens' participation in decision-making processes.

The digital governance approach enables the reorganization of the structural capacities that produce public value, while enabling public policies to become more predictable and evidence-based through data-driven decision-making. However, the contribution of digital governance to public value is not limited to technical intermediation; it also brings with it a governance logic that strengthens participation, accountability and social inclusion (Bannister & Connolly, 2011, p. 3).

Moreover, digital governance has the potential to not only increase efficiency and effectiveness in the delivery of public services, but also to enable faster and more effective responses to citizens' needs and expectations. This makes a significant contribution to increasing public value.

The use of digital technologies in public administration has the potential to make public value generation more “data-driven”, “citizen-centered” and “accountable”. This potential makes the relationship between digital governance and public value increasingly central.

2. LITERATURE REVIEW ON PUBLIC VALUE GENERATION WITH DIGITAL TECHNOLOGIES

Digitalization in public administration represents not only a technical change but also a structural and value-oriented transformation in governance. In this context, public value is being reevaluated through the opportunities created by emerging technologies. Academic interest focuses on the use of artificial intelligence, big data, the Internet of Things, and blockchain in the design and implementation of public services. The current literature examines the social impacts of these technologies and their capacity to create public value in greater detail, emphasizing how digital tools are reshaping governance and service delivery.

2.1. Recent Studies on the Use of Digital Technologies in Public Administration

In recent years, there has been an intense interest in the academic literature on the use and integration of digital technologies in public administration. In particular, the potential of technologies such as artificial intelligence, big data analytics and blockchain to increase efficiency in the delivery of public services has been addressed in many studies. For example, Twizeyimana and Andersson (2019) examined the contribution of e-government applications to public value in six key dimensions and stated that these applications have positive effects in areas such as improving the quality of public services, improving administrative efficiency, strengthening open government capabilities, improving ethical behavior and professionalism, increasing trust in government, and improving social value and welfare (p. 169).

Furthermore, Panagiotopoulos, Klievink, and Cordella (2019) examined how digital government applications play a role in public value creation and emphasized that these technologies offer innovative ways to plan, design, and implement public services (p. 2).

2.2. Digitalization of Public Services: Artificial Intelligence, Big Data, Blockchain

Artificial intelligence, big data, and blockchain are emerging as key technologies in the digitization of public services. Artificial intelligence enables new forms of governance that prioritize the public interest by making decision-making processes faster, more transparent, and data-driven. Babšek et al. (2025) draw on examples from the European Commission to highlight the potential of artificial intelligence to increase internal efficiency and service quality in public institutions, strengthen democratic governance, and support the public interest.

Big data, meanwhile, contributes to the redefinition and more effective production of public value. Fredriksson et al. (2018) note that this technology offers the opportunity to improve service quality, streamline processes, and develop data-driven decision-making capabilities. Kitchin (2014) emphasizes that big data has created a paradigm shift in the public sector with its real-time, dynamic data processing capabilities. Wirtz et al. (2020) also state that big data, combined with artificial intelligence, offers more personalized services, but that this also gives rise to ethical and managerial responsibilities.

Blockchain technology, on the other hand, makes important contributions to e-government applications in terms of security, transparency, and data integrity. Terzi et al. (2019) demonstrate that blockchain can be used in energy and healthcare services in conjunction with artificial intelligence. Sabbagh (2019) argues that blockchain-based systems strengthen citizen trust in public services, especially through data security, transaction transparency and resistance to unauthorized interference. In this framework, it is not only possible for public services to become faster and automated, but also to gain democratic legitimacy.The study emphasizes that blockchain in e-government applications should be evaluated not only from a cost-effectiveness perspective, but also in terms of increasing public value. Thus, blockchain plays a role for public administrators not only as a technology choice but also as a governance tool that prioritizes participation, accountability and public interest.

2.3. Gaps in the Literature and the Contribution of this Study

The literature on the use of digital technologies in public administration has mainly focused on performance-based outcomes such as technical efficiency, service quality and improvement of administrative processes. Most of the studies examine the practices in developed countries; especially e-government systems, artificial intelligence-supported services and open data applications in European Union member states are at the forefront (Twizeyimana & Andersson, 2019, p. 174). In this context, public value is measured only in terms of administrative efficiency, with limited attention to normative dimensions such as citizen participation, digital inclusion, ethical governance and social justice.

Research on the integration of advanced technologies such as artificial intelligence and big data into public policies is mostly centered around technical parameters such as technological capacity, system design and cost-effectiveness. However, in a comprehensive literature review conducted by Misuraca and van Noordt (2020) on behalf of the European Commission, the adoption of AI in the public sector in EU member states was assessed and it was argued that AI technologies can play a strategic role not only as a means of improving managerial efficiency but also in the reconstruction of public value. In addition to its capacity to improve the quality and effectiveness of public services, the study emphasizes that AI can contribute to core public administration values such as transparency, citizen interaction and accountability. In particular, it is stated that the use of artificial intelligence in line with the core principles of public value such as citizen orientation, social impact assessment and contribution to the public good necessitates the ethical and responsible application of technology in the public sphere. In this respect, the literature points out that not only the instrumental but also the normative dimensions of digital technologies should be taken into account.

Similarly, Dunleavy and Margetts (2015) argue that digital transformation in public services offers an opportunity not only for improved performance but also for the redesign of the public good. The capacity of digital public administration to engage citizens, its power to promote participatory governance and its role in strengthening social justice have not yet been systematically assessed. Bekkers and Homburg (2007), while explaining the impact of ICTs on public value, emphasized the need for more empirical studies on the relationship of digital tools with social participation, trust and governance quality.

Taking into account the aforementioned gaps, this study addresses the contribution of digital technologies to public value from the perspective of not only technical efficiency but also social inclusiveness, democratic governance and ethical responsibilities. Contrary to the dominant trend in the literature, this study analyzes the citizen-centered effects of digital public services through country cases with different governance models and focuses on the normative components of public value production. Thus, it aims to deepen the relationship between digitalization and value-based governance in the public administration literature and provide an inclusive roadmap for policymakers. By addressing it more comprehensively, it aims to focus on practices in developing countries and fill the literature gap in this field.

3. THE ROLE OF DIGITAL TECHNOLOGIES IN PUBLIC VALUE GENERATION

Digital technologies have not only created a change and transformation in the structure of public administration, but also reshaped the understanding of how public value is generated. These technologies not only make the delivery of public services more effective and efficient, but also increase the opportunities for citizens to participate in governance, make public policy processes more transparent and accountable, and offer new opportunities for public administrators to design innovative public policy. Given the multidimensional nature of public value, the contribution of digitalization should be considered not only as a technical development but also as a process of managerial, social and normative transformation. In this section, how digital technologies redefine public value is discussed in detail along the axes of service efficiency, citizen participation, co-production, transparency and innovation.

3.1. Efficiency and Automation in Service Delivery

The use of digital technologies in public administration plays a critical role in making service delivery more efficient, faster and cost-effective. According to Dunleavy et al., digitalization brings about a new paradigm in public administration. "Digital age governance" is based on the centralization of public services, automation of processes and reshaping them according to user needs. This approach supports the development of more flexible, transparent and accountable governance models that are different from traditional bureaucratic structures (Dunleavy et al., 2006, pp. 12-30).

Automation technologies not only speed up operations, but also reduce error rates, reduce staff dependency and enable more efficient use of resources. For example, the OECD's 2019 report, The Path to Becoming a Data-Driven Public Sector, states that digital tools save time and costs, improve service quality and accelerate decision-making processes in the public sector. In the same report, the rise of big data and digital technologies is rapidly transforming national economies and societies. They offer enormous advantages for the day-to-day functioning of public administrations, and in the digital age, governments must keep pace with the growing demands and expectations of their citizens, manage increasing pressure on their budgets and respond to new policy challenges. Any failure to adapt to the conjuncture of this new and changing digital age can expose public administrations to serious risks and ultimately to a loss of public trust (OECD, 2019, pp. 24-27).

In this context, effective adoption of digital technologies not only increases operational efficiency, but has also become a strategic imperative that strengthens the legitimacy, credibility and citizen-oriented service approach of public administration.Public institutions that fail to adapt to the digitalization process risk both a decline in service quality and a loss of public trust. Therefore, it is critical for public administrators to consider digital technologies not only as a tool but also as a transformation mechanism that will ensure the sustainability of managerial capacity and public value.

3.2. Co-Production and Citizen Participation

The digital delivery of public services enables more active citizen participation in decision-making processes and co-production processes.Linders (2012) states that the digital age has shaped the "We-Government" concept and that this transformation has embraced the role of citizens not only as information recipients but also as data producers, solution partners and policy makers. Social media, online platforms, open data and open government data applications provide the technical infrastructure for this participation (Linders, 2012, pp. 446-448).

This process increases not only the quality of governance but also the inclusiveness and legitimacy of public services. OECD (2020), Digital Government in Chile: Digital Transformation and Public Sector Innovation, emphasizes that digital platforms contribute to the production of more inclusive public policies by increasing citizen participation. The mainstreaming effect of digital tools on democratic participation enables public administrators to respond more quickly and directly to citizen demands (OECD, 2020, pp. 45-50).

Moreover, Bovaird and Loeffler (2012) argue that co-production is being redefined in the digital environment, which has a transformative effect on enhancing public value. This effect is particularly evident in models where public services are co-designed, implemented and evaluated (Bovaird & Loeffler, 2012, pp. 112-115). Thus, digital participation is not only about sharing information; it is also the basis for the co-production of public good.

In conclusion, the interaction channels provided by digital technologies not only facilitate governance processes but also enable citizens to directly contribute to the shaping of public policies.This new form of participation goes beyond the classical understanding of representation, enabling more accurate identification of social needs and reconstruction of public services on the basis of social legitimacy.Therefore, structuring digital co-production processes in line with institutional capacity has become a strategic necessity for public administrators not only to strengthen participatory democracy but also for sustainable public value creation.

3.3 Innovation, Transparency and Accountability

The diffusion of digital technologies in public administration enables the emergence of innovative practices and the transformation of institutional structures. According to Mergel, Edelmann and Haug, digital transformation is not only a technological transition, but also a strategic and cultural restructuring of public institutions. This transformation integrates elements such as data-driven decision-making, algorithmic governance and digital leadership into public administration practices (Mergel et al., 2019, pp. 2-6). In this framework, digital transformation is not only an instrumental modernization in public administration, but also a multi-layered change process in which managerial values, roles and competencies are redefined. Strategic digital leadership and organizational learning capacity play a critical role in the sustainability of this transformation. Therefore, not only the effective integration of digital technologies, but also how these technologies are internalized into the managerial culture becomes decisive in the production of public value.

In terms of transparency, digital tools have an important role in making public institutions more accountable for data sharing and information openness. According to Janssen, Charalabidis and Zuiderwijk, open data policies increase transparency, build trust in public administration and strengthen citizens' monitoring and judgment capacities. This also allows public policies to be implemented in a fairer and more traceable manner (Janssen et al., 2012, pp. 260-261).

In this context, open data and digital transparency practices have become powerful tools to rebuild trust between citizens and public administration. Equal access to information not only increases the effectiveness of oversight mechanisms but also strengthens the social legitimacy of public decisions. Therefore, treating digital transparency policies as not only a technical but also an ethical and managerial responsibility should be considered as a fundamental strategy to ensure the long-term sustainability of public value.

Accountability becomes more institutionalized and systematized through digital traceability.Citizens can instantly monitor the processes related to public services, provide feedback and demand more transparent governance from public administrators.This strengthens both institutional oversight mechanisms and democratic participation (OECD, 2019, pp. 33-36).

These developments show that accountability in public administration is no longer the monopoly of audit institutions or legislative bodies, but a direct citizen-based and digitally supported audit approach has also emerged.Tools such as instant monitoring, online complaint and suggestion systems, feedback mechanisms and digital performance indicators enable both process- and outcome-oriented evaluation of public services.As emphasized by OECD (2019), such practices enable citizens to be positioned not only as consumers but also as controlling and directive actors. In this respect, digital accountability not only increases administrative transparency, but also contributes to the internalization of public value at the institutional level by deepening the culture of responsibility in public administration. This transformation reveals that accountability in modern public administration is no longer a static obligation but a dynamic and participatory approach to governance.

4. INSTITUTIONAL CAPACITIES AND DYNAMICS OF TRANSFORMATION

Digital transformation processes are not only about implementing technological innovations; they also require restructuring the institutional capacities of public institutions and managing transformation dynamics correctly.In this context, digital capacity building, equipping public employees with digital skills and institutionalizing digital leadership stand out as decisive factors in the success of transformation. However, in this process, not only capacity building but also dealing with organizational resistance, implementing change management strategies and adapting the institutional culture to transformation are vital.On the other hand, in order for digitalization to reach all segments of society equally, eliminating inequalities in access to technology and promoting digital literacy is also a strategic imperative for the inclusive production of public value. In this section, the relationship between digital transformation and institutional capacity in public institutions is assessed along three main axes: developing digital competencies, overcoming institutional resistance and digital inclusion issues.

4.1. Digital Capacity Building and Competence of Public Employees

The sustainability and success of digital transformation largely depends on the internal capacity of public institutions and the digital competencies of their employees.In addition to providing technological infrastructure, it is also critical to train human resources who can use these technologies correctly and effectively.The OECD's Digital Government Index report published in 2020 emphasizes that digital capacity can be achieved not only through hardware and software infrastructure, but also by equipping public employees with digital skills, supporting digital leadership and developing innovative business models (OECD, 2020, pp. 29-32).

In this framework, digital transformation can be completed not only through the establishment of technological systems, but also through a mental transformation that will ensure the integration of human resources with these systems. Increasing the digital competencies of public employees directly affects not only individual performance but also organizational flexibility and innovation capacity.Lack of digital leadership or inadequate digital skills can render even the most advanced infrastructure investments ineffective.Therefore, it has become a strategic imperative for the sustainable production of public value that the vision of digital public administration includes human-centered capacity building as well as technical modernization.

Mergel, Edelmann, and Haug (2019) argue that for digital transformation processes to succeed, public employees' perceptions of technology, learning capacity, and institutional support mechanisms should be evaluated together. According to them, digital governance requires a public organization that is not only instrumental but also learning, experiencing and evolving (Mergel et al., 2019, pp. 3-5). In this context, digital capacity is not only technical knowledge but also strategic thinking, data literacy and agile decision-making capabilities.

The European Digital Competence Framework for Public Sector (DigCompOrg and DigComp 2.2) developed by the European Commission categorizes the basic digital skills that public employees should possess under headings such as data security, online communication, information management and service innovation. Supporting these competencies with corporate learning programs enables digital transformation to evolve into a cultural change (Vuorikari et al., 2022).

4.2. Organizational Resistance and Change Management

Digital transformation is a multifaceted change process in public institutions that has not only technical but also organizational and cultural dimensions. However, this process can encounter resistance, especially due to entrenched norms, habits and hierarchical structures. OECD (2019) emphasizes that one of the main reasons for the failure of digital transformation projects is insufficient planning of organizational change management. Public managers' ability to recognize and transform such resistance depends on their strategic leadership and stakeholder management skills (OECD, 2019, pp. 49-51).

Theoretical frameworks such as Kotter's eight-stage change model show that visioning, quick wins, and institutionalizing change are critical steps to succeed in digital transformation (Kotter, 1996). Margetts and Dorobantu (2019) argue that digitalization in public administration often turns into a "political struggle" rather than a "technical analysis". Therefore, transformation should be supported not only by technology investments but also by internal cultural reforms (Margetts & Dorobantu, 2019, pp. 14-17).

In this context, designing change management strategies in a participatory and inclusive manner not only reduces resistance, but also increases employee engagement and facilitates the internalization of digital transformation. In projects where public employees are not included in the process and their feedback is ignored, resistance increases even more, which causes the transformation process to falter.

4.3. Inequality of Access to Technology and Digital Literacy

One of the most important structural limitations of digital transformation is inequality of access to technology and differences in digital literacy levels.Many factors such as unequal internet access, age, education level, income level and regional differences play a role in the dissemination of digital services. These inequalities constitute a serious obstacle to effective delivery of public services and participatory governance (UNESCO, 2021).

UNESCO's Digital Inclusion report emphasizes that the digital divide is not only a technical but also a social problem and that digital access to public services is limited, especially in rural areas and disadvantaged groups (UNESCO, 2021, pp. 18-21).This situation hinders the equitable provision of public services and makes it difficult to produce public value equally.

Digital literacy is not limited to the ability to use computers, but includes multifaceted skills such as critical thinking, information verification, digital rights and cybersecurity. The DigComp 2.1 framework developed by Carretero et al. (2017) categorizes digital competencies under five main headings: information and data literacy, communication and collaboration, digital content creation, security and problem solving.These topics are critical in understanding citizens' ability to use digital services.

Therefore, for digital transformation to succeed at the societal level, it is not enough to invest only in technology infrastructure. It is also necessary to develop digital inclusion strategies and implement education, awareness and support policies to include disadvantaged groups in digital public life. Otherwise, digitalization may deepen social segregation instead of increasing public value.

5. ETHICAL, LEGAL AND SOCIAL DIMENSIONS

The proliferation of digital technologies in public administration should be evaluated not only in terms of its administrative and technical dimensions, but also with multi-layered issues such as data security, individual rights, social inclusion and ethical governance. Digital public administration practices have a dual nature, both potentially increasing public value and threatening fundamental rights and freedoms when misguided. For this reason, digitalization needs to be considered not only in the context of benefit generation, but also within the framework of ethical, legal and social responsibility. This chapter systematically evaluates various dimensions ranging from data privacy to digital exclusion, from algorithmic decision-making processes to the citizen-state relationship.

5.1. Data Privacy and Algorithmic Accountability

With the rise of digitalization, the capacity of public institutions to collect and analyze big data and make decisions based on algorithms has increased, creating new risk areas for individuals' right to privacy, data security and transparency in governance processes.As Zuboff puts it, in the age of "surveillance capitalism", data is not just information; it is also power. When this power is not properly utilized in public administration, it becomes inevitable that citizens' freedom is narrowed and public trust is damaged (Zuboff, 2019, pp. 377-392).

Data privacy is critical not only for the protection of individual rights but also for the sustainability of the democratic system.The OECD emphasizes that decision-making processes of public institutions should be traceable, explainable and auditable when using AI-based systems.In this context, algorithmic accountability has become one of the fundamental principles that ensure the transparency and legitimacy of AI-enabled public decisions (OECD, 2021, pp. 43-47).

Eubanks demonstrates that algorithmic systems used in the distribution of social benefits can systematically exclude poor and vulnerable groups through data biases and discriminatory coding. Such practices point to a crisis that is not only technological, but also ethical and structural.Therefore, it is essential to adopt a human rights-centered framework, not just a performance-centered one, in the integration of algorithms into decision-making processes.

5.2. Social Justice, Digital Exclusion and Ethical Governance

In addition to the opportunities created by digital transformation in public policies, new types of inequality have also emerged.Regional, socioeconomic and cultural differences in the accessibility of digital services increase the risk of digital exclusion, which directly threatens the principle of social justice (UNESCO, 2021, pp. 18-21).

Ethical governance is an approach to governance that is not limited to compliance with the law but prioritizes values and principles in decision-making processes. In defining the ethical dimensions of digital public governance, the OECD emphasizes criteria such as "reducing algorithmic bias", "protecting the chain of accountability" and "fair participation of different segments of society in digital transformation" (OECD, 2020, pp. 12-15).

In this context, digital governance should be shaped not only by technical competence but also by moral responsibility. Inequalities in access to digital public services for young, old, disabled or low-income individuals undermine the inclusiveness of public value. Therefore, when designing digital policies, public administrators should adopt an approach that ensures equal opportunities, strengthens social inclusion and is sensitive to discrimination.

5.3. Digital Trust Building and Citizen-State Relationship

One of the most sensitive aspects of digitalization's relationship with society is trust. The ability of data sharing, online service use and digital feedback mechanisms to function directly depends on the trust citizens have in public institutions. The European Commission (2022) states that citizen trust in digital public services is linked to data protection practices, transparency and user experience, as well as service quality.

Mayer, Davis, and Schoorman (1995) argue that organizational trust consists of three key elements: competence, good faith, and integrity. These three elements need to be reinterpreted in the context of digital governance. No matter how competent the state is in digital services, data misuse or lack of transparency can undermine the citizen-state relationship. Protecting digital trust is a guarantee not only of individual privacy but also of public legitimacy.

Building trust requires a continuous interaction and oversight relationship between the digital state and citizens. Open data applications, participatory platforms and digital oversight mechanisms enable citizens not only to receive information but also to be involved in shaping public services.In this respect, digital trust has become a fundamental building block of both governance quality and public value.

Consequently, the use of digital technologies in public administration is a critical area of transformation not only in terms of administrative efficiency and service innovation, but also in terms of protecting fundamental rights, ensuring social justice and strengthening democratic governance. Violations of data privacy, lack of algorithmic transparency and digital exclusion can turn digitalization into a tool that can undermine public value rather than enhance it.Therefore, it is imperative that digital transformation policies are not limited to technical or economic dimensions, but should be redesigned on the basis of ethical sensitivity, legal safeguards and social inclusiveness.The sustainability of digital public governance depends on the coherent management of these multi-layered areas of responsibility.Only in this way can digital technologies become the building blocks of a trust-based, fair and participatory public order.

6. PRACTICAL EXAMPLES: INTERNATIONAL GOOD PRACTICE EXPERIENCES

The effectiveness and sustainability of policies in the field of digital public administration should be based not only on conceptual frameworks and normative propositions, but also on the analysis of concrete examples based on practice. In the international context, some countries have considered digital transformation processes not only as technological modernization but also as a tool for strategic production of public value.In this section, the experiences of pioneering countries in digitalization such as Estonia, Singapore and the USA and the current situation in Türkiye are discussed in a comparative manner and how digital public value is constructed.

6.1. Estonia: e-Government and Digital Identity Ecosystem

Estonia is one of the leading countries in the field of digital government initiatives. Thanks to its investments in digital infrastructure and legal regulations since the late 1990s, Estonia has been able to move public services almost entirely online. At the center of Estonia's contribution to digital public value is the data integration infrastructure called “X-Road” and the “digital identity system” that every citizen has (European Commission, 2022). This system enables public institutions to exchange data securely with each other, thus revolutionizing both speed and security in service delivery.

In Estonia, citizens can perform many transactions with their digital identities, from accessing health records to declaring taxes and voting in elections. This situation both increases the quality of service and reinforces trust in public administration. Madise and Martens (2006) emphasize that digital identity is not only a technology in Estonia, but also a digital reflection of democratic participation and citizenship awareness. This success of Estonia is remarkable in terms of showing how public value can be embodied through digital infrastructures.

In this framework, the case of Estonia shows that digital public administration is not only a technical transformation, but also an integrated process with the redesign of institutional structures and the digitalization of citizenship understanding. The holistic legal, ethical and managerial construction of the digital identity system made it possible to simultaneously build public values such as trust, accessibility and efficiency.Estonia's success reveals how decisive the implementation of digital technologies with a strategic vision and within the framework of the principles of social participation, data integrity and service integration from an early stage is in the construction of sustainable digital public value.For developing countries with digitalization processes such as Türkiye, the Estonian model offers a paradigm that should be taken as an example not only in terms of technology transfer but also in terms of governance approach.

6.2. Singapore: Data-Driven Public Strategies and Artificial Intelligence Policies

Singapore has built its digital transformation on public strategies based not only on technology but also on data management.The country prioritized data-driven governance under the Smart Nation initiative, integrating real-time data analysis into many public services, from urban planning to healthcare, traffic management to disaster response (Government of Singapore, 2022). This has enabled public policies to become more evidence-based, goal-oriented and agile.

Singapore's success in increasing digital public value has been driven by three key elements: strong digital leadership, holistic data management infrastructure, and AI-enabled decision systems. In particular, the national platform AI Singapore offers support programs for public institutions to develop data analytics and AI applications. According to Lee and Lim (2020), this model increases the predictive capacity of decision-making in public administration, enabling service delivery to become proactive rather than merely reactive.

Singapore has also taken serious steps on data ethics and established ethical principles for AI applications in the public sector (IMDA, 2019).Thus, technology has become a tool that strengthens not only efficiency but also trust-based governance. In this context, the case of Singapore shows how public value can be generated holistically not only through service digitalization, but also through data-centric governance, proactive service design and ethical use of AI.Singapore's digital strategy presents a sustainable model not only in terms of technological sophistication but also in terms of governance quality and citizen satisfaction.The fact that the state uses its digital capacity not only as a management tool but also for the smart and fair production of the public good is one of the aspects that distinguishes Singapore in this regard. This approach concretely demonstrates how critical data-driven decision-making, holistic policy-making and ethical oversight mechanisms are for countries like Türkiye that are in the process of developing their digital infrastructure.

6.3. USA: Artificial Intelligence and Decision Support Systems

The United States is using artificial intelligence and big data technologies in public administration not only as a tool for service improvement, but also for strengthening strategic decision-making, rationalizing resource allocation and holistically generating public value.Launched in 2019, the American AI Initiative encourages AI research and applications at the federal level, and the National Artificial Intelligence Research and Development Strategic Plan, published in 2023, was updated to ensure that AI is used ethically, accountably and in the public interest (National Science and Technology Council, 2023).

The US transformation in digital public administration is deepening along three main axes in particular:inter-agency data openness, sectoral AI applications, and the establishment of an ethical framework. Artificial intelligence applications function as decision support systems in the operations of many federal agencies, speeding up processes and improving the quality of services. For example, AI-supported systems used within the Ministry of Health contribute to the early detection and prevention of infectious diseases by analyzing health records; during the COVID-19 period, these systems were effectively used to create epidemic maps (Jiang et al. 2021).

Similarly, the Department of Homeland Security automated the evaluation of applications by using natural language processing and algorithmic ranking systems in immigration processing, which increased the consistency and speed of processing (U.S. Government Accountability Office, 2021).The Department of Transportation has developed AI-based simulation and data analysis systems for traffic safety and accident prevention. In addition, the Department of Defense (DoD) has developed guidelines for the ethical use of artificial intelligence in war and defense (Defense Innovation Board, 2019).

The US is not only involved in the application of these technologies, but also in the institutionalization of the principles of transparency and public accountability. In its 2019 guidance, the White House Office of Science and Technology Policy stated that artificial intelligence systems used in public institutions should be designed around principles such as "Fairness and Nondiscrimination, Interagency Coordination, Public Trust, Citizen Engagement, Openness and Transparency" (OSTP, 2019, pp. 4-6).In this respect, the US adopts a multi-layered policy approach that enhances digital public value while at the same time upholding citizen rights and governance ethics.

In this context, the US example demonstrates that digital public governance is not limited to system integration; technological capacity must be balanced with institutional ethics and public safety.Open data strategies, public evaluation of algorithmic systems and ethical guidelines published at the federal level make it possible to generate digital public value on the basis of legitimacy.This multidimensional approach of the United States is a strong example for other countries on the balance that can be struck between technology, governance and ethics.

6.4. Türkiye: Current Situation and Challenges in Public Digitalization

Türkiye has made significant investments in digital public administration in recent years and started to offer many services through the e-Government Gateway (turkiye.gov.tr). The operations of many institutions such as the Population and Citizenship Affairs, Social Security Institution, and Ministry of Justice have been moved online, significantly increasing the speed and prevalence of access to public services. With more than 60 million active users by 2023, the e-Government platform is a concrete reflection of Türkiye's digitalization vision (Republic of Türkiye Digital Transformation Office, 2023).

However, the digital transformation process in Türkiye faces some structural problems in the areas of institutional capacity, regulatory harmonization and public awareness as well as technical infrastructure development.For example, data sharing among public institutions is still fragmented and an integrated data sharing infrastructure similar to X-Road has not yet been established.Moreover, the lack of institutional frameworks in areas such as data security, artificial intelligence applications, and ethical governance complicates the sustainable production of digital public value.Differences in digital literacy levels, capacity disparities in local governments, and legislative gaps in AI integration are the main challenges Türkiye faces in the field of digital public administration.However, the National Artificial Intelligence Strategy published in 2021 provided a framework to address these shortcomings and set targets under the headings of data governance, the use of artificial intelligence in public services, and the development of competent human resources (Republic of Türkiye Ministry of Industry and Technology, 2021).

6.5. Evaluation and Comparative Commentary

International experiences show that digital transformation is not only limited to technological development in public administration, but also requires restructuring in many dimensions such as institutional capacity, data management, ethical governance and citizen trust.While Estonia institutionalizes public trust with digital identity and data integrity, Singapore transforms public strategies with data-centric policy design and artificial intelligence. The US, on the other hand, stands out in transparency, auditing and AI-driven public innovation.In Türkiye, while infrastructure investments are significant, there is still room for improvement in areas such as institutional integration, data sharing, algorithmic accountability and public participation.

In this context, for Türkiye to build digital public value in a sustainable and inclusive manner, a comprehensive digital capacity transformation is needed not only in technical but also in managerial, ethical and social dimensions.

7. POLICY RECOMMENDATIONS AND STRATEGIC ROADMAP

Effective and sustainable use of digital technologies in public administration can only be possible through strategic governance approaches, holistic digital policies and ethical frameworks.At this point, the generation of digital public value requires not only technical investments, but also normative, managerial and legal reforms.

The success of digital transformation strategies in public administration should be designed based on three key principles: inclusiveness, ethical responsibility and effective governance.The OECD (2020) emphasizes that digital strategies should focus not only on technological infrastructure, but also on citizens' digital rights, equality of access and trust building. Accordingly, if public institutions develop policies to reduce digital inequalities between social groups in digital service delivery, it will increase the inclusiveness of public value (OECD, 2020, pp. 14-19).

Furthermore, ethical principles should be clearly defined and implemented in digital public strategies. Since the use of AI, big data and algorithms in public services carries risks such as discrimination, data privacy violations and lack of accountability, governance models should include "ethical oversight" mechanisms (Cath, 2018, pp. 15-18).

7.1 Future Perspectives: Public Value Generation Reshaped by Technology

Autonomous systems, big data analytics and algorithmic decision support mechanisms enable a shift from reactive to proactive service models in public administration. This transformation allows public services to become more predictable, needs-oriented and privatized, while at the same time creating new areas of responsibility on ethical, social and legal levels.

7.1.1. Proactive Service Delivery With Autonomous Decision Systems and Big Data

Artificial intelligence and big data-enabled decision support systems and big data technologies enable public institutions not only to manage the current situation, but also to develop preventive services with insights into the future. According to Janssen et al., the use of big data in public administration supports more efficient allocation of resources, early identification of risks and targeted policy design. Especially in areas such as health, transportation, disaster management and social services, data-driven algorithms can provide tailored and personalized public services (Janssen et al., 2020, pp. 20-22).

The next stage of big data-driven systems is autonomous systems that can make decisions under certain conditions without the need for human intervention. Such systems can, for example, analyze scenarios in real time and self-select the most appropriate solution in traffic management, energy distribution or emergency response planning (Wirtz et al., 2019). While this enables speed, efficiency and effectiveness in public administration, it also necessitates the redefinition of chains of responsibility. The proliferation of autonomous systems in the public sphere requires not only a technological but also a managerial, legal and ethical restructuring.

7.2. The Potential of Digital Technologies to Reshape the Public Sphere

Digitalization has accelerated both the transformation of public spaces and the digitization of citizenship experiences. E-participation platforms, open data portals, digital voting, and AI-supported consultation mechanisms are reshaping forms of participation in governance, making decision-making processes more transparent and interactive; at the same time, they are giving rise to a new political arena known as "algorithmic publicness".

The digitalization of the public sphere increases accessibility, but also has the potential to create new forms of discrimination for groups at risk of digital exclusion. Therefore, the design of digital public space should not only be based on technical competence, but also on the principles of equal representation, the right to access information and freedom of digital expression (UNESCO, 2021, pp. 14-16). Otherwise, digital public platforms may turn into isolating and unsafe spaces of experience.

In this context, the impact of digital technologies on public space is not only a technical transformation but also a socio-political restructuring. Traditionally associated with squares, public buildings or physical forums, the public sphere is now shaped by digital platforms, networks and algorithmic decision structures. While this new public sphere offers democratic opportunities to access information, express opinions and participate in governance, it can also bring new exclusionary boundaries.In particular, individuals with limited digital skills, low-income groups or certain age groups may not have the chance to be represented in the digital public sphere.Therefore, in order to sustain the egalitarian and emancipatory impact of digitalization, the design of digital public spaces should be considered not only as a technological but also as an ethical and social issue.

The fair functioning of the digital public sphere depends not only on the availability of participation tools, but also on participation being meaningful, inclusive, and sustainable. This is because e-participation can exclude certain groups due to the digital divide in terms of access, accessibility, and competence. Furthermore, the lack of transparency in algorithmic decision-making mechanisms can weaken rather than support public value (Mao et al., 2024, p. 483). Therefore, the management of digital public spaces should be based on user-centered design, explainable artificial intelligence, and ethical participation principles. Indeed, explainable artificial intelligence systems can increase public trust by providing transparent, understandable, and reliable explanations in the interaction between the user and the system (Phillips et al., 2021, p. 5).

7.3. Assessment of the Future of Digital Public Administration

The public administration of the future is shaping up to have governance structures that are not only supported by digital tools but also born with digital.According to the OECD's Digital Government 2.0 vision, public administration systems will become increasingly data-driven, agile and user-centered, and the production of public value will be co-constructed with both internal managerial capacity and external citizen engagement (OECD, 2020, pp. 8-12).In this model, technologies such as artificial intelligence, blockchain, Internet of Things (IoT), augmented reality (AR) and quantum computing will be integrated into public administration not only as supporting but also decision-making components.However, the success of digital public administration depends on the ethical and socially compatible use of these technologies.As emphasized in the European Commission's (2020) Ethics Guidelines for Trustworthy AI, the use of AI in the public sphere should be limited by the principles of "respect for ethical principles and values, respecting all applicable laws and regulations, both technically and taking into account its social environment".

In this perspective, digital public administration becomes not only a service delivery model but also a reshaped social contract. This contract should be based on the principles of trust, balance and accountability; public values of the digital age should be redefined and governance principles should be updated in line with this transformation.

From this perspective, the future of digital public administration will depend not only on the pace of technological developments, but also on how these technologies define, structure and redistribute public value. In this context, digital transformation processes should be centered not only on instrumental efficiency, but also on sensitivity to the public good, social justice, governance ethics and democratic participation.The digitalization of public administration not only changes the way institutions produce services, but also redefines the content of the contract between the public and society, what citizens expect from the state and how administrators should be held accountable.

The basic approach advocated in this study considers digital public administration not only as a technological reform area, but also as a multidimensional systemic transformation where public value is strategically and ethically reproduced.Comparative examples from countries such as Estonia, Singapore and the United States show that success in digital public administration is not only possible with technical capacity and digital infrastructure, but also with the digital leadership skills of public administrators, citizens' access to digital participation rights, and the alignment of this whole structure with ethical governance principles. The proliferation of artificial intelligence and big data-based decision-making systems, especially in public services, requires discussing the concept of public interest not with technical accuracy but with normative legitimacy.

While digital technologies have the potential to deliver fast, personalized and predictable public services, they can also create new forms of exclusion, surveillance risks and algorithmic biases.The success of digital public administration is therefore less about how much technology is available and more about the extent to which these technologies are aligned with public ethics and social responsibility.As stated in the European Commission's "Ethical Principles for Trustworthy Artificial Intelligence" report, algorithms carry not only technical but also moral responsibility when used in the public sector (European Commission, 2020). Therefore, the sustainable production of public value in the digital age is possible through accountable algorithms, transparent data use, and securing citizens' digital rights.

However, another important element that will shape the future of digital public administration is the ability to strike a balance between institutional and societal capacity.If the increase in the digital capabilities of institutions is not coordinated with the digital literacy of the society, this can undermine the inclusiveness of services and lead to an erosion of public trust.Therefore, digital public policies should be centered on preventive mechanisms that guarantee access to digital public value, especially for disadvantaged groups such as the elderly, rural residents, low-income citizens and people with disabilities.Inclusive digitalization means not only quantitative access, but also qualified participation and equitable service distribution.

In conclusion, this study makes three main propositions for the strategic design and governance modeling of digital public administration:(1) The production of digital public value should be redefined in relation to managerial ethics, social equity and democratic participation rather than technical efficiency. (2) Technology is a means, not an end in public administration; therefore, it should be constrained, guided and controlled in a way that maximizes the public good. (3) Digital public administration should be treated as a new culture of public citizenship and a new form of social contract, not just an area of reform.

In this context, the task before public administration research and practitioners is not just about managing technology.It is about rethinking how to transform technology for the purposes of public responsibility, ethical reason and social welfare. If this transformation is strategic, inclusive and value-based, the digital age will make public administration not only more efficient, but also more just, democratic and people-centered.

CONCLUSIONS

This study examined how the integration of digital technologies into public administration systems has transformed the production of public value.The analysis shows that digitalization is not only limited to operational efficiency, but also redefines public values such as transparency, participation, accountability and ethical governance.

Comparative analyses of Estonia, Singapore, the United States and Turkey have revealed significant differences in how factors such as digital capacity, data infrastructure, legal regulations and administrative will shape public value in the digital environment. It has been examined that citizen satisfaction and governance quality have increased, especially in countries such as Estonia and Singapore, which have transformed digitalization into holistic strategies.

In order to produce public value sustainably through digital transformation processes, digital technologies need to be evaluated not only instrumentally but also in a governance and ethical framework.In this context, it is important for public institutions to develop their digital capacity not only in terms of technical hardware and software, but also in terms of strategic planning, organizational learning and digital leadership. Unless digital transformation is supported by internal structural reforms, it risks creating a superficial modernization effect rather than deepening public value.

To increase digital public value, citizen participation mechanisms should be multiplied through digital platforms. E-participation systems, open data portals and online consultation processes play a critical role in making public policies more transparent, accountable and user-centered. However, the mere technical availability of these tools is not enough. The accessibility, user-friendliness and functionality of feedback mechanisms of these systems are indispensable for building trust. Since inequalities that deepen the digital divide, especially between social groups, can directly affect the quality of participation, it is of great importance that public policies consider the dimension of digital inclusion.

As public services have become more data-driven, ethical oversight of algorithmic decision systems has become a separate requirement.Therefore, artificial intelligence and automation systems used in public institutions should be compatible with the principles of explainability, non-discriminatory design and auditability. Public administrators should continuously review the impact of digital systems on decision-making processes and build institutional structures to ensure algorithmic accountability. Otherwise, digitalization may undermine public trust instead of strengthening public value.

For digital public strategies to be successful, the legal and ethical infrastructure also needs to be updated.The compatibility of existing legislation with digital public technologies should be reconsidered in terms of data privacy, cybersecurity and digital rights.Especially in developing countries, legislation lagging behind technological developments causes public institutions to shy away from taking risks and slows down innovation processes.This can undermine the potential for increasing public value through technology.

Finally, digital transformation policies should be designed not only at the central level but also with local governments and actors at the field level of public service delivery.Generic digitalization strategies that do not take into account local conditions, user needs and cultural factors do not produce the expected public value. Therefore, digital public policies should be based on coordinated, participatory and contextually flexible models.

REFERENCES

Babšek, M., Ravšelj, D., Umek, L., & Aristovnik, A. (2025). Artificial Intelligence Adoption in Public Administration: An Overview of Top-Cited Articles and Practical Applications. *AI*, *6*(3), 44. DOI: 10.3390/ai6030044

Bannister, F., & Connolly, R. (2011). The trouble with transparency: A critical review of openness in e-government. *Policy and Internet*, *3*(1), 1–30. DOI: 10.2202/1944-2866.1076

Bekkers, V., & Homburg, V. (2007). *The Information Ecology of E-Government: E-Government as Institutional and Technological Innovation in Public Administration*. IOS Press.

Benington, J., & Moore, M. H. (2011). *Public Value: Theory and Practice*. Palgrave Macmillan. DOI: 10.1007/978-0-230-36431-8

Bovaird, T., & Loeffler, E. (2012). From engagement to co-production: The contribution of users and communities to outcomes and public value. *Voluntas*, *23*(4), 1119–1138. DOI: 10.1007/s11266-012-9309-6

Carretero, S., Vuorikari, R., & Punie, Y. (2017). *DigComp 2.1: The Digital Competence Framework for Citizens with eight proficiency levels and examples of use*. Publications Office of the European Union., DOI: 10.2760/38842

Cath, C. (2018). Governing artificial intelligence: Ethical, legal and technical opportunities and challenges. *Philosophical Transactions. Series A, Mathematical, Physical, and Engineering Sciences*, *376*(2133), 20180080. DOI: 10.1098/rsta.2018.0080 PMID: 30322996

Cordella, A., & Bonina, C. M. (2012). A public value perspective for ICT enabled public sector reforms: A theoretical reflection. *Government Information Quarterly*, *29*(4), 512–520. DOI: 10.1016/j.giq.2012.03.004

Denhardt, J. V., & Denhardt, R. B. (2000). The New Public Service: Serving rather than steering. *Public Administration Review*, *60*(6), 549–559. DOI: 10.1111/0033-3352.00117

Dunleavy, P., & Margetts, H. (2015). *Digital Era Governance: IT Corporations, the State, and E-Government*. Oxford University Press.

Dunleavy, P., Margetts, H., Bastow, S., & Tinkler, J. (2006). *Digital Era Governance: IT Corporations, the State, and E-Government*. Oxford University Press. DOI: 10.1093/acprof:oso/9780199296194.001.0001

Eubanks, V. (2018). *Automating Inequality: How High-Tech Tools Profile, Police, and Punish the Poor*. St. Martin's Press.

European Commission. (2020). *Ethics Guidelines for Trustworthy AI*. High-Level Expert Group on Artificial Intelligence.

European Commission. (2022). Digital Public Administration factsheet 2022, European Commission. (2022). eGovernment Benchmark 2022: Trust and User-Centric Services.

Fredriksson, C., Mubarak, F., Tuohimaa, M., & Zhan, M. (2018). Big Data in the Public Sector: A Systematic Literature Review. *Scandinavian Journal of Public Administration*, *22*(3), 39–61. DOI: 10.58235/sjpa.v21i3.11563

Government of Singapore. (2022). Smart Nation: What is it? Hood, C. (1991). A public management for all seasons? *Public Administration*, *69*(1), 3–19.

IMDA. (2019). *Model AI Governance Framework*. Infocomm Media Development Authority.

Janssen, M., Charalabidis, Y., & Zuiderwijk, A. (2012). Benefits, adoption barriers and myths of open data and open government. *Information Systems Management*, *29*(4), 258–268. DOI: 10.1080/10580530.2012.716740

Janssen, M., van der Voort, H., & Wahyudi, A. (2020). Factors influencing big data decision-making quality. *Journal of Business Research*, *70*, 338–345. DOI: 10.1016/j.jbusres.2016.08.007

Jiang, L., Wu, Z., Xu, X., Zhan, Y., Jin, X., Wang, L., & Qiu, Y. (2021). Opportunities and challenges of artificial intelligence in the medical field: Current application, emerging problems, and problem-solving strategies. *The Journal of International Medical Research*, *49*(3), 03000605211000157. DOI: 10.1177/03000605211000157 PMID: 33771068

Kitchin, R. (2014). *The Data Revolution: Big Data, Open Data, Data Infrastructures and Their Consequences*. SAGE Publications.

Kotter, J. P. (1996). *Leading Change*. Harvard Business Press.

Lee, C., & Lim, W. (2020). Governing Smart Nation: Policy, politics and digital innovation in Singapore. *Policy and Society*, *39*(3), 335–351. PMID: 35039726

Linders, D. (2012). From e-government to we-government: Defining a typology for citizen coproduction in the age of social media. *Government Information Quarterly*, *29*(4), 446–454. DOI: 10.1016/j.giq.2012.06.003

Madise, Ü., & Martens, T. (2006). E-voting in Estonia 2005. The first practice of country-wide binding Internet voting in the world. *Electronic Voting*, *86*(3), 15–26.

Mao, Z., Zhang, W., Zou, Q., & Deng, W. (2024). E-katılımın söz hakkı ve hesap verebilirlik Mao, Z., Zhang, W., Zou, Q., & Deng, W. (2024). The effects of e-participation on voice and accountability: Are there differences between countries? *Information Technology for Development*, *31*(2), 473–498. DOI: 10.1080/02681102.2024.2373745

Margetts, H., & Dorobantu, C. (2019). Rethink government with AI. *Nature Human Behaviour*, *3*, 14–16. PMID: 30967667

Mayer, R. C., Davis, J. H., & Schoorman, F. D. (1995). An Integrative Model of Organizational Trust. *Academy of Management Review*, *20*(3), 709–734. DOI: 10.2307/258792

Mergel, I., Edelmann, N., & Haug, N. (2019). Defining digital transformation: Results from expert interviews. *Government Information Quarterly*, *36*(4), 101385. DOI: 10.1016/j.giq.2019.06.002

Misuraca, G., & van Noordt, C. (2020). *AI Watch – Artificial Intelligence in Public Services: Overview of the use and impact of AI in public services in the EU*. Publications Office of the European Union.

Moore, M. H. (1995). *Creating Public Value: Strategic Management in Government*. Harvard University Press.

OECD. (2019). *The Path to Becoming a Data-Driven Public Sector*. OECD Digital Government Studies.

OECD. (2020). Digital Government Index: 2019 Results. OECD Public Governance Policy Papers, No. 03.

OECD. (2020). *Digital Government in Chile: Digital Transformation and Public Sector Innovation*. OECD Digital Government Studies.

OECD. (2020). The Ethical Use of Artificial Intelligence in the Public Sector.

OECD. (2020). The OECD Digital Government Policy Framework.

OECD. (2020). The OECD Digital Government Policy Framework: Six Dimensions of a Digitally-Enabled Public Sector.

OECD. (2021). Principles on Artificial Intelligence.

OECD. (2021). Recommendation of the Council on the Governance of Critical Risks.

OSTP. (2019). *Guidance for Regulation of Artificial Intelligence Applications.* Office of Science and Technology Policy.

Panagiotopoulos, P., Klievink, B., & Cordella, A. (2019). Public value creation in digital government. *Government Information Quarterly*, *36*(4), 101421. DOI: 10.1016/j.giq.2019.101421

Phillips, P. J., Hahn, C. A., Fontana, P. C., Broniatowski, D. A., & Przybocki, M. A. (2021). *Four principles of explainable artificial intelligence* (NIST Interagency/ Internal Report No. 8312). National Institute of Standards and Technology.

Sabbagh, P. (2019). The Public Value of E-Government: A Blockchain-Based Approach. *European Integration Studies and International Conference Proceedings*, University of Verona.

Stoker, G. (2006). Public value management: A new narrative for networked governance? *American Review of Public Administration, 36*(1), 41–57. DOI: 10.1177/0275074005282583

T.C. Sanayi ve Teknoloji Bakanlığı. (2021). National Artificial Intelligence Strategy (2021-2025).

Terzi, S., ... (2019). Blockchain 3.0 Smart Contracts in E-Government 3.0 Applications. arXiv preprint arXiv:1910.06092. https://arxiv.org/abs/1910.06092

Twizeyimana, J. D., & Andersson, A. (2019). The public value of E-Government – A literature review. *Government Information Quarterly*, *36*(2), 167–178. DOI: 10.1016/j.giq.2019.01.001

UNESCO. (2021). Digital Inclusion: Connecting the Unconnected. .

UNESCO. (2021). Re-Shaping Policies for Creativity: Addressing Culture as a Global Public Good.

Vuorikari, R., Kluzer, S., & Punie, Y. (2022). *European Digital Competence Framework for the Public Sector: DigCompOrg*. Publications Office of the European Union.

Wirtz, B. W., Weyerer, J. C., & Geyer, C. (2019). Artificial Intelligence and the Public Sector—Applications and Challenges. *International Journal of Public Administration*, *42*(7), 596–615. DOI: 10.1080/01900692.2018.1498103

Wirtz, B. W., Weyerer, J. C., & Geyer, C. (2020). Artificial Intelligence and the Public Sector Applications and Challenges. *International Journal of Public Administration*, *43*(9), 816–830.

Zuboff, S. (2019). *The Age of Surveillance Capitalism: The Fight for a Human Future at the New Frontier of Power*. PublicAffairs.

Chapter 6
AI in Public Administration:
Transforming Governance and Public Services

Mustafa Kayyali
https://orcid.org/0000-0003-3300-262X
Maaref University of Applied Sciences, Syria

ABSTRACT

Artificial Intelligence is no longer the distant future of public administration—it is the pressing present. This chapter examines how AI is reshaping the machinery of governance, offering unprecedented opportunities for smarter service delivery, predictive policymaking, and real-time responsiveness. It investigates both the technical and human dimensions of this transformation, exploring how automation, data analytics, and machine learning are redefining the roles of public servants, the expectations of citizens, and the core principles of transparency and accountability. At the same time, the chapter does not romanticize technological change. It critically addresses the challenges posed by AI systems—algorithmic opacity, systemic bias, privacy concerns, and the ethical dilemmas inherent in delegating public decisions to machines. Ultimately, this chapter offers a nuanced portrait of AI's role in public administration—not as a neutral tool, but as a transformative force that demands foresight, vigilance, and deep ethical grounding.

INTRODUCTION

There are moments in history when the trajectory of governance shifts so dramatically that it becomes impossible to return to previous models. The rise of

DOI: 10.4018/979-8-3373-1484-6.ch006

Artificial Intelligence represents one such moment—a technological turning point that challenges not only the structures of public administration but also its very principles. We are witnessing the slow but steady erosion of the old bureaucratic model, one built on hierarchy, paper-based workflows, and reactive decision-making, in favor of a new paradigm: one that is data-driven, anticipatory, automated, and, increasingly, algorithmically guided. For decades, public administration has operated with certain assumptions: that decisions are made by humans, that public servants are the conduits between government and society, and that transparency is achieved through procedural rigor and documentation (Dahl, 2018). But these assumptions are now under pressure. AI systems can process vast troves of data in seconds, identify patterns invisible to the human eye, and make decisions or recommendations with breathtaking speed. Whether in detecting tax fraud, predicting traffic congestion, or allocating public resources, AI is not simply an add-on to existing systems—it is reshaping the very logic of how governance works. Yet, this transformation is not occurring in a vacuum. It is unfolding within a social, political, and ethical landscape that is complex and uneven. AI technologies are not neutral; they are developed by humans, trained on historical data that reflects existing biases, and deployed within institutions shaped by power, politics, and legacy structures. In this sense, AI in public administration is not just about tools—it is about values. What kind of governance do we want? What are we willing to delegate to machines? And how do we ensure that the public good remains at the center of this transformation?

There is an urgent need for clarity—not only in how we design and deploy AI systems but also in how we conceptualize their role in the public sphere. The promise of AI lies in its ability to make governance more efficient, more equitable, and more responsive. But the risks are equally real: surveillance creep, algorithmic discrimination, lack of accountability, and the erosion of citizen trust. This chapter does not seek to offer easy answers. Rather, it aims to paint a comprehensive and grounded picture of what it means to integrate AI into public administration. Drawing from global case studies, policy analysis, and critical scholarship, it examines both the opportunities and the pitfalls. It calls for a nuanced approach—one that balances innovation with ethics, automation with accountability, and efficiency with equity. We stand at a threshold. The decisions we make today about AI's role in governance will shape the institutions of tomorrow. Will we create public administrations that are more intelligent, but also more humane? Will we use AI to narrow the gap between citizens and the state—or will we widen it? These are not just technological questions; they are fundamentally human ones. And the answers, as always, will depend on our collective imagination, responsibility, and courage.

REDEFINING BUREAUCRACY: THE ADVENT OF AI IN GOVERNANCE

The word "bureaucracy" rarely evokes enthusiasm (Satkunanandan, 2019). For many, it is synonymous with red tape, inefficiency, impersonality, and long queues in dimly lit government offices. It conjures images of dusty files, complex procedures, and clerks buried in paperwork—an apparatus that seems more concerned with formality than with people. And yet, bureaucracy has been the backbone of modern states, the invisible scaffolding that holds together systems of education, health, law, and welfare. It has ensured predictability, fairness, and continuity in public affairs, often against the odds of political change and social upheaval. But as artificial intelligence begins to take root in public administration, the question becomes unavoidable: what happens to bureaucracy when intelligence is no longer exclusively human?

Artificial Intelligence is not simply automating the tasks of bureaucrats—it is forcing a rethinking of what bureaucracy is and what it could become (Newman et al, 2022). For centuries, bureaucracy was about rules, hierarchies, and standard operating procedures. These mechanisms were designed to minimize human error, arbitrariness, and favoritism. In the Weberian tradition, bureaucracy emerged as the ideal type of rational organization: efficient, rule-bound, and impersonal. But this model was built on the assumption that humans, with their cognitive limits and emotional tendencies, needed structure and constraint. AI disrupts that premise. Machine learning algorithms are not limited by fatigue, mood, or memory. They can process millions of data points in seconds, adjust to new information in real-time, and "learn" from patterns without human intervention. In doing so, they challenge the very foundation of traditional bureaucratic logic. When a chatbot can handle thousands of citizen inquiries without blinking, or when a predictive model can assess risk more accurately than a seasoned caseworker, we are no longer talking about incremental reform. We are talking about a structural shift—a redesign of public administration from the ground up.

One of the most striking changes is the collapse of time and space in administrative processes. Historically, bureaucracy was slow by design. It prioritized procedure over speed, fairness over expedience (Brunsson & Olsen, 2018). With AI, however, speed and personalization become not just possible but expected. Citizens who once braced for delays now expect real-time responses. Processes that took weeks—like benefit approvals or permit applications—can now be completed in hours, sometimes minutes. The traditional bureaucratic virtues of patience and process are being replaced by the values of immediacy and efficiency. And while this shift brings undeniable benefits, it also raises profound questions about accountability and control. Who is responsible when an algorithm denies someone a welfare benefit? What recourse does a citizen have when a machine makes a decision based on data they cannot see or understand? Bureaucracy, for all its flaws, at least provided a face—a person, however distant, who could be held to account. AI, in contrast, operates in a space of abstraction. Decisions are made not by individuals but by systems. The rationale behind those decisions is often hidden in layers of code and statistical inference, opaque even to the developers who built them.

This opaqueness is not just a technical issue—it is a democratic one. Public administration is not merely a service provider; it is a site of public trust. When decisions that affect people's lives are made in ways that are invisible and unexplainable, trust erodes. Bureaucracy, for all its shortcomings, was at least visible (Monteiro, P., & Adler, 2022). Citizens could complain, escalate, or resist. AI, particularly in its current forms, makes resistance difficult. It is hard to argue with a black box. Yet it would be a mistake to romanticize the old model. Bureaucracy has often been guilty of exactly the problems AI now promises to fix: inconsistency, inefficiency, and human bias. Studies have shown that decisions made by public officials can vary significantly depending on time of day, workload, or unconscious prejudice. AI offers a tantalizing solution: standardization without fatigue, fairness without bias. But this promise depends entirely on how the systems are trained, who designs them, and whose interests they serve.

In some cases, AI has already revealed its potential. Consider the use of algorithms in managing urban traffic, predicting crime hotspots, or allocating limited medical resources. These are areas where complexity and scale have outstripped human capacity, and where data-driven insights can make a tangible difference. In these cases, AI does not replace the bureaucratic apparatus—it augments it, offering tools for better decision-making, more precise targeting, and anticipatory governance. But augmentation is not neutral. The moment AI becomes embedded in public decision-making, it starts to shape not just how decisions are made, but what decisions are possible. Predictive models, for instance, tend to reproduce patterns from historical data. If those patterns are shaped by systemic inequalities, the algorithms may perpetuate them. In trying to make bureaucracy more rational, we risk making it more rigid—entrenching existing disparities under the guise of objectivity.

Moreover, the advent of AI changes the skill sets required in public administration (Agarwal, 2018). Traditional bureaucracies valued procedural knowledge, institutional memory, and legal literacy. The new bureaucracies need data scientists, ethicists, interface designers, and machine learning specialists. This shift not only reconfigures the workforce but also changes the culture of governance. There is a growing tension between the values of public service and the logics of tech innovation. Public institutions, traditionally cautious and deliberative, are being asked to move fast and break things—a motto borrowed from Silicon Valley, not civil service. This tension is especially evident in the procurement and deployment of AI systems. Many governments lack the in-house capacity to develop their own tools, and so they turn to private vendors. But outsourcing core administrative functions to proprietary technologies introduces new dependencies and new risks. It becomes difficult to audit the systems, to understand their logic, or to ensure they align with public values. In effect, the bureaucratic state risks becoming a platform operated by external actors whose incentives may not align with democratic governance.

The redefinition of bureaucracy, then, is not just about replacing paper forms with digital ones, or clerks with algorithms. It is about a deeper rethinking of the relationship between the state and its citizens. In traditional models, bureaucracy was a buffer—a space where rules were applied, where discretion was limited, and where fairness was pursued through procedure. In the AI model, discretion re-emerges in new forms—through algorithm design, data selection, and model tuning. These forms are less visible but no less consequential. This brings us to a crucial point: the future of bureaucracy will depend not only on technological capacity but on normative choices. We must ask: What kind of public administration do we want? One that optimizes for speed and efficiency? Or one that preserves space for empathy, discretion, and human judgment? Can we have both? Can we design AI systems that are not only powerful but also accountable, transparent, and aligned with the principles of public service?

Some countries are beginning to grapple with these questions. In Estonia, for instance, digital governance has been pursued as a national strategy, with AI systems used to streamline tax, voting, and legal services. In Canada, the Algorithmic Impact Assessment tool aims to evaluate the potential risks of AI systems before deployment. In the European Union, regulations are being developed to classify AI applications by risk level, with corresponding obligations for transparency and oversight. These examples suggest that a different kind of bureaucracy is possible—one that is not simply automated, but reimagined. A bureaucracy that uses AI not to eliminate the human element but to support it. A bureaucracy that treats data not as a commodity but as a public asset, to be governed with care and responsibility. A bureaucracy that recognizes that fairness is not just a statistical outcome but a moral imperative.

To redefine bureaucracy in the age of AI is not to abandon its core mission (Bullock, 2019). It is to renew it. To remember that at its best, bureaucracy is not an obstacle to justice, but a vehicle for it. That public servants are not just implementers of policy, but stewards of the public good. And that AI, powerful as it is, must remain a tool—not the master—of democratic governance. The challenge is not merely technical. It is philosophical. It is about how we understand the role of the state, the rights of citizens, and the nature of fairness. AI can help us build a more agile, responsive, and informed public administration. But only if we bring to its development the same care, deliberation, and commitment to justice that inspired the bureaucracies of the past. The future of governance lies not in replacing the human with the machine, but in creating new forms of collaboration between them—partnerships that honor the strengths of both, while remaining anchored in the values that define public service at its best.

SMART PUBLIC SERVICES: AUTOMATION, EFFICIENCY, AND ACCESSIBILITY

It's a curious paradox of our time that even as the world grows more connected, many people still struggle to access the services that define a functioning society—those basic provisions that should never feel like privileges: healthcare, education, housing assistance, social security, legal protection. For decades, these systems have carried the weight of complex bureaucracies, often slow, inefficient, and intimidating. Now, as Artificial Intelligence and automation technologies edge their way into the public sphere, we are presented with both a profound opportunity and an equally profound responsibility: to redesign public services not just to be smarter, but to be more just, inclusive, and human-centered. Automation, at first glance, seems to be a cure for many of the ills that plague public service delivery. It promises speed where there was once delay, accuracy where there was once error, and scalability where there was once rigidity. A citizen applying for a disability allowance no longer has to make repeated trips to a government office or wait for weeks to receive confirmation. Instead, automated systems can assess eligibility based on preloaded data, process the request in real time, and issue payments with minimal human intervention. It's not just convenient—it's transformative. It speaks to a new relationship between the state and the citizen, one in which responsiveness and efficiency are not exceptions but expectations.

Figure 1. AI Use-Cases in Public Services (Illustrative Share)

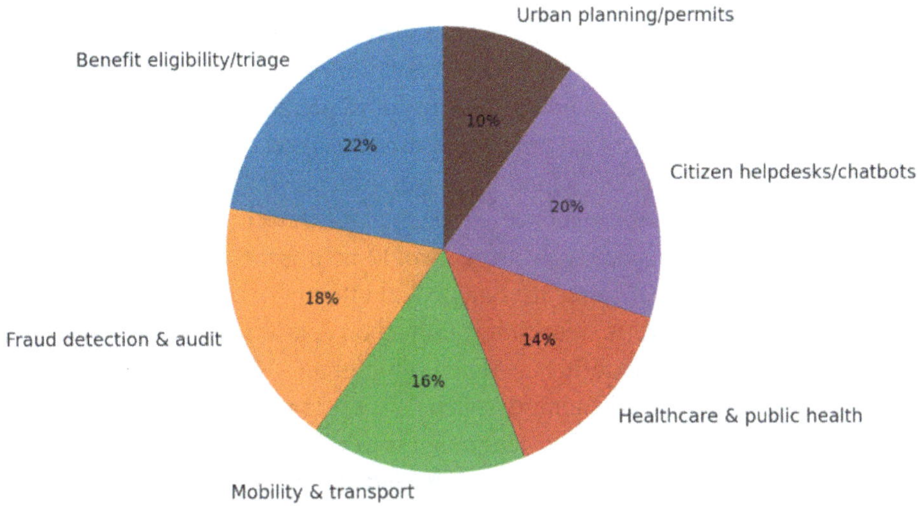

But behind this promise lies a deeper set of tensions. Efficiency, while valuable, is not synonymous with fairness. Automation can streamline processes, but it can also replicate blind spots, magnify inequalities, and leave behind those who are not digitally fluent (Sharma et al, 2024). The same system that swiftly grants housing support to a tech-savvy applicant may inadvertently exclude an elderly person who doesn't own a smartphone. The same chatbot that resolves a tax query in seconds might baffle someone with cognitive impairments or language barriers. These are not mere technical issues—they are ethical dilemmas that strike at the heart of what it means to serve the public. That said, when thoughtfully designed and inclusively implemented, smart public services can be liberating. Consider the example of digital healthcare platforms that use AI to triage symptoms, recommend care pathways, and reduce the burden on overextended hospitals. In rural areas where doctors are scarce, such platforms act as frontline support systems, offering diagnostic insights, reminders for medication adherence, and even mental health check-ins. They don't replace doctors, but they extend the reach of care in ways previously unimaginable. For patients, especially those in underserved communities, this can mean the difference between intervention and neglect.

The same applies to education. Smart learning platforms powered by adaptive algorithms are being used in public schools to support differentiated instruction (Kem, 2022). Rather than teaching to the average, these platforms adjust in real time to a student's learning pace and style, offering extra practice where needed and accelerating progress where possible. For students with learning disabilities, language challenges, or inconsistent attendance due to socio-economic issues, such systems provide a sense of continuity and personalization that traditional one-size-fits-all curricula often fail to achieve. In public transport systems, AI is helping cities predict congestion, optimize routes, and reduce carbon footprints. In emergency response, automated alert systems are mapping wildfire paths, predicting floods, and coordinating evacuation logistics. These are not just conveniences—they are life-saving applications. The intelligence behind them is not magic; it is the product of data, design, and human intention channeled through algorithms that learn and adapt.

Yet, to equate intelligence with justice would be a grave mistake. Smart systems are only as good as the data they are fed and the frameworks that guide their operation. If a public benefit algorithm is trained on datasets that reflect historical discrimination—against minorities, women, immigrants—it will inherit and perpetuate those biases. If automation decisions are made without human oversight, errors can go unnoticed, and grievances may lack a channel for redress. Efficiency without accountability is not progress—it is abdication. That's why accessibility must sit alongside efficiency in the architecture of smart public services. The goal is not just to build systems that work faster, but systems that work for everyone. This means designing interfaces that are multilingual, readable, and navigable for those with disabilities. It means investing in digital literacy programs so that marginalized populations can engage meaningfully with new tools. It means offering analog alternatives where needed—not as an afterthought, but as a deliberate act of inclusion.

The conversation must also include the emotional dimension of public service (Chen et al, 2021). For many people, especially those in distress—whether fleeing domestic violence, seeking asylum, or applying for medical leave—the experience of navigating public services is not just transactional. It is intimate, vulnerable, and deeply human. A system that responds with only logic, devoid of empathy, risks alienating those it seeks to serve. Automation can answer questions, but it cannot yet offer the comfort of a warm tone or the reassurance of shared understanding (Kunze et al, 2019). In these spaces, human interaction remains irreplaceable, and technology must be seen not as a substitute, but as a support. There is also a generational dimension to consider. For digital natives, the idea of managing government services through a smartphone app is not only intuitive—it's expected. But for older populations or those displaced by conflict and unfamiliar with new languages and technologies, even the most well-designed platforms can feel foreign. Public services must therefore exist within a pluralistic ecosystem, where digital tools enhance but do not dominate, where the speed of change is matched by the depth of support.

Moreover, we must resist the urge to measure the success of smart public services solely in terms of cost savings or user satisfaction scores. Yes, it matters that people can renew their driver's licenses faster, access unemployment benefits with fewer hurdles, or track the status of a court case online. But public services are not businesses. Their worth lies not just in how efficiently they operate, but in how they reinforce the social contract—how they make citizens feel seen, heard, and valued. The introduction of AI into this space should deepen, not dilute, this sense of belonging. Some governments have begun to lead by example. In Singapore, the "Moments of Life" platform consolidates different services—childcare, education, health—into a single touchpoint for young families, reducing paperwork and improving coherence. In Denmark, digital service delivery is paired with strong commitments to user privacy and data ethics, ensuring that automation does not come at the expense of citizen autonomy. In Uruguay, chatbots provide real-time legal assistance to women facing domestic violence, guiding them step by step through options, rights, and emergency procedures. These are instances where smart systems meet real needs, and where technology amplifies, rather than replaces, the human voice.

Still, for every success story, there are cautionary tales. In the Netherlands, the use of an AI-driven system to detect welfare fraud led to wrongful accusations and stigmatization of low-income families, particularly those with immigrant backgrounds. The system was eventually scrapped, and the government issued a public apology—but the damage was done. This incident reminds us that smart systems can go terribly wrong when driven by suspicion rather than solidarity, by data without context, and by automation without empathy. As we imagine the future of public service, we must also imagine the public servants of that future. They will not just be policy implementers or desk workers. They will be interpreters of complex systems, stewards of digital ethics, bridge-builders between machine logic and human need. Their role will not be diminished by automation—it will be elevated. But only if we train, support, and trust them to engage meaningfully with the tools at their disposal.

Finally, we must reflect on the philosophical shift that smart public services represent. When a citizen interacts with a government chatbot at midnight, or receives a tax refund calculated by an algorithm, what kind of relationship are we cultivating between the individual and the state? Is it purely transactional? Or is there space for a new kind of trust—one based not on personal familiarity or face-to-face encounters, but on reliability, clarity, and responsiveness? Smart public services should not aim to dazzle. They should aim to serve—quietly, competently, and inclusively. Their success should be measured not in how advanced the technology is, but in how deeply they are rooted in human realities. For public service is, above all, a moral commitment: to care, to include, and to ensure that no one is left behind—not in a queue, not in a database, and not in the silence of a system that does not speak their language. In a world saturated with noise and speed, perhaps the smartest public service is the one that listens. Listens to the rhythms of life as it is lived, to the frustrations of the overlooked, and to the quiet hopes of those who dare to believe that government can still be a force for good. It is here, in this attentiveness, that automation finds its purpose, and efficiency gains its soul. Only then can smart public services fulfill their true promise—not as marvels of innovation, but as instruments of dignity.

ALGORITHMIC DECISION-MAKING: POTENTIALS AND PERILS IN PUBLIC INSTITUTIONS

There is something deeply unsettling about the idea that an invisible set of instructions—a mathematical model, a stream of code—can determine whether a person receives housing, qualifies for welfare, or is flagged as a potential risk. And yet, this is the reality quietly unfolding in public institutions around the world. Algorithmic decision-making is no longer a speculative concept or a futuristic ideal (Pedwell, 2024). It is here, embedded in the very systems that shape our lives, increasingly determining how governments interact with citizens. At its best, it holds the promise of more consistent, efficient, and scalable decisions. But at its worst, it can be impersonal, opaque, and unjust in ways that are difficult to detect and even harder to challenge.

Public administration, by its nature, requires decision-making at scale (Hildreth, 2021). Whether it's distributing public funds, enforcing compliance, managing public health, or allocating limited resources, these tasks demand consistency, speed, and objectivity. For decades, institutions relied on procedural frameworks and human judgment to navigate this complexity. But as demands on public services grew and datasets ballooned beyond human comprehension, the appeal of algorithmic systems became difficult to ignore. Here was a toolset that could not only process massive volumes of data but also extract insights, generate predictions, and offer real-time recommendations. Governments, often under pressure to do more with less, turned to algorithms as both a practical solution and a symbol of modernization (Valentine, 2019). The attraction is understandable. Algorithms, after all, don't get tired. They don't forget, procrastinate, or carry personal grudges. They promise fairness through neutrality, and efficiency through automation. They can be deployed at scale, responding to thousands of queries or applications simultaneously, reducing human workloads and perceived inconsistencies. In theory, algorithmic systems can reduce bias, flag anomalies, catch fraud, and streamline decision-making in ways that no human bureaucracy ever could. But here lies the first great irony: the very qualities that make algorithms so appealing are also what make them dangerous. Their apparent objectivity masks a deeper truth—that no algorithm is truly neutral. Every model is built on data, and data carries the fingerprints of history. When algorithms are trained on datasets shaped by decades of inequality—discriminatory housing policies, racially skewed policing records, biased employment histories—

they learn those patterns. They replicate them. And they do so without awareness or accountability.

Figure 2. Decision Oversight Mix in Public Administration (Illustrative, 2018–2025)

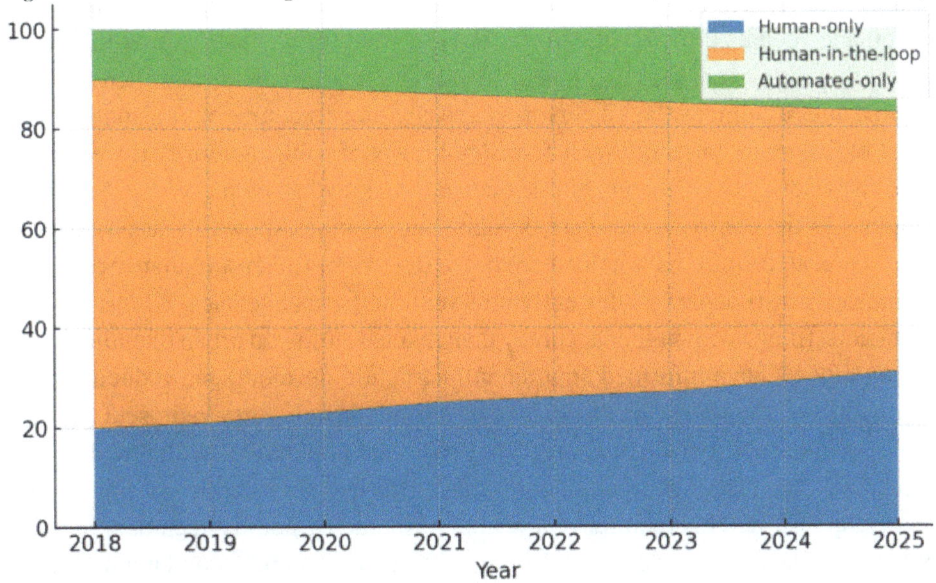

Take, for instance, predictive policing systems used in several cities across the globe. These algorithms analyze historical crime data to determine where crimes are most likely to occur. On paper, this seems like a smart allocation of law enforcement resources. But in practice, it often means that communities historically over-policed continue to be over-policed—not because of actual risk, but because of legacy data. The system becomes a self-fulfilling prophecy. The more police are sent to a neighborhood, the more incidents they report, and the more the algorithm flags it as a hotspot. It's a closed loop of bias masquerading as insight. Or consider welfare eligibility algorithms designed to flag fraud. These systems typically score applicants based on a range of factors—past behavior, income level, household data, and other variables. Those with high scores may face extra scrutiny or be denied benefits altogether.

What makes these cases especially troubling is not just the outcomes, but the opacity. With human decision-makers, flawed as they may be, there is the possibility of explanation, of appeal, of emotional connection. One can ask questions, express concerns, provide context. With algorithms, the logic is hidden—buried in code, protected by intellectual property laws, or lost in the complexity of machine learning models that even their developers struggle to interpret. For the average citizen, there is no face to confront, no voice to plead with. There is only the outcome, cold and unquestionable. This erosion of transparency is not merely a technical issue—it is a democratic one. Public institutions are supposed to be accountable to the people they serve. When decisions are made by systems that cannot explain themselves, or that operate in ways the public cannot understand, the trust that sustains democratic governance begins to fray. Citizens do not just want efficient services—they want to feel that the system sees them, hears them, and treats them fairly. When an algorithm denies a claim or flags a person as a risk without recourse or explanation, that sense of fairness is lost. And with it, the legitimacy of public authority is weakened.

This is not to say that algorithmic decision-making has no place in public institutions. On the contrary, there are domains where it has shown great promise. In healthcare, algorithms have helped predict outbreaks, optimize ambulance dispatch, and identify at-risk patients for early intervention. In tax agencies, AI has flagged suspicious filings with higher accuracy than manual audits. In urban planning, data-driven models have informed smarter infrastructure development, reducing costs and improving livability. These successes are not trivial—they represent genuine progress in the ability of governments to serve their populations with foresight and precision. The challenge, then, is not whether to use algorithms, but how to use them responsibly. This requires a new kind of literacy—not just technical literacy, but ethical, legal, and civic literacy. Public officials must understand not only what the algorithms do, but what they mean. They must be equipped to ask hard questions: Who designed this system? What data was it trained on? What values does it encode? What risks does it pose? And how will we ensure that its decisions are subject to review, challenge, and correction?

Equally important is the need for robust public engagement (Holmes et al, 2019). Too often, algorithmic systems are introduced as fait accompli—technical upgrades presented with little explanation or consultation. But if these tools are to govern public life, then the public must have a say in their design and deployment. This means involving communities, civil society groups, and ethicists in conversations about what values should guide algorithmic decisions. It means ensuring that affected populations are not just consulted after the fact, but involved from the beginning. And it means being honest about trade-offs—not every efficiency gain is worth the social cost it may entail. We also need better legal frameworks. Existing laws on administrative procedure, due process, and discrimination were not built with algorithms in mind. They struggle to address questions like: Can an algorithm be sued? What constitutes due process when a decision is made by code? Who is liable when automated systems cause harm? Some countries are beginning to grapple with these issues—through AI impact assessments, algorithmic auditing standards, and regulations requiring explainability. But much remains uncharted, and the pace of technology continues to outstrip the pace of law.

At the heart of all this is a deeper philosophical question: what does it mean to govern in the age of algorithms? Governance is not just about outcomes—it is about relationships, trust, legitimacy. Public institutions are not factories churning out efficient results. They are arenas of moral judgment, democratic deliberation, and social accountability. Algorithms can support these functions, but they cannot replace them. They do not understand justice. They do not feel compassion. They do not carry the burden of ethical responsibility. That burden remains ours. We must resist the temptation to see algorithms as infallible or inevitable. They are tools—nothing more, nothing less. Their value lies not in their complexity, but in how wisely we choose to use them. A well-designed algorithm, used with care, transparency, and humility, can be a powerful ally in the quest for better governance (Coglianese & Lehr, 2019). A poorly designed one, used without scrutiny or soul, can become a silent force of harm. The true test of algorithmic decision-making in public institutions is not how fast it operates, or how much money it saves, but how well it aligns with our deepest values. Does it uphold dignity? Does it promote equity? Does it enhance trust? These are not technical questions—they are human ones. And they are the questions we must keep asking, again and again, as we navigate this uncertain but vital frontier.

AI-DRIVEN TRANSPARENCY AND ACCOUNTABILITY IN PUBLIC ADMINISTRATION

When we think of transparency and accountability in public administration, the image that often comes to mind is that of a government official standing before a public forum, answering questions about policy decisions, budget allocations, or the distribution of resources. We think of transparency as the ability for citizens to scrutinize actions, understand motives, and demand answers when something goes wrong. It is the bedrock of trust in democratic systems, and it is essential for ensuring that power is not abused and that public resources are used effectively. But as governments increasingly adopt Artificial Intelligence (AI) to manage public services and decision-making, the relationship between transparency, accountability, and public trust has become more complicated (Kuziemski & Misuraca, 2020). AI, in its various forms, offers the tantalizing promise of improving transparency in public administration. With the right implementation, AI systems can provide real-time access to information, offer data-driven insights into government performance, and even enable citizens to track public spending, policy outcomes, or service delivery in ways that were previously unimaginable. For example, AI-powered platforms can sift through massive amounts of data to produce reports on government spending, helping citizens understand where taxpayer money is going and how it is being used.

AI can also help governments detect inefficiencies or fraud in real-time, creating opportunities for rapid corrective action before issues snowball (Bello & Olufemi, 2024). These capabilities, in theory, could drastically improve the transparency of governance by making it easier for the public to access and understand the inner workings of government operations. At the same time, the rise of AI in governance also presents significant challenges to transparency. The very algorithms that promise greater clarity in government processes are also inherently opaque. Machine learning models, in particular, are often referred to as "black boxes" because their decision-making processes are difficult, if not impossible, to fully explain, even to the experts who build them. This opacity poses a serious problem when AI systems are used to make decisions about people's lives, such as determining eligibility for social benefits, assessing tax liabilities, or allocating public health resources. How can we hold a system accountable when we cannot fully understand how it arrived at its conclusions?

The issue becomes even more complex when we consider that many AI systems are not created in-house by governments, but are instead developed by private companies with their own interests, priorities, and biases. When a city uses an AI tool to predict crime patterns or optimize traffic flow, is the company that designed the algorithm transparent about how its model works? Are they willing to disclose the data it was trained on, the assumptions it makes, or the potential risks involved? The more governments rely on third-party AI solutions, the more they outsource their responsibility for transparency to external vendors, who may not be as committed to public accountability as the governments themselves. There is also the risk that AI-driven transparency might be used as a tool for surveillance rather than genuine oversight. Imagine a scenario in which AI algorithms are used not only to improve the efficiency of government services but also to monitor citizens' behavior more closely. Governments could use AI to track online interactions, analyze social media activity, or even predict when citizens are likely to engage in protests or civil disobedience. While this might improve the government's ability to respond quickly to potential threats or unrest, it also raises serious concerns about privacy, civil liberties, and the balance of power between the state and the individual. In these cases, transparency is not a force for empowerment but a mechanism for control. It is important that as we pursue greater transparency in public administration, we ensure that it serves the public, not just those in power.

So how do we reconcile the promise of AI-driven transparency with the potential perils? The answer lies in a combination of careful design, rigorous oversight, and ethical governance. The first step is ensuring that AI systems are developed with transparency as a core principle. Governments must be clear about how and why they are adopting AI, what goals they hope to achieve, and how they will mitigate potential risks. This includes being transparent about the data used to train AI models, the algorithms' design and assumptions, and the potential biases that may be embedded in the system. It also means establishing clear mechanisms for auditing AI systems, ensuring that they remain aligned with public values, and providing channels for citizens to raise concerns when they feel a system is making an unfair or incorrect decision. In many ways, the key to transparency in AI is explainability. If we cannot understand how an algorithm works, we cannot trust it. This is especially important in the context of public administration, where the stakes are high, and the consequences of a flawed decision can be devastating. For example, if an AI system denies a citizen's claim for unemployment benefits, that person deserves to know exactly why that decision was made, how the algorithm reached that conclusion, and what data was used to make the determination. If citizens cannot access this information, they cannot challenge the decision, and the algorithm effectively becomes a black box that operates outside of public scrutiny. By making AI systems more explainable, we give people the ability to understand, question, and, if necessary, appeal decisions that affect their lives.

Figure 3. Organizational Readiness for Responsible AI (Illustrative, 1–5)

One promising development in the field of AI transparency is the movement toward algorithmic accountability (Busuioc, 2021). Governments and organizations are beginning to establish guidelines, best practices, and regulations aimed at ensuring that AI systems are not only effective but also fair, transparent, and accountable. For example, the European Union has introduced the General Data Protection Regulation (GDPR), which mandates that citizens have the right to know how their personal data is being used, including by AI systems (Sartor & Lagioia, 2020). Similarly, the EU's proposed Artificial Intelligence Act seeks to regulate high-risk AI applications by establishing clear rules around transparency, accountability, and oversight. These regulations represent a step in the right direction, but they must go further. Transparency in AI should not be limited to access to information—it should also include the ability to influence how algorithms are designed and deployed. This means involving the public in discussions about how AI is used in governance and what safeguards are necessary to prevent misuse. Public consultations, citizen panels, and independent oversight bodies can all play a role in ensuring that AI systems align with the public interest, rather than serving the interests of powerful corporations or governments alone.

Additionally, AI-driven transparency must be seen as part of a larger effort to promote equitable access to public services. Technology should not exacerbate existing inequalities—it should address them (Imran, 2023). Governments should actively work to ensure that AI systems are inclusive, reaching underserved communities and vulnerable populations who might otherwise be left behind. This involves designing AI systems that account for different levels of digital literacy, ensuring that marginalized groups are not further excluded from the benefits of AI-driven services. It also means investing in digital infrastructure that supports equitable access, such as ensuring that all citizens have access to the internet, devices, and digital literacy training. It is important to remember that transparency is not an end in itself. The goal is to foster a deeper sense of trust between the government and the people it serves. AI has the potential to make government services more efficient, accessible, and responsive—but only if it is built on a foundation of trust. Citizens must believe that AI is being used in their best interest, not just to streamline processes but to enhance their rights, freedoms, and opportunities (Kuziemski & Misuraca, 2020). When governments make transparency and accountability central to their AI strategies, they demonstrate that they understand the delicate balance between technological progress and democratic values. AI-driven transparency in public administration is both a tremendous opportunity and a profound challenge. It has the potential to transform how governments interact with their citizens, offering unprecedented levels of openness, efficiency, and responsiveness. But for this potential to be realized, it must be approached with care, caution, and commitment to ethical governance. The public must not only have access to information but also the ability to understand and challenge the systems that shape their lives. In the end, AI should not only serve the goal of efficiency but also the deeper purpose of empowering citizens, ensuring that government remains accountable, just, and above all, human.

HUMAN-CENTERED DESIGN IN AI SYSTEMS FOR GOVERNANCE

The rapid advancement of Artificial Intelligence (AI) in public administration has led to new and powerful ways to manage the complexities of governance (Young et al, 2019). However, as AI begins to play a larger role in shaping decisions about people's lives, it becomes increasingly clear that the design of these systems must be rooted in a fundamental principle: human-centeredness. If we are to create AI systems that are fair, accountable, and aligned with democratic values, they must be designed with human beings at the core, not just in terms of technical efficiency, but in a way that preserves the dignity, agency, and autonomy of every individual. Human-centered design is not a new concept, but in the realm of AI, it takes on even greater importance. Traditionally, human-centered design refers to an approach in which the needs, experiences, and values of people are prioritized during the creation of products, services, or systems. In the context of AI and governance, this means that the systems should not just be optimized for performance and accuracy, but also for inclusivity, fairness, and respect for human rights. AI in governance should aim to serve people, not just deliver results. It should complement human judgment, not replace it. And it should empower citizens, rather than automate them out of the equation.

One of the fundamental challenges in applying human-centered design to AI systems in governance is the tension between automation and human agency (Ozmen Garibay et al, 2023). AI is often viewed as a way to reduce human intervention in decision-making processes, especially in tasks that require processing large amounts of data or making predictions based on historical patterns. This can bring significant benefits, such as increased efficiency, scalability, and consistency. But when AI systems are designed without human-centered considerations, they risk undermining the very values they are meant to support. For example, AI systems deployed in public administration can automate processes such as benefit claims, eligibility checks, and even legal decisions (Kayyali, 2025). While these processes may be made more efficient, there is a risk that they become dehumanized, with decisions being made solely based on data patterns, without room for context, compassion, or understanding. A human-centered approach, on the other hand, requires designers and policymakers to think deeply about how AI systems interact with the public. How can we ensure that AI systems are designed not just to streamline processes but to serve citizens with empathy and respect? How can we preserve the space for human discretion and judgment, even in automated systems?

At its core, human-centered design in AI for governance means recognizing that people are not data points. Citizens are complex, dynamic beings with unique experiences, needs, and aspirations. Too often, AI systems have been designed to treat individuals as nothing more than sets of data—bits and bytes that can be analyzed, categorized, and predicted. However, AI systems that treat people in this reductive way risk reinforcing existing biases and excluding marginalized groups, who may already be vulnerable to systems that fail to recognize their humanity. Take, for instance, AI systems used to assess eligibility for social services. These systems typically use large datasets—such as income levels, family size, employment history, and health status—to determine whether a person qualifies for benefits. While these algorithms may seem efficient, they also have the potential to overlook the nuances of an individual's situation. A person may be denied benefits because their situation doesn't fit neatly into predefined categories. A single mother struggling to find work after a medical emergency, for example, may not appear eligible for assistance based on the algorithm's rigid criteria, even though their need is urgent and genuine. In this case, the algorithm may fail to account for human dignity and agency—the very qualities that human-centered design seeks to prioritize.

A human-centered approach to AI in governance would look beyond the raw data and seek to understand the broader context in which individuals live (Gentelet & Mizrahi, 2024). This means building systems that not only use data to make decisions but also incorporate human judgment, enabling administrators to apply discretion when necessary. It also means designing AI tools that assist, rather than replace, public servants—empowering them to make better-informed decisions rather than outsourcing their responsibility to a machine. An essential component of human-centered design in AI systems for governance is transparency. If we are asking individuals to trust algorithms with important decisions, they must have the ability to understand how these systems work, how their data is being used, and why certain decisions are being made. In the context of public administration, transparency is more than just a technical requirement—it is a moral imperative. When people cannot access information about how decisions are made, they cannot hold the system accountable. And when citizens are excluded from the decision-making process, trust in public institutions erodes.

This is where explainability becomes key. AI systems, particularly those based on complex algorithms such as machine learning, are often described as "black boxes" because the decision-making process is not easily understood by humans (Pedreschi et al, 2019). The system's reasoning is often hidden beneath layers of mathematical models, making it difficult for people to know why a certain outcome was reached. For AI to be human-centered, it must be explainable. Public servants and citizens alike must be able to understand the rationale behind decisions made by AI systems. If an AI system denies a citizen's claim for assistance, that person should be able to understand how the system arrived at its decision. The ability to explain an AI's reasoning is not just an issue of transparency—it's a matter of ensuring fairness and accountability. Without explainability, people are left in the dark, unable to challenge decisions or seek redress. But transparency and explainability alone are not enough. Human-centered design also requires accountability for the outcomes of AI systems. If an AI system makes a flawed decision, there must be mechanisms in place to correct it. Public institutions must be prepared to intervene when AI systems go wrong, whether by offering an appeals process, correcting errors in the data, or even shutting down the system entirely if it becomes clear that it is not working as intended. Accountability ensures that AI systems are not seen as autonomous or beyond the reach of human judgment. AI should always serve the public good, and humans must remain in control.

To ensure that AI in public administration remains human-centered, governments must also prioritize inclusivity in the design of these systems (Schmager et al, 2024). AI systems that are not designed with inclusivity in mind run the risk of exacerbating social inequalities. Marginalized communities, including low-income populations, racial minorities, and people with disabilities, are often the most vulnerable to discrimination by algorithmic systems. For example, AI models trained on biased data may disproportionately affect communities that have historically been disadvantaged. To avoid this, designers must work with diverse groups of stakeholders to ensure that AI systems are fair, unbiased, and accessible to everyone, regardless of their background or socioeconomic status. Inclusive design goes beyond addressing technical biases—it involves recognizing and addressing power dynamics. In the context of public administration, power is not just about who controls the data or the algorithms, but also about who gets to shape the questions and the decisions. Citizens must have a voice in the creation and deployment of AI systems that impact their lives. This requires not only technical expertise but also ethical and democratic considerations. Governments must involve communities in the design process, soliciting feedback, and ensuring that marginalized voices are heard.

Incorporating participatory design into the development of AI systems is essential to achieving a human-centered approach (Auernhammer, 2020). This means collaborating with citizens, public servants, and other stakeholders in the design and implementation of AI systems, rather than imposing top-down solutions. Participatory design helps ensure that the needs and perspectives of all affected individuals are taken into account. Moreover, it fosters trust and ownership among those who are most affected by AI systems, ensuring that these tools are used to empower, rather than alienate, citizens. In sum, human-centered design in AI for governance is about much more than just making algorithms "work" or improving efficiency. It is about creating systems that are responsive, transparent, inclusive, and accountable to the people they serve. It is about building AI systems that enhance human dignity, respect human rights, and empower individuals to participate in the decisions that shape their lives. It is about recognizing that technology, when designed with humanity at its core, has the potential to not only make government more efficient but to make it more just. As we look toward the future, it is clear that AI will continue to play a significant role in public administration. But its impact will be shaped by how we choose to design and deploy these systems. If we want AI to serve us—rather than the other way around—we must ensure that it is designed with care, attention, and a deep commitment to human values. Only then will AI in governance truly be a force for good.

NAVIGATING ETHICAL, LEGAL, AND SOCIAL FRONTIERS OF AI INTEGRATION

As Artificial Intelligence (AI) continues to integrate into public administration, it becomes increasingly important to understand the ethical, legal, and social dimensions of this technological shift (Wirtz et al, 2019). These dimensions are not just theoretical concerns; they are practical challenges that affect real people's lives. The decisions made by AI systems in public governance are deeply consequential, influencing everything from eligibility for social services to the allocation of public resources. However, as AI enters the realm of public administration, we find ourselves standing at the crossroads of unprecedented opportunities and potential risks. Navigating these ethical, legal, and social frontiers requires more than just technological innovation; it demands careful thought, deliberate action, and a commitment to values that prioritize human dignity, equity, and accountability. The ethical challenges of AI in public administration are manifold. Perhaps the most pressing of these challenges is bias—whether implicit, explicit, or systemic. AI systems are not neutral; they are shaped by the data on which they are trained. Data, by its very nature, is a reflection of the world as it is—often shaped by historical inequalities, prejudices, and structural biases. If the data used to train an AI system reflects these biases, then the AI is likely to replicate them, perpetuating existing disparities in public services.

Table 1. AI Governance Framework for Public Administration

Pillar	Policy actions	Indicators	Risks
Legal basis & mandates	Publish AI registers; define lawful bases; AI impact assessments	AI systems listed; AIA completed; DPIA counts	Shadow IT; legal ambiguity
Accountability & oversight	Assign accountable officials; independent review boards	Named owners; board minutes; audit cycles	Responsibility gaps; capture
Data governance	Quality/lineage standards; privacy-by-design; consent & purpose limits	Data quality scores; access logs; DPIA outcomes	Bias propagation; misuse

continued on following page

Table 1. Continued

Pillar	Policy actions	Indicators	Risks
Model lifecycle	Standards for training, testing, monitoring & drift response	Release notes; bias tests; drift incidents resolved	Unseen drift; brittle models
Human-centered design	Co-design with communities; multilingual & accessible interfaces	User testing reports; accessibility checks	Exclusion; low uptake
Redress & explainability	Right to explanation; appeal & human review channels	Appeal turnaround; explainer coverage	Opaque vendors; delays
Security & resilience	Threat modeling; adversarial tests; continuity plans	Pen-test reports; recovery MTTR	Adversarial attacks; outages

Consider, for example, a predictive policing algorithm designed to allocate police resources based on patterns of past crime data. If the data used to train the system reflects historical over-policing in certain neighborhoods, the algorithm may reinforce these patterns, sending more officers to already heavily policed communities, while overlooking others. In the context of public administration, these kinds of biases are particularly concerning because they have direct consequences for people's lives—decisions about who receives services, who is scrutinized, and who is left behind. To mitigate this risk, the ethical design of AI systems must prioritize fairness. This requires the identification and rectification of bias at every stage of the AI development process. It means critically assessing the datasets used for training, questioning whether they accurately reflect the diversity of the population they are meant to serve. It also means creating models that are flexible enough to account for complexity and nuance, recognizing that human experiences cannot always be reduced to data points. Human-centered design is key to ensuring that AI systems remain accountable to the communities they serve, with a focus on inclusivity and equity. Only by making fairness a central value in AI system design can we begin to address the risks of discrimination and exclusion that accompany the automation of decision-making in governance.

Beyond the ethical challenges, there are profound legal considerations as well (Pozgar, 2023). As AI systems become more embedded in public administration, the question of who is legally accountable for the decisions made by these systems becomes critical. If an AI system wrongly denies an individual's access to housing, social services, or healthcare, who should be held responsible? Is it the government agency that deployed the system? The developers who created the algorithm? The private company that provided the AI tool? The lack of clear legal frameworks around AI accountability raises significant concerns about liability and due process. At present, many existing legal frameworks are ill-equipped to handle the complexities of AI in governance. Traditional laws governing administrative procedures, discrimination, and due process were not designed with AI in mind. In many jurisdictions, there is no clear legal standard for ensuring that AI systems are transparent or explainable, making it difficult for citizens to challenge decisions made by algorithms. If a person's claim for social assistance is denied by an AI system, they may have no clear recourse for appeal if the algorithm is not transparent about how the decision was made. The lack of legal clarity also makes it difficult to establish accountability when AI systems go wrong, leaving individuals vulnerable to harm. To address these challenges, governments must develop comprehensive legal frameworks that govern the use of AI in public administration. These frameworks must include clear accountability mechanisms that outline who is responsible for AI-driven decisions and ensure that citizens have the right to challenge those decisions. In addition, laws must be updated to ensure that AI systems are subject to the same principles of transparency, fairness, and due process that apply to human decision-makers (Kayyali, 2026). One promising development is the European Union's proposed Artificial Intelligence Act, which seeks to regulate high-risk AI applications and establish clear rules for transparency, oversight, and accountability. Similar initiatives should be pursued globally to ensure that the integration of AI into governance is guided by strong legal and ethical standards.

In addition to the ethical and legal dimensions, the integration of AI into public administration also raises important social questions (Wirtz et al, 2020). One of the most pressing of these questions is accessibility. As governments adopt AI-driven systems to deliver public services, there is a real risk of leaving behind those who are not digitally literate or do not have access to the technologies required to interact with these systems. This could exacerbate existing social inequalities, particularly among marginalized groups, such as low-income populations, the elderly, rural residents, and people with disabilities. Imagine a scenario in which a government service, such as applying for unemployment benefits, is fully automated using an AI system. For individuals who are comfortable with technology and have access to a computer or smartphone, this might seem like a convenient and efficient process. But for those who do not have access to these tools—or who lack the digital literacy to navigate them—the system becomes a barrier rather than a facilitator. Digital exclusion could leave many citizens unable to access essential services, deepening social divides and eroding public trust in government.

To ensure that AI systems are socially responsible, governments must make digital inclusion a priority (Elliott et al, 2021). This means investing in infrastructure that ensures access to the internet and technology for all citizens, particularly those in underserved areas. It also means providing digital literacy training to ensure that all citizens, regardless of their background, can engage with AI-powered services. Social inclusion should be at the forefront of AI system design, ensuring that technology works for everyone, not just those who are already digitally connected. Another significant social challenge posed by AI in governance is the potential erosion of privacy. AI systems, particularly those used in public administration, often rely on vast amounts of personal data to make decisions. Whether it's data about income, family composition, medical history, or social behavior, this information is used to assess eligibility for services, predict needs, or even determine risk. While the use of data can improve the efficiency of public services, it also raises significant concerns about surveillance and data privacy.

As AI systems become more pervasive, the scope of data collection expands, and the potential for misuse grows. Governments may be tempted to use AI to monitor citizens more closely, tracking their behaviors, preferences, and movements (Duberry, 2022). If left unchecked, this could lead to a surveillance state, where citizens are constantly monitored and their personal data is exploited for purposes beyond what is necessary for service delivery. To mitigate these risks, governments must adopt strong data protection measures and be transparent about how personal data is collected, used, and stored. Citizens must have the right to control their own data and know exactly how it is being used by AI systems. The social impact of AI in governance cannot be fully understood without considering its effect on democratic values. As AI takes on a larger role in decision-making, there is a risk that the human element of governance—the deliberation, the debate, the dialogue—will be sidelined. Public administration is not just about efficiency and outcomes; it is about ensuring that the voices of citizens are heard and that decisions are made with accountability to the public. If AI systems replace too much of the decision-making process, there is a danger that governance will become more technocratic, with decisions made by machines rather than people. This could erode the public's sense of ownership and participation in governance.

To preserve the democratic character of governance, AI systems must be seen as tools for enhancing, not replacing, human decision-making. Public servants must remain at the center of governance, with AI acting as a support system to help them make more informed, efficient, and equitable decisions. Additionally, citizens must be actively engaged in the design, implementation, and oversight of AI systems, ensuring that these tools remain accountable to the people they serve. Participatory democracy should be an essential principle in the integration of AI into public administration. The ethical, legal, and social challenges of AI integration in public administration are complex and multifaceted. But they are not insurmountable. With careful thought, strong regulations, and a commitment to values of fairness, transparency, and inclusion, AI can be harnessed to improve governance and public service delivery in ways that benefit all citizens. The key is to navigate these frontiers with a sense of responsibility, humility, and respect for human dignity, ensuring that AI remains a tool for good and not a force that undermines the principles of democracy and justice.

CONCLUSION

As we arrive at the close of this exploration into the transformative role of AI in public administration, what emerges is not a singular narrative of progress, but a complex tapestry woven from threads of promise, caution, innovation, and human responsibility. Artificial Intelligence, for all its computational prowess, is not a magic solution. It is a mirror, reflecting both the best and the most troubling aspects of how we govern, whom we serve, and what we prioritize. We have seen how AI can reimagine service delivery—making it faster, more personalized, and more adaptive to citizens' needs. From predictive analytics in healthcare to chatbots streamlining social services, the public sector has begun to embrace a model of governance that is proactive rather than reactive. In theory, this opens the door to a more dynamic and responsive state—one that can foresee problems before they spiral and respond to crises with surgical precision. But technology, left unchecked, rarely bends toward justice. As AI systems become more embedded in the machinery of public decision-making, the risks grow ever more urgent. Algorithms can reinforce historical biases. Automated systems can make decisions that are difficult to audit or explain. Citizens can find themselves caught in bureaucratic loops orchestrated not by indifferent clerks, but by faceless lines of code. And in the name of efficiency, we may quietly normalize a kind of technocratic opacity—where public choices are made not in town halls or legislative chambers, but in servers and datasets far removed from democratic oversight.

It is here that we must return to first principles. Public administration, at its core, is about serving people—not as data points, but as individuals with rights, needs, and dignity. The use of AI in this domain must never lose sight of that. It must be anchored in ethics, guided by law, and shaped through inclusive dialogue. We need frameworks that ensure accountability without stifling innovation. We need public servants who are not only technologically literate but ethically grounded. And we need citizens who are informed, empowered, and involved in shaping how these technologies are used. Perhaps most importantly, we must resist the seduction of inevitability. AI is not destiny. It is a set of tools—powerful ones, yes—but tools nonetheless. How we use them will depend on the stories we tell about progress, the values we hold as a society, and the courage we muster to ask difficult questions. Are we building systems that deepen our humanity, or ones that distance us from it? Are we using AI to democratize knowledge and power, or to consolidate them in the hands of the few? The future of public administration will be written not by algorithms alone, but by the people who design, deploy, and hold them accountable. In this journey, we must strive not only to build smarter governments but also more just ones. The path forward is not just technical—it is moral, social, and deeply human. And that, ultimately, is the real transformation.

REFERENCES

Agarwal, P. K. (2018). Public administration challenges in the world of AI and bots. *Public Administration Review, 78*(6), 917–921. DOI: 10.1111/puar.12979

Auernhammer, J. (2020). Human-centered AI: The role of Human-centered Design Research in the development of AI.

Bello, O. A., & Olufemi, K. (2024). Artificial intelligence in fraud prevention: Exploring techniques and applications challenges and opportunities. Computer science & IT research journal, 5(6), 1505-1520.

Brunsson, N., & Olsen, J. P. (2018). *The Reforming organization: making sense of administrative change*. Routledge. DOI: 10.4324/9781351252188

Bullock, J. B. (2019). Artificial intelligence, discretion, and bureaucracy. *American Review of Public Administration, 49*(7), 751–761. DOI: 10.1177/0275074019856123

Busuioc, M. (2021). Accountable artificial intelligence: Holding algorithms to account. *Public Administration Review, 81*(5), 825–836. DOI: 10.1111/puar.13293 PMID: 34690372

Chen, T., Guo, W., Gao, X., & Liang, Z. (2021). AI-based self-service technology in public service delivery: User experience and influencing factors. *Government Information Quarterly, 38*(4), 101520. DOI: 10.1016/j.giq.2020.101520

Coglianese, C., & Lehr, D. (2019). Transparency and algorithmic governance. *Administrative Law Review, 71*(1), 1–56.

Dahl, R. A. (2018). The science of public administration: Three problems. In *Democracy, bureaucracy, and the study of administration* (pp. 60–76). Routledge. DOI: 10.4324/9780429501036-6

Duberry, J. (2022). Artificial intelligence and democracy: risks and promises of AI-mediated citizen–government relations. In *Artificial Intelligence and Democracy*. Edward Elgar Publishing. DOI: 10.4337/9781788977319

Elliott, K., Price, R., Shaw, P., Spiliotopoulos, T., Ng, M., Coopamootoo, K., & Van Moorsel, A. (2021). Towards an equitable digital society: Artificial intelligence (AI) and corporate digital responsibility (CDR). *Society, 58*(3), 179–188. DOI: 10.1007/s12115-021-00594-8 PMID: 34149122

Gentelet, K., & Mizrahi, S. K. (2024). A Human-Centered Approach to AI Governance: Operationalizing Human Rights Through Citizen Participation. In Human-Centered AI (pp. 215-230). Chapman and Hall/CRC.

Hildreth, W. B. (2021). *Handbook of public administration* (Hildreth, W. B., Miller, G., & Rabin, J., Eds.). Routledge. DOI: 10.4324/9780429270680

Holmes, L., Cresswell, K., Williams, S., Parsons, S., Keane, A., Wilson, C., Islam, S., Joseph, O., Miah, J., Robinson, E., & Starling, B. (2019). Innovating public engagement and patient involvement through strategic collaboration and practice. *Research Involvement and Engagement*, *5*(1), 1–12. DOI: 10.1186/s40900-019-0160-4 PMID: 31646001

Imran, A. (2023). Why addressing digital inequality should be a priority. *The Electronic Journal on Information Systems in Developing Countries*, *89*(3), e12255. DOI: 10.1002/isd2.12255

Kayyali, M. (2025). Digital Transformation in Public Sector Management: An Overview. Enhancing Public Sector Accountability and Services Through Digital Innovation, 289-324.

Kayyali, M. (2026). Digital Transformation in Public Administration: Global Case Studies. In Sustainable Innovation in the Middle East and North Africa (MENA) Region (pp. 1-26). IGI Global Scientific Publishing.

Kem, D. (2022). Personalised and adaptive learning: Emerging learning platforms in the era of digital and smart learning. *International Journal of Social Science and Human Research*, *5*(2), 385–391. DOI: 10.47191/ijsshr/v5-i2-02

Kunze, A., Summerskill, S. J., Marshall, R., & Filtness, A. J. (2019). Automation transparency: Implications of uncertainty communication for human-automation interaction and interfaces. *Ergonomics*, *62*(3), 345–360. DOI: 10.1080/00140139.2018.1547842 PMID: 30501566

Kuziemski, M., & Misuraca, G. (2020). AI governance in the public sector: Three tales from the frontiers of automated decision-making in democratic settings. *Telecommunications Policy*, *44*(6), 101976. DOI: 10.1016/j.telpol.2020.101976 PMID: 32313360

Monteiro, P., & Adler, P. S. (2022). Bureaucracy for the 21st century: Clarifying and expanding our view of bureaucratic organization. *The Academy of Management Annals*, *16*(2), 427–475. DOI: 10.5465/annals.2019.0059

Newman, J., Mintrom, M., & O'Neill, D. (2022). Digital technologies, artificial intelligence, and bureaucratic transformation. *Futures*, *136*, 102886. DOI: 10.1016/j.futures.2021.102886

Ozmen Garibay, O., Winslow, B., Andolina, S., Antona, M., Bodenschatz, A., Coursaris, C., Falco, G., Fiore, S. M., Garibay, I., Grieman, K., Havens, J. C., Jirotka, M., Kacorri, H., Karwowski, W., Kider, J., Konstan, J., Koon, S., Lopez-Gonzalez, M., Maifeld-Carucci, I., & Xu, W. (2023). Six human-centered artificial intelligence grand challenges. *International Journal of Human-Computer Interaction, 39*(3), 391–437. DOI: 10.1080/10447318.2022.2153320

Pedreschi, D., Giannotti, F., Guidotti, R., Monreale, A., Ruggieri, S., & Turini, F. (2019, July). Meaningful explanations of black box AI decision systems. *Proceedings of the AAAI Conference on Artificial Intelligence, 33*(01), 9780–9784. DOI: 10.1609/aaai.v33i01.33019780

Pedwell, C. (2024). Speculative machines and us: More-than-human intuition and the algorithmic condition. *Cultural Studies, 38*(2), 188–218. DOI: 10.1080/09502386.2022.2142805

Pozgar, G. D. (2023). *Legal and Ethical Issues for Health Professionals with Navigate Advantage Access*. Jones & Bartlett Learning.

Sartor, G., & Lagioia, F. (2020). The impact of the General Data Protection Regulation (GDPR) on artificial intelligence.

Satkunanandan, S. (2019). Bureaucratic passions. *Law, Culture and the Humanities, 15*(1), 14–29. DOI: 10.1177/1743872115614801

Schmager, S., Pappas, I., & Vasilakopoulou, P. (2024). Citizens-Focused Design Principles for Human-Centered AI in Public Services. AMCIS 2024 Proceedings.

Sharma, M., Paliwal, T., & Baniwal, P. (2024). Challenges in Digital Transformation and Automation for Industry 4.0. In AI-Driven IoT Systems for Industry 4.0 (pp. 143-163). CRC Press.

Valentine, S. (2019). Impoverished algorithms: Misguided governments, flawed technologies, and social control. *The Fordham Urban Law Journal, 46*, 364.

Wirtz, B. W., Weyerer, J. C., & Geyer, C. (2019). Artificial intelligence and the public sector—Applications and challenges. *International Journal of Public Administration, 42*(7), 596–615. DOI: 10.1080/01900692.2018.1498103

Wirtz, B. W., Weyerer, J. C., & Sturm, B. J. (2020). The dark sides of artificial intelligence: An integrated AI governance framework for public administration. *International Journal of Public Administration, 43*(9), 818–829. DOI: 10.1080/01900692.2020.1749851

Young, M. M., Bullock, J. B., & Lecy, J. D. (2019). Artificial discretion as a tool of governance: A framework for understanding the impact of artificial intelligence on public administration. *Perspectives on Public Management and Governance*, 2(4), 301–313. DOI: 10.1093/ppmgov/gvz014

KEY TERMS AND DEFINITIONS

AI Impact Assessment (AIA): a pre-deployment evaluation of an AI system's risks, benefits, bias, transparency, and redress mechanisms.

Algorithmic Accountability: the duty of public bodies to explain, audit, and take responsibility for AI-driven decisions that affect citizens.

Anticipatory Governance: using AI/analytics to foresee issues (e.g., service demand, public health risks) and act before harms occur.

Data Governance: policies and controls ensuring lawful, high-quality, privacy-preserving data for public-sector AI.

Digital Inclusion: guaranteeing access (devices, skills, alternatives) so AI-enabled services work for everyone, not only the digitally fluent.

Explainability: the ability to communicate how an AI reached its conclusion in terms citizens and caseworkers can understand.

Human-in-the-Loop: workflows where humans oversee and can override automated recommendations before final administrative action.

Chapter 7 Artificial Intelligence-Induced Algorithmic Bias in Public Services: A Framework for Fair and Transparent Governance

Gamze Sinem Özer
https://orcid.org/0000-0003-1073-1707
Akdeniz Üniversitesi, Turkey

ABSTRACT

With the rapid advancement of technology, AI-supported chatbots are increasingly used in public administration to enhance efficiency, provide 24/7 service, reduce costs, and streamline bureaucratic processes. However, these systems may suffer from algorithmic bias—systematic errors in AI models that result in unfair or discriminatory outcomes for certain groups, often due to biased training data or design flaws. Such biases challenge the presumed neutrality of AI and risk reinforcing existing social inequalities, raising ethical and governance concerns. This study examines algorithmic bias in the context of public administration, aiming to explore its sources, impacts on public services, and implications for social justice. By reviewing academic literature, the research proposes a conceptual framework to support the development of more transparent, accountable, and fair AI systems in the public sector.

DOI: 10.4018/979-8-3373-1484-6.ch007

INTRODUCTION

Artificial intelligence and algorithmic decision-making systems are becoming increasingly important in decision-making processes that shape individuals' lives. While these systems promise efficiency, objectivity, and scalability, they also carry significant ethical and social implications. The concept of "algorithmic bias" emerged at a critical moment when the claim that technology is impartial was being scrutinized. It has become clear that this is not simply a technical glitch or a bug in the code, but can stem from a variety of causes.

Algorithmic bias is an inevitable process whereby historical inequalities, cultural biases, and structural injustices in human societies are embedded in digital systems and perpetuated through those same systems. Algorithms provide patterns, assumptions, and contexts in data. As a result, these systems, which appear to operate with mathematical certainty, can produce discriminatory and systematic outcomes against certain social groups, thereby reinforcing existing privileges and further deepening already disadvantaged positions. In this context, the manifestations of algorithmic bias are multi-layered: from representational gaps or distortions in training data (Data Representation Bias); traces of past institutional practices embedded in the data (Data Collection/Historical Bias); errors in feature selection during technical design (Feature Selection Bias); inequities stemming from the mathematical structure of the model (Algorithmic Processing Bias); a situation where the final outputs consistently have negative effects on certain groups (Output Bias); and misinterpretations of these outputs by human decision-makers (Interpretation/Explanation Bias).

Algorithmic bias has gained particular importance and urgency in the field of public administration, as it has in all disciplines within the general framework. This is because the state is characterized by democratic principles such as fundamental rights, equality, justice, transparency, and accountability in its relations with citizens. The use of algorithmic systems in essential areas such as the distribution of social assistance, tax auditing, public safety, the allocation of educational resources, access to health services, and even courts put these principles to the test. The field of public administration is the most obvious example of how algorithms, under the banner of "objectivity," reproduce past injustices; how opacity weakens democratic control; and how technical systems undermine the trust relationship between citizens and the state. Thus, cases such as SyRI, COMPAS, or MI-DSS have shown that algorithms used by public authorities can produce discriminatory outcomes that affect the most vulnerable groups and violate fundamental rights.

The study aims to reveal the many forms that algorithmic bias can take, particularly the dangers it can pose in the field of public administration and the fundamental legitimacy issues it creates for democracies. In this context, the study first establishes a conceptual framework related to algorithmic bias and then attempts to evaluate it from the perspective of public administration.

THE CONCEPT OF ALGORITHMIC BIAS

The increasing prevalence of artificial intelligence systems in decision-making processes has rendered the assumption that these technologies are neutral and objective open to question. In this context, the concept of "algorithmic bias" has been extensively discussed in recent years across both technical disciplines and the social sciences. The term was initially introduced by Friedman and Nissenbaum (1996) as "bias in computer systems." Furthermore, the authors contributed to the literature by classifying algorithmic bias into three categories: preexisting bias, technical bias, and emergent bias.

Algorithmic bias refers to the systematic discrimination against specific individuals or groups that occurs through data-driven decision-making systems. This concept has become a central concern in the literature examining the socio-technical implications of machine learning and artificial intelligence technologies. Although there is no universally accepted definition of algorithmic bias, various scholars have conceptualized and categorized it from different disciplinary perspectives.

Barocas and Selbst (2016) define algorithmic bias as "the unintended reproduction of social inequalities by data-driven decision systems, datasets, or model configurations." According to them, despite the common perception that algorithmic systems are free from human bias, these systems may perpetuate discrimination by embedding historical and structural biases present in the training data.

Cathy O'Neil (2016), by contrast, offers a more critical perspective, describing algorithmic systems as "weaponized mathematical models." In her analysis, algorithms are not merely biased but actively exacerbate social inequalities due to their opacity and lack of accountability: "Algorithms are not only biased, but they are also systems that amplify these biases and make their effects invisible."

Eubanks (2018) also frames algorithmic bias as a broader issue, conceptualizing it as a digital manifestation of structural inequalities. She argues that algorithms serve as mechanisms that reinforce not only individual discrimination but also institutionalized forms of bias. For instance, she highlights how algorithms deployed in public welfare systems disproportionately target and penalize low-income communities.

Similarly, Binns (2018) characterizes algorithmic bias not merely as a form of individual discrimination but as outcomes that engender systemic disadvantage. As he states: "Algorithmic bias is a form of injustice that arises when machine learning models systematically place certain groups at a disadvantage."

In its broadest sense, algorithmic bias can be defined as the systematic and predictable production of discriminatory outcomes by an algorithm stemming from its technical design, the data it is trained on, or the context in which it is implemented.

DIFFERENT DIMENSIONS AND DEFINITIONAL ASPECTS OF THE CONCEPT OF ALGORITHMIC BIAS

Definitions of algorithmic bias converge on the idea of systematic, unfair outcomes produced by algorithms, which are often based on social, data, or institutional factors. The concept is multifaceted, and definitions vary depending on the context; however, all emphasize the importance of fairness and the risks associated with perpetuating discrimination through automated systems. The statements under this heading explain the different dimensions and definitional aspects of the concept of algorithmic bias (Table 1). In this context, each subheading highlights a specific aspect of algorithmic bias.

Unfair Outcomes

Algorithmic bias is commonly defined as the tendency of algorithms to systematically produce unfair or biased outcomes against specific individuals or groups based on protected characteristics such as race, gender, or age (Kim & Cho, 2022; Mavrogiorgos et al., 2024; Castillo, 2019; Fu et al., 2020). This definition aligns with the framework of disparate impact. Barocas and Selbst (2016) emphasize that such discrimination can systematically arise in algorithmic outputs, even when there is no explicit intent to discriminate. The primary focus here is on the harmful consequences of algorithmic decisions for specific social groups. This constitutes an output-oriented definition of bias.

Repeated Errors

Algorithmic bias is also defined as the tendency of computational systems to consistently make errors that result in unfair outcomes, often reflecting underlying societal or data-driven biases (Mavrogiorgos et al., 2024; Johnson, 2020; Fu et al., 2020). This perspective highlights the influence of data bias. Eubanks (2018) underscores the idea that algorithms can "reproduce historical inequalities." In this sense, algorithms internalize the biases present in historical data during training, thereby institutionalizing them. This notion is closely related to the concept of automated inequality.

Embedded Social Models

Algorithms may inherit and reinforce social patterns and biases embedded in their training data, regardless of the developers' explicit intentions (Johnson, 2020; Fu et al., 2020). This perspective highlights the perpetuation of structural inequalities through technological systems. It resonates with scholars such as Latanya Sweeney and Kate Crawford, who argue that algorithms cannot be evaluated in isolation from their broader social context. The central claim here is that algorithms are not "neutral"; instead, they carry the social and historical legacies of the data on which they are trained.

Institutional and Structural Bias

Some scholars broaden the definition of algorithmic bias to encompass not only the algorithmic systems themselves but also the broader institutional and structural contexts within which they are deployed (Danks & London, 2017; Flowerman, 2023). This approach is rooted in the field of critical algorithm studies. It shifts the focus from technical components alone to include the political, legal, and institutional environments surrounding algorithmic decision-making. For instance, Noble (2018) argues that technology is deeply embedded in social structures and demonstrates how search engines can reinforce racial biases.

Table 1. Different Dimensions and Definitional Aspects of the Concept of Algorithmic Bias

Definition Aspect	Description	Citations
Systematic Unfairness	Produces outcomes that are unfair to certain groups	Kim and Cho (2022), Mavrogiorgos ve diğerleri (2024), Castillo (2019), Fu ve diğerleri (2020), Barocas and Selbst (2016).
Recurrent Errors	Repeatedly makes errors that disadvantage specific groups	Mavrogiorgos ve diğerleri (2024), Johnson (2020), Fu ve diğerleri (2020), Eubanks (2018).
Embedded Social Patterns	Reflects or amplifies biases from training data or society	Fu ve diğerleri (2020), Johnson (2020), Crawford (2016).
Institutional/structural context	Biases embedded in broader social or institutional structures	Danks and London (2017), Flowerman (2023), Noble (2018).

TYPES AND EXAMPLES OF ALGORITHMIC BIAS

The fact that algorithmic systems have begun to play a decisive role in social decisions necessitates examining not only the technical aspects of these technologies but also their ethical and sociopolitical implications. Particularly, biases emerging in automated decision-making systems can lead to serious consequences for individuals and groups, exacerbating inequality of opportunity, reproducing discrimination, and carrying the risk of perpetuating existing social inequalities in the digital realm. In this context, algorithmic bias emerges not as a single phenomenon but as a multi-layered issue that can manifest itself in various forms and at different stages. Therefore, identifying the different types of algorithmic bias and understanding how each operates is critical for developing effective intervention strategies. Below, the fundamental types of algorithmic bias are classified, and the topic is explored in depth with explanatory examples for each (Table 2).

Data Representation Bias

Algorithmic systems are not purely technical instruments; instead, they are deeply embedded within social and cultural contexts. Social and cultural patterns may be incorporated into these systems through training data or the design decisions made by developers (Barocas et al., 2019). These embedded patterns challenge the perception of algorithms as neutral information processors, revealing instead their capacity to reproduce existing power dynamics and societal biases (Noble, 2018).

The context in which an algorithm is deployed—whether in education, marketing, healthcare, or public safety—plays a critical role in shaping how bias manifests and which social groups are disproportionately affected (Xu et al., 2022; Akter et al., 2022). In particular, the underrepresentation or misrepresentation of certain groups in datasets—often driven by stereotypes—can hinder an algorithm's ability to make accurate or fair predictions for those groups (Buolamwini & Gebru, 2018). This leads not only to individual-level injustices but also contributes to systematic errors that reinforce structural inequalities. For instance, facial recognition technologies: A study conducted by the MIT Media Lab found that some facial recognition systems achieved 99% accuracy for light-skinned men but only 65% for dark-skinned women. This discrepancy is attributable to the overrepresentation of white men and the underrepresentation of Black women in the training datasets (Buolamwini & Gebru, 2018).

Data Collection Bias (Measurement Bias / Historical Bias)

The datasets used to train algorithmic models often reflect historical prejudices and entrenched social inequalities (Akter et al., 2021). As a result, machine learning systems may inherit and reinforce the structural biases embedded within the data (Noble, 2018).

For example, crime prediction algorithms used in law enforcement may flag specific neighborhoods as high-risk based on historical crime data. However, these same neighborhoods may have been subject to disproportionately intense policing in the past, leading to artificially elevated crime statistics (Richardson et al., 2019). In such cases, the algorithm is not detecting objective crime levels but rather reproducing patterns from historical policing practices.

Moreover, broader societal and cultural dynamics can be encoded into algorithmic systems either through biased training data or through the subjective design choices of developers. The sector in which an algorithm is implemented—such as education, healthcare, security, or marketing—directly influences the nature and consequences of the bias, as well as which populations are most affected. When certain groups are systematically underrepresented or distorted in training datasets due to stereotypes, the algorithm may generate inaccurate generalizations that result in discriminatory outcomes (Baker & Hawn, 2021; Kirkpatrick, 2016; Sun et al., 2020; Akter et al., 2021; Fazelpour & Danks, 2021; Xu et al., 2022; Johnson, 2020).

Therefore, the design and implementation of algorithmic systems must go beyond mere technical accuracy to also consider ethical responsibility and the broader social implications of these technologies (O'Neil, 2016).

Feature Selection Bias

The failure to critically evaluate and appropriately select variables (features) in algorithmic models can result in biased outcomes, particularly when mathematical modeling and optimization processes are detached from contextual considerations (Nishant et al., 2023). These models lack the flexibility and common sense inherent in human decision-making, which can lead to unfair results even when the input data appears unbiased (Mittelstadt et al., 2016). This poses a significant risk of indirect discrimination, especially against socially marginalized or sensitive groups. Variables that appear neutral at first glance may inadvertently disadvantage certain demographic groups. This occurs because algorithms function through formalized and mechanical logic, often neglecting cultural and contextual subtleties (Crawford,

2021). The consequences can be particularly harmful in complex, multidimensional social settings.

A pertinent example is the use of geographic data, such as postal codes or neighborhoods, in credit scoring algorithms. These variables can systematically lower the creditworthiness scores of individuals residing in areas frequently inhabited by ethnic minorities or low-income populations. Even if the model does not explicitly include race or income as features, it can indirectly penalize these groups through spatial proxies (Hurley & Adebayo, 2016). In doing so, the algorithm perpetuates historical patterns of inequality. This phenomenon is commonly referred to in the literature as proxy discrimination (Barocas et al., 2019).

Algorithmic Processing Bias

Algorithmic bias can also arise from the processes through which algorithms are distributed and applied, not just from their training data. Interactive systems—such as personalization filters, active learning models, and adaptive technologies—can reinforce and amplify existing social disparities over time (Binns, 2018; Sun et al., 2020). These systems can create "informational blind spots" by continuously prioritizing certain types of content while marginalizing others, thereby narrowing users' exposure to diverse perspectives (Pariser, 2011).

Moreover, user interactions with biased systems serve as feedback loops that further influence the algorithm's future outputs. This recursive dynamic causes initial biases, however, limited, to escalate over time, producing compounding and self-reinforcing discrimination (Barocas & Selbst, 2016; Sun et al., 2020). Thus, algorithmic bias is not static; it evolves and intensifies as part of a dynamic system.

Bias may also emerge from the design and configuration of technical components such as learning algorithms, classification thresholds, or optimization objectives. For instance, an algorithm optimized solely for overall accuracy may fail to ensure equitable performance across different social groups. In such cases, the pursuit of global optimization can lead to systematic disadvantages for specific populations (Hardt et al., 2016). A well-known example is the COMPAS (Correctional Offender Management Profiling for Alternative Sanctions) algorithm used in the U.S. criminal justice system. Investigative reporting by ProPublica revealed that the algorithm was significantly more likely to incorrectly label Black defendants as high-risk compared to White defendants despite similar overall accuracy rates (Angwin et al., 2016). The disparity in false favorable rates highlights how an ostensibly neutral system can lead to profound inequalities between groups (Dressel & Farid, 2018).

Ultimately, algorithmic systems are shaped not only by data but also by technical architecture, implementation context, and user interaction. These factors collectively determine how bias emerges and persists.

Outcome Bias

Even when algorithmic systems function correctly from a technical standpoint, the social consequences of their outputs may still be unfair. Outcome bias refers to situations where algorithmic decisions systematically produce negative consequences for specific social groups (Aiyer et al., 2024; König-Kersting et al., 2020). This type of bias may stem from variables that are not explicitly discriminatory (e.g., gender or race) but are nonetheless correlated with such characteristics in a way that affects outcomes (Mittelstadt et al., 2016).

A well-known example is Amazon's AI-based recruitment tool, developed in 2014, which aimed to identify the "most qualified" candidates by analyzing résumés submitted over the previous decade. Because the training data predominantly consisted of applications from male candidates, the algorithm systematically disadvantaged female applicants (Dastin, 2018). Although the gender variable was not explicitly included, the system identified specific word patterns commonly used by male candidates—such as "captain," "executed," or "led"—as positive indicators while discounting terms more commonly associated with women (Cowgill et al., 2021). This case has become a prominent example in the literature of how proxy discrimination and learned bias can emerge in algorithmic decision-making. Although Amazon discontinued the tool in 2018, the case highlights how data-driven bias can permeate algorithmic systems and perpetuate historical inequalities (Raji & Buolamwini, 2019).

Interpretation Bias

The outputs of algorithmic systems are not shaped solely by their technical design or accuracy; they are also influenced by how users—exceptionally expert decision-makers—interpret and act upon them. When users uncritically accept algorithmic outputs or, conversely, disregard algorithmic recommendations altogether, the social impact of these systems can deviate significantly from their intended effects (Parasuraman & Riley, 1997). This phenomenon is referred to in the literature as automation bias or overreliance on algorithmic authority (Zerilli et al., 2019).

This issue is particularly evident in healthcare prediction systems. For example, if an algorithm classifies a patient as "high risk," the interpretation of this output can have direct implications for treatment. When clinicians place excessive trust in such predictions, any bias embedded in the training data may directly affect patient outcomes (Obermeyer & Mullainathan, 2019).

In such cases, human-algorithm interaction becomes as critical as the system's technical architecture. Research has shown that when users do not understand the rationale behind an algorithmic decision, they are more likely to conform to its recommendations (Bussone et al., 2015). This underscores the importance of explainability and transparency not only as technical attributes but also as ethical and clinical safeguards (London, 2019). Thus, the fairness and effectiveness of algorithmic decision-support systems depend not only on technical performance metrics but also on the critical and contextual interpretation by their users. In this light, it is emphasized that algorithms should not be treated as autonomous decision-makers but rather as explainable and supportive tools (Binns, 2018).

Table 2. Types and Examples of Algorithmic Bias

Bias Type	Definition	Example	Source
Representation Bias	Algorithms produce inaccurate and unfair results for specific groups due to underrepresentation or stereotypical representation of those groups in the training data.	While facial recognition algorithms are 99% accurate for light-skinned men, this rate drops to 65% for dark-skinned women. This difference is due to the overrepresentation of white men in the data.	Buolamwini & Gebru (2018), Barocas et al. (2019), Noble (2018).
Measurement/ Historical Bias	When algorithms are trained on data that reflects historical inequalities and institutional biases, they systematically reproduce those biases as they are.	Police patrol algorithms identify historically overpoliced neighborhoods as "high risk," a reflection of past practices rather than actual crime rates.	Richardson et al. (2019), Noble (2018), Akter et al. (2021).
Feature Selection Bias	Some variables that appear neutral on the surface (e.g., postal code) may indirectly disadvantage certain demographic groups.	Spatial variables such as postcode in credit scoring systems can indirectly penalize low-income or ethnic minority areas.	Hurley & Adebayo (2016), Nishant et al. (2023), Mittelstadt et al. (2016).
Algorithmic Processing Bias	Algorithms that learn through user interaction may produce biased results over time, and the system's technical architecture may create systematic disadvantages for specific groups.	The COMPAS algorithm incorrectly labeled black defendants as "high risk" more often than whites.	Angwin et al. (2016), Dressel & Farid (2018), Hardt et al. (2016), Binns (2018).
Outcome Bias	If the output consistently produces adverse outcomes for some social groups even when the algorithm is working correctly, this is output-based bias.	Amazon's hiring algorithm systematically under-scored and undervalued women because it was trained on male resumes.	Dastin (2018), Cowgill et al. (2021); Raji & Buolamwini (2019), Aiyer et al. (2024).
Interpretation Bias	Users accepting the algorithm output without questioning it or, conversely, completely ignoring the algorithm may lead to unfair or erroneous results.	Doctors may make incorrect interventions by treating individuals labeled as "high-risk patients" according to the system's recommendations.	Obermeyer & Mullainathan (2019), Bussone et al. (2015), London (2019), Zerilli et al. (2019).

EXAMPLES OF ALGORITHMIC BIAS BY DISCIPLINE

As the areas of use for algorithmic systems expand, it is evident that the biases caused by these technologies also manifest in discipline-specific forms. Since each field has its own data structure, decision processes, and social effects, the type, severity, and consequences of algorithmic bias also vary significantly depending on the context. Algorithms developed in fields such as health, law, education, finance, and public administration have become not only technical tools but also decision-makers that reflect social norms, inequalities, and institutional structures. Therefore, when analyzing the effects of algorithmic bias, it is necessary to consider not only general principles but also the specific dynamics of each discipline. Below, examples of algorithmic bias encountered in various disciplines are examined, and concretely, how these technologies can produce discrimination in practice is demonstrated.

Examples of Algorithmic Bias in the Field of Education

The use of artificial intelligence and data analytics systems in education is expanding rapidly. These technologies offer new possibilities in various domains, such as predicting student performance, identifying risks of absenteeism, estimating graduation probabilities, and providing personalized support services (Baker & Inventado, 2014). However, the algorithms and datasets used by these systems often raise significant ethical and pedagogical concerns by excluding or misrepresenting certain groups of students. For example, students living in rural areas, those with special education needs, or those belonging to minority communities are frequently underrepresented in educational technology datasets or are classified based on narrow patterns. This may result in such students being erroneously labeled by algorithmic systems as "at-risk" or as having "low academic potential" (Slade & Prinsloo, 2013).

Such classifications compromise the principle of educational equity and can negatively affect both student self-confidence and educators' pedagogical decisions. Biases in student assessment algorithms are not limited to demographic variables; they may also stem from factors such as socioeconomic status, disability, or affiliation with military families (Boyarskaya & Diakopoulos, 2020). AI-based grading systems, recommendation engines, and digital resource platforms may inadvertently exacerbate existing inequalities due to these biases (West et al., 2019).

Moreover, such biases can emerge not only in algorithmic outputs but throughout various stages of system development. Processes such as data collection, feature engineering, model training, and deployment can each affect different student groups in disparate ways (Binns, 2018). For instance, if data representing low-income students is insufficient, the unique learning needs of this group may be neglected, leading to solutions that lack inclusivity and contextual adequacy.

Examples of Algorithmic Bias in Finance and Digital Platforms

Algorithms used in financial services play a central role in processes such as credit scoring, risk assessment, and customer evaluation. These systems typically make predictions based on individuals' past financial behavior, credit histories, and consumption patterns. However, the incorporation of indirect variables—such as postal codes, shopping habits, or even social media activity—can increase the risk of structural discrimination and data-driven inequality (Hurley & Adebayo, 2016).

For instance, women entrepreneurs may receive lower credit scores than male entrepreneurs with similar financial profiles, or individuals with immigrant backgrounds may be automatically categorized as "high risk." These are concrete manifestations of algorithmic bias in finance (Citron & Pasquale, 2014). The underrepresentation of historically marginalized groups in financial datasets contributes to the misclassification of these populations (Eubanks, 2018), giving rise to representational bias and undermining fairness.

Similar biases are also prevalent on digital platforms beyond the financial sector. Discriminatory algorithmic outcomes have been documented in online advertising, job postings, and search engine functionalities. For example, high-paying job advertisements are shown more frequently to male users than to female users; search results for executive roles disproportionately feature male figures; and individuals with dark skin tones are more frequently associated with law enforcement or crime-related imagery (Datta et al., 2015; Kirkpatrick, 2016).

These examples illustrate how algorithms can reflect and perpetuate biases based on gender, race, and socioeconomic status. In this context, transparency, auditability, and fair representation in data-driven decision support systems have become essential ethical and legal imperatives in both finance and digital media. The absence of robust algorithmic accountability mechanisms increases the risk that such systems will reinforce discrimination rather than mitigate it (Noble, 2018).

Examples of Algorithmic Bias in Healthcare

The use of AI-assisted diagnostic, screening, and treatment recommendation systems is rapidly expanding in healthcare. These technologies support medical professionals across a wide range of applications—from clinical decision support and medical image analysis to patient triage systems and drug interaction alerts. However, the representativeness of the data used in developing these systems critically influences their accuracy and inclusiveness, raising significant ethical concerns (Obermeyer & Emanuel, 2016).

One of the most common forms of algorithmic bias in healthcare is representational bias. For instance, many imaging algorithms developed for melanoma (skin cancer) diagnosis have been trained predominantly on data from light-skinned individuals. This has resulted in significantly lower diagnostic accuracy for dark-skinned patients and potentially life-threatening delays in detection (Adamson & Smith, 2018). Similarly, some cardiovascular risk scoring systems have been validated primarily on male patients, leading to the underrecognition of atypical symptoms in women and resulting in misdiagnoses (Chapman et al., 2019).

Bias also emerges in applications specific to women's health, such as pregnancy monitoring and prediction of birth complications, due to the lack of diverse and representative data. Furthermore, individuals across the gender and sex spectrum—including transgender and intersex persons—are often underrepresented in medical datasets, limiting the algorithm's ability to make accurate predictions for these groups (Lee et al., 2022).

The development of COVID-19 risk assessment models during the pandemic highlighted how such biases can have severe global consequences in certain hospitals. Algorithms assigned lower risk scores to patients from low-income or minority groups, resulting in their reduced access to intensive care resources (Obermeyer et al., 2019).

In conclusion, for AI applications in healthcare to be ethical, fair, and trustworthy, attention must extend beyond technical accuracy to include principles such as data diversity, social representation, and impact assessment. Transparency in algorithm development, increased demographic diversity in clinical trials, and the establishment of continuous ethical oversight mechanisms are essential steps toward this goal.

Examples of Algorithmic Bias in the Legal Domain

Artificial intelligence (AI) and machine learning systems are being increasingly integrated into judicial decision-making processes. These systems are designed to assist legal actors, such as judges and parole boards, in areas including bail determinations, parole evaluations, risk assessments, and even sentencing recommendations. However, these applications bring significant ethical and justice-related challenges, particularly when producing data-driven predictions (Berk & Hyatt, 2015).

One of the most prominent examples is the Correctional Offender Management Profiling for Alternative Sanctions (COMPAS) algorithm, which is used to estimate the likelihood of recidivism among defendants. A landmark investigation by ProPublica in 2016 revealed that the algorithm systematically assigned higher risk scores to Black defendants compared to White defendants (Angwin et al., 2016). This led to Black individuals being disproportionately classified as "high-risk," while White defendants were more frequently assessed as lower risk.

The root cause of this bias lies in historical data collection bias—the algorithm was trained on criminal justice data reflecting long-standing racial disparities, such as the over-policing of Black communities. As Barocas and Selbst (2016) argue, structural racial inequalities are embedded in historical data, which algorithms may reproduce if left unchecked.

COMPAS is not an isolated case. Other legal algorithms exhibit similar problems. For example, "predictive policing" systems deployed by some police departments aim to identify high-crime areas but often end up targeting neighborhoods that have historically experienced excessive police surveillance—areas predominantly inhabited by Black and Latinx populations (Lum & Isaac, 2016). These systems can create self-reinforcing feedback loops, perpetuating existing biases over time (Ensign et al., 2018).

Furthermore, criticisms have been raised regarding algorithms used in U.S. immigration courts and deportation proceedings, where minority groups appear to be systematically disadvantaged (Brayne, 2021). A recurring concern is the lack of transparency: algorithmic decisions are often opaque, and their underlying reasoning is not accessible to legal practitioners or defendants.

Although the use of AI in legal contexts may enhance efficiency and consistency, its potential to reinforce entrenched social inequalities has been widely criticized. Therefore, any implementation must be accompanied by robust frameworks for accountability, transparency, and fairness to safeguard the principles of justice.

ALGORITHMIC BIAS IN PUBLIC ADMINISTRATION

The use of algorithms in public administration is increasingly widespread in areas such as decision support systems, resource allocation, risk analysis, service prioritization, and citizen classification. However, the assumption that these technologies are impartial and objective cannot prevent the emergence of various biases in their practical application. In particular, the use of incomplete, inaccurate, or unbalanced data regarding historically marginalized communities can lead to algorithmic decisions that work against certain groups. Additionally, the social, economic, and political contexts in which public policies are developed also facilitate the institutionalization of biases embedded in algorithmic processes. The evaluation of citizens by algorithmic systems on sensitive issues, such as security, social assistance, or immigration, raises serious debates in terms of both democratic accountability and governance principles. In this context, the reasons for algorithmic bias in public administration and examples of algorithmic bias seen in the field of public administration will be discussed below, and a general framework will be drawn on the subject.

Causes of Algorithmic Bias in Public Administration

Public administration is increasingly employing algorithmic systems and decision-support tools in critical domains, such as resource allocation, citizen services, welfare programs, and public safety. This digitalization trend is primarily driven by the goals of enhancing efficiency, speed, and objectivity in the delivery of public services (Eubanks, 2018). However, algorithmic bias in public administration arises from a range of structural and institutional factors, including data representational imbalances, lack of transparency, and disparities in institutional capacity. These dynamics reveal that algorithms are not merely neutral technical instruments but can also reflect and reinforce existing structural inequalities.

One primary source of algorithmic bias in public administration is data representational inequality. Public sector datasets are often derived from historically accumulated records that may already encode systemic disparities. For instance, certain ethnic groups may be overrepresented in social welfare applications or regions subject to more frequent inspections or surveillance. When such data are used in algorithmic systems, they can lead to the classification of these groups as "high-risk" or "costly," regardless of individual circumstances (O'Neil, 2016). Similarly, the underrepresentation of minority populations, rural communities, or immigrants can result in inadequate or distorted algorithmic assessments of these groups.

Despite expectations that public sector decision-making should be neutral and equitable, algorithms can inherit normative assumptions from their developers and the context in which they are created. This challenges the principle of political neutrality. For example, automated welfare eligibility assessment systems often reduce complex concepts, such as "deservingness" or "need," to rigid technical criteria, thereby reproducing normative judgments about poverty and marginality in a coded form (Young et al., 2019).

Another critical issue is the lack of transparency and accountability. Many algorithms used in public institutions are developed by private firms and are protected under "trade secret" claims, which restrict public scrutiny. This lack of openness can prevent stakeholders from challenging decisions or seeking recourse, undermining citizens' legal rights (Veale & Brass, 2019). A notable case is the Dutch SyRI (System Risk Indication) algorithm, developed to detect welfare fraud. The system sparked legal and social controversy when it was revealed that the criteria used to assign risk scores were not publicly disclosed (van Eck & Leurs, 2020).

Variations in governance capacity across institutions also contribute to the emergence of algorithmic bias. Public organizations differ in their levels of digital literacy, ethical oversight mechanisms, and abilities to assess the impact of algorithmic tools. In particular, limited capacity at the local government level increases the risk of unmonitored and uncritical algorithm deployment, weakening institutional accountability (Bullock, 2019).

Moreover, policy-embedded biases may manifest algorithmically when algorithms reflect the ideological assumptions of the policies they are designed to enforce. For instance, an algorithm developed to manage immigration control may implement stricter surveillance measures that align with a politically exclusionary agenda. Even if the algorithm appears technically neutral, it may nonetheless produce discriminatory outcomes (Amoore, 2020).

In conclusion, algorithmic bias in public administration emerges from multiple sources throughout the lifecycle of algorithmic systems. A primary cause is biased or unrepresentative training data, which can reflect and perpetuate existing social inequalities or stereotypes, particularly when demographic features correlate with sensitive outcomes or when data collection is flawed or incomplete (Thais et al., 2023; Kirkpatrick, 2016; Fazelpour & Danks, 2021). Bias may also be introduced during problem specification, model design, or deployment contexts, where algorithms mechanically optimize for formalized criteria without accounting for complex social realities. This may result in decisions that are neither contextually appropriate nor ethically fair (Thais et al., 2023; Nishant et al., 2023).

Human factors further complicate this landscape. Public officials may selectively rely on algorithmic outputs that align with their preexisting biases or may over-depend on algorithmic recommendations due to a lack of awareness or institutional pressure (Alon-Barkat & Busuioc, 2021; Adomavicius & Yang, 2022). Additionally, the broader sociotechnical environment—including organizational culture, regulatory frameworks, and prevailing societal norms—shapes how algorithms are interpreted and used. If not carefully governed, these influences may compound algorithmic bias (Kordzadeh & Ghasemaghaei, 2021; Lee, 2022).

Addressing algorithmic bias in public administration, therefore, requires more than just technical interventions. It necessitates attention to human behavior, institutional dynamics, policy intentions, and sustained oversight mechanisms to ensure fairness, accountability, and equity in algorithm-informed public decision-making (Fazelpour & Danks, 2021; Adomavicius & Yang, 2022; Thais et al., 2023).

Examples of Algorithmic Bias in Public Administration

In public administration, algorithms are increasingly employed across various domains, including welfare distribution, tax auditing, immigration control, and risk classification. However, some of these applications have been shown to disadvantage specific social groups systematically—either directly or indirectly. The following cases illustrate such outcomes:

1. The SyRI Case – Netherlands

In 2014, the Netherlands implemented an algorithmic system known as Systeem Risico Indicatie (SyRI) to detect potential social welfare and tax fraud. However, the criteria and logic underpinning the system's risk scoring were not publicly disclosed. Moreover, SyRI was disproportionately deployed in low-income neighborhoods predominantly populated by immigrants. In 2020, the District Court of The Hague ruled that the system violated human rights due to its lack of transparency and discriminatory effects (van Eck & Leurs, 2020). The SyRI case has since become a paradigmatic example of how algorithmic systems can perpetuate bias when transparency and accountability are lacking.

2. MI-DSS – United States (Michigan)

The Michigan Integrated Data Automated System (MI-DSS) was introduced in 2013 to assess the risk of child abuse and neglect. The system disproportionately flagged low-income and African American families as high-risk, leading to numerous unnecessary family separations (Eubanks, 2018). This case highlights how representational imbalances in data and embedded structural biases can lead to discriminatory outcomes, even in systems designed to protect vulnerable populations.

3. COMPAS Algorithm – United States

The Correctional Offender Management Profiling for Alternative Sanctions (COMPAS) algorithm, widely used as a risk assessment tool in the U.S. justice system, has received significant criticism for producing racially biased outcomes. While it is often discussed in the context of legal decision-making, COMPAS also plays a significant role in the administrative functions of public governance, such as resource allocation by state courts and decisions on pretrial detention (Angwin et al., 2016). The case exemplifies how algorithmic tools in the public sector can perpetuate inequality even when used for ostensibly neutral administrative purposes.

4. "No-Fly List" and Immigration Screening – United States

In the U.S., the Department of Homeland Security utilizes algorithms to manage its "No-Fly List" and conduct immigration screenings. These systems operate based on undisclosed criteria, often labeling individuals as security threats without justifying their actions. Numerous reports and critiques have highlighted the disproportionate targeting of individuals from specific ethnic and religious groups—particularly those of Muslim descent (Pasquale, 2015). This illustrates how policy-embedded biases can become institutionalized through algorithmic mechanisms in public administration.

5. Automated Welfare Assessment Systems – United Kingdom

Several local governments in the United Kingdom have adopted automated systems to evaluate social welfare applications. However, investigations have shown that these systems are more likely to subject low-income applicants to intensive scrutiny and request additional documentation more frequently from non-white applicants (Veale & Brass, 2019). These findings reveal how biased classification algorithms can reinforce existing inequalities and hinder equitable access to public services.

CONCLUSION

Algorithmic bias is not merely a technological flaw but rather an inevitable reflection of existing societal structures encoded into digital systems. Within the context of public administration, this phenomenon acquires particular urgency and significance. The state is fundamentally obligated to uphold principles of equality, justice, and transparency in its interactions with citizens. However, the integration of algorithmic decision-support systems into public services poses serious risks to these foundational values.

The core issue underlying algorithmic bias in public governance lies in the widespread misconception that such systems offer "objectivity" and "efficiency," while in reality, they are deeply contextual and political. Case studies such as SyRI, MI-DSS, COMPAS, and the U.S. No-Fly List have made it abundantly clear:

"Technical Objectivity" Is an Illusion: Algorithms are not immune to the historical and social context embedded in the data they consume. Public data—such as police surveillance records, welfare applications, or judicial statistics—often reflect institutional discrimination, uneven resource distribution, and longstanding societal biases. When algorithms are trained on such data, they reproduce and institutionalize existing inequalities under the guise of neutrality. This is not merely a matter of "data bias" but rather an encoding of institutional memory and political choices into technology.

Transparency and Accountability Are Democratic Imperatives: The fact that public sector algorithms are often kept opaque under the pretext of "trade secrets" or "national security" severely undermines democratic oversight. Citizens have the right to understand and challenge decisions that significantly impact their lives—such as being denied welfare benefits, being categorized as high-risk, or being refused immigration status. A lack of transparency is thus not only a technical flaw but a violation of civic rights and a crisis of legitimacy in public administration.

Algorithms Are Vehicles of Political Values: Public policies inherently reflect normative priorities—such as tightening immigration control, combating welfare fraud, or prioritizing certain types of crime. Algorithms, when used to implement these policies, act as tools that conceal their political nature under a veneer of technical neutrality. Far from being passive instruments, they can actively amplify the discriminatory effects of the underlying policies they encode.

Institutional Capacity and Ethical Sensitivity Are Critical: Public institutions vary significantly in their ability to understand, regulate, and ethically evaluate algorithmic systems. Local governments and smaller agencies often lack the resources or expertise to manage these complex tools responsibly. Additionally, excessive reliance on "algorithmic authority" or the legitimization of bureaucrats' personal biases through algorithmic outputs can degrade the quality of public decision-making and reinforce unjust outcomes.

Key Implications for Public Administration

From Data-Centric to Context-Sensitive Approaches: The development and procurement of public algorithms must go beyond technical accuracy to critically assess the historical and societal context of the data used. Methodologies for mapping and correcting potential biases in datasets should be systematically developed and implemented.

Mandatory Transparency and Oversight: The core principles, key variables, and performance metrics of public algorithms—especially their differential impacts across demographic groups—must be made publicly accessible and understandable. Independent audit and ethical oversight mechanisms should be established to ensure transparency and accountability.

Primacy and Responsibility of Human Judgment: Algorithms should serve as decision-support tools, not as final arbiters of judgment. Public officials must be trained to critically evaluate algorithmic outputs through the application of contextual reasoning and ethical judgment. Institutional cultures should encourage such scrutiny, with ultimate responsibility for decisions remaining with humans.

Citizen Participation and Right to Appeal: Citizens affected by algorithmic decisions must be guaranteed the right to understand the rationale behind those decisions and to access meaningful mechanisms for appeal. This should be a standard of public service quality and rights protection in the digital age.

Capacity Building and Ethical Culture: Public institutions must enhance their technical, legal, and ethical capacities to manage algorithmic systems responsibly and effectively. A shift from "technology-driven" to "human-centered" and "rights-based" digital transformation is essential.

Ultimately, algorithmic bias in public administration cannot be solved by simply "better technology." It poses a complex governance and ethical challenge that redefines the relationship between the state and its citizens in the digital age. It raises urgent questions about how democratic values (equality, justice, transparency, and accountability) can be realized in algorithmically mediated systems. Public administration must, therefore, pursue the promise of technological efficiency without compromising its fundamental commitment to public values. Otherwise, algorithms risk becoming tools that erode impartiality and fairness in public services, deepen existing social inequalities, and undermine democratic accountability.

REFERENCES

Adamson, A. S., & Smith, A. (2018). Machine learning and health care disparities in dermatology. *JAMA Dermatology, 154*(11), 1247–1248. DOI: 10.1001/jamadermatol.2018.2348 PMID: 30073260

Adomavicius, G., & Yang, M. (2022). Integrating Behavioral, Economic, and Technical Insights to Understand and Address Algorithmic Bias: A Human-Centric Perspective. [TMIS]. *ACM Transactions on Management Information Systems, 13*(3), 1–27. DOI: 10.1145/3519420

Aiyer, S., Chan, W., & Feldman, G. (2024). Outcome Bias in Evaluations of Ethical Decisions: Replication and Extensions of Gino, Moore, and Bazerman (2009). *Collabra. Psychology, 10*(1), 126266. Advance online publication. DOI: 10.1525/collabra.126266

Akter, S., Dwivedi, Y., Sajib, S., Biswas, K., Bandara, R., & Michael, K. (2022). Algorithmic bias in machine learning-based marketing models. *Journal of Business Research, 144*, 201–216. Advance online publication. DOI: 10.1016/j.jbusres.2022.01.083

Akter, S., McCarthy, G., Sajib, S., Michael, K., Dwivedi, Y., D'Ambra, J., & Shen, K. (2021). Algorithmic bias in data-driven innovation in the age of AI. *International Journal of Information Management, 60*, 102387. DOI: 10.1016/j.ijinfomgt.2021.102387

Alon-Barkat, S., & Busuioc, M. (2021). Human-AI Interactions in Public Sector Decision-Making:"Automation Bias"and"Selective Adherence"to Algorithmic Advice. . .DOI: 10.1093/jopart/muac007

Angwin, J., Larson, J., Mattu, S., & Kirchner, L. (2016). "Machine Bias." *ProPublica*. https://www.propublica.org/article/machine-bias-risk-assessments-in-criminal-sentencing

Baker, R., & Hawn, A. (2021). Algorithmic Bias in Education. *International Journal of Artificial Intelligence in Education, 32*(4), 1052–1092. DOI: 10.1007/s40593-021-00285-9

Baker, R. S., & Inventado, P. S. (2014). Educational data mining and learning analytics. In Larusson, J., & White, B. (Eds.), *Learning analytics: From research to practice* (pp. 61–75). Springer. DOI: 10.1007/978-1-4614-3305-7_4

Barocas, S., Hardt, M., & Narayanan, A. (2019). *Fairness and Machine Learning: Limitations and Opportunities*. https://fairmlbook.org

Barocas, S., & Selbst, A. D. (2016). Big data's disparate impact. *California Law Review*, *104*(3), 671–732.

Berk, R., & Hyatt, J. (2015). Machine learning forecasts of risk to inform sentencing decisions. *Federal Sentencing Reporter*, *27*(4), 222–228. DOI: 10.1525/fsr.2015.27.4.222

Binns, R. (2018). "Fairness in Machine Learning: Lessons from Political Philosophy." *Proceedings of the 2018 Conference on Fairness, Accountability and Transparency (FAT*)*, 149–159.

Boyarskaya, M., & Diakopoulos, N. (2020). Algorithmic bias in student grading: Implications for fairness and equity. *AI & Society*, *35*(4), 897–910.

Brayne, S. (2021). *Predict and Surveil: Data, Discretion, and the Future of Policing*. Oxford University Press.

Bullock, J. B. (2019). Artificial intelligence, discretion, and bureaucracy. *American Review of Public Administration*, *49*(7), 751–761. DOI: 10.1177/0275074019856123

Buolamwini, J., & Gebru, T. (2018). *Gender Shades: Intersectional Accuracy Disparities in Commercial Gender Classification*. In *Proceedings of the Conference on Fairness, Accountability and Transparency (FAT)**, 77–91.

Bussone, A., Stumpf, S., & O'Sullivan, D. (2015). "The Role of Explanations on Trust and Reliance in Clinical Decision Support Systems." *CHI '15 Extended Abstracts on Human Factors in Computing Systems*, 1701–1706. https://doi.org/DOI: 10.1145/2702613.2733313

Castillo, C. (2019). Algorithmic Bias in Rankings. Companion Proceedings of The 2019 World Wide Web Conference. DOI: 10.1145/3308560.3316451

Chapman, A. R.. (2019). High-sensitivity cardiac troponin and the underdiagnosis of myocardial infarction in women: Prospective cohort study. *BMJ (Clinical Research Ed.)*, *363*, k5094.

Citron, D. K., & Pasquale, F. (2014). The scored society: Due process for automated predictions. *Washington Law Review (Seattle, Wash.)*, *89*(1), 1–33.

Cowgill, B., Dell'Acqua, F., & Deng, S. (2021). "Biased Programmers? Or Biased Data? A Field Experiment in Operationalizing AI Ethics." *Columbia Business School Research Paper No. 18-67*. https://doi.org/DOI: 10.2139/ssrn.3614776

Crawford, K. (2016). Artificial intelligence's white guy problem. The New York Times.

Crawford, K. (2021). *Atlas of AI: Power, Politics, and the Planetary Costs of Artificial Intelligence*. Yale University Press.

Danks, D., & London, A. (2017). Algorithmic Bias in Autonomous Systems., 4691-4697. .DOI: 10.24963/ijcai.2017/654

Dastin, J. (2018). "Amazon scraps secret AI recruiting tool that showed bias against women." *Reuters*. https://www.reuters.com/article/us-amazon-com-jobs-automation-insight-idUSKCN1MK08G

Datta, A., Tschantz, M. C., & Datta, A. (2015). Automated experiments on ad privacy settings: A tale of opacity, choice, and discrimination. *Proceedings on Privacy Enhancing Technologies. Privacy Enhancing Technologies Symposium*, *2015*(1), 92–112. DOI: 10.1515/popets-2015-0007

Dressel, J., & Farid, H. (2018). The Accuracy, Fairness, and Limits of Predicting Recidivism. *Science Advances*, *4*(1), eaao5580. Advance online publication. DOI: 10.1126/sciadv.aao5580 PMID: 29376122

Ensign, D., Friedler, S. A., Neville, S., Scheidegger, C., & Venkatasubramanian, S. (2018). Runaway feedback loops in predictive policing. *Proceedings of the 1st Conference on Fairness, Accountability and Transparency (FAT*)*, 160–171.

Eubanks, V. (2018). *Automating Inequality: How High-Tech Tools Profile, Police, and Punish the Poor*. St. Martin's Press.

Fazelpour, S., & Danks, D. (2021). Algorithmic bias: Senses, sources, solutions. *Philosophy Compass*, *16*(8), e12760. Advance online publication. DOI: 10.1111/phc3.12760

Flowerman, C. (2023). (Some) algorithmic bias as institutional bias. *Ethics and Information Technology*, *25*(2), 1–10. DOI: 10.1007/s10676-023-09698-7

Fu, R., Huang, Y., & Singh, P. (2020). AI and Algorithmic Bias: Source, Detection, Mitigation and Implications. *InfoSciRN: Machine Learning (Sub-Topic)*. DOI: 10.2139/ssrn.3681517

Hardt, M., Price, E., & Srebro, N. (2016). "Equality of Opportunity in Supervised Learning." *Advances in Neural Information Processing Systems (NeurIPS)*, 29.

Hurley, M., & Adebayo, J. (2016). Credit Scoring in the Era of Big Data. *Yale Journal of Law and Technology*, *18*(1), 148–216.

Johnson, G. (2020). Algorithmic bias: On the implicit biases of social technology. *Synthese*, *198*(10), 9941–9961. DOI: 10.1007/s11229-020-02696-y

Kim, J., & Cho, S. (2022). An information theoretic approach to reducing algorithmic bias for machine learning. *Neurocomputing*, *500*, 26–38. DOI: 10.1016/j.neucom.2021.09.081

Kirkpatrick, K. (2016). Battling algorithmic bias. *Communications of the ACM*, *59*(10), 16–17. DOI: 10.1145/2983270

König-Kersting, C., Pollmann, M., Potters, J., & Trautmann, S. (2020). Good decision vs. good results: Outcome bias in the evaluation of financial agents. *Theory and Decision*, *90*(1), 31–61. DOI: 10.1007/s11238-020-09773-1

Kordzadeh, N., & Ghasemaghaei, M. (2021). Algorithmic bias: Review, synthesis, and future research directions. *European Journal of Information Systems*, *31*(3), 388–409. DOI: 10.1080/0960085X.2021.1927212

Lee, H.. (2022). Health disparities and bias in machine learning models for medical imaging. *Radiology. Artificial Intelligence*, *4*(2), e210179.

Lee, J. (2022). Algorithmic bias and the New Chicago School. *Law, Innovation and Technology*, *14*(1), 95–112. DOI: 10.1080/17579961.2022.2047520

London, A. J. (2019). Artificial Intelligence and Black-Box Medical Decisions: Accuracy versus Explainability. *The Hastings Center Report*, *49*(1), 15–21. DOI: 10.1002/hast.973 PMID: 30790315

Lum, K., & Isaac, W. (2016). To predict and serve? *Significance*, *13*(5), 14–19. DOI: 10.1111/j.1740-9713.2016.00960.x

Mavrogiorgos, K., Kiourtis, A., Mavrogiorgou, A., Menychtas, A., & Kyriazis, D. (2024). Bias in Machine Learning: A Literature Review. *Applied Sciences (Basel, Switzerland)*, *14*(19), 8860. Advance online publication. DOI: 10.3390/app14198860

Mittelstadt, B. D., Allo, P., Taddeo, M., Wachter, S., & Floridi, L. (2016). The Ethics of Algorithms: Mapping the Debate. *Big Data & Society*, *3*(2), 2053951716679679. Advance online publication. DOI: 10.1177/2053951716679679

Nishant, R., Schneckenberg, D., & Ravishankar, M. (2023). The formal rationality of artificial intelligence-based algorithms and the problem of bias. *Journal of Information Technology*, *39*(1), 19–40. DOI: 10.1177/02683962231176842

Noble, S. U. (2018). *Algorithms of Oppression: How Search Engines Reinforce Racism*. NYU Press. DOI: 10.18574/nyu/9781479833641.001.0001

O'Neil, C. (2016). *Weapons of Math Destruction: How Big Data Increases Inequality and Threatens Democracy*. Crown Publishing Group.

Obermeyer, Z., & Emanuel, E. J. (2016). Predicting the future—Big data, machine learning, and clinical medicine. *The New England Journal of Medicine*, *375*(13), 1216–1219. DOI: 10.1056/NEJMp1606181 PMID: 27682033

Obermeyer, Z., Powers, B., Vogeli, C., & Mullainathan, S. (2019). Dissecting racial bias in an algorithm used to manage the health of populations. *Science*, *366*(6464), 447–453. DOI: 10.1126/science.aax2342 PMID: 31649194

Parasuraman, R., & Riley, V. (1997). Humans and Automation: Use, Misuse, Disuse, Abuse. *Human Factors*, *39*(2), 230–253. DOI: 10.1518/001872097778543886

Pariser, E. (2011). *The Filter Bubble: What the Internet Is Hiding from You*. Penguin Press.

Pasquale, F. (2015). *The Black Box Society: The Secret Algorithms That Control Money and Information*. Harvard University Press. DOI: 10.4159/harvard.9780674736061

Raji, I. D., & Buolamwini, J. (2019). "Actionable Auditing: Investigating the Impact of Publicly Naming Biased Performance Results of Commercial AI Products." *AAAI/ACM Conference on AI, Ethics, and Society*, 429–435. DOI: 10.1145/3306618.3314244

Richardson, R., Schultz, J. M., & Crawford, K. (2019). Dirty Data, Bad Predictions: How Civil Rights Violations Impact Police Data, Predictive Policing Systems, and Justice. *New York University Law Review*, *94*(1), 192–233.

Slade, S., & Prinsloo, P. (2013). Learning analytics: Ethical issues and dilemmas. *The American Behavioral Scientist*, *57*(10), 1510–1529. DOI: 10.1177/0002764213479366

Sun, W., Nasraoui, O., & Shafto, P. (2020). Evolution and impact of bias in human and machine learning algorithm interaction. *PLoS One*, *15*(8), e0235502. Advance online publication. DOI: 10.1371/journal.pone.0235502 PMID: 32790666

Thais, S., Shumway, H., & Saragih, A. (2023). *Algorithmic bias: Looking beyond data bias to ensure algorithmic accountability and equity*. MIT Science Policy Review., DOI: 10.38105/spr.5lwvw66ssy

van Eck, M., & Leurs, K. (2020). Data justice and the welfare state: Lessons from the Dutch SyRI case. *Internet Policy Review*, *9*(4).

Veale, M., & Brass, I. (2019). Administration by algorithm? Public management meets algorithmic governance. *Public Administration Review*, *79*(4), 567–581.

West, S. M., Whittaker, M., & Crawford, K. (2019). *Discriminating Systems: Gender, Race, and Power in AI*. AI Now Institute.

Xu, J., Xiao, Y., Wang, W., Ning, Y., Shenkman, E., Bian, J., & Wang, F. (2022). Algorithmic fairness in computational medicine. *EBioMedicine*, *84*, 104250. Advance online publication. DOI: 10.1016/j.ebiom.2022.104250 PMID: 36084616

Young, M., et al. (2019). Artificial intelligence and public standards: A review by the UK Committee on Standards in Public Life.

Zerilli, J., Knott, A., Maclaurin, J., & Gavaghan, C. (2019). Algorithmic Decision-Making and the Control Problem. *Minds and Machines*, *29*(4), 555–578. DOI: 10.1007/s11023-019-09513-7

Chapter 8
AI-Based Chatbots in Public Service Delivery: The Case of BAGBI in Türkiye

Sebiha Düz
https://orcid.org/0000-0002-1706-6001
Süleyman Demirel University, Turkey

ABSTRACT

This study examines the chatbot application named BAGBI of Bağcılar Municipality, which is an important example of artificial intelligence-supported service delivery in local governments in Türkiye. The role played by chatbot technologies in the digital transformation process of public services is discussed in the contexts of public value production, accessibility, participatory governance and data-based decision-making. In-depth interview technique, which is one of the qualitative research methods, was used in the study; interviews were conducted with experts from the IT Department who took a crucial part in the design and implementation processes of BAGBI. The interview data were analyzed with thematic analysis method, and findings were obtained especially in the project's design process, service quality, institutional capacity, citizen interaction and ethical dimensions. The obtained data reveal that BAGBI is not only a technical innovation, but also a transformation tool that reshapes the administrative and conceptual boundaries of digitalized public services at the local level.

INTRODUCTION

Following the 21st century's onset, technology has reshaped the structures and norms of public administration. Municipalities, with their direct and continuous

DOI: 10.4018/979-8-3373-1484-6.ch008

contact with citizens, are at the forefront of this digitalization. By moving service delivery from physical offices to digital channels, they enhance access to public services, shorten transaction times, and accelerate information flows.

One of the most prominent instruments of this transformation is chatbot technology. Chatbots are rule-based or AI-driven software systems that interact with users via text or speech by employing predefined rules or advanced natural language processing (NLP) techniques, enabling automated yet context-sensitive communication. In public administration, they both facilitate access to information and perform multiple functions such as processing requests, providing guidance, initiating transactions, and collecting feedback.

Given the diversity of local government services, the adaptability, flexibility, and cost-effectiveness of chatbots make them highly attractive for municipalities. Many have adopted them on a pilot or full scale to interact with citizens 24/7, standardize information requests, and reduce workforce demands. Yet, chatbots represent more than technical innovation: they embody a broader transformation that intersects with governance, ethics, equality, and participation.

This study investigates AI-based chatbot use in local governments from conceptual, applied, and critical perspectives. It defines chatbots, explores their functions and potentials, and evaluates their adoption with international examples. In Türkiye, the Bağcılar Municipality's chatbot BAGBI is analyzed through thematic interpretation of interview data with municipal officials.

Bağcılar's digital transformation began in the early 2000s with Management Information Systems and a focus on data-based architecture. In 2012, the municipality launched a process-based MIS enabling online applications and monitoring, which laid the groundwork for AI adoption. In 2019–2020, two major AI products were introduced: the Smart Application System and the BAGBI chatbot, evolving from a rule-based virtual assistant into a generative AI with machine learning and deep learning features.

This research is among the first to examine AI-based chatbots in Türkiye's local administrations, focusing on their role in delivering public services. The central question is: "How does a municipality's AI-based chatbot affect public value creation in the context of services, administrative processes, and citizen relations?"

A distinctive aspect lies in BAGBI, Türkiye's first AI-based municipal chatbot. With its vision of becoming a pioneering municipality, Bağcılar launched the rule-based system on April 21, 2021, and has since advanced to an AI-based assistant. Developed by their IT Department, BAGBI completed testing successfully and now operates via the municipality's website.

This study is explicitly limited in scope to a qualitative case study of Bağcılar Municipality's AI-based chatbot application, BAGBİ, which constitutes a pioneering initiative in the delivery of digital public services at the local government level in

Türkiye. The research does not seek to provide a comprehensive analysis of all AI applications in public administration; rather, it concentrates on this single case in order to examine the opportunities and challenges associated with the integration of AI-based chatbot technologies into municipal service provision. However, the study's concentration on a single AI-based chatbot, together with Bağcılar Municipality's longstanding trajectory of digital transformation and comparatively high level of digital maturity, constitutes a significant limitation for the direct generalization of the findings to other local governments in Türkiye. Municipalities differ considerably in their digital capacity, human resources, and levels of technological adoption, and in some cases chatbot initiatives may serve as little more than symbolic or cosmetic tools. Accordingly, while this study offers valuable insights into the potential and implications of AI-enabled chatbots in the delivery of public services, it also underscores the necessity of further research across diverse institutional and contextual settings to enable broader and more robust generalizations.

THEORETICAL AND CONCEPTUAL FRAMEWORK

Conceptual Foundations of Chatbot Technology and Its Role in Public Services

A chatbot is defined as a type of software that can interact with people through AI-based algorithms. These systems undertake functions such as providing users with rapid responses, providing information, supporting product or service procurement processes, and improving the user experience. Chatbots are digital assistants that can communicate with users in natural language, in written or vocal form. These systems generally work on two main bases: the first is "rule-based" chatbots that respond according to command systems based on fixed rules; the second is "AI-based" chatbots that use artificial intelligence and natural language processing (NLP) techniques and improve themselves with machine learning.

AI-based chatbot technologies have become an increasingly strategic tool in the public sphere and public services. Public institutions are integrating these technologies into their service processes to increase transparency, accessibility, and efficiency in their interactions with citizens. Thus, chatbots are becoming a key component of digital transformation and innovative service delivery in public administration, going beyond simply being a communication tool that instantly responds to citizens' requests for information.

From ELIZA (ELIZA, 1966), one of the first chatbot examples, to the present day, these technologies have both interacted technically and with issues such as management, communication and ethics in social sciences (Makasi et al., 2020). In public administration, chatbots mitigate administrative burden in high-demand service areas while simultaneously enhancing citizen satisfaction. The main function here is automation together with the reproduction of public values such as transparency, accountability, and participation through technology (Senadheera et al., 2024).

Chatbot technology in the public sector can be classified around four basic functions. Chatbots, which can be accessed via municipalities' websites or mobile applications, provide citizens with quick access to information by answering frequently asked questions and directing them to the service they request. Alongside time savings, this function plays a role in minimizing staff workload in public institutions. Some chatbots can initiate or direct transactions such as tax payment, appointment making, and document delivery. This application is one of the most advanced examples of the digital transformation of public services. Chatbots can also integrate citizens' requests and suggestions into municipal systems. In this respect, chatbots become tools that not only provide information, but also collect information and contribute to the governance process.

Various studies in the literature have examined the integration of chatbots into public services from theoretical, experimental and practical perspectives. With the acceleration of digital transformation processes in public administration, AI-based chatbot technologies have begun to transform the way public services are provided. This transformation constitutes a technical innovation together with a range of normative dimensions, including public values, citizen satisfaction, governance principles, and digital inclusiveness. Studies in the literature have addressed how chatbots are positioned in public institutions, for what purposes they are used and what kind of effects they create from different perspectives. In addition to operational functions, chatbot technologies have also brought about many governance issues such as communication with citizens, service quality, public value creation and digital inclusiveness.

Makasi, Nili, Desouza, and Tate (2020) state that chatbots are not just technical tools, but digital actors that should be designed in the context of public service values. The same researchers (2022) propose participatory design principles for the public, addressing the contradictions between developers and citizens' expectations of public values. Dube (2024) also focused on the potential of chatbots to create public value, emphasizing the importance of digital public services that are compatible with ethical principles.

Senadheera et al. (2024) analyzed the factors affecting chatbot adoption in local governments (trust, openness, accessibility), while Ma'rup & Rokhman (2024) demonstrated through meta-analysis that digital infrastructure deficiencies may limit success.

Li and Wang (2024) on the other hand, examined the effects of chatbot identity features on citizen perception, while Wiethölter, Kühl, and Feldmann (2024) defined chatbots as strategic information management tools. Song (2022) showed that voice chatbots increase access opportunities for groups that are digitally excluded.

Huang & Gan (2023) emphasize that chatbots encourage citizen participation in smart cities and are especially effective in processes such as urban planning. Zhou, Liu, and Feng (2024) stated that chatbots with empathic communication skills increase citizen satisfaction. In the study by Abbas, Følstad, and Bjørkli (2023), it is shown that the main factors shaping the intention to use chatbots from user interviews are performance, trust, and effort expectation.

In an experimental study, Aoki (2020) shows that citizens' initial trust in chatbots is directly related to the service area and the communication strategy of the public institution. Wang, Zhang, and Zhao (2022) analyzed the determinants at different stages of AI adoption in China and stated that public portal quality has a positive effect on adoption.

The integration of chatbot technology into public institutions is a process that requires not only technical but also governance and institutional capacity. Medaglia, Mikalef, and Tangi (2024) emphasize that strategic governance, audit mechanisms, and institutional competencies are essential for the effective management of chatbots.

In their study titled "New Wine in Old Bottles", Van Noordt and Misuraca (2019) analyze the disruptions that new generation technologies (especially chatbots) can create in traditional public administration structures. Chatbots can promote new forms of governance that contradict old bureaucratic structures. The "AI Watch" report (Misuraca & Van Noordt, 2020) is one of the pioneering studies examining the use of AI and especially chatbots in public services across Europe. While mapping the development of AI-based services, the study shows that chatbots are preferred especially in terms of cost-effectiveness and service continuity. In another study (2022), the same researchers examine the use of AI throughout the public sector in European Union countries. Chatbots stand out as a common practice in local governments in terms of facilitating communication with citizens, digitizing feedback mechanisms and providing more inclusive services.

Grimmelikhuijsen and Tangi (2024) examined the perceptions of public administrators about chatbots and revealed that these technologies are generally seen as operational tools, while governance and democratic functions remain secondary. Maragno et al. (2023), in their study titled "AI as an Organizational Agent", argues that Chatbots embody a dual role, functioning as practical tools while also symbolizing institutional representation, transforming the way citizens experience the institution.

Kaun and Männiste (2025) addressed the "AI frictions" associated with the data infrastructure of public sector chatbots, stating that the tendency of systems to provide fixed responses that match certain keywords can limit citizen communication. In this context, it is argued that public sector chatbots should also be designed to respond contextually.

Gerontas et al. (2022) emphasize the importance of chatbot integration into digital infrastructures developed for the personalization of public services. Chatbots increase the efficiency of local governments by facilitating the provision of personalized information and services to citizens. Nirala, Singh, and Purani (2022) gave the example of the citizen-focused chatbot "AadhaarBot" developed for the public service AadhaarCard in the Indian context. Rathnayake et al. (2025) A study on e-government chatbots in Sri Lanka revealed that the sense of trust and the design of the bot play an important role in users' perceptions.

Larsen and Følstad (2024) analyzed the effects of chatbots on public service delivery through qualitative interviews with citizens and public officials, emphasizing the functionality of chatbots, especially in feedback and satisfaction mechanisms. Følstad and Bjerkreim-Hanssen (2023) on the other hand, examined user dialogues with a municipal chatbot and made inferences about the quality of communication.

Cortés-Cediel et al. (2023) analyze the trends of e-government chatbots in the areas of open data and citizen participation, especially pointing to issues of access to information and content quality. Dreyling et al. (2024) evaluate the technical, managerial, legal and ethical challenges of using generative (Gen)AI-based chatbots in public services with a holistic review, based on the example of Bürokratt in Estonia, while also offering solutions on user expectations, security, privacy and transparency.

In addition, in the case of Türkiye, while the "Chatbot Application and ChatGPT Example Evaluation Report" (2023), published by the Presidency of the Digital Transformation Office of the Republic of Türkiye, which was dissolved in 2025, aims to evaluate chatbot applications in general and the ChatGPT example in particular. It comprehensively evaluates the history, security risks, benefits and ethical issues of chatbot technology; Tamer (2025) discusses whether AI-based chatbots can be considered as a type of digital civil servant in public service and evaluates this situation from utopian or dystopian perspectives.

The literature shows that beyond facilitating access to information, chatbots have the potential to reshape the representation forms of public institutions, their communication with citizens and the production processes of public value. However, in order to realize this potential, institutional capacity, ethical audit and user-centered design approaches must be adopted in a holistic manner.

In addition to the existing literature, the inclusion of context-specific case examples from local governments would enhance the empirical grounding and practical relevance of the discussion. Over the past years, various local governments around the world have implemented AI-based chatbots in different service areas. Below are some application examples compiled from the Govlaunch platform (defined as "a wiki for government innovation") (Pica-Alfano, n.d.). These application examples are valuable in showing how chatbots are used in practice and what kind of results are achieved.

The first example is a WhatsApp-based chatbot that was launched by the Kolkata Municipality in India in 2021 to speed up the COVID-19 vaccination process. Integrated into a messaging platform that is widely used by the public, this chatbot made it easier for citizens to make vaccination appointments online. Initially integrated with only 3 vaccination centers, the bot was expanded to cover more than 100 centers in a short time to respond to demand. In this way, Kolkata was able to effectively manage appointment processes during the busy vaccination period.

Secondly, the city of Los Angeles has launched a chatbot called "Chip" to help companies and individuals seeking information on public procurement and purchasing processes. Known for "City Hall Internet Personality," Chip has been trained to answer approximately 700 of the most frequently asked questions by contractors looking to do business with the municipality. After going live, this AI assistant has gained great success in a short time by expanding its knowledge through real user interactions. This example is considered a good example of how chatbots can increase efficiency in municipalities' internal business processes.

Another example is the City of Boston, which has made it easier for citizens to access food aid with a permanent SMS-based chatbot, following the success of a food distribution chatbot it developed during the pandemic. This service, implemented by the City's Food Access Office, works via text messaging without requiring an internet connection and provides services in the city's 8 most spoken languages. Using this bot, citizens can learn about the nearest food banks or free food distribution points, and if necessary, they can contact institutions that will donate food. Designed specifically for those who cannot use the internet or do not have a smartphone, this solution is a good example of the use of chatbots as an inclusive tool in social services, aiming to reduce digital exclusion.

The City of Derby in the United Kingdom has implemented a chatbot on Facebook Messenger as part of a public health-related smoking cessation campaign. Created to support the national "Stoptober" campaign, this bot provided instant motivational messages and informative content to citizens who wanted to quit smoking. A small game and distracting activities were also integrated to make the experience more interactive and help reduce users' stress. Many citizens used this digital support line during the campaign; the municipality reported that thanks to the chatbot, participants' retention rates increased. The Derby example shows that chatbots can also be used creatively in the field of behavioral public policies.

Ronneby, a town with a population of 12,000 in Sweden, uses chatbots not only for citizens but also to provide internal services to municipal employees. The internal service chatbot called "BerIT" was developed to answer frequently asked IT (information technology) questions by employees of the institution. During the implementation or updating of new software systems, employees often raise similar concerns or inquiries. BerIT steps in and provides instant answers, thus reducing the burden on the IT department. Ronneby Municipality states that the BerIT project saves time by automating routine IT support requests in particular and allows expert personnel to focus on more complex issues. This application shows that chatbots can also be an important tool for increasing organizational efficiency.

Since 2016, Singapore has positioned itself as a pioneer in digital innovation by declaring its ambition to become the world's first smart city, building upon its already advanced digital infrastructure. In this context, the Municipal Services Office introduced the OneService Kaki chatbot, integrated into the country's most widely used messaging platforms, WhatsApp, Telegram and Instagram. Designed to uphold the city-state's long-standing commitment to cleanliness and order, the chatbot enables residents to easily report issues such as littering, illegal parking, and concerns related to domestic or wild animals. Leveraging AI, OneService Kaki interprets user input with flexibility and directs the information to the relevant public authorities, thereby enhancing efficiency, responsiveness, and citizen-centered service delivery in municipal governance.

Yokosuka, Japan, became the first local government to pilot a ChatGPT-based AI application across all municipal departments in April 2023. The trial period stated that confidential data would be kept out of the system, and tested functions such as creating newsletters, summarizing meeting minutes, editing text, developing project proposals, and contributing to policy processes. The municipal government aims to evaluate whether this initiative offers a new tool for strengthening administrative capacity to improve the quality of life for its citizens (Kyodo News, 2023).

These examples demonstrate how municipalities of varying scales have adopted chatbot technology to support different areas of service delivery. In this spectrum, which extends from big cities to small towns, from health services to internal administrative processes, it is seen that chatbots can be flexibly adapted to many scenarios when designed correctly. Each successful application offers lessons learned for other municipalities; it reveals which approaches are effective and which issues need to be considered. It is emphasized in the literature that the implementation of chatbots in a local government unit may vary depending on contextual factors, therefore each municipality should develop solutions adapted to its own needs and capacities (Chen et al. 2023). However, when viewed in general, the experiences accumulated over the years reveal that AI-based chatbots open a significant window of opportunity for local governments to provide faster, more accessible and satisfaction-oriented services to citizens. Therefore, it is expected that more municipalities will implement their own chatbots by following good practice examples in this field in the future.

AI-based chatbot systems can be conceptualized not merely as technological instruments but as drivers of institutional transformation (Medaglia et al., 2024).

Especially when integrated with decision support systems, chatbots allow municipalities to be managed with data. In addition, chatbots become areas where public value is reproduced with functions such as increasing digital literacy, informing citizens about the operation of public services, and increasing trust in services (Moore, 1995; Wiethölter et al., 2024).

Nevertheless, chatbots can be conceptualized both as technical artifacts and socio-technical systems influenced by their operational and societal environments. In other words, these tools are not just software algorithms; they are also affected by the values of the engineers who design them, the service vision of the institution, and the usage patterns of citizens (Song, 2022). Hence, beyond their technical functions, chatbots represent digital environments through which modes of public engagement are redefined and reconstructed.

Strategic Functions and Sociotechnical Drivers of Chatbot Use in Local Governments

Local governments are confronted with challenges such as maintaining citizen satisfaction, improving service quality, and making governance mechanisms more efficient at a time when global service expectations are increasing and resources are limited. By prioritizing digital innovation in service delivery, local governments aim to both reach more citizens and produce more services with the same resources. For this reason, chatbots stand out as a low-cost and scalable solution. Chatbots function as a strategic tool that enhances municipal responsiveness to public demands, even under conditions of limited workforce availability. In high-demand service environments like metropolitan areas, chatbots facilitate public engagement beyond the physical limits of conventional service delivery systems.

The visibility of chatbot systems plays an important role in citizens' perception of municipal services as contemporary, accessible and inclusive. This can be expressed as institutional legitimacy and digital image. Considering the sensitivity of the young population to digital services in particular, municipalities that use chatbots may have a stronger institutional image. In their study, Li and Wang (2024) show that the identity features of chatbots affect citizens' general perception of the municipality. Chatbots that simulate human interaction (human-like) and reflect institutional identity through logos and names help reinforce the symbolic presence of the state, thus enhancing digital platforms' role in public governance.

This points to the necessity of conceptualizing chatbots simultaneously as technical enablers and as institutional entities situated in the wider framework of public administration (Misuraca & Van Noordt, 2020). In other words, chatbots become digital public servants representing the municipality and establishing one-on-one contact with citizens.

One of the biggest advantages of chatbot systems is that they can provide uninterrupted and timeless services. Chatbots offer an important solution for citizens who want to access municipal services outside of working hours due to the busy pace of daily life. In addition, their user-friendly interfaces make access easier from both mobile and desktop devices (Huang & Gan, 2023). This feature can represent an inclusive service format, especially when evaluated for individuals with disabilities, the elderly, or groups with low digital literacy. From this perspective, it can play an important role in reducing digital inequality in public services. Song (2022) demonstrates how the use of voice chatbots in public services provides convenience for elderly and visually impaired individuals in accessing digital content. This indicates that chatbots contribute both to the speed of digital service provision and to the expansion of service inclusivity. Chatbots stand out as a tool to facilitate access, especially for citizens from different socioeconomic groups, age groups, or those with physical limitations. Misuraca and Van Noordt's (2022) research on AI applications in the European Union emphasizes that local governments' internalization of accessibility principles in the use of chatbots is a strategic step to reduce the digital divide. In this context, chatbots can be effective both in providing ease of service and in ensuring digital justice.

The study conducted by Zhou, Liu, and Feng (2025) underscores that enabling empathetic communication in digital contexts is essential to contemporary chatbot design. Within this framework, chatbots with developed empathic communication capabilities have made digital services encompass not only the technical but also the emotional dimension.

Alongside their practical utility in service provision, chatbots generate valuable data that can inform decision-making and policy development. Each user interaction creates institutional memory about how effective the services are, which information is not understood, or which areas have high demand. Gerontas et al. (2022) emphasize that digital infrastructures developed for the personalization of public services should be integrated with chatbot systems. This points to the fact that every request or complaint received through chatbots turns into strategic data that shapes the future service policies of municipalities.

Wiethölter, Kühl, and Feldmann (2024) suggest in their study that external information management in public administration can be carried out more effectively through chatbots. Especially in municipalities with multi-unit structures, feedback collected through chatbot systems accelerates information sharing between units and supports decision-making processes. This indicates that beyond their service-oriented functions, chatbots also contribute to the construction and preservation of organizational memory.

Local governments, as the closest link in democratic governance, are responsible for encouraging participatory processes. Traditional participation methods—face-to-face meetings, petition mechanisms, or physical complaint boxes—can be limiting in terms of time, space, and access to information. Chatbots, on the other hand, digitalize these limitations and facilitate participation. Notably facilitated by the integration with mobile devices, citizens can provide feedback or express their opinions to the administration from any platform. In this context, Makasi, Nili, Desouza, and Tate (2022) stated in their study that chatbots transfer information as well as actively encourage citizen participation. In particular, the ability of users to share their ideas about municipal services through chatbots supports the development of an interactive and dynamic model in governance.

The conceptual framework developed by Senadheera et al. (2024) reveals that the contribution of chatbots to citizen participation is formed on three axes: accessibility, openness and reliability. In particular, the implementation of the principle of openness is made possible by ensuring the clarity and impartiality of the information provided through chatbots. In this respect, chatbots are considered as digital tools of transparent public administration.

Thus, chatbots emerge as a public value production tool with the characteristics of Public Value Theory (Moore, 1995). Public service delivery evolves by balancing efficiency with citizens' values and expectations. In this light, the effectiveness of a service is measured not just by its technical outputs, but by its broader social relevance and capacity to produce meaningful societal outcomes. Chatbots produce both symbolic and functional values with these theory models. Symbolically, they create a modern, institutional and advanced public administration perception. They play an active role in the public sector by offering performance, fast access, effective management of demands and the opportunity to receive and store public decision changes with feedback. Makasi et al. (2022), the analysis framework they developed on the ways chatbots shape public service values, draws the evaluation of the potential of these technologies to reflect the value set of public administration. In particular, if policy frameworks shaped by transparency, institutional consistency, and the pursuit of public good are adopted in design options, chatbots serve as not just as tools for service provision, but as integral stakeholders in the public sector.

Current Challenges, Potential Risks, and Prospects for the Future

The integration of chatbots into public services is often justified by presenting digitalization as an inevitable and neutral process. However, this approach risks ignoring the limitations of the "instrumental reason" approach that sees technology as a mere tool. Having a critical approach to the use of chatbots in public services is important in order to emphasize that technology should be evaluated not only within the framework of values such as efficiency and speed, but also according to normative principles such as ethics, justice and participation.

Chatbots technically appear to be participation tools, but in reality, the interactions they offer often rely on predefined scenarios. This can replace participatory models where citizens can truly contribute to governance with superficial forms of feedback. Such practices can void the content of democratic participation in governance. Grimmelikhuijsen and Tangi (2024), in their study on the extent to which public administrators use chatbots for democratic governance purposes, found that most administrators see chatbots only as a "tool for filtering citizen demands" and do not include them in strategic decision-making processes. This limits the potential of chatbots as digital tools to generate democratic legitimacy.

The widespread use of chatbot systems can be exclusionary for groups with low digital literacy, the elderly population, or immigrant communities. In particular, visual and text-based chatbot interfaces can create additional barriers to accessing information. In this context, services provided through chatbots can push certain groups out of the system; this creates the risk of "digital exclusion" (Song, 2022). In addition, in the meta-analysis study of Ma'rup and Rokhman (2024), it was stated that many public institutions do not sufficiently consider accessibility and digital inequality issues in chatbot integration. This reveals that investment should be made in the ethical sensitivity of chatbot systems as well as their technical adequacy.

The decision logic of AI-based chatbot systems is often not transparent. It is not clear how and which information is shared with the citizen, with what logic the questions are answered, or what guidance is given. This situation contradicts the principles of transparency and accountability in public administration. Medaglia, Mikalef, and Tangi (2024) emphasize that public institutions do not have the institutional capacity to ensure accountability in AI projects. This deficiency makes it difficult to monitor algorithmic biases in particular. When citizens think that the answer given by the chatbot is incorrect, biased, or incomplete, they may lose trust in the entire system without knowing who made this decision. In line with the observations of Jobin, Ienca, and Vayena (2019), The creation of ethical guidance and algorithmic control mechanisms in AI systems should be understood as a dual imperative in the public sector, encompassing technical requirements alongside democratic principles.

For many years, public administration has gained legitimacy through the image of the state with a human face. However, the proliferation of automated systems such as chatbots may cause public institutions to be represented with cold and anonymous digital faces. This may lead to the erosion of values such as relationality, trust and belonging between public institutions and citizens. The study examining how chatbots affect the citizen experience shows that chatbots that identify with the institutional identity and human-like positively affect the citizen experience;

on the other hand, anonymous and mechanical systems create alienating effects (Li & Wang, 2024). In this context, it should be taken into account that chatbots are functioning simultaneously as technological, emotional, and symbolic agents in socio-digital environments.

METHODOLOGY

This study utilized in-depth interviews as part of a qualitative research approach, and the data obtained were examined through thematic analysis. Qualitative research is a flexible methodology that provides an in-depth understanding of complex social phenomena. Thematic analysis, as defined by Braun and Clarke, is essentially the process of systematically uncovering recurring patterns or themes within qualitative data. This approach involves organizing and interpreting extensive qualitative data—for example, interview and focus group transcripts, online forum content, or open-ended survey responses—into thousands of words through a researcher-developed framework of themes (Braun & Clarke, 2006). In this study, in-depth interview technique was selected as the most appropriate method to understand the effects of AI-based chatbot usage on public value creation. Due to the focused nature of the case and the expertise of the participants, three in-depth interviews were considered sufficient to capture relevant insights. Sound recordings were made as part of the data collection process during the interviews and these recordings were later transcribed and structured for analysis. These interviews started with open-ended questions about the participants' chatbot experiences and then deepened with more specific questions about certain topics such as security, design process, equality and impact on business processes, and future plans. In this way, the participants' reflections on how the chatbot contributed to public value creation were captured comprehensively. This rich data set provides a convenient ground for examining the effects of BAGBI from a multidimensional perspective.

The research focused on collecting the views of critical actors within Bağcılar Municipality who played a role in the design, management, or evaluation of the BAGBİ chatbot system who directly affected and were affected by the implementation and maintenance of the chatbot service. For this purpose, interviews were conducted with the personnel of the IT Department within the Bağcılar Municipality. These personnel have participated in the BAGBI project since its inception (2019-2020 period) and played an active role in the design, development, implementation and continuous improvement processes of the system. In addition, meetings and collaboration with the institutional development teams of 25 directorates within the municipality played an important role in the creation of the knowledge base of the chatbot and the integration of institutional memory. This is consistent with the findings of Larsen and Følstad (2024) that the chatbot maintenance was organized as a team effort and included resources from different municipal departments.

Analysis of the Interviews

The data collection process for the Bağcılar Municipality BAGBI chatbot case study focused on collecting the views of key personnel who directly affect and are affected by the implementation and maintenance of the chatbot. Audio recordings were taken during the interviews, and these recordings were later transcribed and made ready for analysis.

As a result of the thematic analysis, four overarching themes were identified. "Service quality, accessibility and citizen interaction" shows how chatbots enhance accessibility, speed, and continuity of services while enabling feedback and data-driven planning. "Perception of digitalization and trust in AI" reflects citizens' attitudes toward digital tools and confidence in AI, shaping adoption and legitimacy. "Institutional capacity and organizational sustainability" illustrates how chatbots strengthen coordination, standardize processes, and support organizational memory. "Algorithmic neutrality, ethical sensitivity, and public value" highlights normative dimensions such as impartiality, ethical sensitivity, and value generation in governance. This thematic framework shows that chatbot technologies go beyond being a means of interaction with citizens; chatbots transcend technical tools, intersecting with governance capacity, trust, ethics, and data-driven decision-making in public administration.

Service Quality, Accessibility and Citizen Interaction

The adoption of AI-based chatbots in public services is largely motivated by the goal of improving service quality and ensuring continuous access to information. In Bağcılar Municipality, the BAGBI chatbot was developed to provide citizens with fast, easy, and uninterrupted service, overcoming both spatial and temporal barriers. As one employee noted, the chatbot "approaches all citizens in the same way… there is no concept of time or space, 24/7," emphasizing its capacity to deliver equal and uninterrupted service. Citizens confirmed that they could now receive instant answers even on weekends or outside working hours, and this continuity was reflected in high satisfaction levels.

With BAGBI, citizens who previously needed to call repeatedly to track municipal transactions can now resolve requests with a single query. One participant explained, "with the chatbot, frequently asked questions of citizens can be answered instantly. This reduces the load on the call center and increases citizen satisfaction." The automation of routine queries has reduced workloads in call centers and face-to-face units, allowing personnel to focus on more complex issues. As another interviewee stated, "The workload in the call center and counseling units has decreased," highlighting efficiency gains for the municipality alongside faster service for citizens.

BAGBI was designed as a "one-stop" service point, integrating diverse municipal services such as zoning status inquiry, tax debt information, marriage hall appointments, pharmacy duty schedules, garbage collection hours, and event announcements. By consolidating seven different modules into a single interface, citizens save time and experience easier access. Comparative findings support this benefit: a study on Norwegian municipalities (Larsen & Følstad, 2024) noted that citizens appreciated chatbots for simplifying complex websites by acting as "a hub for all the services that are like a forest." In this respect, BAGBI aligns with international experiences by granting continuous and effortless access to information.

Another prominent dimension of BAGBI is its role as a data-driven interaction bridge between citizens and the municipality. Each chatbot exchange produces valuable information on citizen needs, including what topics are most frequently asked about and what words are used. A project official explained, "Each interaction with the chatbot contains valuable data such as what topics citizens seek information on, what questions they ask the most, and what words they use." This data, anonymized and systematically analyzed, supports service improvements and enables administrators to detect frequently raised issues.

Interviewees confirmed that chatbot data functioned as a decision support tool. The most frequently asked questions were regularly reported, allowing managers to identify which services citizens prioritized or which areas required clearer communication. As one participant noted, this method represents "an innovative approach that provides data input to the municipality through e-participation." Beyond providing one-way information, BAGBI thus served as a two-way communication platform, strengthening the municipality's understanding of its community.

Concrete examples illustrate how chatbot data influences service planning. A participant observed, "For example, when social assistance applications are announced, many questions are asked about that subject through the chatbot. This way, we can see what the citizens are curious about." In response, the municipality made relevant information more visible on its website and ensured application processes remained up to date. Similarly, repeated complaints or a high volume of queries about specific services signaled potential bottlenecks, prompting coordination across units to address problems.

BAGBI also introduced direct feedback mechanisms. Users could instantly evaluate chatbot responses (like/dislike), and negative feedback was systematically reviewed. One interviewee stated that "the 76% satisfaction rate regarding BAGBI's answers was calculated from this feedback." Beyond rate monitoring, detailed analysis of comments allowed the municipality to correct errors and enhance chatbot performance. This iterative process illustrates the system's capacity for continuous learning.

The integration of feedback into decision-making reflects broader principles of co-production in public service delivery. Citizens may not directly shape policy, but their daily interactions have become an important input for municipal planning. In effect, BAGBI demonstrates how digital technologies can simultaneously increase service quality, improve accessibility, reduce administrative burdens, and strengthen participatory governance through data-driven insights.

Perception of Digitalization and Trust in AI

The implementation of the BAGBI application has been evaluated as a concrete indicator of Bağcılar Municipality's digital transformation efforts. According to the participants, citizens perceive the use of an AI-based chatbot in the municipality as "an indicator of the municipality's digitalization process." In other words, BAGBI has helped the institution to display an innovative and technology-friendly profile. This creates a positive perception that the municipality is adapting to the requirements of the age and adds value to the corporate image. Indeed, it is emphasized in the public administration literature that the adoption of digital services strengthens the perception of modernity and innovation of institutions in the eyes of citizens (Twizeyimana & Andersson, 2019). In the case of BAGBI, the belief that the municipality is transparent and accessible has been reinforced as citizens can instantly receive information via the chatbot. One participant summarizes this situation by saying, "The perception of transparency increases because citizens can instantly access information." Indeed, a digital assistant that can provide instant and accurate information flow strengthens the municipality's perceived openness and accountability from the citizens' perspective.

The trust dimension is perhaps one of the most critical aspects of the perception of digitalization. In the BAGBI case, the successful performance of the chatbot increased the trust that citizens had in both technology and the institution. Participants stated that the fast and accurate answers provided by the chatbot satisfied the citizens and as a result, "reinforced the trust in the municipality." When a citizen can get a satisfactory answer to his/her own question, his/her trust in the digital service provided increases and his/her belief in the municipality's problem-solving capacity is strengthened. For instance, according to the scenario shared by a participant, a citizen who used to have to search repeatedly to get simple information can now easily reach the result through BAGBI; since he/she sees the municipality as more accessible and transparent, his/her sense of trust in the institution is also nourished. This narrative is important in terms of showing how the concept of trust is built:

Greater transparency, faster service delivery, and improved accessibility collectively reinforce the trust relationship between citizens and the state.

However, the sustainability of trust in technology depends on the accuracy and reliability of the chatbot's answers. The BAGBI team has made serious efforts to keep the accuracy of the system high in order not to shake the trust in AI. In the interviews, it is stated that the answers are checked with regular tests, the content is integrated with the official sources of the municipality, and an accuracy rate of over 90% is targeted. Participants stated that each new user question is recorded by the system and included in the training for the machine learning model, thus minimizing the chatbot's errors over time and starting to give more accurate answers. In fact, the project team stated that they ensured that BAGBI's "reliability increases sustainably" by evaluating citizens' chat histories as a type of feedback and processing them into the model. This proactive approach aims to maintain users' trust in the chatbot in the long term.

On the other hand, citizens' trust in an AI-based system depends both on technical performance and socio-ethical factors. Makasi et al. (2020) state that the use of chatbots in the public sector is sometimes met with social concerns and users may question whether these services carry the necessary public values As emphasized in this study, the extent to which values such as trust, justice, and transparency are perceived through the use of chatbots constitutes a significant factor in shaping citizens' attitudes toward technology. The effort made to establish the element of trust in the BAGBI project is of critical importance for this very reason. The participants succeeded in building technological trust by ensuring that the system serves everyone equally and consistently, provides transparent information, and is responsive to citizen feedback. As a result, BAGBI increased the trust in the digital capabilities of the municipality in the eyes of citizens; this contributed positively to the trust in public institutions in general. This finding is in line with the predictions in the literature that the successful implementation of digital services can positively reflect on the legitimacy of public authorities and the public willingness to participate in decision-making.

Institutional Capacity and Organizational Sustainability

The success of AI-based chatbot projects must be evaluated not only by external benefits but also by their impact on internal operations and institutional sustainability. In Bağcılar Municipality, the BAGBI project required significant coordination and capacity building, particularly in uniting fragmented knowledge across directorates. A team of representatives from each unit compiled citizens' frequently asked questions, producing a knowledge inventory of 500 questions from 22 directorates and 4,500 user questionnaires. This process integrated siloed institutional knowledge into a common platform. As one participant explained, "While creating BAGBI's knowledge base, institutional knowledge of all units was integrated; siloed knowledge accumulations were combined on a common platform. This is also an important step towards creating institutional memory within the municipality."

The project thus strengthened institutional memory and increased information sharing across units, providing a concrete example of how e-government initiatives enhance management capacity. Another contribution was the standardization and efficiency of business processes. Participants noted that automation redefined certain procedures and accelerated routine operations, particularly in citizen application management. Document classification errors were significantly reduced, as one participant emphasized: "This was the most critical area in the system... The texts written by the citizen are analyzed, the subject is predicted... We made our first artificial intelligence application there."

By automating repetitive tasks, BAGBI also transformed workload distribution. Routine queries once handled by staff are now answered by the chatbot, reducing pressure on call centers. One participant noted: "Since routine and repetitive citizen questions are now primarily answered by the chatbot, a certain burden has been lifted off call center personnel or relevant unit employees. Thanks to this, staff have had the opportunity to focus on more complex or exceptional issues that the chatbot cannot answer." This shift enabled more efficient use of human resources, directing expert staff toward high-value tasks and improving both motivation and problem-solving capacity.

Sustainability was ensured through institutional mechanisms for system maintenance. The IT Department conducts technical monitoring, content is updated periodically, and citizen feedback is reviewed systematically. Participants reported that BAGBI's language perception is continually refined with new terms, and organizational changes are instantly reflected in the knowledge base. Importantly, while the system was initially implemented with external support, municipal staff later internalized operations, signaling a learning organization model.

The success of BAGBI also encouraged broader digital transformation within the municipality. Interviewees emphasized that it set an example for other units and inspired more ambitious initiatives, such as smart city projects and a digital twin. Moreover, knowledge of technologies like natural language processing and machine learning expanded internally, fostering data-driven decision-making practices. In the long term, BAGBI's implementation is expected to support the development of evidence-based policies across service areas, embedding innovation into the municipality's institutional culture.

Algorithmic Neutrality, Ethical Sensitivity, and Public Value

In AI-based public services, compliance with ethical principles and impartiality play a critical role in the adoption and success of the technology. Interview findings show that special importance was given to values such as equality, inclusiveness, impartiality, and transparency in the design and implementation stages of the BAGBI project. For example, participants frequently emphasized that the chatbot provides services to all citizens at an equal distance. A municipality employee stated that BAGBI is based on the principles of "equality and inclusiveness" when explaining its service logic, that it offers a "simple, user-friendly interface" and that it uses "appropriate response language according to different literacy levels". This statement reveals that conscious choices were made in the design of the chatbot in order not to exclude any segment and to appeal to the widest possible user base. By the deliberate simplicity of BAGBI's interface and the language configuration based on user-friendly and everyday terms, it was aimed that including citizens with low levels of digital competence could use the system.

In the context of algorithmic neutrality, it is an important principle that BAGBI exhibits a standard approach to all users. In the interviews, one participant stated that the chatbot "approaches all citizens in the same way and provides a standard" service. Indeed, a well-designed public chatbot is expected to provide answers of the same quality and content regardless of who the user is. Since BAGBI is based on the official data of the municipality in terms of the information it contains, it does not produce personalized or arbitrary answers; it provides consistent and verified information to everyone. This is the provision of fairness and neutrality in public service through technology. Algorithmic neutrality also includes the system not producing biased or discriminatory results when producing answers. Since BAGBI's knowledge base consists of the municipality's institutional content and was developed around frequently asked questions, care was taken to ensure that its answers did not contain discriminatory language or attitudes towards any group. Participants stated that the data used in the training of the chatbot was compiled from a wide range, included different forms of expression and scenarios, and that the system was adapted to diversity. In this way, BAGBI can understand users who do not use official languages or write with different accents, for example, and tries to interpret everyone's questions correctly. This approach points to linguistic inclusiveness, which can be considered as a dimension of algorithmic neutrality.

There are several prominent elements in the BAGBI project regarding ethical sensitivity. First of all, it is seen that the principles of privacy and security are respected in the use of citizen data. The collected data is analyzed by anonymizing and aggregating it, and no individual tracking or intervention is made in personal data. For example, a specific citizen is not profiled in BAGBI's reports, but instead the common tendencies of all users are examined. This approach shows the importance given to the protection of personal data and its ethical use. Secondly, the accuracy and reliability of the information provided by the chatbot are considered as an ethical issue. Since the possibility of providing false or misleading information can have serious consequences in public service, the contents of BAGBI are constantly kept up-to-date and the possibility of giving wrong answers is tried to be minimized. It was stated in the interviews that the system is subjected to regular tests, and any detected errors are immediately corrected. This means that the principles of accountability and honesty towards the public are observed in technological application. In addition, it is ethically important that BAGBI includes a feedback mechanism and that users can convey their dissatisfaction; because citizens can make their voices heard and contribute to the improvement of the system.

The issue of access to digital services, especially for vulnerable groups such as the disabled and the elderly, is an important indicator of ethical inclusiveness in public services. Some public chatbot projects around the world have been criticized for not adequately meeting the needs of individuals with disabilities. For example, a chatbot called Nadia, developed in Australia for a service for the disabled, was stopped due to public pressure on the grounds that it was not suitable for the needs of this segment. The BAGBI project aimed to facilitate access to services for disabled and elderly citizens. Participants emphasized that citizens who cannot physically go to the municipality can receive services from anywhere with an internet connection using the chatbot, and that this is "revolutionary in terms of accessibility," especially for individuals with limited mobility. Indeed, BAGBI has provided a location-independent service, giving those who cannot leave their homes the opportunity to access public information. This means a concrete contribution to the principle of equality in service. As one participant put it, thanks to the chatbot, "disabled individuals, elderly people or citizens living in different neighborhoods can access the same service with the same quality." In other words, when digital technology is applied correctly, it can reduce geographical or physical barriers and strengthen equal opportunities in public services. The BAGBI example demonstrates that designing technological innovations in a socially inclusive manner increases public value.

The concept of public value, in Mark H. Moore's classic framework, refers to the total value that public institutions can create for society (including benefit, trust, justice, legitimacy, etc.). In this case, BAGBI has produced a multidimensional public value by improving service quality (pragmatic value), increasing citizen satisfaction and trust (societal value), and ensuring internal efficiency (administrative value). In particular, values such as trust, justice, and transparency have played a central role in BAGBI's success. As Makasi et al. (2020) emphasize, when innovations such as chatbots fail to reflect public service values, their acceptance by the public becomes difficult. In the Bağcılar example, on the contrary, the BAGBI project has been adopted and appreciated by citizens because it draws a profile that overlaps with public service values from its design to its implementation. The high user satisfaction and increased trust achieved are an indicator of this. Moreover, BAGBI has strengthened citizen-state interaction by democratizing access to information and simplifying communication. This is an effect that somewhat flattens the traditional hierarchical structure of public service, empowers citizens, and is an important part of public value.

Of course, it is also accepted by the participants that we should always be vigilant about ethical sensitivity and impartiality. It is an important governance issue to monitor AI systems over time and verify that they do not contain bias. Participants stated that they manage this risk by paying attention to the diversity of data used in the development process of BAGBI and by monitoring the system for "mislearnings". In particular, the feedback mechanism helps to quickly detect and correct possible systematic errors. In the future, as the chatbot's capabilities increase and it is used in more complex services, issues such as protecting privacy, maintaining trust in government-citizen relations, and explaining AI decisions will become even more important. Bağcılar Municipality has demonstrated its determination to observe these values with the BAGBI project. As a result, BAGBI has presented an example of innovation that increases public value in public service by adhering to the principles of algorithmic impartiality and ethical sensitivity. It has both gained the satisfaction and trust of citizens receiving the service and demonstrated the capacity to reflect the values of the institution providing the service to technology. In this respect, the BAGBI project emerges as a success that is at once technical and value-oriented in terms of digital transformation.

DISCUSSION AND CONCLUSION

The integration of AI technologies into public services is transforming local governance. Chatbot systems, central to this transformation, reshape citizen–government interaction by making services faster, more accessible, personalized, and cost-effective. Beyond their technical role, they function as new public actors that influence governance, creating symbolic thresholds in service delivery and redefining institutional capacity. Literature highlights both opportunities—accessibility, efficiency, data-driven governance, and participatory value production—and risks, including ethical concerns, trust, security, and dependency (Makasi et al., 2020; Senadheera et al., 2024).

This study confirms that chatbots in local governments are not merely digital tools but governance practices supporting citizen participation and public value. The BAGBI chatbot of Bağcılar Municipality demonstrates this impact in practice through 24/7 access, automatic response capacity, and multilingual support, showing the progress of Türkiye's municipalities in digital transformation.

Chatbots, when well-designed, facilitate citizens' participation in decision-making and provide democratic platforms for problem-solving (Zhou et al., 2024; Makasi et al., 2022). However, this participation must also be supported by social design. Empathic communication capabilities, personalization capacity, and sensitivity to citizen expectations are the aspects of chatbots that increase their public value (Zhou et al., 2024). Literature also warns that digital gaps can exacerbate inequalities, particularly for the elderly, low-income groups, or those with limited literacy (Song, 2022). Thus, chatbots simultaneously hold potential for inclusion and exclusion. Issues such as data protection, privacy, and algorithmic ethics remain critical for sustaining public trust (Grimmelikhuijsen & Tangi, 2024; Medaglia et al., 2024).

The efficiency of chatbot projects depends not only on technical infrastructure but also on administrative and cultural adoption. Factors such as human resource capacity, internal process compatibility, staff training, and feedback integration determine success (Misuraca & Van Noordt, 2020; Wiethölter et al., 2024). It may be inferred that many municipalities lack such capacity, limiting chatbots to showcase innovations. By contrast, BAGBI exemplifies sustainability through nearly two decades of digital strategy, institutional memory integration, and reinforcement of governance principles.

BAGBI evolved from rule-based systems to generative AI, with its knowledge base built from 500 FAQs and 4,500 user scenarios. Continuous feedback enhanced flexibility at technical and managerial levels, while usage data—783,000 messages and 250,000 users by 2024—demonstrates rapid citizen adoption. BAGBI thus functions as both an informative tool and a decision-support mechanism, providing valuable data for planning and highlighting deficiencies. Its plain language and 24/7 design also enable inclusive services for citizens with different literacy levels.

Ethical and sustainability challenges remain. BAGBI avoids personal data collection and uses double-factor authentication for sensitive processes, but issues such as coordination gaps, dependency on external vendors, and evolving information needs pose risks. The municipality's acquisition of international security certifications, however, illustrates institutional awareness in mitigating these risks. Future plans envision expanding services, integrating with digital city twin platforms, and deepening the role of chatbots as building blocks of digital urbanism.

The BAGBI initiative exemplifies how AI-based chatbots in public administration represent more than technical innovation—they demand rethinking governance and value production. Moore's (1995) public value framework emphasizes government's role as both legislator and creative actor. BAGBI contributes directly to value creation by enhancing service quality, accessibility, transparency, and satisfaction, showing how algorithmic intermediaries now shape value alongside human labor. This shift requires renewed discussion of the criteria for public value.

Chatbots also enable “shadow participation” by converting citizen queries into decision-making inputs, thus acting as hybrid actors in governance. BAGBI illustrates how citizen interactions feed data-based feedback loops, reshaping traditional definitions of participation. At the same time, its simple language design promotes egalitarian digitalization by ensuring elderly and digitally disadvantaged groups benefit, embedding principles of equality and inclusiveness into service provision.

Finally, BAGBI highlights ethical and governance implications. The need for impartiality in handling politically sensitive content raises questions of algorithmic public servants and the ethical boundary between decision support and decision making. As repositories of institutional knowledge, chatbots digitize organizational memory and push decision-making toward evidence-based methods. They also raise questions of digital sovereignty, as reliance on external suppliers challenges autonomy. Bağcılar’s internalization of operations shows how local governments can build digital autonomy.

In conclusion, BAGBI represents a pioneering model of AI-based service provision in Türkiye. It operationalizes normative principles such as accessibility, transparency, evidence-based governance, and public value. For wider adoption, national AI standards, regulatory frameworks rooted in open governance, and inter-institutional cooperation are essential. A human-centered digitalization vision, rather than technology-centered approaches, is critical for democratizing AI in the public sector.

REFERENCES

Abbas, N., Følstad, A., & Bjørkli, C. A. (2023). Chatbots as part of digital government service provision – A user perspective. In A. Følstad, T. Araujo, S. Papadopoulos, E. L.-C. Law, E. Luger, M. Goodwin, & P. B. Brandtzaeg (Eds.), Chatbot Research and Design: 6th International Workshop, CONVERSATIONS 2022 Amsterdam, The Netherlands, November 22–23, 2022 Revised Selected Papers (pp. 66–82). Springer. DOI: 10.1007/978-3-031-25581-6_5

Aoki, N. (2020). An experimental study of public trust in AI chatbots in the public sector. *Government Information Quarterly*, *37*(4), 101490. DOI: 10.1016/j.giq.2020.101490

Braun, V., & Clarke, V. (2006). Using thematic analysis in psychology. *Qualitative Research in Psychology*, *3*(2), 77–101. DOI: 10.1191/1478088706qp063oa

Chen, T., Gascó-Hernandez, M., & Esteve, M. (2023). The adoption and implementation of artificial intelligence chatbots in public organizations: Evidence from US state governments. *American Review of Public Administration*, *54*(3), 255–270. DOI: 10.1177/02750740231200522

Cortés-Cediel, M. E., Segura-Tinoco, A., Cantador, I., & Rodríguez Bolívar, M. P. (2023). Trends and challenges of e-government chatbots: Advances in exploring open government data and citizen participation content. *Government Information Quarterly*, *40*(4), 101877. DOI: 10.1016/j.giq.2023.101877

Dreyling, R. M., Koppel, T., Tammet, T., & Pappel, I. (2024). Challenges of generative AI chatbots in public services – An integrative review. Available at *SSRN*: https://ssrn.com/abstract=4850714 or DOI: 10.2139/ssrn.4850714

Dube, I. (2024). Chatbots: A tool to improve public service delivery and create public value. Journal of Public Administration and Development Affairs, 1(1), Article. .DOI: 10.55190/JPADA.2024.341

ELIZA. (1966). ELIZA: a very basic Rogerian psychotherapist chatbot. Retrieved from: https://web.njit.edu/~ronkowit/eliza.html, June 2025.

Følstad, A., & Bjerkreim-Hanssen, N. (2023). User interactions with a municipality chatbot—Lessons learnt from dialogue analysis. *International Journal of Human-Computer Interaction*, *40*(18), 4973–4986. DOI: 10.1080/10447318.2023.2238355

Gerontas, A., Zeginis, D., Promikyridis, R., Androš, M., Tambouris, E., Cipan, V., & Tarabanis, K. (2022). Enhancing core public service vocabulary to enable public service personalization. *Information (Basel)*, *13*(5), 225. DOI: 10.3390/info13050225

Govlaunch. (n.d.). Ten local government chatbots that are making a difference. Retrieved from https://govlaunch.com/stories/ten-local-government-chatbots-that-are-making-a-difference

Grimmelikhuijsen, S., & Tangi, L. (2024). What factors influence perceived artificial intelligence adoption by public managers? Publications Office of the European Union. JRC138684.

Huang, C., & Gan, K. (2023). Enhancing citizen engagement in smart cities with chatbot. *International Journal of Smart Systems*, *1*(1), 34–39. https://ijss.etunas.com/index.php/ijss/article/view/6. DOI: 10.63876/ijss.v1i1.6

Jobin, A., Ienca, M., & Vayena, E. (2019). The Global Landscape of AI Ethics Guidelines. *Nature Machine Intelligence*, *1*(9), 389–399. DOI: 10.1038/s42256-019-0088-2

Kaun, A., & Männiste, M. (2025). Public sector chatbots: AI frictions and data infrastructures at the interface of the digital welfare state. *New Media & Society*, *27*(4), 1962–1985. DOI: 10.1177/14614448251314394

Kyodo News. (2023). Yokosuka becomes 1st local gov't in Japan to begin ChatGPT trial use. Retrieved From: https://english.kyodonews.net/articles/-/40065

Larsen, A. G., & Følstad, A. (2024). The impact of chatbots on public service provision: A qualitative interview study with citizens and public service providers. *Government Information Quarterly*, *41*(2), 101927. DOI: 10.1016/j.giq.2024.101927

Li, X., & Wang, J. (2024). Should government chatbots behave like civil servants? The effect of chatbot identity characteristics on citizen experience. *Government Information Quarterly*, *41*(3), 101957. Advance online publication. DOI: 10.1016/j.giq.2024.101957

Ma'rup, M., & Rokhman, A. (2024). Utilization of Artificial Intelligence (AI) Chatbots in Improving Public Services: A Meta-Analysis Study. *Open Access Indonesia Journal of Social Sciences*, *7*(4), 1610–1618. DOI: 10.37275/oaijss.v7i4.255

Makasi, T., Nili, A., Desouza, K., & Tate, M. (2020). Chatbot-mediated public service delivery: A public service value-based framework. *First Monday*, *25*(12). Advance online publication. DOI: 10.5210/fm.v25i12.10598

Makasi, T., Nili, A., Desouza, K., & Tate, M. (2022, January). Public service values and chatbots in the public sector: Reconciling designer efforts and user expectations. In *Proceedings of the 55th Hawaii International Conference on System Sciences*. DOI: 10.24251/HICSS.2022.292

Maragno, G., Tangi, L., Gastaldi, L., & Benedetti, M. (2023). AI as an organizational agent to nurture effectively introducing chatbots in public entities. *Public Management Review*, *25*(11), 2135–2165. DOI: 10.1080/14719037.2022.2063935

Medaglia, R., Mikalef, P., & Tangi, L. (2024). Competences and governance practices for artificial intelligence in the public sector. Publications Office of the European Union. JRC138702.

Misuraca, G., & Van Noordt, C. (2020). AI Watch - Artificial Intelligence in public services, EUR 30255 EN, Publications Office of the European Union, Luxembourg. ISBN 978-92-76-19540-5, , JRC120399.DOI: 10.2760/039619

Moore, M. H. (1995). *Creating Public Value: Strategic Management in Government*. Harvard University Press.

Nirala, K. K., Singh, N. K., & Purani, V. S. (2022). AI-Chatbot to determine citizen centric solution of Aadhaar Card services in Public Administration: Aadhaarbot. *Bengal, Past & Present*, *140*(VII), 37–48.

Pica-Alfano, L. (n.d.). Ten local government chatbots that are making a difference. Retrieved from: https://govlaunch.com/stories/ten-local-government-chatbots-that-are-making-a-difference, June 2025.

Rathnayake, A. S., Nguyen, T. D. H. N., & Ahn, Y. (2025). Factors Influencing AI Chatbot Adoption in Government Administration: A Case Study of Sri Lanka's Digital Government. *Administrative Sciences*, *15*(5), 157. DOI: 10.3390/admsci15050157

Song, J. (2022). The implications of providing voice-based chatbots in public service for digital inclusion and public communication. OMNES. *The Journal of Multicultural Society*, *12*(2), 26–68. DOI: 10.14431/omnes.2022.07.12.2.26

Tamer, H. Y. (2025). AI-Based Chatbots as Civil Servants: A Utopia or a Dystopia? In Sevinç Çubuk, E. (Ed.), *Digital Competency Development for Public Officials: Adapting New Technologies in Public Services* (pp. 121–152). IGI Global Scientific Publishing., DOI: 10.4018/979-8-3693-6547-2.ch006

Twizeyimana, J. D., & Andersson, A. (2019). The public value of e-government: A literature review. *Government Information Quarterly*, *36*(2), 167–178. DOI: 10.1016/j.giq.2019.01.001

Van Noordt, C., & Misuraca, G. (2019). New wine in old bottles: Chatbots in government – Exploring the transformative impact of chatbots in public service delivery Proceedings of the 11th IFIP WG 8.5 international conference on electronic participation, Springer, pp. 49-59.

Van Noordt, C., & Misuraca, G. (2022). Artificial intelligence for the public sector: Results of landscaping the use of AI in government across the European Union. *Government Information Quarterly*, *39*(3), 101714. DOI: 10.1016/j.giq.2022.101714

Wang, Y., Zhang, N., & Zhao, X. (2022). Understanding the determinants in the different government AI adoption stages: Evidence of local government chatbots in China. *Social Science Computer Review*, *40*(2), 534–554. DOI: 10.1177/0894439320980132

Wiethölter, J., Kühl, L., & Feldmann, C. (2024). AI-based chatbots as enabler for efficient external knowledge management in public administration. In Proceedings of the 7th Conference on Legal and Administrative Informatics (RVI 2024): New Approaches to Collaboration and Networking for Digital Transformation and Administrative Modernization (pp. 149–160). Gesellschaft für Informatik e.V. DOI: 10.18420/rvi2024-12

Zhou, M., Liu, L., & Feng, Y. (2025). Building citizen trust to enhance satisfaction in digital public services: The role of empathetic chatbot communication. *Behaviour & Information Technology*, •••, 1–20. DOI: 10.1080/0144929X.2025.2585328

ADDITIONAL READING

Jung, H., & Camarena, L. (2024). Street-Level Bureaucrats & AI Interactions in Public Organizations: An Identity Based Framework. *Public Performance & Management Review*, •••, 1–30. DOI: 10.1080/15309576.2024.2447352

Nam, J., & Bell, E. (2024). Efficiency or Equity? How Public Values Shape Bureaucrats' Willingness to Use Artificial Intelligence to Reduce Administrative Burdens. *Public Performance & Management Review*, •••, 1–34. DOI: 10.1080/15309576.2024.2419132

Rulandari, N., & Silalahi, A. D. K. (2025). Achieving effectiveness of public service in AI-enabled service from public value theory: does human–AI collaboration matters? Transforming Government: People. *Process and Policy*, *19*(2), 428–452.

Yuan, Q., & Chen, T. (2025). Holding AI-Based Systems Accountable in the Public Sector: A Systematic Review. *Public Performance & Management Review*, *48*(6), 1–34. DOI: 10.1080/15309576.2025.2469784

KEY TERMS AND DEFINITIONS

Algorithmic Neutrality: Chatbot systems must provide services in an impartial and unbiased manner, ensuring that no form of discrimination occurs based on gender, age, socioeconomic status, or other personal attributes.

Chatbot: Chatbots are AI- or rule-based systems that interact with citizens in real time, improving service efficiency and reducing staff workload.

Data-Driven Decision Making: Data obtained through chatbot interactions is systematically collected, processed, and analyzed to inform and support the design, implementation, and evaluation of public policies. This approach enables evidence-based decision-making, enhances transparency, and allows local governments to tailor services more effectively to citizen needs.

Digital Service Delivery: The process of delivering public services to citizens online and through technology encompasses not only information dissemination but also the provision of interactive services such as applications, transactions, and support. This approach aims to increase accessibility, efficiency, and transparency in the provision of government services.

Institutional Capacity: It is the ability of a municipality to implement, maintain, and effectively manage digital technologies, including the necessary human, technical, and organizational resources. Strong institutional capacity ensures that digital initiatives such as AI-based chatbots are sustainable, scalable, and capable of producing measurable public value.

Participatory Governance: It refers to the ability of citizens to contribute to public decision-making processes through digital tools, platforms, or interfaces in order to foster transparency, accountability, and a sense of civic empowerment among citizens.

User Experience (UX): The general satisfaction, accessibility, and ease of interaction experienced by citizens during their engagement with the chatbot reflects the overall quality of the service. A positive user experience can enhance citizen trust, encourage repeated use, and improve the effectiveness of digital service provision.

Chapter 9
Artificial Intelligence (AI) Policies in Public Administration:
The Case of Estonia

Aysun Öcal
https://orcid.org/0000-0003-4552-4521
Aksaray University, Turkey

Mustafa Zihni Tunca
https://orcid.org/0000-0003-2315-905X
Suleyman Demirel University, Turkey

ABSTRACT

As a pioneer in digital governance, Estonia exemplifies how AI can revolutionize public service delivery, with 99% of services accessible online, including AI-driven platforms like the federated virtual assistant network Bürokratt. Estonia's success stems from its phased infrastructure development, multi-stakeholder collaboration, and regulatory frameworks that balance efficiency with fundamental rights. However, challenges such as algorithmic bias risks, legacy system integration, and bureaucratic resistance persist. The study provides a conceptual framework for understanding Estonia's milestones while offering actionable recommendations for policymakers. By analyzing Estonia's model, this research highlights transferable lessons for nations pursuing digital sovereignty, particularly in harmonizing AI innovation with democratic values. Future research should explore longitudinal societal impacts and comparative governance models, especially in the context of the EU's evolving AI policies.

DOI: 10.4018/979-8-3373-1484-6.ch009

INTRODUCTION

Estonia's accession to the European Union in 2004, achieved after six years of rigorous negotiations, marked a pivotal turning point in the nation's modernization trajectory. This milestone catalyzed a series of transformative reforms, from joining the Schengen Area in 2007 to adopting the euro in 2011, each reinforcing Estonia's alignment with European institutions. The "*2023-2025 European Union Policy Priorities*", ratified in June 2023, exemplify Estonia's sustained commitment to innovation, positioning digital transformation as a cornerstone of its EU integration strategy.

Renowned as a global pioneer in digital governance, Estonia has redefined public service delivery through visionary policies. Nearly all public services (99%) are accessible online, supported by universal digital identities, creating a seamless interface between citizens and the state. The *Digital Agenda 2030* further articulates Estonia's ambition to harness emerging technologies—particularly artificial intelligence (AI)—to advance economic, administrative, and societal progress.

This study investigates Estonia's pioneering integration of AI into public administration, analyzing its implications for governance efficacy and democratic resilience. It establishes a conceptual framework to elucidate AI's role in the public sector, traces the historical evolution of AI adoption within Estonia's institutional architecture, and evaluates concrete implementations—from the *Bürokratt* virtual assistant network to AI-driven judicial and environmental management systems. By synthesizing these dimensions, the research distills transferable insights for nations aspiring to leverage AI's potential while safeguarding inclusivity and accountability. The findings aim to inform policy frameworks that balance technological innovation with ethical governance, offering a model for responsive and future-ready public administration.

CONCEPTUAL FRAMEWORK

The integration of Artificial Intelligence (AI) into e-governance has emerged as a transformative force in contemporary public administration, offering significant opportunities to enhance service delivery, decision-making, and citizen engagement. This synthesis of recent literature, spanning studies from 2019 to 2025, explores the multifaceted applications, benefits, challenges, and governance needs associated with AI in e-governance, drawing insights from systematic reviews, empirical case studies, and policy analyses. By consolidating diverse perspectives, this review provides a cohesive examination of AI's role in reshaping governance while addressing persistent ethical, technical, and regulatory complexities.

E-governance, defined as the application of information and communication technologies to improve government services and democratic participation, increasingly leverages AI tools such as machine learning, natural language processing (NLP), and predictive analytics. These technologies automate administrative tasks, optimize resource allocation, and enable real-time citizen interactions. For instance, AI-powered chatbots have been deployed by local governments, such as the London Borough of Barking and Dagenham, to reduce bureaucratic delays and improve user satisfaction by providing 24/7 support for inquiries related to taxes, permits, or public services (Zuiderwijk et al., 2021; Equality and Human Rights Commission, 2021). Similarly, predictive analytics has demonstrated efficacy in addressing complex societal challenges, such as homelessness prevention initiatives in Maidstone and Kent, where data-driven insights enabled proactive resource allocation and targeted interventions (Zuiderwijk et al., 2021; Al-Ansi et al., 2024). These applications underscore AI's capacity to streamline governance processes, though their effectiveness often depends on robust data infrastructure and seamless integration with legacy systems.

The benefits of AI in e-governance are well-documented across the literature. Automation of routine administrative tasks, such as processing citizen requests or managing public records, reduces operational burdens and costs while freeing human resources for strategic activities. Studies report reductions of up to 40% in processing times for functions like permit approvals or welfare claims, significantly enhancing governmental efficiency (Kankanhalli et al., 2019; Zuiderwijk et al., 2021). AI also enhances decision-making by extracting actionable insights from large datasets, enabling evidence-based policymaking. For example, predictive modeling has been employed to anticipate public health emergencies, economic downturns, or urban planning needs, facilitating proactive interventions and resource optimization (Fatima et al., 2020; Desouza et al., 2020). Furthermore, AI fosters personalized citizen engagement through tools like virtual assistants, which provide tailored responses and round-the-clock support, thereby improving accessibility and trust in public services (Androutsopoulou et al., 2019; Moreira & Naranjo-Zolotov, 2023). Cost reductions are another notable advantage, particularly in large-scale initiatives such as smart cities, where AI-driven resource optimization minimizes manual labor and operational expenditures (Wirtz et al., 2019; Al-Mushayt, 2019). Collectively, these benefits highlight AI's potential to enhance public value by making governance more responsive, efficient, and inclusive.

Despite these advantages, the adoption of AI in e-governance faces significant challenges, many of which stem from ethical, technical, and governance-related complexities. Ethical concerns, particularly algorithmic bias and privacy violations, are recurrent themes in the literature. Biased training data can perpetuate inequalities in critical areas such as welfare allocation, predictive policing, or social service delivery, disproportionately affecting marginalized groups (Zuiderwijk et al., 2021; Bullock, 2019). For instance, AI systems trained on historical data may replicate past discriminatory practices, leading to unfair outcomes in resource distribution or law enforcement (Aoki, 2020). Privacy risks are heightened by AI's reliance on vast datasets containing sensitive citizen information, with inadequate data protection frameworks in many jurisdictions exacerbating vulnerabilities (Wang & Siau, 2018; Saura et al., 2022). Technical barriers further complicate implementation, as legacy systems in public administrations often lack compatibility with modern AI architectures, necessitating costly upgrades (Al-Ansi et al., 2024; Hakimi et al., 2023). Poor data quality, such as incomplete or outdated records, undermines the accuracy of AI models, while a persistent skills gap in AI literacy among public servants limits effective deployment (Fatima et al., 2020; Medaglia et al., 2023). Governance and accountability issues also persist, with fragmented regulatory frameworks creating uncertainty about liability for AI-driven decisions. For example, the absence of standardized guidelines for auditing AI systems or addressing algorithmic errors raises questions about transparency and public trust (Thierer et al., 2017; Ashok et al., 2022). These challenges underscore the need for comprehensive oversight mechanisms to ensure AI's benefits are realized without compromising equity or democratic principles.

Governance frameworks are critical to mitigating these risks, and recent studies advocate for multi-level approaches that prioritize fairness, transparency, and human oversight. International initiatives, such as the European Union's AI Act and the OECD's ethical guidelines, emphasize the importance of stakeholder accountability, risk management, and public participation in AI governance (Etscheid, 2019; IAPP Report, 2025). These frameworks advocate for explainable algorithms, rigorous impact assessments, and mechanisms to ensure human oversight of AI systems, particularly in high-stakes domains like criminal justice or social services (Zuiderwijk et al., 2021; Ashok et al., 2022). However, regulatory fragmentation remains a significant obstacle, as jurisdictions adopt divergent approaches to AI governance. For instance, the United States favors market-driven innovation with minimal intervention, while China prioritizes state-controlled AI deployment for surveillance and social governance (Medaglia et al., 2023). Scholars stress the need for interdisciplinary collaboration to develop standardized ethical frameworks that balance innovation with accountability, incorporating insights from public administration, computer science, and legal studies (Schiff et al., 2020; Leiser & Murray, 2016). Additionally, non-state actors, including tech companies and civil society organizations, are increasingly recognized as vital partners in governance, contributing technical expertise and advocating for citizen-centric AI policies

(Butcher & Beridze, 2019; Vrabie, 2023). These efforts highlight the importance of inclusive, multi-stakeholder approaches to ensure AI aligns with public values and democratic norms.

The literature reveals notable research gaps that hinder a comprehensive understanding of AI's long-term implications for e-governance. Most existing studies are conceptual or qualitative, with limited empirical evidence on AI's societal impacts over time (Zuiderwijk et al., 2021). Western-centric perspectives dominate the discourse, often overlooking the unique challenges faced by developing nations, where infrastructural limitations, digital divides, and weaker regulatory capacities shape AI adoption (Schiff et al., 2020; Hakimi et al., 2023). For example, while AI-driven chatbots may enhance service delivery in well-resourced municipalities, their feasibility in regions with limited internet access or digital literacy remains understudied. Furthermore, there is a paucity of technology-specific analyses, particularly regarding emerging tools like generative AI, computer vision, or large language models, which have transformative potential but raise distinct ethical and operational questions (Jha & Jha, 2024; Totonchi, 2025). The literature also calls for longitudinal studies to assess AI's impact on public trust, bureaucratic efficiency, and democratic participation, as well as comparative assessments of governance models across different political and cultural contexts (Zuiderwijk et al., 2021; Mihus et al., 2024). Addressing these gaps is essential to develop context-sensitive strategies that ensure equitable AI deployment.

Future research directions proposed in the literature emphasize the need for empirical rigor, global inclusivity, and interdisciplinary collaboration. Longitudinal studies tracking the implementation of AI tools in public administrations could provide insights into their long-term efficacy and unintended consequences, such as workforce displacement or shifts in power dynamics between governments and citizens (Zuiderwijk et al., 2021). Comparative analyses of AI governance frameworks across regions, such as the EU's regulatory approach versus the U.S.'s innovation-centric model, could identify best practices for balancing accountability and technological advancement (Medaglia et al., 2023). Additionally, technology-specific investigations into tools like generative AI could explore their applications in drafting policies, simulating public feedback, or enhancing participatory governance, while addressing risks related to misinformation or bias (Jha & Jha, 2024; Totonchi, 2025). Scholars also advocate for greater focus on AI literacy programs for public servants, ensuring they possess the skills to critically evaluate AI systems and mitigate risks (Ashok et al., 2022). Finally, the literature underscores the importance of inclusive innovation, urging policymakers to engage marginalized communities in AI design and deployment to prevent exacerbating existing inequalities (Schiff et al., 2020; Vrabie, 2023). These priorities collectively highlight the need for a holistic research agenda that bridges technical, ethical, and sociopolitical dimensions.

In conclusion, AI holds transformative potential for e-governance, offering tools to enhance efficiency, decision-making, and citizen engagement. However, its successful integration hinges on addressing ethical dilemmas, technical barriers, and governance challenges through robust frameworks, empirical research, and global cooperation. The literature emphasizes that AI's benefits can only be realized through cautious, inclusive, and transparent implementation strategies that prioritize public trust, equity, and democratic values. As governments worldwide continue to experiment with AI-driven tools, interdisciplinary collaboration and context-sensitive policies will be essential to navigate the complexities of this technological paradigm shift. By synthesizing these insights, this review underscores the imperative of aligning AI innovation with the principles of accountability, fairness, and citizen-centric governance to foster equitable and effective public administration.

ESTONIA'S HISTORY OF DIGITAL DEVELOPMENT AND TRANSFORMATION

It must first be noted that Estonia's AI strategy bears a distinctive name with significant brand value: *Kratt*. This term derives from a renowned figure in Estonian mythology and folklore—an animated helper crafted from household objects and brought to life by drops of blood given to the devil. According to legend, the Kratt serves its owner by performing tasks but must be kept constantly occupied to prevent it from directing its energy against its master (Robinson et al., 2022). To elucidate Estonia's digital evolution, the process is divided into thematic sections. Initial efforts from the 1990s are briefly addressed, while the 2000s—marking a pivotal phase in the proliferation of digital identities and services—are examined under a separate heading. This section also details Estonia's transformative advancements in AI and cutting-edge technologies, supported by notable case studies.

The 1990s: Laying the Foundation

Following five decades of foreign domination, Estonia regained independence in 1991. Despite limited legacy technological systems and scarce resources, the nation seized the opportunity to build its technological infrastructure from the ground up. In 1994, the first draft of the *Principles of Estonian Information Policy* was published. This policy document aimed to harness technological capabilities to advance Tallinn's social, economic, and political objectives (Khalid et al., 2024). Consequently, 1% of GDP was allocated as state funding for information technology (Larsson, 2019).

The *Tiger Leap Initiative*, launched in 1996, sought to establish nationwide IT infrastructure. This program enabled 99% of the population to regularly use the internet, positioning Estonia first in the Digital Development Index. That same year, pioneering e-banking services—developed by private banks as a digital banking solution—were introduced. This system catalyzed the creation of high-quality e-banking services, incentivizing citizens to engage online and later adopt e-governance and digital ID solutions.

The 2000s: Proliferation of Digital Identity Services and Adoption of Advanced Technologies

The decade marked transformative milestones, beginning with the inaugural e-Cabinet Meeting in 2000. This digital governance initiative streamlined bureaucratic processes, reducing average cabinet meeting duration from five hours to 30 minutes. Concurrently, the e-Tax Board was established, enabling Estonians to declare taxes online—a system adopted by 99% of citizens for income reporting.

Further innovations included the 2000 launch of m-Parking, a mobile payment system for urban parking fees. Its global replication underscored Estonia's pioneering role. In 2001, the X-Road data exchange layer interconnected public and private sector information systems, facilitating 24/7 digital access to *100% ofpublic services*.

A cornerstone achievement was the 2002 implementation of e-ID and digital signatures, an AI-integrated system providing 99% of citizens with identity cards. This solution yields annual savings equivalent to *2% of GDP* (Government of Estonia, 2023).

Electoral innovation emerged in 2005 with i-Voting, boosting participation by enabling online ballots. By 2023, *one-third of all votes* were cast digitally from over 110 countries. Cybersecurity became critical after April 2007, when Estonia weathered the *world's largest coordinated cyberattack* against a single nation. This precipitated the development of world-class cyber defenses, cementing Estonia's status as a key cybersecurity partner for the EU and NATO. Presently, Tallinn hosts both the EU Agency for Cybersecurity (ENISA) and NATO's Cooperative Cyber Defence Centre of Excellence.

Notably, Estonia adopted blockchain technology in 2008—predating its global prominence—and remains a recognized pioneer in this domain. In healthcare, the nationwide e-Health system (2008) integrated provider data, followed by e-Prescriptions (2010), through which *100% of medical prescriptions* are now digitally processed.

2013 – Present: Sustainable Governance and Frontier Technologies

To ensure the sustainability and future evolution of its e-state, Estonia implemented the Green Paper for Public Services in 2013. This framework established clear objectives and principles to "better understand citizen needs and enhance e-service development" (Estonian Government, 2013).

A paradigm shift occurred in 2014 with e-Residency, creating the world's first transnational digital society. This initiative grants global citizens access to Estonian e-services, redefining notions of citizenship and governance. That same year, the Road Administration's e-Portal simplified bureaucratic procedures and reduced administrative costs.

In 2017, Estonia pioneered the world's first data embassy in Luxembourg, securing critical databases in a high-security cloud facility. The Nordic Institute for Interoperability Solutions (NIIS) consortium, co-founded with Finland, advanced cross-border e-governance through shared X-Road infrastructure.

The 2018 Flawless Services Roadmap optimized public service efficiency under the motto *"Less bureaucracy, fewer human resources."* Estonia then became the first nation to adopt an official Government AI Strategy in 2019, providing a framework for public and private sector AI implementation.

Key social innovations include:

- Proactive Child Care System (circa 2020): Leveraging state data to automatically identify and address childcare needs for newborns.
- Remote Notarization (2020): Enabled real estate transactions without physical presence, accelerated during the pandemic.
- e-Marriage (2022) and e-Divorce (2024): Digitized 100% of civil procedures.

Technological milestones feature the world's first autonomous hydrogen vehicle Liisu (Auve Tech/University of Tartu, 2021), developed as an eco-friendly transport alternative. By 2024, the eesti.ee state app enabled mobile access to all public services, achieving 100% digitalization of government functions (e-Estonia, 2025).

This evolution reflects Estonia's distinctive approach: convening multi-stakeholder expertise while avoiding overly ambitious strategies (Kaska et al., 2021).

ESTONIA'S NATIONAL DIGITALIZATION STRATEGIES

The UN explicitly highlights Estonia's trajectory as demonstrating how "strategic digital policies and investments substantially enhance e-government services and infrastructure" (United Nations, 2024:120), positioning the country as an exemplary model for nations pursuing integrated digital transformation. This recognition reflects Estonia's consistent advancement from eighth to second position globally within a four-year period, underscoring the efficacy of its governance approach.

Estonia's advancements in digital governance are anchored by robust legal and policy frameworks, including the following key statutes (*Riigi Teataja*, 2025):

- **Information Society Services Act (2004)**: Regulates digital service providers and establishes accountability mechanisms for violations.
- **Electronic Communications Act (2005)**: Promotes development of digital infrastructure for electronic communications.
- **Payment Institutions and E-Money Institutions Act (2010)**: Governs payment/e-money services, operational requirements, and supervisory frameworks for financial entities.
- **Electronic Identification and Trust Services Act (2016)**: Implements secure standards for electronic transactions and aligns with EU regulations (eIDAS).
- **Cybersecurity Act (2018)**: Mandates critical information system enhancements to prevent cybercrime.
- **Crypto-Assets Markets Act (2024)**: Regulates market participant activities, liability, termination procedures, and oversight in crypto-asset markets (newest legislative update).

ESTONIA'S NATIONAL ARTIFICIAL INTELLIGENCE STRATEGY AND POLICY FRAMEWORK

Estonia has emerged as a global exemplar in artificial intelligence (AI) governance, as evidenced by the Organisation for Economic Co-operation and Development's (OECD) recognition of its AI ecosystem (OECD, 2025). Central to this achievement is the National Artificial Intelligence Strategy (2019–2022), which was explicitly designed to operationalize international principles for trustworthy and human-centric AI (OECD, 2019) by embedding them within a coherent policy framework. This strategy, mobilizing over €10 million in public-private investments and later supplemented by funding commitments of €20 million by 2023 and €85 million for 2024–2026 (Robinson et al., 2022; Riisalo, 2023), positioned AI as "a transformative instrument for elevating economic productivity and public service potential." In crafting this strategy, Estonia drew directly from OECD guidance on public sector integration (OECD, 2021) and inclusive growth through private sector deployment (OECD Economic Surveys: Estonia, 2022), thereby exceeding baseline recommendations through targeted initiatives such as the Privacy-Enhancing

Technologies (PETs) Action Plan (Estonian Ministry of Economic Affairs and Communications, 2021; OECD, 2020).

Underpinning these policy ambitions is a robust technical infrastructure characterized by interoperable public sector information systems that translate abstract governance principles into concrete administrative mechanisms. The Public Sector Information Systems Catalogue (RIHA) serves as the official registry of the state's information assets, ensuring that AI deployments comply with OECD recommendations on interoperability and transparent governance (OECD Digital Government Studies, 2020; Government of Estonia, 2023). Complementing RIHA, the Estonian Open Data Portal provides an accessible platform for data consumption, visualization, and reuse scenarios, thereby catalyzing innovation across both public and private sectors while adhering to OECD data governance frameworks (World Bank, 2022; OECD, 2020). The X-Road data exchange layer, overseen by the Estonian Information System Authority, further exemplifies practical implementation of OECD data governance principles by balancing accessibility with security (Estonian Information System Authority, 2023; OECD, 2020).

Concurrent with the National AI Strategy, the Digital Agenda 2030 (Estonian Government, 2021) articulates a broader vision for digital transformation through seven ethical principles—respect for human dignity and autonomy, equitable treatment and justice, robust privacy protection, system reliability and safety, operational transparency, clear accountability, and commitments to social and environmental welfare—that directly respond to the OECD's call for responsible stewardship of AI technologies (OECD AI Policy Observatory, 2022; OECD, 2019). Implemented through an inter-ministerial collaboration between the Ministry of Economic Affairs and Communications and the Ministry of Justice (OECD Public Governance Reviews, 2023), the Agenda situates AI within a multilateral context, notably through Estonia's leadership in the Nordic-Baltic Declaration on AI (Nordic Council of Ministers, 2019), which extends human-centric governance principles across ten nations. These ethical commitments are institutionalized through rigorous oversight mechanisms that have been recognized by international bodies, including the Council of Europe, UNESCO, and the Freedom Online Coalition, underscoring Estonia's dual role as practitioner and innovator in ethical digital governance.

Among the most tangible manifestations of Estonia's AI governance is the Bürokratt Network, a federated system of interoperable virtual assistants that leverages conversational AI to streamline citizen–agency communication. Developed under the aegis of AI Empowering Estonia (2025) and aligned with OECD recommendations for interoperable digital government services (OECD, 2022), the Bürokratt Network exemplifies how localized AI solutions can scale to nationwide platforms. In parallel, the National AI Project Repository functions as a centralized database documenting public sector AI use cases and deployments, enabling transparent knowledge sharing as advocated by OECD transparency guidelines (OECD, 2021; OECD.AI, 2025). These infrastructure components illustrate how Estonia has translated abstract governance principles into replicable technical architectures.

The National Artificial Intelligence Strategy's four strategic pillars—public sector integration, private sector deployment, R&D capacity building, and adaptive regulatory frameworks—have catalyzed a broad ecosystem of programs and partnerships. Industrial adoption is driven by initiatives such as AI & Robotics Estonia, which supports the integration of intelligent digital solutions in manufacturing and services (OECD.AI, 2025). Public-facing programs like SUVE: AI-Powered Crisis Response, deployed during the COVID-19 pandemic to disseminate real-time public health information via chatbot, demonstrate Estonia's agility in leveraging AI for crisis management. Technical assistance is provided through the AI Support Portfolio, which offers human-centric guidance to public institutions, while the AI Task Force Report articulates policy recommendations for scalable nationwide implementation. The Open-Source AI Components initiative has produced reusable toolsets, lowering barriers to entry for both public and private stakeholders, and reinforcing the strategic emphasis on transparency and collaboration. Concurrently, the Privacy-Enhancing Technologies (PETs) Action Plan continues to guide secure data usage in alignment with OECD Privacy Guidelines (2013), minimizing personal data exposure while optimizing processing capabilities.

Building on these operational programs, Estonia has sequenced its strategic priorities through successive iterations of its National AI Strategy. The foundational National AI Strategy 1.0 (2019–2021) laid the groundwork for promoting AI usage across sectors, enhancing R&D capabilities, and establishing preliminary regulatory frameworks. National AI Strategy 2.0, effective since 2022, shifts the focus toward ethical AI governance and cross-sectoral scaling, emphasizing iterative refinement based on empirical insights from early adopters and case studies, as documented in the AI Task Force Report (OECD.AI, 2025). This evolution in strategy underscores Estonia's commitment to a dynamic governance model in which localized pilot successes inform national policy adjustments.

Looking forward, the AI Leap 2025 (TI-Hüpe 2025) initiative, set to launch on 1 September 2025, represents a groundbreaking effort to democratize AI access within the educational ecosystem (e-Estonia, 2025). Combining technology access, teacher training, and ethical frameworks, the program will provide universal free access to world-class AI applications, comprehensive pedagogical support, and targeted skill development for students across all educational levels. In doing so, AI Leap 2025 directly addresses OECD warnings about AI readiness gaps by integrating the OECD Skills Outlook (2023) and insights from OECD AI in Work, Innovation, Productivity and Skills (2022) into its design. By positioning itself as a testbed for OECD-aligned AI governance in education, Estonia further cements its status as a global reference point for responsible AI adoption, with active engagement in standard-setting bodies such as UNESCO and the Freedom Online Coalition providing a backdrop for international collaboration (Education Estonia, 2021).

Estonia's experience offers valuable lessons for other nations seeking to operationalize abstract governance principles through tangible mechanisms such as interoperable infrastructure (RIHA), dynamic funding models (Riisalo, 2023), and privacy-preserving technologies (OECD, 2020). The country's initiatives illustrate how balancing innovation with regulation—particularly through the implementation of PETs—can foster trust without stifling technological progress. Moreover, Estonia's multilateral governance models, exemplified by participation in the Nordic-Baltic Declaration on AI and adherence to the OECD International Regulatory Cooperation framework (2021), demonstrate how small, digitally advanced nations can exert outsized influence in the global AI arena. In sum, the Estonian case underscores the necessity of integrating policy, technical architecture, and ethical considerations into a cohesive, iterative strategy, thereby offering a replicable template for public sector AI governance that aspires to be both trustworthy and human-centric.

EU INTEGRATION PROCESS AND AI POLICY HARMONIZATION WITH EU FRAMEWORKS

Estonia's substantive engagement with the European Union commenced upon receiving its formal accession invitation in 1999. Former Foreign Minister Toomas Hendrik Ilves highlighted the protracted effort required to build public consensus, noting that dismantling preconceptions about European integration constituted the most significant challenge (Demirtaş, 2020). During the pre-accession phase, Estonia strategically joined key European institutions including the Organization for Security and Co-operation in Europe (OSCE) and the Council of Europe. Following the 1993 local elections, President Mart Laar consistently prioritized deepening economic and political integration with EU member states, framing this alignment as essential for national development (Eravcı, 2020).

The post-accession period involved complex institutional learning through three key processes: membership negotiation experience, participation in the European Convention's constitutional treaty development, and ultimately the ratification of the Lisbon Treaty in 2007 after the rejection of the Constitutional Treaty. Estonia formally acceded to the EU in 2004 alongside nine other states, including Latvia, Lithuania, and Slovenia. Subsequent integration milestones included accession to the Schengen Area in 2007, adoption of the Euro in 2011, and assuming the Presidency of the Council of the EU in 2017.

During Estonia's 2017 Presidency of the Council of the EU, the European Commission Authentication System (ECAS) recognized its success in elevating digitalization and technological advancement to the forefront of the Union's agenda. ECAS particularly commended Estonia's ambitious vision to "extend beyond the negotiated Digital Single Market," "harness the digital revolution for greater citizen benefit," and establish free data flow as the EU's fifth fundamental freedom. An ECIPE study underscored the economic rationale, projecting that implementing cross-border data flows could yield €8 billion annually while preventing €52 billion in losses from data localization measures. However, ECAS also cautioned that digitalization must transcend economic and public service benefits to strengthen democratic processes—notably through electoral innovations—assigning Estonia a pivotal role in this transformation (ECAS, 2017).

The European Commission's 2018 definition of artificial intelligence fundamentally anchors Estonia's regulatory approach: "Artificial intelligence denotes systems that exhibit intelligent behavior by analyzing their environment and acting autonomously toward objectives" (European Commission, 2018). This conceptualization directly informs Estonia's governance frameworks for emerging technologies. The Commission further delineates dual implementation pathways for AI systems: software-based applications (virtual assistants, image analysis tools, search engines, and biometric systems) and hardware-embedded solutions (advanced robotics, autonomous vehicles, drones, and IoT applications).

Estonia's implementation reflects both modalities, as evidenced by its virtual assistant networks like Bürokratt (software-based) and autonomous hydrogen vehicle initiatives like Liisu (hardware-embedded). This alignment demonstrates Estonia's commitment to the EU's technological governance paradigm while allowing room for national innovations that exceed baseline requirements, such as the 2024 Crypto-Assets Act which extends beyond the EU's MiCA regulation framework.

Quantitative analysis reveals significant shifts in public perception throughout the integration process. Eurobarometer data indicates that public support for EU membership rose from 36% during pre-accession (1999) to 67% post-accession (2004). The 2017 EU Council Presidency enabled Estonia to advance its digital governance agenda, directly influencing key policy instruments including the 2018 AI definition (Veebel, 2009). This strategic positioning allowed Estonia to transform from policy adopter to agenda-setter in domains like cybersecurity, where it now hosts both ENISA (EU Agency for Cybersecurity) and NATO's Cooperative Cyber Defence Centre of Excellence.

Ibrus et al. (2022) identify four critical requirements for sustaining Estonia's digital cultural autonomy in their *Digital Culture Manifesto*: enhanced understanding of platformization mechanisms and consequences; systematic strategic engagement with EU platform regulation frameworks; platform-aware development of public services, particularly within cultural and educational institutions; and pursuit of systematic decentralization pathways for internet infrastructures and services. This manifesto is distinguished by its integration of ethical and social considerations, emphasizing the imperative to transform cultural metadata into interconnected datasets through ethically rigorous methodologies. Crucially, it advocates for data justice—demanding that data collection, commodification, and algorithmic decision-making processes be developed, analyzed, and regulated according to their impact on societal equity, specifically examining whether individuals and groups receive fair treatment when categorized by activity-derived data.

The manifesto outlines key implementation priorities: ensuring universal accessibility of digital governance channels; strengthening local digital cultural industries as vital to Estonian identity; providing targeted support for digital arts; establishing a centralized digital cultural heritage platform; and developing long-term digital archiving strategies. It further mandates rigorous assessment of AI applications' alignment with national cultural interests and concurrently urges Estonia's proactive engagement with European green AI certification frameworks to address digitalization's ecological dimensions.

The European Commission's 2023 Country Report highlighted persistent productivity constraints in Estonia, attributing slower growth to below-average business investment in R&D (relative to EU norms) and delayed adoption of big data and AI technologies—partially due to shortages of qualified specialists. To address these gaps, Estonia established a National Innovation Agency to enhance industry-academia collaboration and launched large-scale grant programs supporting corporate R&D. Concurrently, it created a Centre of Excellence for Data Management and Open Data to improve the quality, accessibility, and reuse of public sector data. These institutional reforms aim to make digital transition policies more accessible while strengthening e-governance capabilities (European Commission, 2023).

On 22 June 2023, the Estonian government approved its European Union Policy Priorities for 2023-2025. This policy document centers on foreign affairs, security, and defense while emphasizing digital transitions and energy security. Key technological and digitalization provisions critical to understanding Estonia's integration with the EU include four core imperatives. First, evolving security threats, technological advancements, and environmental shifts necessitate enhanced European crisis resilience and operational continuity. Second, disrupted relations with an aggressive and revisionist Russia require strengthening strategic energy, transport, and communication links. Third, successful implementation of green and digital reforms must anchor the EU's four fundamental freedoms (movement of goods, services, capital, and people) alongside data flows, leveraging EU funds optimally. Fourth, modern data-driven solutions should replace burdensome corporate reporting requirements, with Estonia committing to extend stakeholder engagement principles to draft EU legislation negotiations (Republic of Estonia Government, 2023).

Under its Recovery and Resilience Plan, Estonia committed to critical digital infrastructure milestones by 2024: 1) Migrating core digital services—including data embassy functions—to national cloud infrastructure; and 2) Deploying ultra-high-capacity broadband (≥100 Mbps) to 4,000 new households and socioeconomically significant institutions (hospitals, schools, public services, businesses). These deliverables align with the European Commission against Racism and Intolerance's (ECRI) 2024 recommendations, emphasizing digital inclusion as foundational for societal resilience (European Commission, 2023; ECRI, 2024).

The European Commission's 2024 "Cohesive Estonia Strategy 2030" highlights Estonia's promotion of virtual workspaces alongside facilitation of short-term labor mobility and digital nomadism. Estonia pioneers initiatives like the *digital nomad visa* and *e-residency program*, attracting approximately 1,800 annual visa applications. This advances Estonia's internationalization through the "Global Estonia" concept while creating opportunities to redefine national identity in the digital age. The strategy further emphasizes human-centered e-service optimization, requiring public services to adapt to evolving user needs and habits through simplified digital interfaces.

The strategy outlines preparations for digitizing integration services—including adaptation programs—to develop modern, intelligent pathways for efficient client-centered delivery. Concurrently, Estonia continues developing inclusive digital language-learning platforms for all age groups. Cross-sectoral objectives for digital society and cybersecurity establish prerequisites for achieving population registry goals. Estonia's EU policy priorities further prioritize building an integrated society through enhanced cultural access via digital tools and competences (European Commission, 2024).

ESTONIA'S LEADING AI INITIATIVES

The UN E-Government Survey (2020) establishes that robust political will, strategic leadership, and commitment to expanding digital service delivery are fundamental determinants of success in the E-Government Development Index (EGDI). Estonia exemplifies this through its articulation of shared digital vision, adoption of holistic strategies, implementation of resilient platforms, and cultivation of dynamic digital ecosystems. The nation ranked eighth globally in both the 2020 and 2022 surveys, while achieving third position in the E-Participation Index and fifth place among

European states. By 2024, Estonia ascended to second place globally in the EGDI rankings, surpassed only by Denmark (United Nations, 2024:22).

The UN explicitly highlights Estonia's trajectory as demonstrating how “strategic digital policies and investments substantially enhance e-government services and infrastructure” (United Nations, 2024:120), positioning the country as an exemplary model for nations pursuing integrated digital transformation. This recognition reflects Estonia's consistent advancement from eighth to second position globally within a four-year period, underscoring the efficacy of its governance approach.

Estonia's commitment to enhancing governance and public service accessibility through digital technologies is evidenced by its tangible achievements and exemplary applications. The implementation of AI-driven solutions—such as SUVE, a real-time informational chatbot, and Bürokratt, an interoperable virtual assistant network—demonstrates AI's capacity to increase public sector efficiency while maintaining citizen-centric service delivery.

Estonia's public sector AI deployments span multiple domains. Financial systems utilize AI for tax fraud detection, while environmental management employs computer vision for remote monitoring of forests, crops, snow cover, ice, floods, and wildlife. Transportation innovations include autonomous museum buses in Tallinn and Tartu, alongside hospital transport robots optimizing medical logistics. Educational initiatives feature personalized learning solutions for students, and legal processes leverage AI for online notarial services through remote authentication. Linguistic applications encompass machine translation and text-to-speech systems, with national broadcasting using real-time automated subtitling. Government transparency is enhanced through automated transcription of court proceedings and parliamentary sessions.

The e-Cabinet system streamlines governmental decision-making, while the e-Tax Board enables 100% online tax declarations. Citizen participation is institutionalized via Rahvaalgatus.ee, a platform allowing citizens to draft proposals, create digitally signed collective petitions, facilitate policy discussions, and formally submit initiatives to Parliament (United Nations, 2020). These integrated applications collectively exemplify Estonia's model of embedding AI to optimize administrative functions while expanding democratic engagement (e-Estonia, 2025).

In addition to these projects, Table 1 was created to showcase other initiatives implemented in Estonia using artificial intelligence, in order to highlight the country's progress in digital transformation. The table particularly emphasizes notable projects, specifying the institutions that developed them, their starting years, and their current status (AI Empowering Estonia, 2025).

Table 1. List of AI initiatives in Estonia

Institution	Year	Project Name	Project Status
North Estonia Medical Centre	2015	Speech recognition in radiology	Completed
	2022	Chatbots in hospitals	In development
Institute of the Estonian Language	2016	EstNLTK	In development
	2022	Word cloud generator	In use
Estonian Public Broadcasting	2020	Automated real-time subtitling	In use
State Forest Management Centre	2020	Automatic tool for planning felling	Completed
Tallinn Transport Department	2018	Better traffic management	Completed
Enterprise Estonia	2018	E-Residency Bot	In use
	2019	EIA	In use
National Archives of Estonia	2018	Transkribus	In use
	2018	FOTIS	In use
	2020	Ilme	In use
Chancellery of the Riigikogu	2018	HANS	In use
Statistics Estonia	2018	ITI	In use
Environment Agency	2018	Keeping records of forest resources with remote sensing methods	In use
	2019	Information system for ice map preparation	In use
	2019	Water level monitoring	Completed
	2020	Detecting clear cutting of forests	Completed
	2021	Calculating the height of a forest	In use
	2021	Identifying tree species in the forests	In use
	2021	Distance monitoring of forests	Completed
	2022	Remote monitoring of snow	In development

continued on following page

Table 1. Continued

Institution	Year	Project Name	Project Status
University of Tartu	2018	Neurokõne	In use
	2018	Neurotõlge	In use
	2019	MAITT - Work Package 3 (Health)	Completed
	2021	SayEst	In use
Estonian Unemployment Insurance Fund	2018	OTT	In use
	2019	Transcription and analysis of customer calls	In use
	2019	MAITT - Work Package 1 (Employment)	In use
ARIB	2018	SATIKAS	In use
Ministry of Education and Research	2018	Texta Toolkit	In use
	2022	Personalised learning pathway	In development
Estonian Road Administration	2018	Traffic sign detection	Completed
	2020	Improving traffic safety	Completed
Estonian Tax and Customs Board	2019	Creating a risk model from bulk data	In use
	2019	Tool detecting possible envelope wage payers	In use
	2021	Tool detecting possible VAT fraud	In use
Estonian Health Insurance Fund	2019	Tool for customer calls	Completed
	2019	Verification of treatment invoices	In use
	2019	Forecasting the health and treatment needs of chronically ill patients	Completed
	2019	Treatment invoice database	Completed
Emergency Response Centre	2019	Transcription of emergency calls	Completed
	2020	Transcription of crisis hotline 1247	Completed
	2020	Threat assessment assistant	Completed

continued on following page

Table 1. Continued

Institution	Year	Project Name	Project Status
Department of Marine Systems	2019	Flood detection prototype	Completed
Agency of Medicines	2019	Monitoring medicinal product pricing	Completed
	2019	INNA - medicinal product name assessment	Completed
Chamber of Notaries	2019	Identification of a person in remote authentication	In use
Information System Authority	2019	Identifying data exchange anomalies in the X-Road system	Completed
Rescue Board	2019	MAITT - Work Package 2 (Fire Safety)	Completed
Tallinn University of Technology	2019	MAITT - Work Package 4 (Cyber security)	Completed
	2021	Online speech recognition	In use
Ministry of Economic Affairs and Communications	2019	Remote monitoring in the construction sector	Completed
	2021	Siimuke: customer enquiry classifier	Completed
	2022	Business viability index and tool	In development
	2022	Early warning service for businesses	Completed
Estonian Courts	2019	Salme	In use
National Heritage Board	2019	Sälli	Completed
	2022	Folli	Completed
National Library of Estonia	2019	Vesta	Completed
	2022	Marta: Automated keywording of articles	Completed
Ministry of the Interior	2019	Wildfire risk reduction	Completed

continued on following page

Table 1. Continued

Institution	Year	Project Name	Project Status
Centre of Registers and Information Systems	2020	Machine translation of official notices of the Riigi Teataja	In use
	2020	Translation tool in e-Business Register	In use
	2021	Business name checker	In development
	2021	Translation tool in Land Register search portal	In use
Education and Youth Board	2020	Marakratt	Completed
Ministry of Rural Affairs	2020	Identifying crops using satellite imagery	Completed
Estonian Academy of Security Sciences	2020	Kotkas	Completed
Enterprise Estonia, Ministry of Justice, Ministry of Economic Affairs and Communications, North Estonia Medical Centre, Ministry of Social Affairs, Consumer Protection and Technical Regulatory Authority, Ministry of Culture, Health Board	2020	SUVE	Completed
Consumer Protection and Technical Regulatory Authority	2021	Enquiry tagger	In use
Social Insurance Board	2021	Customer enquiries automation	Completed
National Audit Office of Estonia	2021	Detecting prohibited election campaigns	Completed
TalTech Laboratory of Language Technology	2021	Tekstiks.ee	In use
Ministry of Social Affairs	2022	Pay Mirror	In development
Ministry of Education and Research, Register of Economic Activities, Police and Border Guard Board, National Library of Estonia, Statistics Estonia, Consumer Protection and Technical Regulatory Authority, Viimsi rural municipality government	2022	Bürokratt	In development
Ministry of Justice	2022	Removing personal data from court decisions	In development
Tartu University Hospital	2021	Robot Pepper	In use
	2022	Transport robots in the hospital	In development
Police and Border Guard Board	2018	Calls transcription	Completed
Rae Municipality, Tartu City Government / Estonian National Museum	2022	Iseauto	Completed

continued on following page

Table 1. Continued

Institution	Year	Project Name	Project Status
Defence Forces	2022	KrattWorks target drones	In use
Teede Tehnokeskus AS	2022	Superhands - Road salinity derivation	In development
State Information System Authority	2023	LLM trained on national legislation	In use

Initiated from 2015 onward, the projects referenced in Table 1 exhibit substantial thematic diversity across implementation phases—ranging from completed deployments to operational systems and ongoing developments. Foundational to Estonia's citizen-centric e-governance are core applications including i-Voting for secure digital elections, e-Health for remote medical service delivery, e-ID for identity verification, and e-Marriage/e-Divorce platforms enabling fully digital civil procedures. These systems collectively establish the infrastructure for Estonia's digital public services.

Foremost among efficiency initiatives is Bürokratt, an interoperable network of AI-powered chatbots facilitating citizen interactions with government agencies through conversational interfaces, significantly reducing administrative burdens as documented by AI Empowering Estonia. Complementing this system, Enterprise Estonia's EMMA (Electronic Multimedia Assistant), launched in 2020, enhances public sector marketing capabilities through natural language processing. Critical infrastructure includes the X-Road data exchange layer, operational since 2017, which detects data anomalies while supporting open data compliance across public institutions through its secure interoperability framework (Enterprise Estonia, 2018).

Environmental monitoring leverages the AI Detecting Wild Animals system, active since 2020, which classifies trail camera imagery via computer vision and applies Random Encounter Modelling to quantify wildlife populations. Educational transformation is evidenced by the AI in Education initiative (2020), where machine learning models analyze digital learning patterns to generate assessment prototypes and pedagogical data science methodologies. Regulatory efficiency advanced through the 2022 Ads Scraper in Social Media project, automating detection of non-compliant advertisements.

Data-driven public services feature collaborative projects such as the Analysis of Customer Calls pilot (Social Insurance Board and Feelingstream, 2020), applying speech analytics to service interactions; the Estonian Biobank's 2019 Analysis of Health Data project structuring medical records via ML; and the State Portal Usability Analytics system (2020) optimizing citizen interface design. Data protection is strengthened through the Anonymiser tool (2022), a GDPR-compliant solution minimizing personal data exposure risks during processing.

Security applications include the Automated Border Control Gates deployed at Tallinn Airport and Narva border crossing in 2021, alongside the National Library's Automated Book Keywording system (2019) enhancing cultural accessibility. Defense integration focuses on AI-enhanced military training systems as analyzed by Jermalavičius (2024:149-150), with universities incubating specialized firms: Milrem Robotics (unmanned ground vehicles), Threod Systems (UAVs), and Marduk Technologies (counter-drone solutions).

Cybersecurity leadership manifests through Cybernetica's cryptographic AI development, notably its PAI-MACHINE project with U.S. Naval Research funding enabling "secure collaborative AI without classified data compromise" (Cybernetica, 2023). Strategic partnerships include the CR14 Foundation-NATO CCDCOE alliance and the EU-funded iMUGS/iMUGS2 initiatives—Europe's ambitious defense robotics programs led by Milrem Robotics (European Commission, 2020; iMUGS, 2025). This ecosystem collectively demonstrates Estonia's cross-sectoral integration of digital solutions within governance frameworks.

CRITICAL PERSPECTIVES ON ESTONIA'S DIGITAL TRANSFORMATION

While Estonia's global leadership in digital governance is widely recognized, its approach has not been immune to criticism. Several key challenges and critiques have emerged, reflecting tensions between innovation and practical implementation.

One significant critique centers on bureaucratic inertia, where some officials appear content with existing systems rather than pushing for continuous improvement. More substantively, concerns have been raised about the limitations of Estonia's flagship X-Road (X-tee) data exchange platform. Critics argue that while the system is technologically advanced, it cannot single-handedly ensure comprehensive data protection under current legislation, particularly regarding the principle that citizens should only need to provide their data to one government entity (Dreyling et al., 2024).

The architecture of Estonia's AI-assisted services has also faced scrutiny. Rather than relying on a centralized government chatbot, experts suggest that a more effective model would involve interoperable, localized chatbots linked to individual government agencies and their respective databases. This decentralized approach could potentially offer greater precision, accountability, and user-specific functionality.

It is important to contextualize these critiques—while relevant for Estonia's advanced digital ecosystem, they represent concerns that are not yet urgent priorities for nations like Turkey, which are still developing their foundational digital governance frameworks. Estonia's challenges largely reflect the complexities of refining an already mature system rather than addressing basic implementation gaps.

These criticisms do not diminish Estonia's achievements but rather highlight the ongoing need for evolution in digital governance—particularly in balancing efficiency with robust data protection, and centralized systems with localized functionality. The debates surrounding Estonia's model provide valuable insights for other nations anticipating similar developmental trajectories in their digital transformation journeys.

ETHICAL AND SOCIAL CONSIDERATIONS IN AI IMPLEMENTATION

The integration of artificial intelligence (AI) into public administration presents both opportunities and challenges that require careful consideration (Guckelberge, 2019; Pilving & Mikiver, 2020). While the benefits are frequently highlighted, this section focuses on the critical issues that emerge from AI adoption in governance.

Algorithmic Bias and Governance Challenges

Algorithmic bias represents a primary governance challenge in Estonia's adoption of automated decision-making (ADM) systems, recognized as a significant risk to equitable public service delivery. The central concern revolves around whether automation can uphold fairness, transparency, and accountability in governmental decision processes. Biased algorithms risk generating inequitable outcomes—such as discriminatory access to social benefits or biased hiring practices—undermining public trust in digital governance. Critical unresolved issues include establishing effective appeal mechanisms for citizens to challenge automated decisions, defining clear oversight responsibilities for algorithmic monitoring, and ensuring regulatory alignment between GDPR and the EU AI Act—particularly regarding transparency mandates, accountability structures, and human oversight requirements.

Estonia acknowledges that efficiency gains alone are insufficient for legitimate public administration; institutional trust remains equally vital. To address these challenges, Estonia has launched initiatives like *EquiTech*, a TalTech Law School project funded by the European Commission (2024–2026). This initiative specifically targets the mitigation of discrimination and bias in ADM systems through technical audits and ethical framework development, exemplifying Estonia's proactive approach to balancing innovation with fundamental rights protection (e-Estonia, 2025).

The Digital Divide

Estonia's proactive approach to bridging the digital divide—defined as disparities in access, affordability, and competency with digital technologies—exemplifies its commitment to inclusive governance. Since the late 1990s, the Tiger Leap Foundation has spearheaded nationwide efforts to eliminate technological inequities, equipping all schools with internet connectivity and modern computer infrastructure (Roonemaa, 2017). This foundational investment catalyzed a generational shift in digital literacy, positioning Estonia as Europe's most digitally skilled society by 2023 (Eurostat, 2023). By 2023, 93.2% of Estonian households had broadband access (e-Estonia, 2025), an achievement fueled by targeted policies including the Rural Broadband Program which subsidized fiber-optic rollout to remote areas (Ministry of Economic Affairs and Communications [MEAC], 2021), the establishment of over 1,200 public access points offering free Wi-Fi and computing facilities in libraries and community centers (Estonian Librarians Association, 2024), and VAT exemptions on computers for low-income families (Ministry of Finance, 2020).

Despite these advances, significant disparities persist. Elderly populations (aged 65+) exhibit 32% lower digital service adoption rates compared to the national average (Statistics Estonia, 2023), while regional gaps endure in Ida-Viru County due to socioeconomic factors and shortages of Russian-language digital content (UNICEF, 2022). Estonia addresses these challenges through multifaceted interventions: the Digital Champions Network, comprising over 500 volunteers who provide peer-to-peer digital tutoring (Tiger Leap Foundation, 2025); multilingual interfaces on e-governance platforms, particularly in Ukrainian and Russian (MEAC, 2023); and stringent accessibility mandates requiring all public sector websites to comply with WCAG 2.1 standards (Digital Affairs Act, 2022).

The e-Residency program further redefines digital inclusion by extending access to Estonia's digital services to over 110,000 global citizens since 2014, transforming digital divides into bridges for transnational engagement (e-Residency Annual Report, 2024). However, emerging challenges such as algorithmic literacy gaps—where 68% of citizens lack awareness of AI decision-making in public services (TalTech, 2024)—and heightened cybersecurity vulnerabilities among marginalized groups (Consumer Protection Board, 2023) indicate that inclusion efforts must continually evolve. Estonia's journey from connectivity to capability reflects its core philosophy, articulated in the Digital Agenda 2030: "Inclusion is the precondition for innovation" (Government of Estonia, 2021, p. 17). This principle continues to guide refinements to its inclusion architecture, ensuring digital transformation empowers rather than excludes.

Enhancing Citizen Participation

Estonia stands out in addressing citizen engagement gaps through digital solutions. Platforms like Rahvaalgatus.ee empower citizens to participate more actively in democracy, fostering a more inclusive and participatory governance model. By integrating AI effectively, Estonia has

Estonia's approach to AI in public administration highlights the importance of balancing innovation with ethical considerations. While challenges such as algorithmic bias and digital exclusion persist, Estonia's proactive measures—from regulatory alignment to educational investments—demonstrate a commitment to equitable and transparent governance. These efforts position Estonia as a model for other nations navigating the complexities of AI integration in public services.

Broader Implications of Estonia's AI Strategy

Estonia's pioneering integration of artificial intelligence into digital governance offers valuable insights for nations navigating digital transformation. The country's experience reveals several critical implications that extend beyond its borders, demonstrating how technology can enhance governance while preserving democratic values. At its core, Estonia's model proves that digital innovation and citizen-centric governance are not mutually exclusive, but rather mutually reinforcing when implemented thoughtfully.

The Estonian approach has significantly strengthened democratic participation through digital tools. Platforms like i-Voting and e-Cabinet have transformed citizen-state interactions by enabling secure remote voting and transparent decision-making processes. These innovations have achieved measurable impacts, including increased voter participation and greater accessibility for traditionally marginalized groups. Perhaps more importantly, they have enhanced institutional legitimacy by making governance more inclusive and responsive. The success of these digital participation mechanisms suggests that technology, when properly designed, can help reverse global declines in democratic engagement.

In public service delivery, Estonia's AI implementations have set new benchmarks for efficiency and accessibility. Solutions such as the Bürokratt virtual assistant network and X-Road data exchange system have dramatically reduced bureaucratic delays while expanding service availability. The results speak for themselves - from near-universal digital service access to significant cost savings in government operations. These achievements demonstrate how AI can eliminate administrative bottlenecks without sacrificing service quality, providing a compelling case for digital transformation in public sectors worldwide.

Estonia's cybersecurity framework offers particularly relevant lessons in an era of increasing digital threats. The country's comprehensive approach, developed in response to major cyberattacks, combines innovative infrastructure like data embassies with robust international cooperation through organizations like NATO's Cyber Defence Centre. This multilayered strategy shows how nations can build digital resilience while maintaining openness and innovation. The Estonian experience underscores that effective cybersecurity requires both technical solutions and strong governance frameworks.

What truly distinguishes Estonia's model is its commitment to human-centered AI governance. The country has institutionalized safeguards like algorithmic transparency measures and mandatory digital literacy programs, ensuring that technological advancement doesn't come at the expense of public trust. Initiatives like the EquiTech project, which audits automated decision-making systems for bias, exemplify Estonia's proactive approach to ethical challenges. This focus on responsible innovation provides a template for balancing efficiency with accountability in AI implementation.

The transferability of Estonia's success lies in its foundational principles rather than specific technologies. Three key conditions enabled Estonia's achievements: phased implementation that built necessary infrastructure and skills over time, productive collaboration between government and private sector innovators, and regulatory frameworks that adapt to technological change. These elements suggest that successful digital transformation requires more than just technical solutions - it demands holistic governance approaches tailored to each nation's unique context. As countries like Finland and Singapore have shown through their own adaptations of the Estonian model, the real value lies not in copying specific solutions, but in understanding and applying the underlying principles of inclusive, ethical digital governance.

CONCLUSION AND RECOMMENDATIONS

Estonia's experience in integrating AI into public policy stands as one of the most compelling case studies for nations pursuing digital governance transformation. By strategically leveraging AI and digital technologies while maintaining a strong commitment to ethical principles, Estonia has demonstrated how innovation can enhance administrative efficiency, democratic participation, and national resilience. Its success is not merely technological but institutional—rooted in a governance philosophy that prioritizes accessibility, transparency, and adaptability. The Nordic-Baltic AI Declaration of May 2018, which Estonia co-signed alongside Denmark, Finland, Sweden, and other regional partners, further underscores its leadership in fostering collaborative AI ecosystems. This initiative highlights the importance of cross-border knowledge-sharing and policy alignment in advancing responsible AI adoption.

However, Estonia's model also raises critical questions about the broader implications of digital sovereignty. While its Data Envoy program exemplifies how technology can strengthen governance resilience—ensuring institutional continuity even in scenarios of territorial disruption—it also invites scrutiny over how digital governance structures may evolve. As Rice (2019) cautions, the same tools that enhance democratic legitimacy in one context could, if misapplied, contribute to more centralized or surveillance-oriented governance models elsewhere. This duality suggests that the replication of Estonia's successes requires more than technical adoption; it demands a parallel commitment to safeguarding democratic norms and preventing AI from becoming an instrument of control rather than empowerment.

For other nations, Estonia's journey offers actionable insights. The development of comprehensive AI policies must go beyond efficiency gains to explicitly address ethical risks, including algorithmic bias and digital exclusion. Investments in infrastructure should prioritize not only technical robustness but also equitable access, ensuring that marginalized communities are not left behind in the transition to digital governance. Moreover, international collaboration—whether through multilateral agreements like the Nordic-Baltic Declaration or sector-specific partnerships—can accelerate learning curves and mitigate shared challenges, from cybersecurity threats to workforce readiness.

Future research should explore the long-term societal impacts of Estonia's AI integration, particularly how automated decision-making influences public trust and institutional accountability over time. Comparative studies between Estonia and other digital leaders—such as Singapore or South Korea—could yield nuanced insights into how cultural, political, and economic contexts shape AI governance outcomes. Additionally, the ethical dimensions of digital sovereignty warrant deeper examination, especially as nations balance resilience against risks of over-centralization. By addressing these gaps, policymakers and scholars can refine the global playbook for AI in public administration, ensuring that innovation serves as a catalyst for inclusive democracy rather than a tool of exclusion.

Estonia's achievements affirm that AI, when guided by visionary leadership and participatory design, can redefine the social contract between states and citizens. Its legacy lies not in providing a one-size-fits-all solution but in proving that technological progress and democratic values can—and must—advance in tandem. The challenge for other nations is not merely to emulate Estonia's tools but to embrace its underlying ethos: that the ultimate measure of digital transformation is not efficiency alone, but the empowerment of every citizen it serves.

REFERENCES

Al-Ansi, A. M., Garad, A., Jaboob, M., & Al-Ansi, A. (2024). Elevating e-government: Unleashing the power of AI and IoT for enhanced public services. *Heliyon, 10*(23), e40591. DOI: 10.1016/j.heliyon.2024.e40591 PMID: 39654738

Al-Mushayt, O. (2019). Automating E-Government Services with Artificial Intelligence. *IEEE Access : Practical Innovations, Open Solutions*, *7*, 146821–146829. DOI: 10.1109/ACCESS.2019.2946204

Androutsopoulou, A., Karacapilidis, N., Loukis, E., & Charalabidis, Y. (2019). Transforming the communication between citizens and government through AI-guided chatbots. *Government Information Quarterly*, *36*(2), 358–367. DOI: 10.1016/j.giq.2018.10.001

Aoki, N. (2020). Challenges of AI use in government. *Government Information Quarterly*, *37*(3), 101486. DOI: 10.1016/j.giq.2019.101486

Ashok, M., Madan, R., Joha, A., & Sivarajah, U. (2022). Ethical framework for artificial intelligence and digital technologies. *International Journal of Information Management*, *62*, 102433. DOI: 10.1016/j.ijinfomgt.2021.102433

Bullock, J. B. (2019). Artificial intelligence, discretion, and bureaucracy. *American Review of Public Administration*, *49*(7), 751–761. DOI: 10.1177/0275074019856123

Butcher, J., & Beridze, I. (2019). *Lessons from governing emerging technologies.* AI Governance Journal., DOI: 10.1080/03071847.2019.1694260

Consumer Protection Board. (2023). *Annual report on consumer vulnerabilities in the digital environment.* https://www.tarbijakaitseamet.ee

Cybernetica. (2023). Cybernetica signs contract to develop cryptographically secure artificial intelligence with US Office of Naval Research. https://cyber.ee/resources/news/ONR- 2024/

Demirtaş, İ. (2020). Baltık ülkelerinin AB'ye entegrasyon sürecinde Rusya faktörü, (Yayımlanmamış yüksek Lisans Tezi). İstanbul Üniversitesi Sosyal Bilimler Enstitüsü, İstanbul. https://tez.yok.gov.tr/UlusalTezMerkezi/tezDetay.jsp?id=H9xIDamkop_QRtFFgvWUWQ&no=NHS9eR0ybTNb68yfnJLcpQ

Desouza, K. C., Dawson, G. S., & Chenok, D. (2020). AI practices and digital transformation strategies. *Public Administration Review*, *80*(4), 547–553. DOI: 10.1111/puar.13218

Dreyling, R., Tammet, T., Pappel, I., & McBride, K. (June 01, 2024). Navigating the AI Maze: Lessons from Estonia's Bürokratt on public sector aı digital transformation. DOI: 10.2139/ssrn.4850696

e-Estonia. (2025). Estonia and automated decision-making: Challenges for public administration. https://e-estonia.com/estonia-and-automated-decision-making-challenges-for-public-administration/

e-Estonia. (2025). Estonia's groundbreaking national initiative: AI Leap programme to bring AI tools to all schools. https://e-estonia.com/estonia-announces-a-groundbreaking-national-initiative-ai-leap-programme-to-bring-ai-tools-to-all-schools/

e-Estonia. (2025). Factsheet ai strategy. https://e-estonia.com/wp-content/uploads/factsheet-ai-strategy.pdf

e-Residency. (2024). e-Residency annual report 2024. https://e-resident.gov.ee/annual-report

Ecas. (2017). Estonia brings digital focus to EU presidency. https://ecas.org/estonia-eu-presidency/

ECRI. (European Commission against Racism and Intolerance). (2024). Ecri conclusions on the implementation of the recommendations in respect of Estonia subject to interim follow-up. https://rm.coe.int/ecri-conclusions-on-the-implementation-of-the-recommendation-in-respec/1680b1e954

Education Estonia. (2021). ProgeTiger-Estonian way to create interest in technology. https://www.educationestonia.org/progetiger/

Empowering Estonia, A. I. (2025). AI use cases. https://www.kratid.ee/ai-use-cases

Enterprise Estonia. (2018). Estonia invites new cyber security startups - a unique cyber security and AI accelerator to be opened. https://investinestonia.com/estonia-invites-new-cyber-security-startups-a-unique-cyber-security-and-ai-accelerator-to-be-opened/

Equality and Human Rights Commission. (2021). Artificial intelligence case studies: Good practice by local authorities. https://www.equalityhumanrights.com/en/publication-download/artificial-intelligence-case-studies-good-practice-local-authorities

Eravcı, A. (2020). Estonya tarihinin güncel Eston dış politikasına etkisi. *Academic Social Resources Journal*, *5*(19), 710–724. DOI: 10.31569/ASRJOURNAL.127

Estonian Librarians Association. (2024). *Public access infrastructure in Estonia: 2024 assessment.* https://www.ell.ee/en/publications

Etscheid, J. (2019). AI governance and policy issues. *IEEE Transactions on Technology and Society*, *1*(1), 30–37. DOI: 10.1109/TTS.2019.2946204

European Commission. (2018). Artificial intelligence for Europe. https://eur-lex.europa.eu/legal-content/EN/TXT/?uri=COM%3A2018%3A237%3AFIN

European Commission. (2023). 2023 Country report ESTONIA. https://economy-finance.ec.europa.eu/publications/2023-country-report-estonia_en

European Commission. (2024). Cohesive Estonia strategy 2030. https://commission.europa.eu/system/files/202210/1_2_cohesive_estonia_strategy_2030_en.pdf

Eurostat. (2023). *Digital economy and society statistics - households and individuals.* https://ec.europa.eu/eurostat/databrowser/view/isoc_ci_in_h

Fatima, S., Desouza, K. C., & Dawson, G. S. (2020). Maximizing public value with AI. *Government Information Quarterly*, *37*(4), 101579. DOI: 10.1016/j.giq.2020.101579

Government of Estonia. (2021). *Digital agenda 2030.* https://www.riigikantselei.ee/en/digital-agenda-2030

Government of Estonia. 2023, (2023). Estonia's European Union policy priorities 2023–2025. https://www.riigikantselei.ee/sites/default/files/documents/2023-07/Estonia's EU policy priorities for 2023-2025.pdf

Hakimi, M., Hamidi, M. S., Miskinyar, M. S., & Sazish, B. (2023). Integrating artificial intelligence into e-government: Navigating challenges, opportunities, and policy implications. *International Journal of Academic and Practical Research*, *2*(2), 11–21. DOI: 10.5281/zenodo.13142637

IAPP. (2025). AI Governance Profession Report 2025. https://iapp.org/resources/article/ai-governance-profession-report/

Ibrus, I., Tamm, M., & Tiidenberg, K. (January 4, 2022). Estonia's digital culture manifesto. DOI: 10.2139/ssrn.4000959

iMUGS (The Integrated Modular Unmanned Ground System), (2025). https://imugs.eu/

Jermalavičius, T. (2024). Caught Between Today and Tomorrow: Defence AI in Estonia. In Borchert, H., Schütz, T., & Verbovszky, J. (Eds.), *The Very Long Game. Contributions to Security and Defence Studies*. Springer., DOI: 10.1007/978-3-031-58649-1_7

Jha, R. K., & Jha, M. (2024). Optimizing E-Government Cybersecurity through Artificial Intelligence Integration. *Journal of Trends in Computer Science and Smart Technology*, *6*(1), 67–87. DOI: 10.36548/jtcsst.2024.1.005

Kankanhalli, A., Charalabidis, Y., & Mellouli, S. (2019). AI in government: Opportunities and challenges. *Public Management Review*, *21*(2), 122–140. DOI: 10.1080/14719037.2018.1524352

Kaska, K., Rebane, L., & Vask, T. (2021). Lessons from Estonia's national cybersecurity strategy: How to succeed or fail in delivering value. In Rõigas, H., & Jermalavičius, T. (Eds.), *So far, yet so close: Japanese and Estonian cybersecurity policy perspectives and cooperation* (pp. 12–21). International Centre for Defence and Security., https://icds.ee/wp-content/uploads/2021/05/ICDS_Report_So_Far_Yet_So_Close_Roigas_Jermalavicius_May_2021.pdf

Khalid, H., Khan, M. F., & Qureshi, S. (2024). Technological Leapfrogging: Estonia's E-Governance Odyssey by using Emerging Technologies and Lesson for Developing States. *Pakistan Languages and Humanities Review*, *8*(2), 406–414. DOI: 10.47205/plhr.2024(8-II-S)40 PMID: 38256300

Leiser, M., & Murray, A. (2016). Non-state actors in AI governance. Technology and Regulation Journal, 2016, 1–14. https://doi.org/DOI: 10.26116/techreg.2016.001

Medaglia, R., Gil-García, J. R., & Pardo, T. A. (2023). Artificial intelligence in government: Taking stock and moving forward. *Social Science Computer Review*, *41*(1), 123–140. DOI: 10.1177/08944393211034087

Mihus, I., Zahorskyi, V., & Lipentsev, A. (2024). Navigation in e-government: The role of artificial intelligence in the formation of the legal framework for the protection of intellectual property rights. *Public Administration and Law Review*, *3*(19), 17–34. DOI: 10.36690/2674-5216-2024-3-17-34

Ministry of Economic Affairs and Communications. (2021). *Estonian rural broadband initiative: Final implementation report*. https://www.mkm.ee/en/reports

Ministry of Economic Affairs and Communications. (2023). *Multilingual accessibility framework for digital public services*. https://www.mkm.ee/en/reports

Ministry of Finance. (2020). *Tax policy for digital inclusion*. https://www.rahandusministeerium.ee/en/publications

Moreira, J., & Naranjo-Zolotov, M. (2023). Exploring potential drivers of citizen's acceptance of artificial intelligence use in e-government. In *Proceedings of the 16th International Conference on Theory and Practice of Electronic Governance* (pp. 336–345). Springer. DOI: 10.1007/978-3-031-45648-0_33

OECD. (2025). AI in Estonia. https://oecd.ai/en/dashboards/countries/Estonia

Pilving, I., & Mikiver, M. (2020). A Kratt as an administrative body: Algorithmic decisions and principles of administrative law. *Juridica International*, *29*, 47–61. DOI: 10.12697/JI.2020.29.05

Rice, N. F. (2019). Estonia's digital embassies and the concept of sovereignty. https://georgetownsecuritystudiesreview.org/2019/10/10/estonias-digital-embassies-and-the-concept-of-sovereignty/

Riigi Teataja. (2025). Consolidated texts of English translations of Estonian legislation. https://www.riigiteataja.ee/en/

Riisalo, T. (2023, October 18). Artificial Intelligence is part of the next chapter in Estonia's Digital Story. PublicTechnology. https://www.publictechnology.net/2023/10/18/government-and-politics/artificial-intelligence-is-part-of-the-next-chapter-in-estonias-digital-story/

Robinson, N., Hardy, A., & Ertan, A. (2022). Estonia: A Curious and Cautious Approach to Artificial Intelligence and National Security (2021). *SSRN*, *2021*. Advance online publication. DOI: 10.2139/ssrn.4105328

Roonemaa, M. (2017). Global lessons from Estonia's tech-savvy government. *UNESCO Courier*. https://courier.unesco.org/en/articles/global-lessons-estonias-tech-savvy-government

Saura, J. R., Ribeiro-Soriano, D., & Palacios-Marqués, D. (2022). Assessing behavioral data science privacy issues in government artificial intelligence deployment. *Government Information Quarterly*, *39*(4), 101679. DOI: 10.1016/j.giq.2022.101679

Schiff, D., Rakova, B., Ayesh, A., Fanti, A., & Lennon, M. (2020). Principles to practices for responsible AI: Closing the gap. *AI and Ethics Journal*, *1*(1), 1–17. DOI: 10.1007/s43681-020-00007-2

Statistics Estonia. (2023). *Information society yearbook 2023*. https://www.stat.ee/publication-2023

TalTech. (2024). *Public understanding of algorithmic governance in Estonia*. https://www.taltech.ee/publications

Thierer, A., Castillo O'Sullivan, A., & Russell, R. (2017). AI policy and regulatory issues. Mercatus Center Working Paper. https://www.mercatus.org/publications/technology-and-innovation/artificial-intelligence-policy-and-regulatory-issues

Tiger Leap Foundation. (2025). *Digital champions initiative: Impact evaluation*. https://www.tiigrihype.ee/reports

Totonchi, A. (2025). Artificial intelligence in e-government: Identifying and addressing key challenges. *Malaysian Journal of Information and Communication Technology, 10*, 10–24. https://myjict.utm.my/index.php/myjict/article/view/1234

UNICEF. (2022). *Bridging the digital divide in Ida-Viru County*. https://www.unicef.org/estonia/reports

United Nations. (2020). E-Government Survey 2020 Digital Government in the Decade of Action for Sustainable Development With addendum on COVID-19 Response. https://publicadministration.un.org/egovkb/Portals/egovkb/Documents/un/2020-Survey/2020 UN E-Government Survey (Full Report).pdf

United Nations. (2022). E-Government Survey 2022 The Future of Digital Government. https://desapublications.un.org/sites/default/files/publications/2022-09/Web version E-Government 2022.pdf

United Nations. (2024). E-Government Survey 2024 Department of Economic and Social Affairs Accelerating Digital Transformation for Sustainable Development. https://www.unsdsn.org/resources/the-sustainable-development-report-2024/?gad_source=1&gad_campaignid=13253704546&gbraid=0AAAABdu6wyw9vKRJNI8dFZR-maQbMFcW&gclid=CjwKCAiA55rJBhByEiwAFkY1QLudyWMeUkXsVieJ_eKGesxIV8PJCQ0NPaj7ogiwIhDYWfuKJS-n8hoCdaMQAvD_BwE

Veebel, V. (2009). Estonia's Involvment in eu Policy-Making. In Lisonova, Z. (Ed.), *Preference Formation in the New eu Member States* (pp. 53–73). Comenius University.

Vrabie, C. (2023). E-Government 3.0: An AI model to use for enhanced local democracies. *Sustainability (Basel), 15*(12), 9572. DOI: 10.3390/su15129572

Wang, Y., & Siau, K. (2018). AI in public administration: Challenges and opportunities. *International Journal of Public Administration, 41*(13), 1121–1127. DOI: 10.1080/01900692.2018.1498103

Wirtz, B. W., Weyerer, J. C., & Sturm, B. J. (2019). AI in e-governance: A review. *Government Information Quarterly, 36*(2), 201–209.

Zuiderwijk, A., Chen, Y. C., & Salem, F. (2021). Implications of the use of artificial intelligence in public governance: A systematic literature review and a research agenda. *Government Information Quarterly, 38*(3), 101577. DOI: 10.1016/j.giq.2021.101577

Chapter 10
Organizational Dynamics of AI Integration in Italian Public Administration: A Case Study of INPS

Davide de Gennaro
https://orcid.org/0000-0001-6002-6200
University "Parthenope" of Naples, Italy

Ludovica Del Barone
https://orcid.org/0009-0000-1961-0317
University of Salento, Italy

Filomena Buonocore
https://orcid.org/0009-0008-4610-9550
University "Parthenope" of Naples, Italy

ABSTRACT

The integration of Artificial Intelligence (AI) in public administration is reshaping governance, improving efficiency, and transforming service delivery. This chapter examines the case of Italy's National Institute for Social Security (INPS), which has adopted AI to enhance administrative processes, fraud detection, and citizen engagement. While AI implementation presents significant opportunities—such as increased efficiency, predictive analytics, and data-driven decision-making—it also poses organizational challenges related to bureaucratic inertia, workforce adaptation, regulatory compliance, and ethical concerns. By analysing the INPS case, this study highlights the organizational barriers to AI adoption, the need for digital upskilling, the importance of transparent governance, and the broader benefits AI

DOI: 10.4018/979-8-3373-1484-6.ch010

can bring to public administration. The findings contribute to the broader discourse on digital transformation in the public sector, emphasizing the balance between technological innovation and institutional constraints.

1. INTRODUCTION

The integration of Artificial Intelligence (AI) into public administration marks a pivotal shift in governance, redefining how public institutions operate, deliver services, and interact with citizens (Wirtz & Müller, 2019). Over the past decade, AI has evolved from an emerging technological innovation to a fundamental driver of administrative transformation (Neumann *et al.*, 2024), with governments worldwide increasingly relying on AI-powered tools to optimize decision-making, enhance efficiency, and manage the complexities of large-scale bureaucratic systems (Madan & Ashok, 2023). AI implementation in the public sector is particularly significant as it intersects with multiple dimensions of governance, including policy formulation, regulatory compliance, workforce management, and citizen engagement. Unlike private organizations, which often adopt AI for competitive advantage (Kemp, 2024), public institutions operate within frameworks of accountability, transparency, and democratic oversight, requiring AI deployment to align with legal, ethical, and societal expectations (Vesnic-Alujevic *et al.*, 2020).

The rise of AI-driven public administration is embedded within broader technological, economic, and social transformations reshaping governance worldwide (Chen *et al.*, 2024). Governments are increasingly leveraging AI to streamline bureaucratic workflows, reduce administrative burdens, and enhance institutional responsiveness to citizens' needs. AI applications such as machine learning for fraud detection, natural language processing for automated service provision, and predictive analytics for policy forecasting have already demonstrated their capacity to transform key areas of public administration. However, transitioning to AI-powered governance also presents significant challenges beyond technological integration (Campion *et al.*, 2022; Rane *et al.*, 2024). AI adoption in the public sector is shaped by organizational and structural constraints, including resistance to change, the need for workforce upskilling, and ethical concerns surrounding algorithmic decision-making (Cath, 2018; Kulal *et al.*, 2024). Further complicating adoption are concerns over algorithmic bias, data privacy, and the accountability of AI systems, necessitating comprehensive governance frameworks to ensure AI serves the public interest while mitigating risks associated with automation and digital surveillance (Wirtz *et al.*, 2019). Furthermore, employee resistance remains a common organizational barrier, as AI disrupts established routines, challenges existing expertise, and shifts decision-making power (Budhwar *et al.*, 2022). Addressing these concerns requires cultural transformation within public sector organizations (Wirtz *et al.*, 2019), supported by investments in workforce training, leadership engagement, and adaptive strategies that integrate AI into institutional priorities (Babashahi *et al.*, 2024). Additionally, AI implementation raises operational challenges, such as interdepartmental coordination, workflow restructuring, and the redistribution of administrative responsibilities (Babashahi *et al.*, 2024). Public sector organizations must design new operational frameworks to facilitate AI-human collaboration, ensuring AI systems enhance rather than replace human expertise. Simultaneously, AI's capacity to improve administrative efficiency, enable data-driven decision-making, and foster service innovation offers significant opportunities for public institutions willing to embrace organizational change (Akter *et al.*, 2023). By automating routine processes, AI allows public sector employees to focus on higher-value tasks, including policy analysis, complex case management, and citizen engagement. AI-driven analytics also equip public administrators with real-time insights, improving decision-making and resource allocation.

Within this evolving landscape, Italy's public administration is undergoing a significant digital transformation (Datta *et al.*, 2020), driven by national policy initiatives and broader European Union efforts to modernize government operations (Scantamburlo *et al.*, 2024). The National Recovery and Resilience Plan (PNRR) has allocated substantial resources to digital transformation, including AI-driven projects aimed at enhancing administrative efficiency, service accessibility, and fraud detection (Fabbrini, 2022). However, the implementation of AI in Italian public administration remains constrained by bureaucratic inertia, rigid governance structures, and a historically cautious approach to technological change, all of which influence the pace and effectiveness of AI adoption (Ongaro, 2006).

At the forefront of this transformation is the National Institute for Social Security (INPS), Italy's largest public social security agency, which has embraced AI to enhance administrative functions, optimize resource allocation, and improve service delivery. As a key institution managing vast volumes of data related to pensions, unemployment benefits, and social assistance programs, INPS faces substantial operational challenges that AI can help address. However, its experience with AI implementation also reveals broader tensions and organizational obstacles associated with the digital transformation of public administration. Operating within a highly bureaucratic governance framework, INPS provides valuable insights into how institutional structures, political considerations, and public sector culture influence the adoption of emerging technologies. Furthermore, it highlights the organizational challenges AI adoption may generate, alongside the benefits and opportunities it presents. As a leading example of digital transformation within the Italian public sector, INPS serves as a benchmark for understanding both the complexities and the potential of AI-driven innovation.

This chapter examines the case of INPS to explore the broader implications of AI-driven transformation in Italian public administration. The analysis is guided by two key research questions: *What organizational challenges arise during the introduction of AI in public administration? What benefits and impacts could AI bring to public administration?* By addressing these questions, the study contributes to the ongoing academic and policy debate on AI's role in public governance, offering insights that are both theoretically relevant and practically applicable.

As a pioneering case of digital transformation in Italian public administration, INPS offers critical insights into the challenges that arise during AI adoption and the broader organizational benefits and opportunities AI can unlock.

This chapter employs a qualitative research design, leveraging case study methodology to analyse AI implementation at INPS. Drawing on official documents, policy reports and secondary literature, the study investigates the institutional, regulatory, and organizational dimensions of AI adoption in public administration. The findings contribute to the broader discourse on digital transformation by highlighting both the opportunities and constraints associated with AI-driven innovation. By synthesizing theoretical perspectives on technology adoption with empirical insights from INPS, the study provides a comprehensive analysis of the factors enabling or hindering AI's successful implementation into public administration.

To provide a comprehensive understanding of AI adoption in public administration, this chapter is structured as follows. The next section presents the AI in public administration, outlining key technological advancements, policy frameworks, and governance models that shape AI integration in public institutions. Following this, the chapter delves into the organizational challenges of AI adoption, examining the structural, cultural, and managerial obstacles that public institutions face when integrating AI into their operations. Issues such as resistance to change, workforce adaptation, ethical concerns, and regulatory constraints are analysed to provide insight into the factors that hinder AI implementation. The subsequent section explores the organizational benefits and impacts of AI, emphasizing how AI-driven innovations can enhance efficiency, decision-making, and service delivery. This analysis highlights how AI applications can streamline administrative processes, improve citizen engagement, and foster data-driven governance while also considering potential risks and unintended consequences. The methodology section details the research approach adopted in this study, which employs a qualitative case study method to examine AI implementation in a public sector organization. The rationale for selecting the case study approach, data collection strategies, and analytical methods will be explained. The core of the chapter is the case study of INPS, which provides an in-depth analysis of how AI has been introduced in one of Italy's largest public institutions. This section explores the AI initiatives implemented at INPS, the challenges encountered during adoption, and the organizational transformations that have taken place as a result. The discussion section synthesizes the findings, comparing the INPS case with global trends in AI adoption and drawing broader conclusions on AI's role in public administration. Finally, the conclusion summarizes the key insights from the study, emphasizing the balance between AI's potential to optimize public sector operations and the necessity of addressing governance, ethical, and organizational challenges. The chapter closes by considering future research directions and the implications of AI adoption for the evolving landscape of public administration.

2. AI IN PUBLIC ADMINISTRATION

The introduction of AI into public administration has been heralded as a transformative innovation capable of addressing inefficiencies, enhancing transparency, and improving service delivery (Kulal *et al.*, 2024; Phuangthuean & Nuansang, 2024). AI encompasses a range of technologies, including machine learning, natural language processing, robotics, and predictive analytics, which collectively hold the potential to revolutionize public sector operations (Kuziemski & Misuraca, 2020).

AI in public administration builds upon a rich theoretical foundation rooted in technology adoption models, public sector innovation theories, and governance frameworks. Central to this discourse is the idea that technology serves as both a tool and a driver of institutional change (Pencheva *et al.*, 2020; Wirtz *et al.*, 2019). Theories such as the Technology-Organization-Environment (TOE) framework provide valuable insights into how public organizations adopt and integrate AI (Madan & Ashok, 2023). These theories emphasize the interplay between technological capabilities, organizational readiness, and external environmental factors (Bhuiyan, 2024).

Beyond the TOE framework, alternative conceptual perspectives offer valuable insights into the integration of AI in public administration. Socio-technical systems theory emphasizes that technological adoption is not merely a matter of technical capability but emerges from the interaction between technological infrastructures and social structures, including organizational culture, employee attitudes, and governance traditions (Bostrom & Heinen, 1977; Baxter & Sommerville, 2011). This perspective is particularly relevant in highly bureaucratic contexts, where cultural resistance and institutional inertia shape the trajectory of digital transformation. Digital maturity models further contribute by highlighting the stages through which public institutions progress as they integrate new technologies, from initial experimentation to full institutionalization (Kane *et al.*, 2017; Vial, 2019). These models help explain why some organizations, such as INPS, experience uneven progress across departments or functions, depending on their level of digital readiness. Finally, participatory governance approaches stress the importance of citizen involvement and stakeholder engagement in shaping the design and implementation of AI systems (Ansell & Gash, 2008; Meijer *et al.*, 2019). They underscore that the legitimacy and effectiveness of AI in public services depend not only on technical efficiency but also on inclusiveness, accountability, and responsiveness to societal needs. Integrating these perspectives provides a more comprehensive lens through which to examine AI adoption, one that complements the TOE framework by connecting technological innovation to broader organizational and democratic dynamics. This multi-framework approach also enriches the analysis of the INPS case study, where AI implementation reflects not only technological and organizational readiness but also cultural, institutional, and citizen-related factors.

Globally, AI adoption in public administration is gaining momentum (Mikalef *et al.*, 2022; Neumann *et al.*, 2024). Governments in countries such as the United States, the United Kingdom, China, and the European Union have launched ambitious initiatives to integrate AI into public services. These include automating administrative processes, enhancing decision-making through data-driven insights, and improving citizen engagement through AI-powered chatbots and virtual assistants (Dar, 2024). Estonia's e-Residency program and Singapore's Smart Nation initiative are notable examples of how AI can underpin digital governance and citizen-centric services.

AI applications in public administration are diverse and impactful (Phuangthuean & Nuansang, 2024). Process automation, for instance, streamlines repetitive and time-consuming tasks such as processing tax returns, managing benefits claims, and monitoring compliance (Mishra *et al.*, 2024). Predictive analytics enable governments to analyze vast datasets to forecast trends and allocate resources more effectively (Kulal *et al.*, 2024). For example, predictive models can identify areas at risk of natural disasters, allowing for proactive measures and improved disaster response. In the realm of fraud detection and prevention, AI systems analyze patterns and anomalies in transactions to detect fraudulent activities, which is particularly relevant in social security and tax administration. Citizen engagement has also been transformed through AI-powered chatbots and virtual assistants, which enhance interactions by providing instant responses to queries and guiding users through complex administrative procedures (Guo, 2024). These tools improve accessibility and reduce wait times. Furthermore, AI plays a critical role in policy development and decision support by analyzing complex datasets, simulating policy scenarios, and evaluating potential outcomes, thereby supporting evidence-based decision-making and improving governance quality (Loukis *et al.*, 2020; Valle-Cruz *et al.*, 2020).

The integration of AI into public administration offers numerous opportunities. Automation significantly reduces processing times, eliminates redundancies, and enhances overall productivity (Mishra *et al.*, 2020). AI-driven tools provide more accurate and personalized services, meeting citizens' needs more effectively and efficiently (Madan & Ashok, 2023). Transparency and accountability are enhanced through AI systems that audit and document processes in real-time, fostering trust in public institutions (Kuziemski & Misuraca, 2020). Additionally, the adoption of AI can result in substantial cost savings by automating routine tasks and optimizing resource allocation, freeing up funds for other priorities (Valle-Cruz *et al.*, 2020). Moreover, AI acts as a catalyst for innovation within public administration, encouraging experimentation with new technologies and practices that can redefine how public services are delivered (Madan & Ashok, 2023; Salah *et al.*, 2023).

Despite its transformative potential, the adoption of AI in public administration is accompanied by significant challenges. Ethical dilemmas related to privacy, algorithmic bias, and accountability pose serious concerns that public institutions must address to ensure the responsible deployment of AI systems (Bracci, 2023; Busuioc, 2021). Workforce impacts represent another major challenge, as the automation of tasks may lead to job displacement and necessitate significant investments in reskilling and upskilling employees (Dar, 2024). Effective AI systems depend on high-quality data, but issues such as data silos, inconsistencies, and security risks can hinder their effectiveness (Plantinga, 2024). Resistance to change, often rooted in cultural and institutional inertia, can slow the adoption of new technologies, particularly in hierarchical and bureaucratic environments (Reginato *et al.*, 2016). Additionally, the development and maintenance of AI systems require robust technological infrastructure and financial resources, which may be limited in public sector contexts (Madan & Ashok, 2023).

As AI continues to evolve, its role in public administration will expand, offering new possibilities for innovation and efficiency (Dar, 2024). Future research and practice should focus on ensuring that AI systems uphold fairness, transparency, and accountability through ethical development (Phuangthuean & Nuansang, 2024). Citizen-centric design must be prioritized to create AI applications that enhance accessibility and address user needs effectively (Körner-Wyrtki *et al.*, 2024). Collaborative governance models that promote partnerships between governments, academia, and industry can drive AI innovation and facilitate its integration into public administration (Wirts *et al.*, 2020). Examining the societal and organizational implications of AI adoption over time will provide valuable insights into its long-term impacts. Indeed, the integration of AI in public administration is not merely a technological shift but a transformative process that redefines the relationship between governments and citizens.

3. ORGANIZATIONAL CHALLENGES OF AI

The integration of AI into public administration represents a profound shift in how institutions operate, but it is not without its challenges. These challenges arise from the interplay of technological, organizational, and human factors that shape the adoption process.

One of the most significant challenges is resistance to change (Madan & Ashok, 2023). Public administration, often characterized by its hierarchical structure and rigid processes, tends to be cautious in adopting disruptive innovations (Damar *et al.*, 2024). Employees may fear that AI will render their roles redundant, leading to job insecurity and decreased morale (Young *et al.*, 2019). Such concerns are particularly acute in settings where automation is perceived as a direct threat to traditional workflows. Resistance can also stem from a lack of familiarity with AI technologies, resulting in skepticism about their effectiveness and reliability (Alon-Barkat & Busuioc, 2023; Sienkiewicz-Małyjurek, 2023). Addressing this resistance requires comprehensive change management strategies that emphasize the benefits of AI and actively involve employees in the transformation process.

Another major challenge is the digital skills gap (McQuiston & Manoharan, 2021). The successful implementation of AI demands a workforce equipped with the knowledge and technical expertise to manage, operate, and interpret AI systems (Ahn & Chen, 2022). However, public administrations often face significant shortages in these competencies, particularly among employees accustomed to legacy systems and traditional methods of operation (Febiandini & Sony, 2023). Bridging this gap requires substantial investment in training and capacity-building initiatives. Programs focused on digital literacy, technical upskilling, and fostering a culture of lifelong learning are essential to prepare employees for the evolving demands of AI-integrated environments (see Kamukapa *et al.*, 2024).

Ethical concerns also present formidable barriers to the adoption of AI in public administration (Henman, 2020; Wirtz *et al.*, 2020). Issues such as data privacy, algorithmic bias, and accountability raise critical questions about the responsible use of AI technologies (Bignami, 2022). Public institutions must ensure that AI systems adhere to ethical principles, safeguarding the rights and interests of citizens (Pakhnenko & Kuan, 2023). For instance, algorithmic transparency is vital to avoid biases that could disproportionately affect certain groups. Additionally, mechanisms for accountability must be established to clarify the roles and responsibilities of both humans and machines in decision-making processes (Busuioc, 2021). These ethical considerations necessitate the development of robust governance frameworks and regulatory standards tailored to the unique context of public administration.

Infrastructure readiness is another critical factor influencing the adoption of AI (Madan & Ashok, 2023). Public administrations often rely on outdated legacy systems that are ill-suited for integrating advanced AI technologies (e.g., Irani *et al.*, 2023). These systems may lack the computational power, interoperability, and scalability required to support AI applications. Upgrading infrastructure to meet these demands involves significant financial investment, which can be a daunting challenge given budgetary constraints (Agarwal, 2018). Furthermore, ensuring the security of AI systems is paramount, as public administrations are custodians of sensitive citizen data (Wirtz *et al.*, 2020). Cybersecurity measures must be robust and adaptive to mitigate risks associated with AI adoption (Mishra *et al.*, 2024; Phuangthuean & Nuansang, 2024).

Cultural barriers within public administration further complicate the introduction of AI (see Campion *et al.*,, 2022). Bureaucratic inertia and a lack of innovation-friendly environments can hinder progress (Wang *et al.*, 2024). Traditional decision-making processes, often characterized by slow approvals and risk aversion, are at odds with the dynamic nature of AI technologies (Yun, 2020). Encouraging a culture of innovation requires leadership that champions change, fosters collaboration, and aligns organizational goals with the opportunities presented by AI.

Lastly, public trust plays a pivotal role in determining the success of AI adoption (Aoki, 2020). Citizens may harbor concerns about the implications of AI for transparency, fairness, and accessibility in public services (e.g., Criado *et al.*, 2022). Building trust requires consistent communication, participatory approaches, and demonstrable evidence of AI's benefits. Public administrations must prioritize citizen engagement, ensuring that AI systems are designed and implemented in ways that enhance trust and inclusivity (Al-Ansi *et al.*, 2024).

4. ORGANIZATIONAL BENEFITS AND IMPACTS

The implementation of AI in public administration offers a range of organizational benefits and impacts, reshaping how institutions function and deliver services to citizens. These benefits extend across multiple dimensions, from efficiency and resource optimization to enhanced decision-making and citizen satisfaction.

One of the most immediate and measurable benefits of AI integration is the significant improvement in operational efficiency (Agarwal, 2018; Young *et al.*, 2019). AI technologies automate routine and repetitive tasks, such as data entry, document processing, and compliance checks, which traditionally consume substantial time and human resources (see van Noordt & Tangi, 2023). By eliminating these manual processes, public administrations can redirect their workforce toward more strategic and value-added activities (Alshahrani *et al.*, 2024; Hjaltalin & Sigurdarson, 2024). For example, automating the processing of social benefits claims reduces backlogs and accelerates service delivery, ensuring that citizens receive timely assistance. This efficiency gain not only improves the overall productivity of public institutions but also fosters a more agile and responsive administrative framework (Looks *et al.*, 2024).

AI also enhances the accuracy and reliability of public sector operations (Nirala *et al.*, 2022). By minimizing human error, AI systems ensure that administrative tasks, such as tax assessments or eligibility evaluations, are conducted with a higher degree of precision (Kulal *et al.*, 2024). This level of accuracy is particularly critical in areas where errors can have far-reaching consequences, such as healthcare or social security. For instance, predictive analytics tools can identify potential fraud patterns in real-time, enabling agencies to take proactive measures while minimizing false positives. Such advancements not only safeguard public resources but also enhance the credibility and trustworthiness of public institutions (Berman *et al.*, 2024).

Another transformative impact of AI lies in its ability to improve decision-making processes (Schwarz *et al.*, 2022). AI-driven analytics and machine learning models process vast amounts of data, uncovering patterns and insights that inform evidence-based policymaking (Filgueiras, 2022; Henman, 2020). By analyzing historical trends and simulating various scenarios, AI tools empower policymakers to make informed decisions that address complex societal challenges. For example, AI can predict traffic congestion patterns, enabling urban planners to design more efficient transportation systems. Similarly, public health agencies can use AI to track disease outbreaks and allocate resources effectively, mitigating the impact on vulnerable populations. This data-driven approach ensures that public policies are both effective and adaptive to changing circumstances (Longo, 2022).

Citizen engagement and satisfaction (see Wong *et al.*, 2011) represent another area where AI generates substantial benefits (Cortés-Cediel *et al.*, 2023). AI-powered chatbots and virtual assistants provide citizens with instant access to information and support, streamlining interactions with public services (Dar, 2024; Guo, 2024). These tools are particularly valuable in addressing common queries, guiding users through complex procedures, and offering personalized recommendations based on individual needs (Mishra *et al.*, 2024). By reducing wait times and enhancing accessibility, AI-driven solutions improve the overall citizen experience, fostering trust and confidence in public institutions (Kulal *et al.*, 2024; Maciejewski, 2017). For instance, virtual assistants that assist with filing taxes or applying for permits not only simplify bureaucratic processes but also make them more transparent and user-friendly.

In addition to improving service delivery, AI fosters greater transparency and accountability within public administration (Bignami, 2022). Advanced AI systems can audit and document processes in real-time, creating a comprehensive digital record of administrative actions (Kumar, 2024). This level of transparency is instrumental in combating corruption and ensuring that public officials are held accountable for their decisions (Busuioc, 2021). Moreover, AI's ability to analyze vast datasets and detect anomalies enhances oversight and governance, enabling institutions to identify inefficiencies or irregularities promptly (Bouchetara *et al.*, 2024). By promoting a culture of transparency, AI strengthens public trust and reinforces the legitimacy of public administration.

AI also contributes to significant cost savings and resource optimization in public administration (Nzobonimpa, 2023). Automating labor-intensive processes reduces operational costs while enabling more efficient allocation of financial and human resources (Kulal *et al.*, 2024). For example, AI systems that streamline procurement processes or optimize supply chain management can result in substantial cost reductions, freeing up funds for other critical initiatives. Furthermore, AI-driven resource allocation tools ensure that limited resources, such as emergency response teams or healthcare supplies, are deployed where they are needed most. This level of optimization not only enhances the effectiveness of public services but also demonstrates a commitment to fiscal responsibility.

The integration of AI in public administration serves as a catalyst for organizational innovation (Ahn & Chen, 2022; van Noordt & Tangi, 2023). By introducing cutting-edge technologies and methodologies, AI fosters a culture of experimentation and continuous improvement (Chen *et al.*, 2024; Young *et al.*, 2019). Public institutions that embrace AI are better positioned to explore innovative solutions to persistent challenges, such as urbanization, climate change, and social inequality (e.g., Wolniak & Stecuła, 2024). For instance, AI-powered environmental monitoring systems can track air quality or water usage, enabling governments to implement sustainable policies and practices. This innovative mindset ensures that public administrations remain at the forefront of technological and social advancements, adapting to the dynamic needs of their constituencies (David *et al.*, 2024).

Moreover, the adoption of AI has profound implications for workforce development and organizational culture (Ahn & Chen, 2022). While AI automates certain tasks, it also creates opportunities for employees to engage in more meaningful and strategic roles (Criado & Gil-Garcia, 2019). By alleviating administrative burdens, AI allows public sector workers to focus on complex problem-solving, creative thinking, and policy formulation. This shift in job responsibilities requires a parallel investment in training and professional development, ensuring that employees are equipped with the skills needed to thrive in an AI-driven environment (Androniceanu, 2024). Organizations that successfully navigate this transition not only enhance employee satisfaction and retention but also build a resilient and future-ready workforce.

The broader societal impacts of AI adoption in public administration cannot be overlooked (Young *et al.*, 2019). By improving the efficiency, transparency, and responsiveness of public services, AI enhances the overall quality of governance, contributing to social cohesion and economic development (Kuziemski & Misuraca, 2020; Sigfrids *et al.*, 2022). Citizens who experience seamless and reliable public services are more likely to participate in civic activities and support government initiatives (Ahn & Chen, 2022; Wong *et al.*, 2011). Additionally, AI-driven innovations in areas such as education, healthcare, and transportation have the potential to address systemic inequalities, ensuring that the benefits of technological progress are distributed equitably across society.

5. METHOD

This chapter adopts a qualitative research design to explore the implementation of AI within the Italian National Institute of Social Security (INPS). A qualitative approach is particularly suited to uncovering the nuanced organizational dynamics and contextual factors influencing AI adoption. By employing a case study methodology (Yin, 2009), the research provides an in-depth analysis of INPS's experiences, capturing insights that may inform broader applications in public administration.

The case study approach focuses on the INPS as a single, illustrative example of AI integration in public administration. INPS was selected due to its pioneering role in deploying AI technologies within the Italian public sector and its relevance as a large, complex organization dealing with vast amounts of citizen data and administrative processes. This focus allows the study to examine the practicalities, challenges, and impacts of AI implementation in a real-world setting.

The study draws on multiple sources of data to ensure a comprehensive understanding of the AI implementation process at INPS. The primary sources of data include the following:

1. Official documents and policy reports: The analysis involves a detailed examination of official documents, policy reports, and internal memos related to the AI rollout at INPS. These materials provide critical insights into the strategic objectives, milestones, and challenges encountered during the implementation process. They also shed light on the governance structures and decision-making processes that guided the adoption of AI.
2. Secondary literature review: A systematic review of secondary literature on AI in the public sector situates the findings within the broader academic and policy discourse. This includes scholarly articles, government reports, and international case studies that highlight global trends, best practices, and theoretical frameworks relevant to AI integration in public administration. By comparing the INPS case with existing literature, the study identifies commonalities and divergences that enrich the analysis.

Thus, the methodological approach combines thematic analysis with comparative insights to draw meaningful conclusions. Thematic analysis is employed to identify recurring patterns, themes, and insights within the data. This approach enables the study to explore key dimensions of AI implementation, including organizational readiness, technological integration, and stakeholder engagement. Comparative insights are derived by positioning the INPS case within the broader context of AI adoption in public administration, highlighting its unique contributions and implications.

To ensure the validity and reliability of the findings, the study employs triangulation by integrating data from multiple sources. Cross-referencing official documents, policy reports, and secondary literature reduces potential biases and enhances the robustness of the analysis. The selection of INPS as a case study is further justified by its representativeness as a public organization undergoing digital transformation, ensuring that the findings are relevant and transferable to similar contexts.

6. CASE STUDY: INPS

The INPS stands as a pivotal case study in the integration of AI within Italian public administration. As Italy's largest social security institution, INPS is responsible for managing a vast and complex network of pensions, unemployment benefits, and welfare programs that affect millions of citizens. The increasing demand for efficiency, transparency, and rapid service delivery has driven the institution to embrace AI as a strategic tool for digital transformation. The adoption of AI within INPS aligns with broader national and European policies aimed at modernizing public administration and improving the accessibility and effectiveness of government services. As one of the most bureaucratically complex institutions in the country, INPS provides valuable insights into both the organizational challenges and the benefits and opportunities that AI adoption can bring to public sector institutions.

6.1 AI as Part of INPS's Digital Strategy

The implementation of AI at INPS is embedded within the institution's Digital Strategic Plan (2022–2024), which prioritizes innovation to optimize resource allocation, improve service quality, and enhance the efficiency of administrative processes. The AI-driven transformation is structured around several key objectives, including the automation of repetitive tasks, improved decision-making through predictive analytics, fraud detection and prevention, and the personalization of citizen services. AI has been introduced gradually, with an emphasis on ensuring compliance with ethical and regulatory standards, particularly within the framework of European Union AI governance policies. By focusing on a phased approach, INPS has sought to balance technological advancement with institutional adaptation, minimizing disruptions while maximizing the benefits of AI integration.

6.2 AI Applications in INPS: From Automation to Fraud Detection

One of the most impactful applications of AI within INPS has been the automation of customer service interactions. AI-powered chatbots, such as Masterbot and Skillbot, have been deployed to handle high volumes of citizen inquiries, reducing waiting times and improving accessibility. These virtual assistants leverage Natural Language Processing (NLP) to provide real-time, automated responses to frequently asked questions, enabling a more efficient interaction between citizens and the institution. By offloading routine queries to AI, INPS has been able to reallocate human resources to more complex cases that require personalized assistance.

Beyond customer service, AI has played a crucial role in fraud detection and risk management. Given the vast scale of financial transactions processed by INPS, AI-driven analytics have been deployed to detect irregularities in benefit claims and financial disbursements. These AI models analyse large datasets in real time, identifying suspicious patterns that may indicate fraudulent activity. By leveraging AI in fraud prevention, INPS has strengthened its ability to safeguard public resources, ensuring that social security funds are distributed fairly and responsibly. Additionally, AI has been integrated into legal and compliance operations, supporting the verification of insurance account balances and facilitating administrative dispute resolution. AI-driven tools have allowed INPS to process legal cases more efficiently, reducing backlogs and improving the accuracy of compliance assessments.

6.3 Barriers to AI Integration at INPS: Organizational and Institutional Challenges

The integration of AI within INPS, however, has not been without challenges. As a historically bureaucratic institution, INPS has faced internal resistance to AI adoption. Employees accustomed to traditional workflows have expressed concerns about the impact of automation on job security and decision-making autonomy. Many public sector workers perceive AI as a disruptive force that could alter established work routines and shift responsibilities away from human administrators. Addressing this resistance has required investment in digital upskilling and training programs, equipping employees with the knowledge and competencies needed to work alongside AI systems rather than seeing them as a replacement. The implementation of AI has necessitated a cultural shift within the organization, requiring leadership engagement to foster trust in new technologies and encourage workforce adaptability.

Another major challenge has been interdepartmental coordination. Like many large public institutions, INPS operates across multiple departments, each with its own legacy systems, procedural frameworks, and data management structures. The lack of seamless integration between departments has posed barriers to AI adoption, requiring significant restructuring of organizational workflows. AI implementation has demanded new governance mechanisms to facilitate cross-functional collaboration and ensure that AI-driven processes align with institutional goals. Overcoming these silos has been a gradual process, requiring strategic leadership and adaptive management practices to ensure smooth AI integration across different operational units.

Regulatory and ethical considerations have also played a crucial role in shaping AI adoption at INPS. The European Union AI Act imposes strict guidelines on the deployment of AI in public administration, particularly concerning algorithmic transparency, fairness, and non-discrimination. Given the sensitive nature of social security benefits, ensuring that AI-driven decision-making processes remain explainable and accountable has been a priority for INPS. The institution has had to navigate complex compliance requirements, ensuring that AI models used for fraud detection, benefit eligibility, and administrative decision-making operate in a manner that upholds public trust and legal standards. The challenge lies in maintaining AI efficiency while addressing the ethical implications of automated governance, a balancing act that requires continuous oversight and regulatory adaptation.

6.4 Organizational Benefits and Opportunities of AI at INPS

Despite these challenges, the benefits of AI adoption at INPS are substantial, positioning the institution as a leader in the digital transformation of public administration. One of the most immediate advantages has been the significant reduction in administrative workload. AI-powered automation has allowed employees to shift their focus from repetitive, manual processes to high-value tasks such as complex case management, policy analysis, and direct citizen engagement. By streamlining operations, AI has enhanced overall institutional efficiency, enabling faster response times and improving the quality of public service delivery. Citizens now experience reduced processing delays for claims and requests, while administrative personnel can allocate more time to cases that require human discretion and expertise.

The introduction of AI-driven tools has also led to notable improvements in fraud detection and risk management. The ability of AI to analyse vast amounts of data in real time has strengthened INPS's capacity to detect irregular patterns in benefit claims, financial disbursements, and social security contributions. By leveraging machine learning algorithms, the institution has reduced the incidence of fraud while optimizing oversight mechanisms, ensuring that public resources are allocated fairly and responsibly. This proactive approach has not only minimized financial losses but has also reinforced public trust in INPS's ability to manage social security funds transparently and equitably.

Beyond operational efficiency, AI has introduced new opportunities for personalized service delivery, transforming the way INPS interacts with citizens. Traditional public sector services often suffer from a one-size-fits-all approach, which fails to accommodate the diverse needs of different beneficiaries. AI has enabled INPS to tailor responses and interventions based on citizen profiles, historical data, and real-time behavioural insights. By anticipating needs and offering proactive solutions, the institution has enhanced citizen engagement, ensuring that individuals receive timely and relevant information about their benefits, eligibility status, and administrative obligations. AI-driven chatbots and virtual assistants, for instance, are capable of providing citizens with customized guidance, answering queries instantly, and simplifying bureaucratic procedures, making interactions with INPS more intuitive and user-friendly.

Another major advantage of AI implementation has been its role in cost reduction and resource optimization. By automating numerous administrative functions, INPS has significantly decreased operational costs, freeing up resources that can be reinvested in further digital transformation initiatives. The institution can now allocate funding more strategically, focusing on infrastructure upgrades, workforce training programs, and the development of advanced AI solutions that further improve service delivery. AI-driven process optimization has also allowed INPS to make more data-informed policy decisions, ensuring that social security measures are responsive to emerging trends and societal needs.

Additionally, the implementation of AI at INPS has contributed to a cultural shift in public administration, challenging traditional bureaucratic inefficiencies and fostering a more agile, innovation-driven institutional mindset. The integration of AI has demonstrated the potential of data-driven governance, where decisions are not only based on regulatory frameworks but also informed by dynamic, real-time insights. This evolution marks a significant departure from the historically rigid structures of Italian public administration, opening new possibilities for adaptive policymaking and more responsive governance models.

While AI has already brought tangible benefits to INPS, its full potential is yet to be realized. As the institution continues to refine its AI strategies, new advancements in machine learning, predictive analytics, and automation will further shape the future of public administration. The long-term sustainability of AI-driven transformation will depend on ongoing investments in technology, regulatory adaptation, and workforce readiness. Ensuring that AI remains a tool for enhancing citizen trust, reducing inefficiencies, and improving service accessibility will be crucial for maintaining the momentum of digital reform at INPS.

Ultimately, the experience of INPS highlights how AI, when implemented strategically, can serve as a catalyst for efficiency, transparency, and innovation in public administration. By capitalizing on AI's capabilities, INPS has not only modernized its operations but has also set a precedent for other public institutions seeking to navigate the complexities of digital transformation. The institution's ability to balance technological advancements with ethical governance, regulatory compliance, and human-cantered policymaking will serve as a benchmark for future AI-driven reforms in the public sector.

7. DISCUSSION

The findings from the case study of INPS provide a nuanced understanding of the organizational dynamics associated with the adoption of AI in public administration. The experience of INPS serves as a valuable case study for AI-driven transformation in public administration, illustrating both the opportunities and obstacles associated with large-scale AI integration. The case highlights the importance of strategic leadership, institutional adaptability, and regulatory alignment in ensuring that AI adoption does not merely enhance efficiency but also strengthens public trust and accountability. The successful implementation of AI at INPS underscores the necessity of a balanced approach, where technological innovation is accompanied by governance mechanisms that mitigate risks and uphold ethical standards.

As governments worldwide continue to experiment with AI-driven administrative models, the INPS case provides key insights into best practices for AI implementation in public institutions. The challenges faced and solutions adopted by INPS offer lessons for policymakers and public administrators seeking to navigate the complexities of digital transformation in government operations. Moving forward, the continued refinement of AI strategies at INPS will provide a critical reference point for how AI can be harnessed to modernize public administration while preserving institutional integrity, social equity, and citizen trust.

This section contextualizes the findings within the broader literature on digital transformation in public administration, discusses their theoretical and practical implications, and outlines avenues for future research.

7.1 AI in Public Administration: A Transformative Yet Complex Shift

The INPS case study reinforces the notion that AI is not merely a technological tool but a transformative force that reshapes organizational structures, decision-making processes, and public service delivery models (Phuangthuean & Nuansang, 2024). Consistent with previous research (Wirtz *et al.*, 2019; Neumann *et al.*, 2024), the findings suggest that AI enables greater efficiency, transparency, and data-driven governance, allowing public institutions to enhance their service quality while reducing administrative burdens. However, the case of INPS also illustrates that the successful deployment of AI in public administration requires significant institutional adaptation.

AI's integration at INPS aligns with the broader trend of AI-driven governance observed across various countries (Mikalef *et al.*, 2022). Like AI adoption efforts in Estonia's digital government framework and Singapore's Smart Nation initiative, INPS's AI strategy has focused on automating routine processes, enhancing decision-making through predictive analytics, and improving citizen interactions. However, the implementation challenges at INPS highlight the context-specific factors that influence AI adoption in highly bureaucratic public institutions. Unlike Estonia or Singapore, where digital transformation has been integrated into governance models from the outset, Italy's AI implementation at INPS has had to navigate pre-existing administrative silos, overcome cultural resistance, and align AI-driven innovations with a legal framework rooted in traditional bureaucratic processes. Additionally, the regulatory complexity surrounding AI deployment in Italy has further constrained the speed of adoption. Public sector institutions operate within a highly codified legal framework that demands strict adherence to procedural norms, data protection laws, and ethical guidelines. While these regulations are essential for ensuring transparency and accountability, they can also create obstacles to the rapid implementation of AI-driven reforms. The introduction of AI at INPS has therefore required a delicate balancing act between innovation and compliance, where technological advancements must align with both national and European Union regulatory frameworks. This contrasts with Estonia and Singapore, where AI governance is more agile and innovation-friendly, allowing for faster prototyping and implementation of AI-driven public services. In these countries, regulatory environments are designed to facilitate technological experimentation, enabling a smoother transition to AI-powered public administration.

These findings underscore that AI in public administration operates within a complex socio-technical ecosystem, where technological capabilities must be aligned with institutional realities, regulatory requirements, and cultural considerations (Chen *et al.*, 2024). This suggests that AI governance frameworks should not be solely technology-centric but should incorporate organizational change management strategies that address institutional resistance and ensure sustainable adoption.

While the INPS case demonstrates clear efficiency gains and operational improvements, a more critical perspective highlights the potential long-term implications of AI adoption on core public sector values. AI-driven automation risks reinforcing inequalities if citizens with limited digital literacy or access to technology are excluded from digitalized services (Eubanks, 2018; Henman, 2020). Similarly, algorithmic opacity may undermine transparency and democratic accountability, as decisions increasingly rely on systems that are difficult for both administrators and citizens to fully understand (Busuioc, 2021; Yeung, 2019). From a citizen perspective, the shift toward AI-mediated interactions may enhance convenience but also risks reducing opportunities for human contact, which remains a critical element in building trust in public institutions (Aoki, 2020; Criado & Gil-García, 2019). Moreover, the socio-political consequences of automation extend beyond organizational efficiency: reliance on AI in welfare administration, for example, can reshape the relationship between state and citizen by emphasizing control and risk management over empathy and equity (Veale & Brass, 2019). These dynamics suggest that evaluating AI adoption in public administration requires not only an assessment of institutional readiness and organizational benefits but also a careful consideration of its broader societal impacts and implications for democratic governance.

7.2 Theoretical Contribution

From a theoretical standpoint, the findings contribute to organizational and public management theories by highlighting how AI acts as both an enabler and a disruptor in institutional settings characterized by bureaucratic rigidity. Traditional technology adoption models, such as the Technology-Organization-Environment (TOE) framework (Madan & Ashok, 2023), emphasize the role of organizational readiness and external environmental factors in driving digital transformation (Twizeyimana & Andersson, 2019).The INPS case suggests that while technological capabilities and policy support are critical, organizational culture, leadership engagement, and workforce adaptation play equally significant roles in shaping AI's institutional impact.

Additionally, the findings contribute to the literature on public sector innovation by demonstrating how AI adoption in public institutions is not a linear process but an iterative and contested transformation. The implementation of AI at INPS has required continuous adaptation, with iterative refinements to align AI applications with legal, ethical, and institutional constraints. This supports arguments within institutional theory (Ongaro, 2006; Pollitt & Bouckaert, 2017) that emphasize path dependency and resistance to change as key challenges in public sector reform. Public organizations often exhibit strong inertia due to deeply embedded administrative traditions, procedural formalities, and regulatory complexities (Christensen *et al.*, 2020). The INPS case aligns with these perspectives, illustrating that even when AI-driven efficiency gains are evident, institutional constraints can slow down or complicate the implementation process.

The study also contributes to the growing body of research on AI accountability and ethics in governance (Busuioc, 2021; Wirtz *et al.*, 2020; Bovens & Zouridis, 2002). AI-driven decision-making at INPS, particularly in fraud detection and administrative compliance, raises critical questions about algorithmic transparency, accountability, and bias mitigation. These findings align with previous studies on AI ethics in public administration, which highlight the need for regulatory safeguards and human oversight mechanisms to prevent unintended consequences such as algorithmic discrimination or loss of public trust (Mittelstadt *et al.*, 2016). Research on algorithmic governance (Danaher *et al.*, 2017; Zouridis *et al.*, 2020) has demonstrated that while AI can improve efficiency and objectivity in decision-making, it also introduces risks related to opacity, procedural fairness, and challenges in assigning responsibility when automated systems fail.

Furthermore, the INPS case study contributes to ongoing discussions in public sector digitalization (Janssen & Van den Broek, 2022) and the role of AI in e-government transformation (Scholta *et al.*, 2019). While AI has the potential to enhance administrative efficiency and service delivery, it must be integrated within a broader governance framework that ensures its legitimacy, transparency, and alignment with democratic values. Previous studies (Young *et al.*, 2019; Yeung, 2019) have cautioned against the risks of excessive automation in public administration, arguing that AI should be designed to complement, rather than replace, human decision-making. The INPS experience echoes these concerns, reinforcing the argument that AI implementation in public institutions requires continuous monitoring, regulatory oversight, and participatory governance mechanisms to maintain accountability and public trust.

The INPS case also illustrates how different theoretical frameworks can be applied to interpret the dynamics of AI adoption in public administration. The TOE framework is reflected in the interplay between technological readiness (e.g., deployment of chatbots and fraud detection systems), organizational readiness (e.g., digital upskilling and interdepartmental coordination), and environmental pressures (e.g., EU regulations and national digital agendas). From a socio-technical perspective, the challenges faced by INPS—such as employee resistance and the need for cultural adaptation—highlight that AI integration is as much a social and organizational process as it is a technological one (Baxter & Sommerville, 2011). Insights from digital maturity models suggest that INPS is positioned at an intermediate stage of digital transformation: while significant advances have been made in automating services and fraud prevention, gaps remain in achieving seamless integration across departments and functions (Kane et al., 2017; Vial, 2019). Finally, the relative absence of robust participatory governance mechanisms in the INPS case underscores the importance of involving citizens and stakeholders in AI design and implementation to ensure legitimacy, trust, and accountability (Ansell & Gash, 2008; Meijer et al., 2019). Taken together, these frameworks enrich the analysis by demonstrating that AI adoption is a multidimensional process that combines technological innovation with organizational transformation, regulatory alignment, and citizen-centered governance.

7.3 Practical Implications for Public Administration

The findings hold significant implications for policymakers and public sector leaders seeking to implement AI in bureaucratic environments. First, the INPS case underscores that AI adoption should not be treated as a purely technological upgrade but as an organizational transformation process. This means that investments in AI infrastructure must be complemented by investments in workforce upskilling, change management, and cross-departmental coordination mechanisms. AI's potential to enhance efficiency and accuracy is contingent on public sector employees' ability to collaborate with AI tools, rather than viewing them as a threat to job security.

Second, the study highlights the importance of regulatory clarity and AI governance frameworks in ensuring ethical and responsible AI deployment. While INPS has made progress in integrating AI-driven automation and predictive analytics, concerns regarding algorithmic opacity and fairness remain. Public institutions adopting AI must prioritize explainability and public accountability, ensuring that AI-driven decisions remain transparent, contestable, and aligned with democratic values.

Third, the case study points to the need for stronger interdepartmental collaboration and digital governance structures. One of the challenges INPS faced was the lack of seamless integration across departments, which led to fragmentation in AI adoption efforts. Governments seeking to maximize the benefits of AI in public administration should establish centralized AI governance units that facilitate interagency collaboration, standardize AI implementation protocols, and ensure interoperability across public sector digital infrastructures.

Finally, the findings highlight the role of citizen engagement in AI governance. As AI increasingly mediates interactions between citizens and government services, public institutions must develop mechanisms for citizen participation and feedback in AI decision-making. The successful adoption of AI at INPS demonstrates that user-cantered design principles should be incorporated into AI service delivery models to enhance trust, accessibility, and inclusivity.

7.4 Limitations and Directions for Future Research

While this study provides important insights into AI adoption at INPS, several limitations should be acknowledged. First, the study is based on a single case analysis, which, while rich in detail, limits the generalizability of findings to other public institutions. Future research could adopt a comparative case study approach, examining how AI adoption differs across public agencies with varying institutional structures, governance models, and technological capabilities.

Second, the study primarily relies on document analysis and secondary data sources. While these sources provide valuable insights, future research could incorporate qualitative interviews with policymakers, AI developers, and frontline public administrators to capture the lived experiences of AI adoption in public administration.

Third, the long-term impacts of AI adoption at INPS remain an open question. While AI has demonstrated short-term efficiency gains, its broader impact on institutional resilience, workforce dynamics, and public trust requires further investigation. Longitudinal studies tracking the evolution of AI governance at INPS and other public institutions would provide a deeper understanding of AI's long-term implications.

Future research should also explore the intersection of AI and human discretion in public administration. While AI optimizes decision-making, its interactions with human expertise, judgment, and ethical considerations remain underexplored. Investigating hybrid AI-human governance models could offer valuable insights into how AI can complement, rather than replace, human decision-making in public institutions.

8. CONCLUSION

The case of INPS illustrates that AI adoption in public administration is not a one-time implementation but an evolving process. While AI offers unprecedented opportunities to enhance efficiency, transparency, and service delivery, its successful deployment requires organizational readiness, adaptive governance, and continuous stakeholder engagement. The findings reinforce the view that public sector AI adoption should be framed not as a technological revolution but as an institutional evolution—one that balances innovation with accountability, efficiency with equity, and automation with human oversight.

As AI continues to reshape public administration, policymakers must navigate its promise and perils with careful planning, regulatory foresight, and a commitment to democratic governance principles. The experience of INPS serves as a valuable reference point for governments worldwide, offering both lessons learned and best practices for ensuring that AI-driven transformation is both effective and ethically sound.

REFERENCES

Agarwal, P. K. (2018). Public administration challenges in the world of AI and bots. *Public Administration Review*, *78*(6), 917–921. DOI: 10.1111/puar.12979

Ahn, M. J., & Chen, Y. C. (2022). Digital transformation toward AI-augmented public administration: The perception of government employees and the willingness to use AI in government. *Government Information Quarterly*, *39*(2), 1–14. DOI: 10.1016/j.giq.2021.101664

Akter, S., Hossain, M. A., Sajib, S., Sultana, S., Rahman, M., Vrontis, D., & McCarthy, G. (2023). A framework for AI-powered service innovation capability: Review and agenda for future research. *Technovation*, *125*, 1–17. DOI: 10.1016/j.technovation.2023.102768

Al-Ansi, A. M., Garad, A., Jaboob, M., & Al-Ansi, A. (2024). Elevating e-government: Unleashing the power of AI and IoT for enhanced public services. *Heliyon*, *10*(23), 1–14. DOI: 10.1016/j.heliyon.2024.e40591 PMID: 39654738

Alon-Barkat, S., & Busuioc, M. (2023). Human–AI interactions in public sector decision making: 'Automation bias' and 'selective adherence' to algorithmic advice. *Journal of Public Administration: Research and Theory*, *33*(1), 153–169. DOI: 10.1093/jopart/muac007

Alshahrani, A., Griva, A., Dennehy, D., & Mäntymäki, M. (2024). Artificial intelligence and decision-making in government functions: Opportunities, challenges and future research. *Transforming Government: People. Transforming Government*, *18*(4), 678–698. DOI: 10.1108/TG-06-2024-0131

Androniceanu, A. (2024). Artificial intelligence in administration and public management. *Administration & Public Management Review*, *175*(1), 99–114. DOI: 10.24818/amp/2024.42-06

Ansell, C., & Gash, A. (2008). Collaborative governance in theory and practice. *Journal of Public Administration: Research and Theory*, *18*(4), 543–571. DOI: 10.1093/jopart/mum032

Aoki, N. (2020). An experimental study of public trust in AI chatbots in the public sector. *Government Information Quarterly*, *37*(4), 1–10. DOI: 10.1016/j.giq.2020.101490

Babashahi, L., Barbosa, C. E., Lima, Y., Lyra, A., Salazar, H., Argôlo, M., de Almeida, M. A., & Souza, J. M. D. (2024). AI in the Workplace: A Systematic Review of Skill Transformation in the Industry. *Administrative Sciences*, *14*(6), 127. DOI: 10.3390/admsci14060127

Baxter, G., & Sommerville, I. (2011). Socio-technical systems: From design methods to systems engineering. *Interacting with Computers*, *23*(1), 4–17. DOI: 10.1016/j.intcom.2010.07.003

Berman, A., de Fine Licht, K., & Carlsson, V. (2024). Trustworthy AI in the public sector: An empirical analysis of a Swedish labor market decision-support system. *Technology in Society*, *76*, 1–15. DOI: 10.1016/j.techsoc.2024.102471

Bhuiyan, M. R. I. (2024). Industry Readiness and Adaptation of Fourth Industrial Revolution: Applying the Extended TOE Framework. *Human Behavior and Emerging Technologies*, *2024*(1), 1–14. DOI: 10.1155/hbe2/8830228

Bignami, F. (2022). Artificial intelligence accountability of public administration. *The American Journal of Comparative Law*, *70*(1, Supplement_1), i312–i346. DOI: 10.1093/ajcl/avac012

Bostrom, R. P., & Heinen, J. S. (1977). MIS problems and failures: A socio-technical perspective, Part II: The application of socio-technical theory. *Management Information Systems Quarterly*, *1*(4), 11–28. DOI: 10.2307/249019

Bouchetara, M., Zerouti, M., & Zouambi, A. R. (2024). Leveraging artificial intelligence (AI) in public sector financial risk management: Innovations, challenges, and future directions. *EDPACS*, *69*(9), 124–144. DOI: 10.1080/07366981.2024.2377351

Bovens, M., & Zouridis, S. (2002). From street-level to system-level bureaucracies: How information and communication technology is transforming administrative discretion and constitutional control. *Public Administration Review*, *62*(2), 174–184. DOI: 10.1111/0033-3352.00168

Bracci, E. (2023). The loopholes of algorithmic public services: An "intelligent" accountability research agenda. *Accounting, Auditing & Accountability Journal*, *36*(2), 739–763. DOI: 10.1108/AAAJ-06-2022-5856

Budhwar, P., Malik, A., De Silva, M. T., & Thevisuthan, P. (2022). Artificial intelligence–challenges and opportunities for international HRM: A review and research agenda. *International Journal of Human Resource Management*, *33*(6), 1065–1097. DOI: 10.1080/09585192.2022.2035161

Busuioc, M. (2021). Accountable artificial intelligence: Holding algorithms to account. *Public Administration Review*, *81*(5), 825–836. DOI: 10.1111/puar.13293 PMID: 34690372

Campion, A., Gasco-Hernandez, M., Jankin Mikhaylov, S., & Esteve, M. (2022). Overcoming the challenges of collaboratively adopting artificial intelligence in the public sector. *Social Science Computer Review*, *40*(2), 462–477. DOI: 10.1177/0894439320979953

Cath, C. (2018). Governing artificial intelligence: Ethical, legal and technical opportunities and challenges. *Philosophical Transactions. Series A, Mathematical, Physical, and Engineering Sciences*, *376*(2133), 1–8. DOI: 10.1098/rsta.2018.0080 PMID: 30322996

Chen, T., Gascó-Hernandez, M., & Esteve, M. (2024). The adoption and implementation of artificial intelligence chatbots in public organizations: Evidence from US state governments. *American Review of Public Administration*, *54*(3), 255–270. DOI: 10.1177/02750740231200522

Christensen, J., Aarøe, L., Baekgaard, M., Herd, P., & Moynihan, D. P. (2020). Human capital and administrative burden: The role of cognitive resources in citizen-state interactions. *Public Administration Review*, *80*(1), 127–136. DOI: 10.1111/puar.13134 PMID: 32025058

Cortés-Cediel, M. E., Segura-Tinoco, A., Cantador, I., & Bolívar, M. P. R. (2023). Trends and challenges of e-government chatbots: Advances in exploring open government data and citizen participation content. *Government Information Quarterly*, *40*(4), 1–15. DOI: 10.1016/j.giq.2023.101877

Criado, J. I., & de Zarate-Alcarazo, L. O. (2022). Technological frames, CIOs, and Artificial Intelligence in public administration: A socio-cognitive exploratory study in Spanish local governments. *Government Information Quarterly*, *39*(3), 1–13. DOI: 10.1016/j.giq.2022.101688

Criado, J. I., & Gil-Garcia, J. R. (2019). Creating public value through smart technologies and strategies: From digital services to artificial intelligence and beyond. *International Journal of Public Sector Management*, *32*(5), 438–450. DOI: 10.1108/IJPSM-07-2019-0178

Damar, M., Aydın, Ö., Nihal Cagle, M., Özoğuz, E., Ömer Köse, H., & Özen, A. (2024). Navigating the digital frontier: Transformative technologies reshaping public administration. *EDPACS*, *69*(9), 41–69. DOI: 10.1080/07366981.2024.2376792

Danaher, J., Hogan, M. J., Noone, C., Kennedy, R., Behan, A., De Paor, A., Felzmann, H., Haklay, M., Khoo, S.-M., Morison, J., Murphy, M. H., O'Brolchain, N., Schafer, B., & Shankar, K. (2017). Algorithmic governance: Developing a research agenda through the power of collective intelligence. *Big Data & Society*, *4*(2), 1–21. DOI: 10.1177/2053951717726554

Dar, S. A.Showkat Ahmad Dar. (2024). Unleashing the power of artificial intelligence and automation in public administration. *Journal of Public Administration Research*, *1*(1), 1–13. DOI: 10.32996/jpar.2024.1.1.1

Datta, P., Walker, L., & Amarilli, F. (2020). Digital transformation: Learning from Italy's public administration. *Journal of Information Technology Teaching Cases*, *10*(2), 54–71. DOI: 10.1177/2043886920910437

David, S., Zinica, D., Bărbu ă-Mi u, N., Savga, L., & Virlanuta, F. O. (2024). Public administration managers' and employees' perceptions of adaptability to change under "the future of work" paradigm. *Technological Forecasting and Social Change*, *199*, 1–13. DOI: 10.1016/j.techfore.2023.123088

Eubanks, V. (2018). *Automating inequality: How high-tech tools profile, police, and punish the poor*. St. Martin's Press.

Fabbrini, F. (2022). Italy's national recovery and resilience plan: Context, content and challenges. *Journal of Modern Italian Studies*, *27*(5), 658–676. DOI: 10.1080/1354571X.2022.2124672

Febiandini, V. V., & Sony, M. S. (2023). Analysis of public administration challenges in the development of artificial intelligence industry 4.0. *IAIC Transactions on Sustainable Digital Innovation*, *4*(2), 164–168. DOI: 10.34306/itsdi.v4i2.586

Filgueiras, F. (2022). New Pythias of public administration: Ambiguity and choice in AI systems as challenges for governance. *AI & Society*, *37*(4), 1473–1486. DOI: 10.1007/s00146-021-01201-4

Guo, Y. (2024). *Digital Government and Public Interaction: Platforms, Chatbots, and Public Satisfaction: Platforms, Chatbots, and Public Satisfaction*. IGI Global. DOI: 10.4018/979-8-3693-3665-6

Henman, P. (2020). Improving public services using artificial intelligence: Possibilities, pitfalls, governance. *Asia Pacific Journal of Public Administration*, *42*(4), 209–221. DOI: 10.1080/23276665.2020.1816188

Hjaltalin, I. T., & Sigurdarson, H. T. (2024). The strategic use of AI in the public sector: A public values analysis of national AI strategies. *Government Information Quarterly*, *41*(1), 1–16. DOI: 10.1016/j.giq.2024.101914

Irani, Z., Abril, R. M., Weerakkody, V., Omar, A., & Sivarajah, U. (2023). The impact of legacy systems on digital transformation in European public administration: Lesson learned from a multi case analysis. *Government Information Quarterly, 40*(1), 1–14. DOI: 10.1016/j.giq.2022.101784

Kamukapa, T. D., Lubinga, S., Masiya, T., & Sono, L. (2024). Assessing the integration of AI competencies in undergraduate public administration curricula in selected South African higher education institutions. *Teaching Public Administration, Ahead-of-print*, 1–18. DOI: 10.1177/01447394241266443

Kane, G. C., Palmer, D., Phillips, A. N., Kiron, D., & Buckley, N. (2017). Achieving digital maturity. *MIT Sloan Management Review, 59*(1), 1–29.

Kemp, A. (2024). Competitive advantage through artificial intelligence: Toward a theory of situated AI. *Academy of Management Review, 49*(3), 618–635. DOI: 10.5465/amr.2020.0205

Körner-Wyrtki, K., Buck, C., Krombacher, A., & Röglinger, M. (2024). Exploring success factors for developing citizen-centric digital public services-insights from a case study. *Electronic Government, an International Journal, 20*(5), 591–620. DOI: 10.1504/EG.2024.140777

Kulal, A., Rahiman, H. U., Suvarna, H., Abhishek, N., & Dinesh, S. (2024). Enhancing public service delivery efficiency: Exploring the impact of AI. *Journal of Open Innovation, 10*(3), 1–16. DOI: 10.1016/j.joitmc.2024.100329

Kumar, D. (2024). AI-driven automation in administrative processes: Enhancing efficiency and accuracy. *International Journal of Engineering Science and Humanities, 14*(1), 256–265. DOI: 10.62904/qg004437

Kuziemski, M., & Misuraca, G. (2020). AI governance in the public sector: Three tales from the frontiers of automated decision-making in democratic settings. *Telecommunications Policy, 44*(6), 1–13. DOI: 10.1016/j.telpol.2020.101976 PMID: 32313360

Longo, J. (2022). When artificial intelligence meets real public administration. *Canadian Public Administration, 65*(2), 384–388. DOI: 10.1111/capa.12465

Looks, H., Fangmann, J., Thomaschewski, J., Escalona, M. J., & Schön, E. M. (2024). Towards improving agility in Public Administration. *Software Quality Journal, 32*(1), 283–311. DOI: 10.1007/s11219-023-09657-x

Loukis, E. N., Maragoudakis, M., & Kyriakou, N. (2020). Artificial intelligence-based public sector data analytics for economic crisis policymaking. *Transforming Government: People. Transforming Government, 14*(4), 639–662. DOI: 10.1108/TG-11-2019-0113

Maciejewski, M. (2017). To do more, better, faster and more cheaply: Using big data in public administration. *International Review of Administrative Sciences, 83*(1), 120–135. DOI: 10.1177/0020852316640058

Madan, R., & Ashok, M. (2023). AI adoption and diffusion in public administration: A systematic literature review and future research agenda. *Government Information Quarterly, 40*(1), 1–18. DOI: 10.1016/j.giq.2022.101774

McQuiston, J., & Manoharan, A. P. (2021). E-government and information technology coursework in public administration programs in Asia. *Teaching Public Administration, 39*(2), 210–226. DOI: 10.1177/0144739420978249

Meijer, A., Curtin, D., & Hillebrandt, M. (2019). Open government: Connecting vision and voice. *International Review of Administrative Sciences, 85*(2), 311–316. DOI: 10.1177/0020852311429533

Mikalef, P., Lemmer, K., Schaefer, C., Ylinen, M., Fjørtoft, S. O., Torvatn, H. Y., Gupta, M., & Niehaves, B. (2022). Enabling AI capabilities in government agencies: A study of determinants for European municipalities. *Government Information Quarterly, 39*(4), 1–14. DOI: 10.1016/j.giq.2021.101596

Mishra, A. K., Tyagi, A. K., Dananjayan, S., Rajavat, A., Rawat, H., & Rawat, A. (2024). Revolutionizing government operations: The impact of artificial intelligence in public administration. In Rawat, R., Chakrawarti, R. K., Sarangi, S. K., Rajavat, A., Alamanda, M. S., Srividya, K., & Sankaran, K. S. (Eds.), *Conversational Artificial Intelligence* (pp. 607–634). John Wiley & Sons., DOI: 10.1002/9781394200801.ch34

Mittelstadt, B. D., Allo, P., Taddeo, M., Wachter, S., & Floridi, L. (2016). The ethics of algorithms: Mapping the debate. *Big Data & Society, 3*(2), 1–21. DOI: 10.1177/2053951716679679

Neumann, O., Guirguis, K., & Steiner, R. (2024). Exploring artificial intelligence adoption in public organizations: A comparative case study. *Public Management Review, 26*(1), 114–141. DOI: 10.1080/14719037.2022.2048685

Nirala, K. K., Singh, N. K., & Purani, V. S. (2022). A survey on providing customer and public administration based services using AI-chatbot. *Multimedia Tools and Applications, 81*(16), 22215–22246. DOI: 10.1007/s11042-021-11458-y PMID: 35002470

Nzobonimpa, S. (2023). Artificial intelligence, task complexity and uncertainty: Analyzing the advantages and disadvantages of using algorithms in public service delivery under public administration theories. *Digital Transformation and Society*, *2*(3), 219–234. DOI: 10.1108/DTS-03-2023-0018

Ongaro, E. (2006). The dynamics of devolution processes in legalistic countries: Organizational change in the Italian public sector. *Public Administration*, *84*(3), 737–770. DOI: 10.1111/j.1467-9299.2006.00610.x

Pakhnenko, O., & Kuan, Z. (2023). Ethics of digital innovation in public administration. *Business Ethics and Leadership*, *7*(1), 113–121. DOI: 10.21272/bel.7(1).113-121.2023

Pencheva, I., Esteve, M., & Mikhaylov, S. J. (2020). Big data and AI–transformational shift for government: So, what next for research? *Public Policy and Administration*, *35*(1), 24–44. DOI: 10.1177/0952076718780537

Phuangthuean, P., & Nuansang, J. (2024). The transforming public administration: The role of AI in shaping the future. *Journal of Social Science and Multidisciplinary Research*, *1*(3), 21–41.

Plantinga, P. (2024). Digital discretion and public administration in Africa: Implications for the use of artificial intelligence. *Information Development*, *40*(2), 332–352. DOI: 10.1177/02666669221117526

Pollitt, C., & Bouckaert, G. (2017). *Public management reform: A comparative analysis-into the age of austerity*. Oxford university press.

Rane, N., Choudhary, S. P., & Rane, J. (2024). Acceptance of artificial intelligence: Key factors, challenges, and implementation strategies. *Journal of Applied Artificial Intelligence*, *5*(2), 50–70. DOI: 10.48185/jaai.v5i2.1017

Reginato, E., Fadda, I., & Paglietti, P. (2016). The influence of resistance to change on public-sector reform implementation: The case of Italian municipalities' internal control system. *International Journal of Public Administration*, *39*(12), 989–999. DOI: 10.1080/01900692.2015.1068325

Salah, M., Abdelfattah, F., & Al Halbusi, H. (2023). Generative artificial intelligence (ChatGPT & bard) in public administration research: A double-edged sword for street-level bureaucracy studies. *International Journal of Public Administration, Ahead-of-print*, 1–7. DOI: 10.1080/01900692.2023.2274801

Scantamburlo, T., Cortés, A., Foffano, F., Barrué, C., Distefano, V., Pham, L., & Fabris, A. (2024). Artificial intelligence across europe: A study on awareness, attitude and trust. *IEEE Transactions on Artificial Intelligence*, •••, 1–14. DOI: 10.1109/TAI.2024.3461633

Scholta, H., Mertens, W., Kowalkiewicz, M., & Becker, J. (2019). From one-stop shop to no-stop shop: An e-government stage model. *Government Information Quarterly*, *36*(1), 11–26. DOI: 10.1016/j.giq.2018.11.010

Schwarz, G., Christensen, T., & Zhu, X. (2022). Bounded rationality, satisficing, artificial intelligence, and decision-making in public organizations: The contributions of Herbert Simon. *Public Administration Review, Ahead-of-print*, 1–9. DOI: 10.1111/puar.13540

Sienkiewicz-Małyjurek, K. (2023). Whether AI adoption challenges matter for public managers? The case of Polish cities. *Government Information Quarterly*, *40*(3), 1–19. DOI: 10.1016/j.giq.2023.101828

Sigfrids, A., Nieminen, M., Leikas, J., & Pikkuaho, P. (2022). How should public administrations foster the ethical development and use of artificial intelligence? A review of proposals for developing governance of AI. *Frontiers in Human Dynamics*, *4*, 1–19. DOI: 10.3389/fhumd.2022.858108

Twizeyimana, J. D., & Andersson, A. (2019). The public value of E-Government–A literature review. *Government Information Quarterly*, *36*(2), 167–178. DOI: 10.1016/j.giq.2019.01.001

Valle-Cruz, D., Criado, J. I., Sandoval-Almazán, R., & Ruvalcaba-Gomez, E. A. (2020). Assessing the public policy-cycle framework in the age of artificial intelligence: From agenda-setting to policy evaluation. *Government Information Quarterly*, *37*(4), 1–12. DOI: 10.1016/j.giq.2020.101509

van Noordt, C., & Tangi, L. (2023). The dynamics of AI capability and its influence on public value creation of AI within public administration. *Government Information Quarterly*, *40*(4), 1–14. DOI: 10.1016/j.giq.2023.101860

Veale, M., & Brass, I. (2019). Administration by algorithm? Public management meets public sector machine learning. In Lodge, M., & Wegrich, K. (Eds.), *The problem-solving capacity of the modern state* (pp. 413–432). Oxford University Press. DOI: 10.31235/osf.io/mwhnb

Vesnic-Alujevic, L., Nascimento, S., & Polvora, A. (2020). Societal and ethical impacts of artificial intelligence: Critical notes on European policy frameworks. *Telecommunications Policy*, *44*(6), 1–14. DOI: 10.1016/j.telpol.2020.101961

Vial, G. (2019). Understanding digital transformation: A review and a research agenda. *The Journal of Strategic Information Systems*, *28*(2), 118–144. DOI: 10.1016/j.jsis.2019.01.003

Wang, C. W., Hsu, B. Y., & Chen, D. Y. (2024). Chatbot applications in government frontline services: Leveraging artificial intelligence and data governance to reduce problems and increase effectiveness. *Asia Pacific Journal of Public Administration*, *46*(4), 488–511. DOI: 10.1080/23276665.2024.2397677

Wirtz, B. W., & Müller, W. M. (2019). An integrated artificial intelligence framework for public management. *Public Management Review*, *21*(7), 1076–1100. DOI: 10.1080/14719037.2018.1549268

Wirtz, B. W., Weyerer, J. C., & Geyer, C. (2019). Artificial intelligence and the public sector: Applications and challenges. *International Journal of Public Administration*, *42*(7), 596–615. DOI: 10.1080/01900692.2018.1498103

Wirtz, B. W., Weyerer, J. C., & Sturm, B. J. (2020). The dark sides of artificial intelligence: An integrated AI governance framework for public administration. *International Journal of Public Administration*, *43*(9), 818–829. DOI: 10.1080/01900692.2020.1749851

Wolniak, R., & Stecuła, K. (2024). Artificial intelligence in smart cities—applications, barriers, and future directions: A review. *Smart Cities*, *7*(3), 1346–1389. DOI: 10.3390/smartcities7030057

Wong, S. L., Liu, H. T., & Cheng, L. J. (2011). Elucidating the relationship between satisfaction and citizen involvement in public administration. *Public Management Review*, *13*(4), 595–618. DOI: 10.1080/14719037.2010.525032

Yeung, K. (2019). Regulation by blockchain: The emerging battle for supremacy between the code of law and code as law. *The Modern Law Review*, *82*(2), 207–239. DOI: 10.1111/1468-2230.12399

Yin, R. K. (2009). *Case Study Research: Design and methods*. Sage Publishing.

Young, M. M., Bullock, J. B., & Lecy, J. D. (2019). Artificial discretion as a tool of governance: A framework for understanding the impact of artificial intelligence on public administration. *Perspectives on Public Management and Governance*, *2*(4), 301–313. DOI: 10.1093/ppmgov/gvz014

Yun, C. (2020). Early innovation adoption: Effects of performance-based motivation and organizational characteristics. *Public Performance & Management Review*, *43*(4), 790–817. DOI: 10.1080/15309576.2019.1666725

Zouridis, S., van Eck, M., & Bovens, M. (2020). Automated Discretion. In Evans, T., & Hupe, P. (Eds.), *Discretion and the Quest for Controlled Freedom*. Palgrave Macmillan., DOI: 10.1007/978-3-030-19566-3_20

Chapter 11
The Artificial Intelligence Policy of Italy

Çiğdem Pank Yildirim
https://orcid.org/0000-0002-7084-313X
Muğla Sıtkı Koçman University, Turkey

ABSTRACT

Artificial intelligence is known as systems that imitate human intelligence in order to perform certain tasks and can improve themselves by renewing the information they obtain. The ability to imitate human intelligence distinguishes artificial intelligence from today's technologies. Increasing the economic volumes of countries has made artificial intelligence a strategic value in international competition. Italy is also among the countries that see dealing with artificial intelligence as a strategic need, as it is among the countries that want to show their claim in technology. The aim of the study is to reveal the change that Italy's artificial intelligence policies have created on Italy and to evaluate its impact. In line with this purpose, the study examines the regulations regarding the use of artificial intelligence systems in Italy and evaluates the artificial intelligence strategy developed by Italy in the processes of creating public policy and providing public services. The document analysis method is used in the study.

1. INTRODUCTION

The concept of artificial intelligence was introduced in 1856. The increase in data volumes, the importance of algorithms and calculations, and advances in science and technology have made artificial intelligence important. In the early days of its emergence, artificial intelligence was generally associated with topics such as problem solving and symbolic methods. Later, it continued to develop with

DOI: 10.4018/979-8-3373-1484-6.ch011

machine learning and deep learning, which allows it to perform operations such as speech, recognition, and prediction. Artificial intelligence is known as systems that imitate human intelligence in order to perform certain tasks and can improve themselves by renewing the information they obtain. The ability to imitate human intelligence distinguishes artificial intelligence from today's technologies. Artificial intelligence processes certain tasks given to it with fast and intelligent algorithms by observing existing situations. Artificial intelligence works together with methods and technologies such as machine learning, artificial neural network, deep learning technology, cognitive computing, and advanced algorithms. The importance of artificial intelligence is increasing today in terms of analyzing more data in depth.

Operations of artificial intelligence are revolutionizing not just the realm of technology but also societal and executive functions. Noteworthy exemplifications include healthcare (AlphaFold), education (ChatGPT), transportation (Tesla, Waymo), finance (BloombergGPT), and public administration (Estoniane-government), which are leading inventions worldwide. On a global position, AI has surfaced as a pivotal tool in public administration, especially in the areas of policymaking and smart megacity development. The Estoniane-government system is stressed as one of the most successful cases of AI in public services (Margetts and Dunleavy, 2013). Singapore's Smart Nation Project incorporates AI into the operation of business, energy, and security. Although controversial, China's Social Credit System exemplifies the operation of AI in covering social geste (Creemers, 2018).

Countries that exceed in AI showcase their leadership not just through technological exploration and development investments but also via their nonsupervisory structures and public programs. The United States has a longstanding and technological leadership position in AI. Major tech companies like Google DeepMind (firstly innovated in the UK but now part of the US- grounded Alphabet), OpenAI, Microsoft, and IBM are creating advanced AI operations worldwide (Marcus, 2022). A unified AI ecosystem was formed at the civil position with the National AI Initiative Act (2020). In terms of defense and security, AI exploration receives support from DARPA (Allen & Chan, 2017). The US's leadership is a result of both private- sector invention and strategic government investments. In addition to the US, China, the EU, and leading countries similar as Canada, Japan, and South Korea have also advanced in AI operations. The tradition of preparing an artificial intelligence strategy document began in Canada in 2017 and was quickly accepted by different countries around the world (Okçu & Akman, 2022). Canada, in particular, is among the countries that are highly developed in terms of digitalization (Öztürk & Durukal, 2022).

Amidst the global race in artificial intelligence, Italy has emerged as a key player on the world stage with its comprehensive AI strategies, enhancing its innovative efforts. The country has gained recognition through its collaborations with European nations on AI and its policies concerning the deployment of its own AI systems. The Italian government views AI systems as a strategic advantage in international competition and is actively pursuing research in this area. The scarcity of studies examining Italy's AI policy has prompted the development of this research.

This study aims to reveal the changes that Italy's artificial intelligence policies have created in Italy and to evaluate their impact. To this end, the regulations regarding the use of artificial intelligence systems in Italy are examined, and the artificial intelligence strategy developed by Italy in the processes of creating public policy and providing public services is evaluated. First, the historical development of artificial intelligence and the meaning of the concept are discussed. Second, the advantages and disadvantages of artificial intelligence are explained. Third, the policies and strategies of countries on artificial intelligence are mentioned in general, and after providing general information about Italy, the policies developed by Italy in this direction and the digitalization process of Italy are discussed. Finally, the artificial intelligence strategy developed by Italy in the economic, cultural and political fields, its studies on the use of artificial intelligence systems are evaluated, the use of artificial intelligence in public service delivery processes are discussed and suggestions are made. The document analysis method was used in this study. In this direction, the legal and judicial regulations made by Italy on artificial intelligence are used, and the documents on Italian websites on this subject are examined. In addition, domestic and foreign literature information was used.

2. HISTORICAL DEVELOPMENT OF THE CONCEPT OF ARTIFICIAL INTELLIGENCE

The most basic requirement for adapting public administration to technology is the safe preservation of information. The correct and rapid realization of management activities depends on the development of preservation methods and the secure processing and transmission of the information held to the addressees (Durukal&Öztürk, 2019). Artificial intelligence is considered one of the main icons of digitalization processes (Aksu & Akman, 2022). Artificial Intelligence is a complex generality that influences not just technology but also various fields like ethics, sociology, economics, and law. The idea of artificial intelligence (AI) has roots in ancient philosophy, but it began to take shape technically in themid- 20th century, significantly impacting numerous aspects of social life in the 21st century (Russell & Norvig, 2021). The origins of AI can be traced back to Alan Turing's 1950 paper," Computing Machinery and Intelligence," where he asked," Can machines suppose?" The Turing Test surfaced as a standard for assessing AI systems (Turing, 1950). John McCarthy first introduced the term artificial intelligence at the

Dartmouth Conference in 1956, marking a period when logical conclusion systems and representational AI were developed (McCarthy et al., 1956).

During the 1970s and 1980s, expert systems (e.g. MYCIN) were developed. These systems were systems that could make opinions by recycling expert knowledge in a certain field into rules (Buchanan & Shortliffe, 1984). Machine literacy (ML) brought a new direction to artificial intelligence with statistical models and data analysis styles. In this period, ways similar as support vector machines (SVM), decision trees and Bayesian networks came to the fore (Mitchell, 1997). The deep literacy revolution began with AlexNet winning the ImageNet competition in 2012(Krizhevsky et al., 2012).

The use of artificial intelligence systems in decision- timber has brought with it issues similar as translucency, bias, and sequestration (Eubanks, 2018). The ethical dilemmas of independent systems (e.g. independent vehicles) have brought Isaac Asimov's Three Laws of Robotics back to the docket (Asimov, 1950). The European Union espoused a threat- grounded nonsupervisory approach with the Artificial Intelligence Act in 2021(European Commission, 2021). In Turkey, the National Artificial Intelligence Strategy (2021- 2025) document was published in 2021 and targets were determined for the use of artificial intelligence in public services (Ministry of Industry and Technology, 2021).

When we look at its areas of use and styles, artificial intelligence contributes to artificial product stages with styles similar as image recognition and bracket, and is extensively used in different diligence with its prophetic approach (Temel & Coşkun, 2024). While artificial intelligence threatens some lines of work by automating product processes, it also leads to the emergence of new professions. This metamorphosis has needed the restructuring of education programs (OECD, 2020). The future of artificial intelligence is taking shape under headlines similar asmulti-level governance, ethical algorithms, and artificial general intelligence (AGI) quests. With the development of models approaching original intelligence, the philosophical and legal confines of mortal- AI commerce will be questioned again (Bostrom, 2014).

3. ADVANTAGES AND DISADVANTAGES OF ARTIFICIAL INTELLIGENCE

The Internet of Things (IoT) has become a revolutionary technological trend, linking billions of devices and facilitating effortless communication and data sharing (Aksu&Akman, 2023). Moment, artificial intelligence is n't simply a technological advancement but also a complex tool for metamorphosis with social, ethical, and legal ramifications. With its capabilities in robotization, decision support systems, big data analysis, and mortal- suchlike relations, artificial intelligence presents promising prospects in colorful fields similar as healthcare, education, security, and the frugality (Russell & Norvig, 2021). Nevertheless, these openings are accompanied by significant challenges, including changes in employment, ethical breaches, translucency issues, and prejudiced algorithms (Crawford, 2021).

The advantages of artificial intelligence are listed as effectiveness and robotization, decision support systems, substantiated services, and use in parlous surroundings

- effectiveness and robotization Artificial intelligence enables the mortal pool to be directed to further strategic areas by automating repetitious and time-consuming tasks. For illustration, in the manufacturing sector, error-free and fast product has come possible thanks to robotic process robotization (RPA) (Brynjolfsson & McAfee, 2014).
- Decision Support Systems In the healthcare field, croakers can make further accurate opinions thanks to AI- supported individual systems (e.g. IBM Watson Health) (Topol, 2019). Also, decision support systems grounded on big data analysis are being developed in areas similar as law and finance.
- Personalized Services By assaying individual preferences, AI can give individualized education, advertising, and healthcare services. For illustration, adaptive literacy systems give content acclimatized to scholars' learning styles (Luckin et al., 2016).
- Use in Risky surroundings Artificial intelligence can be used in surroundings where it's dangerous for humans to work (e.g. mines, war zones). Autonomous drones and robotic arms play life- saving places in these areas (Lin et al., 2012).

The disadvantages of artificial intelligence focus on employment and pool metamorphosis, ethical issues and prejudiced algorithms, lack of translucency and responsibility, security and cyber pitfalls

- Employment and Workforce Transformation Artificial intelligence can lead to the robotization of jobs in numerous sectors, causing some professions to vanish. Low- professed workforces are particularly negatively affected by this metamorphosis (Frey & Osborne, 2017). According to OECD (2020) data, 14 of the pool is at high threat of robotization.
- Ethical Issues and Poisoned Algorithms AI systems can carry impulses in the datasets they're developed on. For illustration, facial recognition algorithms have been set up to have advanced error rates on black individualities (Buolamwini & Gebru, 2018). This can lead to serious ethical violations, especially in security and justice systems.

- Lack of translucency and Responsibility The "black box" nature of decision-making processes makes it delicate to understand why algorithms reach certain conclusions. This creates query in determining legal liabilities (Pasquale, 2015).
- Security and Cyber pitfalls AI can be used to automate cyber attacks, and it also poses the threat of unethical military use through independent munitions systems (UNIDIR, 2018). Also, AI- supported deepfakes pose a serious trouble in terms of intimation.

When examining artificial intelligence from legal and political perspectives, the European Union and Turkey stand out. The EU has established its guidelines on translucency and mortal oversight by calling checkups for high- threat operations through the Artificial Intelligence Law (2021) (European Commission, 2021). Meanwhile, Turkey's National Artificial Intelligence Strategy, released in 2021, has embraced an approach to artificial intelligence that considers ethical, legal, and social aspects (Ministry of Industry and Technology, 2021).

4. POLICIES AND REGULATIONS DEVELOPED BY ITALY ON ARTIFICIAL INTELLIGENCE

European Union member countries are trying to direct their work on artificial intelligence by exhibiting a common approach (Coşkun, 2022). Italy is also developing strategic programs in the field of artificial intelligence and is harmonizing its regulations in this field with the European Union frame. The country is embracing the eventuality of AI for social and profitable metamorphosis, while also taking a comprehensive approach concentrated on managing ethical and legal pitfalls.

Italy's approach to AI policy is told by both its public priorities and the regulations set by the European Union. Specifically, EU directives like the General Data Protection Regulation (GDPR) and the lately executed Artificial Intelligence Act (AI Act) play a significant part in shaping Italy's public laws and practices. Italy has been laboriously involved in the drafting and concession of the AI Act, which is the EU's first comprehensive AI legislation, and has conducted studies to align with this regulation while also taking fresh public measures (Borocci, 2025). Likewise, the Italian data protection authority, Garante (Garante per la Protezione dei Dati Personali), keeps a close watch on AI operations under the GDPR frame and way in when necessary. For case, in 2023, Garante temporarily halted the ChatGPT service handed by the Microsoft- supported company OpenAI due to suspected GDPR breaches, subsequently blocking access until demanded conduct were taken

(Pollina and Armellini, 2025). These cases illustrate Italy's visionary nonsupervisory approach in the AI sector.

4.1. Italy's National Artificial Intelligence Strategies

Italy has clarified its roadmap by preparing public strategic plans on artificial intelligence. Two important strategy documents, especially published in recent times, reveal the country's vision for artificial intelligence the" National Artificial Intelligence Strategy 2022- 2024" and its follow- up, the" National Artificial Intelligence Strategy 2024- 2026." These strategies reflect a holistic approach that covers different confines of artificial intelligence, from the R&D ecosystem to public administration, from the private sector to education. At the same time, they concentrate on a mortal-centered and dependable understanding of artificial intelligence that's compatible with EU programs (European Commission, Joint Research Centre, 2021).

National Artificial Intelligence Strategy (2022-2024)

The first comprehensive strategy document, the "National Artificial Intelligence Strategy 2022-2024", was published in November 2021 (European Commission, Joint Research Centre, 2021). This strategy defined Italy's main goals and areas of action in the field of artificial intelligence. The document highlights three main areas of action (Borocci, 2025):

- *Strengthening the Ecosystem and Attracting Talent:* Italy aims to increase its expert human resources and attract talented researchers and entrepreneurs to the country in order to develop the AI ecosystem. In this context, it is aimed to increase financing for AI research and innovation, support national research centers and prevent brain drain.
- *Investment in Advanced Research:* The strategy foresees allocating resources to support advanced research and innovation in the field of artificial intelligence. Within this framework, it is planned to encourage collaborations between universities, research institutes and the private sector and to invest in basic and applied artificial intelligence research.
- *Artificial Intelligence Applications in Public and Private Sectors:* The strategy aims to encourage the adoption of artificial intelligence solutions in both public administration and the manufacturing sector in general. In this context, it is envisaged to develop pilot projects for the use of artificial intelligence in public services and to create guidance and support mechanisms for companies to integrate artificial intelligence technologies into their processes.

This strategy document also emphasized the need to harmonize sectoral regulations with AI policies (Borocci, 2025). It was put forward that the use of AI in regulated sectors such as banking and insurance should be encouraged in a way that does not conflict with existing legislation, and that special guidelines should be prepared in these areas if necessary. The publication of the strategy document is also an important step for Italy to fulfill its obligation to create a national roadmap within the framework of the EU's "Coordinated Plan on AI".

Efforts to enhance the integration of artificial intelligence in smart cities have been driven by this strategy. In this regard, the Municipality of Milan, along with its local governments adopting AI or digital twins, initiated an urban "digital twin" project during 2022–2023 in collaboration with the Cyclomedia/Esri/CGR consortium. This design utilizes road mapping and AI- driven image processing algorithms. These technologies have eased prophetic analysis for managing business lights and road signs, thereby boosting data- driven capabilities in original governance. Similar operations have contributed to advancements that align with the objects of smart metropolises and the improvement of public service quality (Network360, 2025).

National Artificial Intelligence Strategy (2024-2026)

Italy has revised its approach to align with the evolving AI terrain and new EU- position regulations, unveiling the National Artificial Intelligence Strategy 2024- 2026 in July 2024. This streamlined strategy builds upon former objects while outlining a more holistic and ambitious vision. It aims to enhance citizens' quality of life and drive the nation's profitable and social growth by employing the transformative eventuality of AI. A crucial focus of the strategy is the establishment of an ethical, mortal- centered, and responsible AI ecosystem. It also underscores the sensitive operation of AI operations, particularly in areas analogous as insulation, security, gender equality, and environmental sustainability (Lexology, 2024).

The 2024-2026 strategy is structured around four main pillars (Lexology, 2024):

- *Scientific Research and Innovation (R&D Ecosystem):* The goal is to foster scientific research in artificial intelligence across the nation and enhance the quality of research outcomes. To achieve this, sweats will concentrate on establishing a robust AI exploration ecosystem that fosters collaboration among universities, exploration institutions, and the private sector.
- *Public Administration and Public Services:* Artificial intelligence is viewed as an essential instrument for transforming public administration and enhancing citizen-centered services. The strategy promotes the relinquishment of artificial intelligence within the public sector to boost internal effectiveness and deliver services acclimatized to the specific requirements of citizens.

- *Private Sector and Economy:* AI is set to play a crucial role in transforming Italy's manufacturing and business sectors, enhancing their competitiveness. Given the manufacturing- driven nature of Italian assiduity, which thrives on product and process excellence, strategically integrating AI technologies into these disciplines is essential.
- *Education and Skills Development:* In Italy, the shortage of skilled professionals in the field of artificial intelligence has been recognized as a key obstacle to the widespread adoption of innovative solutions.

Italy's public strategies demonstrate a strong commitment to erecting a competitive yet responsible AI ecosystem, aligned with broader EU objects. The country is laboriously engaging in common enterprise and networks across Europe. A notable trouble includes the planned establishment of the Italian Institute of Artificial Intelligence(I3A) in Turin, which will serve as a mecca for public exploration and technological advancements. I3A aims to bolster AI development across fields like 5G, Assiduity 4.0, and cybersecurity. Likewise, Italy seeks to establish a public knowledge exchange network linked with the CLAIRE network, an action fostering collaboration among AI exploration centers in Europe, alongside digital invention capitals. On an transnational position, Italy is also a crucial party in enterprise similar as the Global Partnership on Artificial Intelligence (GPAI), championing for inclusive and responsible AI growth that upholds mortal rights and shares global principles and moxie (European Commission, Joint Research Centre, 2021).

4.2. EU Regulations and Italy's Harmonization Efforts

Italy's approach to AI programs is heavily told by regulations established at the European Union position. Specifically, the EU Artificial Intelligence Act and the General Data Protection Regulation serve as the crucial fabrics guiding Italy's legislative and practical measures in the field. This member provides an overview of these EU- position regulations before probing into Italy's enterprise to align with them and apply fresh programs acclimatized to the public setting.

The European Union Artificial Intelligence Act (AI Act) and Italy

The European Union's Artificial Intelligence Act officially came into effect in July 2024, following its publication in the EU Official Journal. Marking a global corner, it stands as the first comprehensive legislation devoted to AI. The Act takes a risk-based approach to regulate the development, deployment, and use of AI systems within the EU market. It classifies AI systems based on their risk levels, assigning unique obligations to each category. Certain AI operations are outright banned, similar as those exercising deceptive styles to unconsciously impact geste or systems like social credit scoring. High- threat AI systems particularly those employed in crucial sectors similar as critical structure, education, employment, finance, and security are subject to strict conditions and robust request surveillance measures. Also, the regulation features a strong enforcement frame, stipulating significant penalties fornon-compliance. Companies failing to meet these scores could face forfeitures of over to 7 of their periodic global development or€ 35 million, showcasing the Act's emphasis on responsibility and safety (Hickman et al., 2024).

Personal Data Protection (GDPR) and Artificial Intelligence

An essential aspect of artificial intelligence applications revolves around personal data protection and privacy. The EU General Data Protection Regulation (GDPR), which has been directly applicable in all member countries, including Italy, since 2018, establishes the guidelines for recycling particular data within AI systems. This regulation introduces crucial principles similar as responsibility, translucency, purpose limitation, data minimization, and data security for data regulators. Also, it includes specific measures to guard individual rights in processes involving automated decision- timber and profiling. In Italy, the GDPR is executed at the public position through the Personal Data Protection Law (Legislative Decree No. 196/2003, harmonized with the GDPR in 2018) (Borocci, 2025).

Garante, Italy's data protection authority, has surfaced as a crucial player in Europe, laboriously driving the perpetration of GDPR vittles within the realm of artificial intelligence (Pollina and Armellini, 2025). Since 2021, a unit specialized in artificial intelligence has been established within the institution and developments in artificial intelligence have been nearly covered (Borocci, 2025). Garante provides both general principle- grounded guidance and enforces warrants in specific cases related to artificial intelligence operations. For case, in February 2023, Italy banned the AI converse operation Replika, developed by a US- grounded company, citing pitfalls to children. Examinations revealed that Replika demanded a licit legal base for recycling stoner data and failed to apply age verification measures to cover minors. As a result, the inventor was fined€ 5 million. Also, in March 2023, Garante temporarily confined OpenAI's ChatGPT service due to GDPR violations, calling that the platform remain suspended until applicable measures were enforced to guard stoner data. This decision marked a significant first in Europe, setting an important precedent for other nations. OpenAI proceeded operations after meeting Garante's conditions, which included age verification, bettered translucency, and furnishing druggies with the option to correct their data. Still, by late 2024, Garante determined that ChatGPT's data processing practices still fell suddenly of full GDPR compliance, leading to the duty of 15 million fine on OpenAI (Pollina, 2025). Garante offers guidance embedded in general principles and imposes warrants in specific cases related to artificial intelligence operations. Specially, in February 2023, Garante initiated an disquisition into the data processing practices of" DeepSeek," a Chinese AI- powered converse operation. Likewise, at the launch of 2025, it issued a public warning pressing the implicit sequestration pitfalls associated with this platform (Pollina & Armellini, 2025).

Alongside its enforcement sweats, Garante adopts a visionary nonsupervisory strategy by issuing guidelines and recommendations regarding the operation of AI across colorful diligence. The association provides precious guidance to professionals, pressing the significance of bedding ethical principles into AI systems right from the original stages of their development (European Commission, Joint Research Centre, 2021). A practical illustration includes a comprehensive ten- composition companion on applying AI in healthcare services, released in October 2023 under the title Decalogue on the Provision of Health Services with Artificial Intelligence. The companion outlines crucial principles, emphasizing translucency, securing patient sequestration, precluding algorithmic bias, and icing mortal oversight in the development and application of AI systems within healthcar. In a similar vein, Garante has also issued several guidance documents on diverse topics. These include the implementation of facial recognition technologies by law enforcement agencies, the use of algorithmic tools to tackle tax fraud, integrating electronic health records with AI systems, managing deepfake content moderation, and deploying intelligent digital assistants (Borocci, 2025). These efforts are part of Italy's policy of raising awareness and responsibility in the AI ecosystem through ethical guidelines and best practices.

4.3. Italy's National Artificial Intelligence Legislation: "Artificial Intelligence Bill of Law"

Following the guidelines set by the EU AI Act along with Italy's domestic priorities, the country has been working on drafting an extensive law to oversee artificial intelligence on a national scale. This action is embodied in the proposed regulation named" Law on vittles and Delegation of Power to the Government on Artificial Intelligence" (Senate Bill No. S.1146), was approved by the Senate at first reading in March 2025(Borocci, 2025). The final enactment of the bill requires the blessing of the Chamber of Deputies, and the process is presently ongoing (Olivi, 2025). The proposed bill seeks to establish fresh public- position regulations in areas not addressed by EU legislation or delegated to member countries, icing alignment with the AI Act. The Italian Council of Ministers has stressed that the bill will round, rather than conflict with, EU laws by furnishing a coherent frame within the compass of public legislation. Its primary ideal is to outline principles aiming to balance the advantages of arising technologies with the implicit pitfalls associated with their abu (Borocci, 2025).

The proposed legislation encompasses a wide- ranging compass, addressing the operation of artificial intelligence across multiple sectors. Crucial areas targeted by this regulation include public healthcare services, the broader health sector, scientific exploration, plant conditions and practices, intellectual professions like law, public administration and the bar, state governance, brand operation, legal processes (both civil and felonious), and public cybersecurity (Borocci, 2025). Some pivotal points of the regulations introduced for these sectors can be epitomized as follows:

- *Governance and Institutional Structure:* The bill introduces a governance framework for artificial intelligence on a national scale, appointing the Agency for Digital Italy (AgID) and the National Cybersecurity Agency (ACN) as the primary overseeing authorities (Olivi, 2025).
- *General Principles and Rights:* Articles 3 to 6 of the bill outline the fundamental principles that should guide the development and application of artificial intelligence systems.
- *Data Management and National Security:* The bill also includes regulations on the management of data, which is the basic input of artificial intelligence systems (Olivi, 2025). In this environment, it's imaged to develop artificial intelligence- grounded discovery and defense tools against possible pitfalls.
- *Health Sector:* The bill emphasizes the significant role of artificial intelligence in the healthcare sector, explicitly stating that AI systems are designed to assist medical professionals rather than take the place of doctors (Olivi, 2025). In this way, while paving the way for artificial intelligence exploration in the field of health, balancing measures are taken to cover sequestration.
- *Artificial Intelligence in Working Life and the Workplace:* The bill highlights the potential of artificial intelligence to enhance working conditions and boost productivity, while firmly prioritizing the protection of workers' dignity and rights as a key principle. In line with this, employers will be required to notify their employees whenever AI-driven automated decision-making or monitoring systems are implemented in the workplace (Olivi, 2025).
- *Copyright and Artificial Intelligence Productions:* The bill also considers the position of content generated through artificial intelligence within the framework of intellectual property laws. Specifically, it stipulates that workshop developed with the backing of AI tools can qualify for brand protection, handed that the creation stems from the author's intellectual trouble (Olivi, 2025). This regulation is noteworthy as one of the first public legal way towards barring the misgivings at the crossroad of artificial intelligence and brand.

- *Public Administration and Judiciary:* The proposed law allows for the integration of artificial intelligence into public administration and the judiciary system while clearly emphasizing that the ultimate decision-making power will remain in the hands of public officials and judges (Olivi, 2025).

Italy's legal and institutional frame for artificial intelligence remains in the experimental stage. The final replication of the Artificial Intelligence Bill might still see emendations as conversations in Parliament progress. Nevertheless, the overarching structure of the bill reveals that Italy has embraced the conception of" responsible invention" in managing artificial intelligence. Basically, this means the country aims to foster invention by using AI's implicit benefits while contemporaneously mollifying pitfalls through clear legal and ethical guidelines. This approach offers a notable illustration of balancing public policy with effective regulation.

4.4. Artificial Intelligence Applications in the Public Sector: Opportunities and Risks

Artificial intelligence plays a vital part in the public sphere by enhancing decision- making processes in policymaking, boosting the effectiveness of public services, perfecting citizen engagement and translucence, and supporting extremity and emergency operation. When it comes to policymaking, AI leverages big data analysis to offer substantiation- grounded druthers, enabling the medication of public programs through soothsaying and script modeling (OECD, 2019). For illustration, it's used in areas similar as business viscosity soothsaying, social backing demand protrusions, or migration inflow analysis (OECD, 2021). Enhancing the effectiveness of public services can be achieved by automating repetitious regulatory tasks, similar as classifying desires and recycling duty returns. This approach facilitates briskly and more cost-effective service delivery to the public (Sun & Medaglia, 2019). Chatbots and digital sidekicks enhance citizen commerce by addressing their questions, thereby perfecting both availability and translucency. Exercising artificial intelligence to dissect data from open data doors further boosts the responsibility of public administration (UNe-Government Survey, 2022). It plays a part in extremity and exigency operation, disaster early warning systems similar as those for earthquakes and cataracts, as well as in covering pandemics, including the use of contact dogging operations during the COVID- 19 epidemic (WHO, 2021).

The most generally used AI functions in public administration are" natural language processing (NLP),"" prophetic analysis,"" computer vision,"" robot process robotization (RPA)," and" decision support systems." Natural language processing (NLP) includes classifying and automatically responding to citizen desires, emails, and social media announcements. For example, in Italy, INPS reduces workload by sorting millions of emails per year using AI (INPS, 2023). Predictive analytics involves predicting risk areas for tax evasion, social security fraud, and crime. It has been used in IRS (Internal Revenue Service) tax audits in the USA and in social security audits in the Netherlands (although this has sparked ethical debate) (Eubanks, 2018). Computer vision is used in the analysis of city surveillance cameras, intelligent urban traffic management, and border security. China, the United Kingdom, and France are making expansive use of these capabilities (Foucault and Papadopoulos, 2021). Robotic process robotization (RPA) frees mortal coffers from routine tasks, speeding up document processing and data entry. In the Estonian e-government system, tax refunds and licensing processes are accelerated in this way (Dunleavy, 2020). Decision support systems, diagnostic software in healthcare, and initial case assessment (risk assessment algorithms) in the justice system are creating personalized learning models in education. In Canada, risk assessment systems similar to COMPAS are used in courts, and in Denmark, early diagnosis systems in healthcare (Veale & Brass, 2019).

Artificial intelligence (AI) enables governments to operate briskly, more efficiently, and further data- centrically. Crucial exemplifications include natural language processing, prophetic analytics, computer vision, robotic robotization, and decision support systems. Still, without an ethical frame, translucency, and responsibility, the sustainable use of these capabilities for the public good can be parlous.

Italian AI strategies and regulations are being enforced with specific operations in the public sector. Public administration has begun to estimate the possibilities offered by artificial intelligence (AI) technologies to give better services to citizens and increase executive effectiveness. This section will bandy exemplifications of AI operations in the Italian public sector, assaying the openings and pitfalls associated with AI.

Examples of Artificial Intelligence Applications in the Public Sector

Chatbots in Citizen Services: As in numerous countries, the Italian government has also introduced artificial intelligence (AI) operations in its citizen relations. Specifically, in 2019, colorful ministries launched AI- grounded chatbot systems to give citizens with faster and further nonstop access to information. For illustration, the Italian Ministry of Labor and Social Policy launched a chatbot that handed information about the" Citizenship Income" program (Reddito di Cittadinanza) for low- income citizens. This bot allowed citizens to learn about the program's terms, operation procedures, and other details of interest 24/7. The ministry reported that this operation was a success and significantly reduced the workload of its call centers (Stempeck, 2024).

Artificial Intelligence in the Fight Against Tax Evasion: Italy has turned to the logical power of artificial intelligence to combat duty elusion, a longstanding problem. One interesting illustration in this regard is the tool for AI-supported analysis "Anonimometro" implemented by tax compliance units. Operated by the Italian Revenue Administration (Agenzia delle Entrate) and the Guardia di Finanza, this system carries out automatic cross-referencing between citizens' tax declarations and their possessions (Stempeck, 2024).

Smart Infrastructure Management (Rome Water Network Project): Artificial intelligence inventions have also begun to show themselves at the original government position. Especially in large metropolises, artificial intelligence- grounded results are drawing attention in the monitoring and conservation of structure systems. A airman design enforced in the megacity of Rome combines machine literacy and Internet of effects (IoT) technologies in covering the civic water network. As part of the design, low- cost detectors were placed at colorful points in the network and the data produced by these detectors were anatomized with artificial intelligence algorithms. The machine literacy model, which was developed specifically to descry abnormal patterns in water inflow and pressure, can identify water leaks and leaks in pipes in real time. Since the inflow of water creates a certain characteristic sound, artificial intelligence can dissect this sound using the aural data from the detectors and prognosticate when and where a leak may do. In this way, external brigades can intermediate before any water bursts or leaks beget serious damage. This operation reduces the need to dig up thoroughfares and check pipes one by one, as in traditional styles, therefore reducing both costs and dislocations in megacity life (Stempeck, 2024). The Rome illustration is a success story that underlines that original governments can produce innovative results with limited coffers. The reduction of losses and leaks, especially in critical architectures similar as water networks, provides both profitable gain and prevents the waste of a precious resource similar as water.

In addition to these exemplifications, there are other enterprise in Italy regarding the use of artificial intelligence in the public sector. Colorful artificial intelligence systems are being carried out in areas similar as business operation, waste collection optimization, and balancing energy networks within the compass of smart megacity operations. It's known that in the justice system, artificial intelligence software that can help in case operation processes has been tested in some courts, but these systems are being carried out cautiously so as not to undermine the independence of decision- makers. In the field of education, there are airman artificial intelligence operations that aim to cover pupil performance and give substantiated feedback. In the field of public health, artificial intelligence tools similar as data- grounded decision support systems and case vaticination models were used during the COVID- 19 epidemic. All these exemplifications show that Italy is experimenting with artificial intelligence in the public sector through airman systems with a "literacy by doing" approach (European Commission, Joint Research Centre, 2021).

Opportunities

Considering the above applications, the main opportunities that artificial intelligence offers for the Italian public sector can be summarized as follows:

Service Quality and Accessibility: Artificial intelligence can increase the speed and quality of public services reaching citizens. As seen in the illustration of chatbots, citizens can incontinently pierce the information they need thanks to smart sidekicks that give 24/7 service (Stempeck, 2024).

Efficiency and Cost Savings: Public institutions can increase pool effectiveness and reduce functional costs by automating their processes with artificial intelligence operations. For illustration, chatbots lighten the cargo of telephone discussion services, allowing staff to concentrate on more complex tasks (Stempeck, 2024).

Increased Revenue and Maximized Public Benefit: When used rightly, AI can directly profit public finances. As in the case of Anonimometro, AI tools that increase duty compliance can help billions of euros in misplaced duty earnings (Stempeck, 2024). This strengthens the public's financial capacity, allowing for better public service investments. Also, structure monitoring systems reduce resource losses similar as water and electricity, performing in both environmental and profitable earnings.

Data-Driven Decision Making and Forecasting Capacity: One of the topmost strengths of AI is its capability to prize meaningful patterns from large and complex data sets and make prognostications. These perceptivity are extremely precious in the design and perpetration of public programs. For illustration, in social backing programs, AI analyses can optimize resource planning by prognosticating which regions will witness the most demand (European Commission, Joint Research Centre, 2021).

Innovation and Technology Ecosystem Development: The involvement of the public sector in AI systems can boost the overall invention ecosystem in the country. Government- supported AI tenders or competitions encourage original startups and technology companies to develop GovTech results. To this end, Italy also plans acceleration programs and awards to support enterprise that can offer AI results for the requirements of public administration (European Commission, Joint Research Centre, 2021). Therefore, the public's input into the sector as a "first client" contributes to the growth of the original assiduity in the field of AI.

Risks and Challenges

The integration of AI into the public sector presents a number of pitfalls and challenges as well as openings. In the Italian case, the main points to consider are as follows:

Algorithmic Bias and Discrimination: AI systems may reflect impulses and crimes essential in the data they're trained on. In public services, this can lead to demarcation against underprivileged groups (Stempeck, 2024). Analogous pitfalls live in Italy. For illustration, an algorithm used by a megacity to allocate aid may intentionally disadvantage ethnical nonages or certain regions (Borocci, 2025).

Lack of Transparency and Accountability: When AI models are used, especially in decision- making processes, it can be delicate to understand how these models work. This situation, appertained to as a "black box" can undermine citizens' right to object to executive opinions or understand the decision (Borocci, 2025).

Data Privacy and Security: Since the public sector processes large- scale data belonging to citizens, the protection of particular data is a critical issue in AI operations. In the case of Anonimometro, the use of pseudonymous data was done with the blessing of Garante (Stempeck, 2024).

In-house Talent Shortage and Change Management: In order for artificial intelligence systems to be successful, public institutions need mortal coffers that can understand and apply these technologies. In Italy, the average age of public labor force is high and it's known that there are scarcities in digital capabilities. Reclamation restrictions that have lasted for numerous times have limited the participation of youthful pool with new technological chops in the public sector (Stempeck, 2024).

Ethical Dilemmas and Social Acceptance: As AI becomes more effective in public services, the issue of public trust in algorithms becomes more important. If citizens find it cold or unfair to see a machine as their interlocutor, trust in public services may decrease (European Commission, Joint Research Centre, 2021).

Legal Liability and Accountability: In the event that AI systems make miscalculations or beget unlooked-for damages, it may be unclear who's responsible. In the case of a business operation AI causing an accident due to incorrect signaling or an AI making a mistake in a health opinion, who'll the citizen sue? Will the manufacturer or the public institution be responsible? In order to fill the gaps in this area, the Artificial Intelligence Legal Liability Directive is being bandied in the EU, and Italy is also putting forward ideas similar as mandatory insurance mechanisms and indispensable disagreement resolution in its public strategy (European Commission, Joint Research Centre, 2021).

In the case of Italy, the active station of nonsupervisory authorities (similar as the Garante), the visionary development of justice by judicial bodies on the subject and clear reference to these pitfalls in strategy documents show that threat operation is at the heart of policy. Indeed, the Italian government states that placing the use of AI within an ethical and legal frame is essential to erecting trust in society (European Commission, Joint Research Centre, 2021). Without this trust, neither public officers can borrow AI tools nor citizens can use these services with peace of min.

5. CONCLUSION

Digital metamorphosis is reconsidering the generalities of data- driven decision- timber, citizen- centric service design, and effective governance in public administration. Artificial intelligence plays a critical part in this metamorphosis; it stands out not only as a specialized tool but also as a governance actor that enhances executive capacity (Margetts & Dunleavy, 2013; Wirtz et al., 2019). The abecedarian places of AI in public administration focus on data analytics and policymaking, citizen- centric service delivery, executive effectiveness and robotization, ethics, translucency, and responsibility. AI creates effectiveness and effectiveness through the robotization of business processes in public institutions. It particularly provides advantages in areas similar as optimization in resource allocation and budget planning, and the capability of public labor force to concentrate on further strategic areas by freeing them from routine tasks.

Numerous approaches have been developed in transnational literature and practice to produce AI- related results and enhance governance capacities in public administration. These approaches generally address specialized, governance, and ethical confines together. These approaches include "Algorithmic Governance," "Ethical and Responsible AI Approaches," "Regulatory Sandboxes and Experimental Policy Approach," "mortal Machine Collaboration Models" "Proactive Public Services" and "Cross-Technology Integration Approach" Algorithmic Governance is the prosecution of decision- making processes in public administration, incompletely or entirely, through algorithms (Janssen & Kuk, 2016). The EU Artificial Intelligence Ethics Principles have been developed by the European Commission as a frame for the use of AI in the public sector, grounded on principles similar as translucency, mortal oversight, data security, and fairness (Floridi, 2021). The "Responsible AI in the Public Sector" action called on OECD countries to apply the principles of mortal- centeredness, trust, and responsibility in the use of AI in public services (OECD, 2021). Regulatory Sandboxes and the Policy Experimental Approach give mechanisms for testing new AI results in a controlled terrain (Gasser & Almeida, 2017). Mortal Machine Collaboration Models endorse that AI should n't fully replace public workers, but rather play a supporting part (Wirtz et al., 2019). In visionary Public Services, AI provides service delivery grounded on anticipated requirements without staying for citizen requests (Margetts & Dunleavy, 2013). In theCross-

Technology Integration Approach, AI is integrated with big data, blockchain, IoT, and pall computing to produce more robust public results (Batty et al., 2012).

Approaches to developing results with AI in public administration must encompass not only technological invention but also rudiments of ethics, governance, and citizen trust. Algorithmic governance and visionary services give effectiveness and speed. Ethical approaches and sandboxing foster legality and trust. Mortal machine collaboration models strengthen the part of public workers. Thus, AI serves as both a specialized machine and a governance catalyst for the integration of digital technologies in public administration.

Public administrations aim to give citizens with effective, presto, and data- driven services by decreasingly using AI. Still, the use of AI in the public sector brings with it both auspicious and pessimistic scripts for the future, as well as doable/ middle-ground scripts. Each of these scripts should be considered within the environment of ethics, governance, technological capacity, and citizen trust (Wirtz et al., 2019; OECD, 2021). The auspicious script is the "Digital Welfare State." In this digital weal state, intimately handed AI results make life easier for citizens and make the state- citizen relationship more transparent, accessible, and participatory. In this environment, citizen trust should be strengthened through ethical canons and transparent algorithms (Floridi, 2021). Open data and open- source AI results should be encouraged. AI Citizen Assemblies or discussion mechanisms should be established for citizen participation (Janssen & Kuk, 2016). The pessimistic script is the "Digital Surveillance State." In the Digital Surveillance State, intimately handed AI, rather than empowering citizens, becomes a tool for surveillance, control, and rejection (Creemers, 2018). In this environment, the explanation for algorithmic opinions should cleave to resolvable AI principles. Algorithmic ombudsmen or independent ethics panels should be established in the public sector. A feasible/ Middle Ground script is "mongrel and Balanced Public AI." Public AI operations neither slide into a full weal state Cockaigne nor a surveillance dystopia; they operate within a balanced frame. In this environment, controlled testing surroundings similar as nonsupervisory sandboxes (AESIA in Spain, Data Ethics Sandbox in Denmark) should be expanded (Gasser & Almeida, 2017). AI ethics training and algorithmic mindfulness programs should be developed for public workers. Common norms should be espoused through transnational cooperation (OECD, EU, United Nations)

The future of intimately handed AI can enhance social weal when conceived in agreement with ethics, governance, and societal values. Still, to help worst- case scripts, translucency and responsibility mechanisms must be established, algorithmic ombudsman and independent oversight bodies must be put in place, citizens' rights to demand algorithmic justice must be fairly guaranteed, and mortal- centered design principles must be at the core of public AI programs. In light of these recommendations, the future of AI operations in the public sector can be aligned with the popular values of societies and citizen trust.

Artificial intelligence operations are in a rapid-fire elaboration process around the world. While advanced countries are guiding this process with strategic documents, developing countries have started to use the openings offered by artificial intelligence more effectively in public programs. still, observing ethical, legal and social confines will insure the sustainable and fair development of this technology.

Across EU countries, AI is progressing through multiple leadership positions rather than a single" leading country" tribune. Denmark, Sweden, and Belgium are among the countries with the loftiest rates of AI relinquishment in Europe. Germany, France, Spain, Finland, and Italy are also prominent policy and structure leaders in AI. Countries with lower AI relinquishment rates include Romania, Poland, and Bulgaria. Estonia is a high illustration for the public sector. An AI- grounded virtual adjunct called" Bürokratt (KrattAI)" has been developed in Estonia to pierce public services. For illustration, when an Estonian citizen wants to apply for social backing, rather of using traditional forms, they tell Bürokratt," I want to apply for educational support for my child." The AI system verifies their identity and automatically fills out the applicable form. The citizen completes the documents with a digital hand (Rebublic of Estonia Information System Authority, 2025).

This review of Italy's AI programs and regulations has handed a comprehensive picture of public strategies, EU adjustment sweats, and concrete practices. In conclusion, the Italian illustration teaches us several important assignments from a public policy perspective:

- First, it is n't possible to make progress in an area like AI without strategic vision and political will. Italy has made it clear that it has made AI a policy precedence by publishing and streamlining public strategies. These strategies are n't only statements of intent, but also include concrete pretensions and action plans. This vision, which covers a wide range from education to assiduity, from public services to ethical fabrics, demonstrates a holistic approach that can be an illustration for other countries.
- Secondly, the balance between nonsupervisory proactivity and responsible invention is pivotal. Italy has taken a pioneering station in this area by drafting public legislation in its own precedence areas rather than staying for EU regulations. At the same time, it has not dithered to respond snappily to developments and cover citizens' rights through institutions similar as the Garante. This approach shows that it's possible to precisely guide invention without fully unleashing it, but without fear or inhibition. An terrain of trust is essential for the healthy development of the AI ecosystem, and Italy has

placed the necessary way to make this trust (translucency, responsibility, ethical principles) at the heart of its policy.

- Third, the significance of operation- acquainted literacy and airman systems should be emphasized. The success of strategies on paper will only be possible if they're tested and gauged in real life. Systems similar as chatbot, Anonimometro, and smart structure launched in the public sector in Italy have revealed the palpable benefits and sins of AI. In this way, policymakers have further concrete information about what works and what poses pitfalls. Other countries can develop AI results that suit their own capacities and needs with analogous small- scale trials.
- Fourth, the precedence of the mortal factor should noway be ignored. As Italy has constantly emphasized in both its strategies and its laws, artificial intelligence should n't be a tool that replaces humans but rather a tool that strengthens them. This understanding is an important principle, especially in the provision of public services. An artificial intelligence that does n't replace the croaker but advises him, an algorithm that does n't take over the authority of the judge but classifies him, a software that controls the decision of the civil menial but eases his routine work. All these balances will maximize social benefit with the harmony of artificial intelligence and humans. Else, no matter how advanced the technology is, it'll be delicate for it to be accepted by society.

When we look at Italy's strategy and regulations regarding artificial intelligence, we can say that the country adopts a visionary but conservative approach. On the one hand, it sets ambitious pretensions, allocates coffers and goes on a literacy path with airman systems in order not to miss the openings brought by artificial intelligence technologies. On the other hand, it's trying to draw the frame with principles and rules by foreknowing the goods of these technologies on society and law. This hunt for balance is nearly related to Italy's unique structural conditions and its position in the European environment.

Still, Italy's AI trip also faces significant challenges. One of the biggest pitfalls to perpetration is the implicit slowness in enforcing what's written in the strategy. Italy's bureaucracy has traditionally been blamed for being slow; reforms and new systems can take time to find a response on the ground. In a fleetly advancing field like AI, detainments between planning and perpetration can hold the country back. For illustration, it's delicate to say that numerous of the enterprise included in the 2022- 2024 strategy have been completely enforced. In order to avoid a analogous fate in the new strategy, monitoring and evaluation mechanisms will need to work effectively. However, it may fill this gap, If the Artificial Intelligence Foundation imaged for this purpose is established and becomes functional. Still, the political and fiscal independence of this foundation will also be critical; else, it may not go beyond adding another subcaste of bureaucracy.

Another issue is education and artistic adaption. Artificial intelligence requires not only a specialized metamorphosis but also a artistic metamorphosis. The mindset of public retainers and citizens must be ready to accept and interact with algorithmic processes. This means a literacy wind that will take time. Italy may profit from EU finances, similar as the Digital Europe Program, to carry out digital knowledge systems. Still, care must be taken not to consolidate the digital peak, especially in regions with a large senior population.

Eventually, Italy's experience also shows the significance of transnational co-operation. The country contributes to AI programs in platforms similar as the G7 and OECD, as well as the EU. Italy also participated its own good practices in the G7 Toolkit for AI in the Public Sector document published by the G7 countries in 2023. Similar knowledge sharing allows countries to learn from each other and make better regulations. Italy is in a position to both contribute to this exchange of experience and benefit from it.

As a result, Italy's AI programs constitute a frame that's compatible with EU regulations, takes into account public interests and perceptivity, and is concentrated on the public interest. Themulti-stakeholder andmulti-dimensional approach, appertained to as "governance" in academic literature and transnational practice, is being tried to be enforced in the Italian illustration. Of course, the success of this trouble will be tested in the coming times with the perpetration of strategies, the enactment of laws, and the development of the AI ecosystem. Still, it can formerly be said that with the way it has taken, Italy has begun to place itself as a country that embraces the openings of AI while also managing its pitfalls. This provides an illustration of the "cotillion of harmony between invention and regulation" being precisely executed in terms of public policy.

REFERENCES

Aksu, D., & Akman, E. (2022). South Korea's Artificial Intelligence Policies. In Akman, E., Topçu, T. B., & Chiftchi, A. (Eds.), *Artificial Intelligence and Public Policy: Country Studies*. Nobel Publishing.

Aksu, D., & Akman, E. (2023). Analysis of Global Research Trends in the Internet of Things (IoT) Using Network Mapping Technique. *Kafkas University Journal of Economics and Administrative Sciences*, *27*(14), 506–524.

Allen, G., & Chan, T. (2017). *Artificial intelligence and national security*. Harvard Kennedy School.

Asimov, I. (1950). *I, Robot*. Gnome Press.

Batty, M., Axhausen, K. W., Giannotti, F., Pozdnoukhov, A., Bazzani, A., Wachowicz, M., Ouzounis, G., & Portugali, Y. (2012). Smart Cities of the Future. *The European Physical Journal. Special Topics*, *214*(1), 481–518. DOI: 10.1140/epjst/e2012-01703-3

Borocci, S. (2025). AI watch: Global Regulatory Tracker – Italy. *White & Case LLP.* https://www.jdsupra.com/legalnews/ai-watch-global-regulatory-tracker-6844025/ (Accessed: May 9, 2025).

Bostrom, N. (2014). *Superintelligence: Paths, Dangers, Strategies*. Oxford University Press.

Brynjolfsson, E., & McAfee, A. (2014). *The Second Machine Age*. W. W. Norton & Company.

Buchanan, B. G., & Shortliffe, E. H. (1984). *Rule-Based Expert Systems*. Addison-Wesley.

Buolamwini, J., & Gebru, T. (2018). Gender Shades: Intersectional Accuracy Disparities in Commercial Gender Classification. In *Proceedings of the Conference on Fairness, Accountability and Transparency (FAT)*.

Coşkun, B. (2022). Germany's Artificial Intelligence Policies. In Akman, E., Topçu, T. B., & Chiftchi, A. (Eds.), *Artificial Intelligence and Public Policy: Country Studies*. Nobel Publishing.

Crawford, K. (2021). *Atlas of AI: Power, Politics, and the Planetary Costs of Artificial Intelligence*. Yale University Press.

Creemers, R. (2018). China's Social Credit System: An Evolving Practice of Control. SSRN *Electronic Journal.* DOI: 10.2139/ssrn.3175792

Dunleavy, P. (2020). *Digital-Era Governance: IT Corporations, the State, and E-government*. Oxford University Press.

Durukal, O., & Öztürk, N. K. (2019). Blockchain Technology in the Provision of Public Services. *Ege Academic Review*, *23*(77), 449–456.

Eubanks, V. (2018). *Automating Inequality*. St. Martin's Press.

European Commission. (2021). Proposal for a Regulation on Artificial Intelligence.

European Commission, Joint Research Centre. (2021). *Italy: Public Sector Dimension of AI Strategy. AI Watch Report.* https://ai-watch.ec.europa.eu/topics/public-sector/public-sector-dimension-ai-national-strategies/italy-public-sector-dimension-ai-strategy_en (Accessed: May 9, 2025).

Floridi, L. (2021). AI and Its New Regulatory Framework in Europe. *Philosophy & Technology*, *34*, 1–7. PMID: 33717860

Foucault, M., & Papadopoulos, D. (2021). Artificial Intelligence, Surveillance and the Politics of Visibility. *Information Communication and Society*, *24*(1), 1–17.

Frey, C. B., & Osborne, M. A. (2017). The Future of Employment: How Susceptible are Jobs to Computerisation? *Technological Forecasting and Social Change*, *114*, 254–280. DOI: 10.1016/j.techfore.2016.08.019

Gasser, U., & Almeida, V. A. F. (2017). A Layered Model for AI Governance. *IEEE Internet Computing*, *21*(6), 58–62. DOI: 10.1109/MIC.2017.4180835

Hickman, T., ... (2024). Long Awaited EU AI Act Becomes Law After Publication in the EU's Official Journal. *White & Case LLP.* https://www.whitecase.com/insight-alert/long-awaited-eu-ai-act-becomes-law-after-publication-eus-official-journal (Accessed: May 9, 2025).

INPS. (2023). *Use of artificial intelligence for certified e-mail classification.* Italian National Social Security Institute Project Report.

Janssen, M., & Kuk, G. (2016). The Challenges and Limits of Big Data Algorithms in Technocratic Governance. *Government Information Quarterly*, *33*(3), 371–377. DOI: 10.1016/j.giq.2016.08.011

Krizhevsky, A., Sutskever, I., & Hinton, G. E. (2012). ImageNet Classification with Deep Convolutional Neural Networks. *Advances in Neural Information Processing Systems (NeurIPS)*, 25.

Lexology. (2024). Innovation Law insights. https://www.lexology.com/library/detail.aspx?g=0e955715-4e58-450d-8ffe-d6dccd4117d5 (Accessed: May 9, 2025).

Lin, P., Abney, K., & Bekey, G. A. (2012). *Robot Ethics: The Ethical and Social Implications of Robotics*. MIT Press.

Luckin, R., Holmes, W., Griffiths, M., & Forcier, L. B. (2016). *Intelligence Unleashed: An Argument for AI in education*. Pearson.

Marcus, G. (2022). Artificial Intelligence: The Challenges of Trustworthy AI. *Daedalus*, *151*(2), 130–144.

Margetts, H., & Dunleavy, P. (2013). The Second Wave of Digital-Era Governance. *Philosophical Transactions of the Royal Society A: Mathematical, Physical and Engineering Sciences*, 371(1987), 20120382.

McCarthy, J., Minsky, M., Rochester, N., & Shannon, C. E. (1956). *A Proposal for the Dartmouth Summer Research Project on Artificial Intelligence*. Dartmouth College.

Ministry of Industry and Technology. (2021). *National Artificial Intelligence Strategy (2021–2025)*.

Mitchell, T. M. (1997). *Machine Learning*. McGraw-Hill.

Network360. (2025). Smart City: Comune di Milano with Cyclomedia for Mapping the City into a Digital Twin. https://www.zerounoweb.it/iot/smart-city-comune-di-milano-con-cyclomedia-per-mappare-il-capoluogo-in-un-digital-twin/ (Accessed: August 18, 2025).

OECD. (2019). *Artificial Intelligence in Society*. OECD Publishing.

OECD. (2020). *AI and the Future of Skills*. OECD Publishing.

OECD. (2021). *Recommendation on Artificial Intelligence in the Public Sector*. OECD Publishing.

Okçu, M., & Akman, Ç. (2022). Türkiye's Artificial Intelligence Policy. In Akman, E., Topçu, T. B., & Chiftchi, A. (Eds.), *Artificial Intelligence and Public Policy: Country Studies*. Nobel Publishing.

Olivi, G. (2025). Seeds and Sparks: Italy's Journey to AI. *Dentons*. https://www.dentons.com/en/insights/articles/2025/march/27/seeds-and-sparks-italys-journey-to-ai (Accessed: May 9, 2025).

Öztürk, N. K., & Durukal, O. (2022). Canada's Artificial Intelligence Policy. In Akman, E., Topçu, T. B., & Chiftchi, A. (Eds.), *Artificial Intelligence and Public Policy: Country Studies*. Nobel Publishing.

Pasquale, F. (2015). *The Black Box Society: The Secret Algorithms that Control Money and Information*. Harvard University Press. DOI: 10.4159/harvard.9780674736061

Pollina, E. (2025, May 19). Italy's Data Watchdog Fines AI Company Replika's Developer €5.6 million. *Reuters*. https://www.reuters.com/sustainability/boards-policy-regulation/italys-data-watchdog-fines-ai-company-replikas-developer-56-million-2025-05-19 (Accessed: May 20, 2025).

Pollina, E., & Armellini, A. (2025, January 28). Italy Regulator Seeks Information from DeepSeek on Data Protection. *Reuters*. https://www.reuters.com/technology/artificial-intelligence/italy-regulator-seeks-info-deepseek-data-protection-2025-01-28 (Accessed: May 9, 2025).

Republic of Estonia Information System Authority. (2025). The Vision of Bürokratt. https://www.ria.ee/en/state-information-system/personal-services/burokratt (Accessed: August 18, 2025).

Russell, S., & Norvig, P. (2021). *Artificial Intelligence: A Modern Approach* (4th ed.). Pearson.

Stempeck, M. (2024). How Italy's Government is Using AI. *Innovation in Politics Institute – Democracy Technologies*. https://democracy-technologies.org/ai-data/how-italys-government-uses-ai-data/ (Accessed: May 9, 2025).

Sun, T. Q., & Medaglia, R. (2019). Mapping the Challenges of Artificial Intelligence in the Public Sector: Evidence from Public Healthcare. *Government Information Quarterly*, *36*(2), 368–383. DOI: 10.1016/j.giq.2018.09.008

Temel, Y., & Coşkun, B. (2024). A Review on Artificial Intelligence Applications in Education in Some Countries and Türkiye. *International Technology and Education Journal*, *8*(1), 9–23.

Topol, E. (2019). *Deep Medicine: How Artificial Intelligence can Make Healthcare Human Again*. Basic Books.

Turing, A. M. (1950). Computing Machinery and Intelligence. *Mind*, *59*(236), 433–460. DOI: 10.1093/mind/LIX.236.433

UN. (2022). *United Nations E-government Survey 2022: The Future of Digital Government*. United Nations Publishing.

UNIDIR. (2018). *The Weaponization of Increasingly Autonomous Technologies*. United Nations Institute for Disarmament Research.

Veale, M., & Brass, I. (2019). Administration by Algorithm? Public Management Meets Public Sector Machine Learning. *Public Administration Review*, *79*(6), 811–825.

WHO. (2021). *Ethics and Governance of Artificial Intelligence for Health: WHO Guidance*. World Health Organization.

Wirtz, B. W., Müller, W. M., Weyerer, J. C., & Geyer, C. (2020). Public Administration in the Age of Artificial Intelligence. *Public Management Review*, *22*(5), 733–751.

Wirtz, B. W., Weyerer, J. C., & Geyer, C. (2019). Artificial Intelligence and the Public Sector: Applications and Challenges. *International Journal of Public Administration*, *42*(7), 596–615. DOI: 10.1080/01900692.2018.1498103

KEY TERMS AND DEFINITIONS

Artificial Intelligence and Efficiency: refers to the process by which artificial intelligence technologies increase productivity by accelerating business processes, reducing mortal error, and optimizing resource use. This conception aims to achieve advanced affair with smaller coffers.

Artificial Intelligence and Public Administration: the process of making decision timber, service planning and citizen commerce more effective and effective by using artificial intelligence technologies in the delivery of public services. This conception aims to increase translucency, speed, cost- effectiveness and data-grounded governance openings in public administration.

Artificial Intelligence Application: the practical use of artificial intelligence technologies to break problems or perform tasks in a specific area. These operations increase effectiveness with functions similar as decision timber, robotization and data analysis in numerous sectors similar as health, education, public administration, finance, and manufacturing.

Artificial Intelligence in Education: the use of artificial intelligence technologies in educational surroundings to ameliorate literacy and tutoring processes. This conception aims to increase effectiveness and effectiveness in areas similar as substantiated literacy, automatic assessment, pupil shadowing and education operation.

Legal Artificial Intelligence: refers to artificial intelligence operations that dissect, interpret and automate legal deals. This conception covers technologies developed for use in areas similar as case analysis, prognosticating court opinions, contract review and accelerating legal exploration.

Perception of Artificial Intelligence: refers to the studies, stations and prospects of individualities and societies regarding artificial intelligence. This perception is shaped by whether the technology is seen as an occasion or a trouble, ethical enterprises, position of trust and operation gests.

Strategic Artificial Intelligence: the planned, coordinated and sustainable use of artificial intelligence in line with long- term pretensions. This conception refers to the evaluation of artificial intelligence as a strategic tool, especially by countries and large institutions, in critical areas similar as profitable development, security, competitiveness and social metamorphosis.

Compilation of References

Abbas, N., Følstad, A., & Bjørkli, C. A. (2023). Chatbots as part of digital government service provision – A user perspective. In A. Følstad, T. Araujo, S. Papadopoulos, E. L.-C. Law, E. Luger, M. Goodwin, & P. B. Brandtzaeg (Eds.), Chatbot Research and Design: 6th International Workshop, CONVERSATIONS 2022 Amsterdam, The Netherlands, November 22–23, 2022 Revised Selected Papers (pp. 66–82). Springer. DOI: 10.1007/978-3-031-25581-6_5

Abdullah Alhujaylan, L. C. & M. R. (2021). Towards an Integrated Conceptual Model for Open Government Data in Saudi Arabia. *Intelligent Sustainable Systems, pp 741–764.*

Abujaber, A. A., & Nashwan, A. J. (2024). Ethical framework for artificial intelligence in healthcare research: A path to integrity. In World Journal of Methodology (Vol. 14, Issue 3). DOI: 10.5662/wjm.v14.i3.94071

Adamopoulos, T., Brandt, L., Chen, C., Restuccia, D., & Wei, X. (2024). Land Security and Mobility Frictions. *The Quarterly Journal of Economics*, *139*(3), 1941–1987. DOI: 10.1093/qje/qjae010

Adamson, A. S., & Smith, A. (2018). Machine learning and health care disparities in dermatology. *JAMA Dermatology*, *154*(11), 1247–1248. DOI: 10.1001/jamadermatol.2018.2348 PMID: 30073260

Adie, B. U., Tate, M., & Valentine, E. (2024). Digital leadership in the public sector: a scoping review and outlook [Review of Digital leadership in the public sector: a scoping review and outlook]. International Review of Public Administration, 29(1), 42. Taylor & Francis. DOI: 10.1080/12294659.2024.2323847

Adomavicius, G., & Yang, M. (2022). Integrating Behavioral, Economic, and Technical Insights to Understand and Address Algorithmic Bias: A Human-Centric Perspective. [TMIS]. *ACM Transactions on Management Information Systems*, *13*(3), 1–27. DOI: 10.1145/3519420

Agarwal, P. K. (2018). Public administration challenges in the world of AI and bots. *Public Administration Review*, *78*(6), 917–921. DOI: 10.1111/puar.12979

Aguilera, U., Peña, O., Belmonte, O., & López-de-Ipiña, D. (2017). Citizen-centric data services for smarter cities. *Future Generation Computer Systems*, *76*, 234–247. https://doi.org/https://doi.org/10.1016/j.future.2016.10.031. DOI: 10.1016/j.future.2016.10.031

Ahern, D. (2021). Regulatory Lag, Regulatory Friction and Regulatory Transition as FinTech Disenablers: Calibrating an EU Response to the Regulatory Sandbox Phenomenon. *European Business Organization Law Review*, *22*(3), 395–432. DOI: 10.1007/s40804-021-00217-z

Ahmadi, S. (2024). Systematic Literature Review on Cloud Computing Security: Threats and Mitigation Strategies. *Journal of Information Security*, *15*(2), 148–167. DOI: 10.4236/jis.2024.152010

Ahn, M. J., & Chen, Y. C. (2022). Digital transformation toward AI-augmented public administration: The perception of government employees and the willingness to use AI in government. *Government Information Quarterly*, *39*(2), 1–14. DOI: 10.1016/j.giq.2021.101664

Aiyer, S., Chan, W., & Feldman, G. (2024). Outcome Bias in Evaluations of Ethical Decisions: Replication and Extensions of Gino, Moore, and Bazerman (2009). *Collabra. Psychology*, *10*(1), 126266. Advance online publication. DOI: 10.1525/collabra.126266

Akaba, T. I., Norta, A., Udokwu, C., & Draheim, D. (2020). A Framework for the Adoption of Blockchain-Based e-Procurement Systems in the Public Sector. In Lecture notes in computer science (p. 3). Springer Science+Business Media. DOI: 10.1007/978-3-030-44999-5_1

Aksu, D., & Akman, E. (2022). South Korea's Artificial Intelligence Policies. In Akman, E., Topçu, T. B., & Chiftchi, A. (Eds.), *Artificial Intelligence and Public Policy: Country Studies*. Nobel Publishing.

Aksu, D., & Akman, E. (2023). Analysis of Global Research Trends in the Internet of Things (IoT) Using Network Mapping Technique. *Kafkas University Journal of Economics and Administrative Sciences*, *27*(14), 506–524.

Akter, S., Dwivedi, Y., Sajib, S., Biswas, K., Bandara, R., & Michael, K. (2022). Algorithmic bias in machine learning-based marketing models. *Journal of Business Research*, *144*, 201–216. Advance online publication. DOI: 10.1016/j.jbusres.2022.01.083

Akter, S., Hossain, M. A., Sajib, S., Sultana, S., Rahman, M., Vrontis, D., & McCarthy, G. (2023). A framework for AI-powered service innovation capability: Review and agenda for future research. *Technovation, 125*, 1–17. DOI: 10.1016/j.technovation.2023.102768

Akter, S., McCarthy, G., Sajib, S., Michael, K., Dwivedi, Y., D'Ambra, J., & Shen, K. (2021). Algorithmic bias in data-driven innovation in the age of AI. *International Journal of Information Management*, *60*, 102387. DOI: 10.1016/j.ijinfomgt.2021.102387

Al-Ababneh, H. A., Fedorchuk, Y., Tymchyshyn, A., Pishchenko, G., & Hrytsai, S. (2024). THE USE OF BIG DATA IN THE DETECTION OF ECONOMIC CRIMES IN PUBLIC PROCUREMENTS. *Journal of Theoretical and Applied Information Technology*, *102*(24), 8860–8871.

Al-Ansi, A. M., Garad, A., Jaboob, M., & Al-Ansi, A. (2024). Elevating e-government: Unleashing the power of AI and IoT for enhanced public services. *Heliyon*, *10*(23), e40591. DOI: 10.1016/j.heliyon.2024.e40591 PMID: 39654738

Albano, C. S. (2013). Open government data: A value chain model proposal. *ACM International Conference Proceeding Series,* June 2013, 285–286. DOI: 10.1145/2479724.2479775

Alenezi, M. (2022). Understanding digital government transformation. *arXiv preprint arXiv:2202.01797*. https://doi.org//arXiv.2202.01797DOI: 10.48550

Aliti, A., Leka, E., Luma, A., & Trpkovska, M. A. (2022). A Systematic Literature Review on Using Blockchain Technology in Public Administration. In *2022 45th Jubilee International Convention on Information, Communication and Electronic Technology (MIPRO)* (pp. 1031-1036). IEEE. DOI: 10.23919/MIPRO55190.2022.9803797

Allen, G., & Chan, T. (2017). *Artificial intelligence and national security*. Harvard Kennedy School.

Almarabeh, T., & AbuAli, A. (2010). A general framework for e-government: Definition maturity challenges, opportunities, and success. *European Journal of Scientific Research, 39*(1), 29–42.

Almuqrin, A., Mutambik, I., Alomran, A., Gauthier, J., & Abusharhah, M. (2022). Factors Influencing Public Trust in Open Government Data. *Sustainability (Basel)*, *14*(15), 9765. Advance online publication. DOI: 10.3390/su14159765

Al-Mushayt, O. (2019). Automating E-Government Services with Artificial Intelligence. *IEEE Access : Practical Innovations, Open Solutions*, *7*, 146821–146829. DOI: 10.1109/ACCESS.2019.2946204

Alon-Barkat, S., & Busuioc, M. (2021). Human-AI Interactions in Public Sector Decision-Making:"Automation Bias"and"Selective Adherence"to Algorithmic Advice. . .DOI: 10.1093/jopart/muac007

Alshahrani, A., Griva, A., Dennehy, D., & Mäntymäki, M. (2024). Artificial intelligence and decision-making in government functions: Opportunities, challenges and future research. *Transforming Government: People. Transforming Government, 18*(4), 678–698. DOI: 10.1108/TG-06-2024-0131

Alteneiji, H. R., Ahmed, V., & Saboor, S. (2020). A qualitative approach to investigate emergency preparedness state for the built environment in the UAE. *Engineering, Construction, and Architectural Management, 28*(7), 2005–2022. DOI: 10.1108/ECAM-05-2020-0296

Androniceanu, A. (2024). Artificial intelligence in administration and public management. *Administration & Public Management Review, 175*(1), 99–114. DOI: 10.24818/amp/2024.42-06

Androutsopoulou, A., Karacapilidis, N., Loukis, E., & Charalabidis, Y. (2019). Transforming the communication between citizens and government through AI-guided chatbots. *Government Information Quarterly, 36*(2), 358–367. DOI: 10.1016/j.giq.2018.10.001

Angwin, J., Larson, J., Mattu, S., & Kirchner, L. (2016). "Machine Bias." *ProPublica.* https://www.propublica.org/article/machine-bias-risk-assessments-in-criminal-sentencing

Ansell, C., & Gash, A. (2008). Collaborative governance in theory and practice. *Journal of Public Administration: Research and Theory, 18*(4), 543–571. DOI: 10.1093/jopart/mum032

Anthes, G. (2015). Estonia. *Communications of the ACM, 58*(6), 18–20. DOI: 10.1145/2754951

Anwa, S. M. A. A. M. I. N. (2022). *Challenges in Open Government Data Implementation: A Systematic Literature Review*. IEEE.

Aoki, N. (2020). An experimental study of public trust in AI chatbots in the public sector. *Government Information Quarterly, 37*(4), 101490. DOI: 10.1016/j.giq.2020.101490

Aoki, N. (2020). Challenges of AI use in government. *Government Information Quarterly, 37*(3), 101486. DOI: 10.1016/j.giq.2019.101486

Aria, M., & Cuccurullo, C. (2017). bibliometrix : An R-tool for comprehensive science mapping analysis. *Journal of Informetrics*, *11*(4), 959–975. DOI: 10.1016/j.joi.2017.08.007

Aryanto, E., Mabruk, H., & Narendroputro, W. (2023). Artificial Intelligence Implementation Strategy to Make It Happen Smart Government Indonesia Gold 2045. *The International Journal of Science in Society*, *5*(5), 172–197. DOI: 10.54783/ijsoc.v5i5.877

Ashok, M., Madan, R., Joha, A., & Sivarajah, U. (2022). Ethical framework for artificial intelligence and digital technologies. *International Journal of Information Management*, *62*, 102433. DOI: 10.1016/j.ijinfomgt.2021.102433

Asimov, I. (1950). *I, Robot*. Gnome Press.

Auernhammer, J. (2020). Human-centered AI: The role of Human-centered Design Research in the development of AI.

Aust, K., & Harmash, O. (2024). Predictive Analytics, Emerging Trends and Future of State Governance. *Science of Law*, *2024*(2), 16–27. DOI: 10.55284/sol.v2024i2.129

Babaoğlu, C., & Duman, H. (2025). Afet Yönetimi Açısından Sosyal Medya: Fırsatlar ve Riskler. *Türk Deprem Araştırma Dergisi*, *7*(1), 25–35. DOI: 10.46464/tdad.1538677

Babashahi, L., Barbosa, C. E., Lima, Y., Lyra, A., Salazar, H., Argôlo, M., de Almeida, M. A., & Souza, J. M. D. (2024). AI in the Workplace: A Systematic Review of Skill Transformation in the Industry. *Administrative Sciences*, *14*(6), 127. DOI: 10.3390/admsci14060127

Babšek, M., Ravšelj, D., Umek, L., & Aristovnik, A. (2025). Artificial Intelligence Adoption in Public Administration: An Overview of Top-Cited Articles and Practical Applications. *AI*, *6*(3), 44. DOI: 10.3390/ai6030044

Bäckström, K. (2023). New technology and in-store service encounters: An analysis of coping practices and work experiences among frontline employees. *International Review of Retail, Distribution and Consumer Research*, *33*(5), 494–518. DOI: 10.1080/09593969.2023.2271191

Bakar, K. A., Ibrahim, R., & Yunus, Y. (2020). Digital government evolution and maturity models: A review. *Open International Journal of Informatics*, *8*(2), 70–87.

Baker, R. S., & Inventado, P. S. (2014). Educational data mining and learning analytics. In Larusson, J., & White, B. (Eds.), *Learning analytics: From research to practice* (pp. 61–75). Springer. DOI: 10.1007/978-1-4614-3305-7_4

Baker, R., & Hawn, A. (2021). Algorithmic Bias in Education. *International Journal of Artificial Intelligence in Education, 32*(4), 1052–1092. DOI: 10.1007/s40593-021-00285-9

Bannister, F., & Connolly, R. (2011). The trouble with transparency: A critical review of openness in e-government. *Policy and Internet, 3*(1), 1–30. DOI: 10.2202/1944-2866.1076

Bannister, F., & Connolly, R. (2012). Defining e-governance. *E-government, 29*(1), 1–12.

Barocas, S., Hardt, M., & Narayanan, A. (2019). *Fairness and Machine Learning: Limitations and Opportunities*. https://fairmlbook.org

Barocas, S., & Selbst, A. D. (2016). Big data's disparate impact. *California Law Review, 104*(3), 671–732.

Batty, M., Axhausen, K. W., Giannotti, F., Pozdnoukhov, A., Bazzani, A., Wachowicz, M., Ouzounis, G., & Portugali, Y. (2012). Smart Cities of the Future. *The European Physical Journal. Special Topics, 214*(1), 481–518. DOI: 10.1140/epjst/e2012-01703-3

Baxter, G., & Sommerville, I. (2011). Socio-technical systems: From design methods to systems engineering. *Interacting with Computers, 23*(1), 4–17. DOI: 10.1016/j.intcom.2010.07.003

Bekkers, V., & Homburg, V. (2007). *The Information Ecology of E-Government: E-Government as Institutional and Technological Innovation in Public Administration*. IOS Press.

Belkhamza, Z. (2023). Cybersecurity in Digital Transformation applications: Analysis of Past Research and Future Directions. *International Conference on Cyber Warfare and Security, 18*(1), 19–24. DOI: 10.34190/iccws.18.1.1005

Bello, O. A., & Olufemi, K. (2024). Artificial intelligence in fraud prevention: Exploring techniques and applications challenges and opportunities. Computer science & IT research journal, 5(6), 1505-1520.

Bello, S. A., Wada, I., Ige, O. B., Chianumba, E. C., & Adebayo, S. A.Sakiru Folarin BelloIfeoluwa Uchechukwu WadaOlukayode B IgeErnest C ChianumbaSamod Adetunji Adebayo. (2024). AI-driven predictive maintenance and optimization of renewable energy systems for enhanced operational efficiency and longevity. *International Journal of Science and Research Archive, 13*(1), 2823–2837. DOI: 10.30574/ijsra.2024.13.1.1992

Benington, J., & Moore, M. H. (2011). *Public Value: Theory and Practice*. Palgrave Macmillan. DOI: 10.1007/978-0-230-36431-8

Benuyenah, V., & Pandya, B. (2020). Meaning of "employee happiness" within the context of complex organisations? An explanatory review on the UAE labour force. *Rajagiri Management Journal*, *14*(2), 169–180. DOI: 10.1108/RAMJ-04-2020-0012

Berk, R., & Hyatt, J. (2015). Machine learning forecasts of risk to inform sentencing decisions. *Federal Sentencing Reporter*, *27*(4), 222–228. DOI: 10.1525/fsr.2015.27.4.222

Berman, A., de Fine Licht, K., & Carlsson, V. (2024). Trustworthy AI in the public sector: An empirical analysis of a Swedish labor market decision-support system. *Technology in Society*, *76*, 1–15. DOI: 10.1016/j.techsoc.2024.102471

Bhole, K., Galphat, Y., Bathija, K., Saini, T., & Bhosale, A. (2021). Allocation and Tracking of Public Funds using Blockchain. *2021 4th Biennial International Conference on Nascent Technologies in Engineering (ICNTE)*, 1–4. DOI: 10.1109/ICNTE51185.2021.9487782

Bhuiyan, M. R. I. (2024). Industry Readiness and Adaptation of Fourth Industrial Revolution: Applying the Extended TOE Framework. *Human Behavior and Emerging Technologies*, *2024*(1), 1–14. DOI: 10.1155/hbe2/8830228

Bibri, S. E., Huang, J., Jagatheesaperumal, S. K., & Krogstie, J. (2024). The synergistic interplay of artificial intelligence and digital twin in environmentally planning sustainable smart cities: A comprehensive systematic review. *Environmental Science and Ecotechnology*, *20*, 100433. DOI: 10.1016/j.ese.2024.100433 PMID: 38831974

Bignami, F. (2022). Artificial intelligence accountability of public administration. *The American Journal of Comparative Law*, *70*(1, Supplement_1), i312–i346. DOI: 10.1093/ajcl/avac012

Binhammad, M. H. Y., Alqaydi, S., Othman, A., & Abuljadayel, L. H. (2024). The Role of AI in Cyber Security: Safeguarding Digital Identity. *Journal of Information Security*, *15*(2), 245–278. DOI: 10.4236/jis.2024.152015

Binns, R. (2018). "Fairness in Machine Learning: Lessons from Political Philosophy." *Proceedings of the 2018 Conference on Fairness, Accountability and Transparency (FAT*)*, 149–159.

Bittencourt, C., Estima, J., & Pestana, G. (2019). Open Data Initiatives in Brazil. *2019 14th Iberian Conference on Information Systems and Technologies (CISTI), June*, 1–4. DOI: 10.23919/CISTI.2019.8760592

Björklund, F. (2016). E-government and moral citizenship: The case of Estonia. *Citizenship Studies*, *20*(6–7), 914–931. DOI: 10.1080/13621025.2016.1213222

Bonomi Savignon, A., Zecchinelli, R., Costumato, L., & Scalabrini, F. (2024). Automation in public sector jobs and services: a framework to analyze public digital transformation's impact in a data-constrained environment. *Transforming Government: People. Transforming Government*, *18*(1), 49–70. DOI: 10.1108/TG-04-2023-0044

Borocci, S. (2025). AI watch: Global Regulatory Tracker – Italy. *White & Case LLP.* https://www.jdsupra.com/legalnews/ai-watch-global-regulatory-tracker-6844025/ (Accessed: May 9, 2025).

Bostrom, N. (2014). *Superintelligence: Paths, Dangers, Strategies*. Oxford University Press.

Bostrom, R. P., & Heinen, J. S. (1977). MIS problems and failures: A socio-technical perspective, Part II: The application of socio-technical theory. *Management Information Systems Quarterly*, *1*(4), 11–28. DOI: 10.2307/249019

Bouchelouche, K., Ghomari, A., & Zemmouchi-Ghomari, L. (2024). From Barriers to Boosters: Optimizing Open Government Data through Publishing Guidelines and Data Protection Strategies. *Recent Research Reviews Journal*, *3*(1), 56–69. DOI: 10.36548/rrrj.2024.1.004

Bouchetara, M., Zerouti, M., & Zouambi, A. R. (2024). Leveraging artificial intelligence (AI) in public sector financial risk management: Innovations, challenges, and future directions. *EDPACS*, *69*(9), 124–144. DOI: 10.1080/07366981.2024.2377351

Bovaird, T., & Loeffler, E. (2012). From engagement to co-production: The contribution of users and communities to outcomes and public value. *Voluntas*, *23*(4), 1119–1138. DOI: 10.1007/s11266-012-9309-6

Bovens, M., & Zouridis, S. (2002). From street-level to system-level bureaucracies: How information and communication technology is transforming administrative discretion and constitutional control. *Public Administration Review*, *62*(2), 174–184. DOI: 10.1111/0033-3352.00168

Bovens, M., & Zouridis, S. (2023). From street-level to system-level bureaucracies: How information and communication technology is transforming administrative discretion and constitutional control. *Public Administration Review*, *83*(2), 234–245. DOI: 10.1111/puar.13345

Boyarskaya, M., & Diakopoulos, N. (2020). Algorithmic bias in student grading: Implications for fairness and equity. *AI & Society*, *35*(4), 897–910.

Bracci, E. (2023). The loopholes of algorithmic public services: An "intelligent" accountability research agenda. *Accounting, Auditing & Accountability Journal, 36*(2), 739–763. DOI: 10.1108/AAAJ-06-2022-5856

Braun, V., & Clarke, V. (2006). Using thematic analysis in psychology. *Qualitative Research in Psychology, 3*(2), 77–101. DOI: 10.1191/1478088706qp063oa

Brayne, S. (2021). *Predict and Surveil: Data, Discretion, and the Future of Policing*. Oxford University Press.

Brown, M. M., & Brudney, J. L. (2001). Achieving advanced electronic government services: An examination of obstacles and implications from an international perspective. *Journal of Public Administration: Research and Theory, 11*(1), 1–11. DOI: 10.22259/2642-8318.0101001

Brunsson, N., & Olsen, J. P. (2018). *The Reforming organization: making sense of administrative change*. Routledge. DOI: 10.4324/9781351252188

Brynjolfsson, E., & McAfee, A. (2014). *The Second Machine Age*. W. W. Norton & Company.

Brzozowska-Rup, K., Nowakowska, M., & Zdradzisz, M. (2024). Cloud computing in the Polish public administration: Current state and development prospects. *Technological Forecasting and Social Change, 205*, 123500. DOI: 10.1016/j.techfore.2024.123500

Buchanan, B. G., & Shortliffe, E. H. (1984). *Rule-Based Expert Systems*. Addison-Wesley.

Budhwar, P., Malik, A., De Silva, M. T., & Thevisuthan, P. (2022). Artificial intelligence–challenges and opportunities for international HRM: A review and research agenda. *International Journal of Human Resource Management, 33*(6), 1065–1097. DOI: 10.1080/09585192.2022.2035161

Bullock, J. B. (2019). Artificial intelligence, discretion, and bureaucracy. *American Review of Public Administration, 49*(7), 751–761. DOI: 10.1177/0275074019856123

Buolamwini, J., & Gebru, T. (2018). *Gender Shades: Intersectional Accuracy Disparities in Commercial Gender Classification*. In *Proceedings of the Conference on Fairness, Accountability and Transparency (FAT)**, 77–91.

Buolamwini, J., & Gebru, T. (2018). Gender Shades: Intersectional Accuracy Disparities in Commercial Gender Classification. In *Proceedings of the Conference on Fairness, Accountability and Transparency (FAT)*.

Bussone, A., Stumpf, S., & O'Sullivan, D. (2015). "The Role of Explanations on Trust and Reliance in Clinical Decision Support Systems." *CHI '15 Extended Abstracts on Human Factors in Computing Systems*, 1701–1706. https://doi.org/DOI: 10.1145/2702613.2733313

Busuioc, M. (2021). Accountable artificial intelligence: Holding algorithms to account. *Public Administration Review*, *81*(5), 825–836. DOI: 10.1111/puar.13293 PMID: 34690372

Butcher, J., & Beridze, I. (2019). *Lessons from governing emerging technologies.* AI Governance Journal., DOI: 10.1080/03071847.2019.1694260

Çaldağ, M. T., Gokalp, M. O., & Gokalp, E. (2019). Open Government Data: Analysing Benefits and Challenges. *1st International Informatics and Software Engineering Conference: Innovative Technologies for Digital Transformation, IISEC 2019 - Proceedings.* DOI: 10.1109/UBMYK48245.2019.8965581

Calzada, I. (2023). Disruptive Technologies for e-Diasporas: Blockchain, DAOs, Data Cooperatives, Metaverse, and ChatGPT. *Futures*, *154*, 103258. DOI: 10.1016/j.futures.2023.103258

Campion, A., Gasco-Hernandez, M., Jankin Mikhaylov, S., & Esteve, M. (2022). Overcoming the challenges of collaboratively adopting artificial intelligence in the public sector. *Social Science Computer Review*, *40*(2), 462–477. DOI: 10.1177/0894439320979953

Carretero, S., Vuorikari, R., & Punie, Y. (2017). *DigComp 2.1: The Digital Competence Framework for Citizens with eight proficiency levels and examples of use.* Publications Office of the European Union., DOI: 10.2760/38842

Casalino, N., Rubichi, V., Gasparri, C., & Pizzolo, G. (2017). Organization of Processes Digitization and E-Invoicing Services for an Effective Digital Transformation of Public Sector. *DigitCult – Scientific Journal on Digital Cultures, 2*(1), 53–62.

Castillo, C. (2019). Algorithmic Bias in Rankings. Companion Proceedings of The 2019 World Wide Web Conference. DOI: 10.1145/3308560.3316451

Cath, C. (2018). Governing artificial intelligence: Ethical, legal and technical opportunities and challenges. *Philosophical Transactions. Series A, Mathematical, Physical, and Engineering Sciences*, *376*(2133), 20180080. DOI: 10.1098/rsta.2018.0080 PMID: 30322996

Çeliksoy, E. (2021). Kurumsal Bilgi Yönetimi: Teknolojik Eğitilmler. In Kocaoğlu, M., & Usta, S. (Eds.), *Kamuda Büyük Veri* (Vol. 1, pp. 119–135). Eğitim Yayınevi.

Ceray Aldemi, E. Ş. (2021). A Model Proposal for Local Governments to Increase Citizen Involvement in the Age of Information Society and E-Government: Crowdsourcing. *Handbook of Research on Global Challenges for Improving Public Services and Government Operations, 19.*

Chapman, A. R.. (2019). High-sensitivity cardiac troponin and the underdiagnosis of myocardial infarction in women: Prospective cohort study. *BMJ (Clinical Research Ed.), 363*, k5094.

Charalabidis, Y., Alexopoulos, C., & Loukis, E. (2016). A taxonomy of open government data research areas and topics. *Journal of Organizational Computing and Electronic Commerce, 26*(1–2), 41–63. DOI: 10.1080/10919392.2015.1124720

Chatfield, A. T., & Reddick, C. G. (2018). All hands on deck to tweet #sandy: Networked governance of citizen coproduction in turbulent times. *Government Information Quarterly, 35*(2), 259–272. DOI: 10.1016/j.giq.2017.09.004

Chen, T., Gascó-Hernandez, M., & Esteve, M. (2023). The adoption and implementation of artificial intelligence chatbots in public organizations: Evidence from US state governments. *American Review of Public Administration, 54*(3), 255–270. DOI: 10.1177/02750740231200522

Chen, T., Guo, W., Gao, X., & Liang, Z. (2021). AI-based self-service technology in public service delivery: User experience and influencing factors. *Government Information Quarterly, 38*(4), 101520. DOI: 10.1016/j.giq.2020.101520

Choi, S., & Park, S. (2023). Governmental Transformation in the Era of the Post Pandemic: Analyzing the Impacts of the Pandemic on Organizational Cultural Change in Government. *Public Organization Review, 23*(2), 451–467. DOI: 10.1007/s11115-023-00703-7

Cho, J. (2023). Comparative analysis of open government data topics and usability. *Quality & Quantity, 57*(6), 5655–5671. DOI: 10.1007/s11135-023-01630-x PMID: 36811111

Cholyshkina, O., Karnaukh, A., Volianiuk, O., Ostapenko, M., & Holishevska, A. (2024). Public participation and innovative technologies: the role of artificial intelligence in public administration and sustainable development. *Salud, Ciencia y Tecnología - Serie de Conferencias, 3*, 974. DOI: 10.56294/sctconf2024974

Christensen, J., Aarøe, L., Baekgaard, M., Herd, P., & Moynihan, D. P. (2020). Human capital and administrative burden: The role of cognitive resources in citizen-state interactions. *Public Administration Review, 80*(1), 127–136. DOI: 10.1111/puar.13134 PMID: 32025058

Ciancarini, P., Giancarlo, R., & Grimaudo, G. (2023). Digital Transformation in the Public Administrations: A Guided Tour For Computer Scientists. *ArXiv. Abs, 2305*, 05551. DOI: 10.1109/ACCESS.2024.3363075

Citron, D. K., & Pasquale, F. (2014). The scored society: Due process for automated predictions. *Washington Law Review (Seattle, Wash.), 89*(1), 1–33.

Coglianese, C., & Lehr, D. (2019). Transparency and algorithmic governance. *Administrative Law Review, 71*(1), 1–56.

Consumer Protection Board. (2023). *Annual report on consumer vulnerabilities in the digital environment*. https://www.tarbijakaitseamet.ee

Cordella, A., & Bonina, C. M. (2012). A public value perspective for ICT enabled public sector reforms: A theoretical reflection. *Government Information Quarterly, 29*(4), 512–520. DOI: 10.1016/j.giq.2012.03.004

Cortés-Cediel, M. E., Segura-Tinoco, A., Cantador, I., & Rodríguez Bolívar, M. P. (2023). Trends and challenges of e-government chatbots: Advances in exploring open government data and citizen participation content. *Government Information Quarterly, 40*(4), 101877. DOI: 10.1016/j.giq.2023.101877

Cossette-Lefebvre, H., & Maclure, J. (2022). AI's fairness problem: Understanding wrongful discrimination in the context of automated decision-making. *AI and Ethics, 3*(4), 1255–1269. DOI: 10.1007/s43681-022-00233-w

Cowgill, B., Dell'Acqua, F., & Deng, S. (2021). "Biased Programmers? Or Biased Data? A Field Experiment in Operationalizing AI Ethics." *Columbia Business School Research Paper No. 18-67*. https://doi.org/DOI: 10.2139/ssrn.3614776

Crawford, K. (2016). Artificial intelligence's white guy problem. The New York Times.

Crawford, K. (2021). *Atlas of AI: Power, Politics, and the Planetary Costs of Artificial Intelligence*. Yale University Press.

Creemers, R. (2018). China's Social Credit System: An Evolving Practice of Control. SSRN *Electronic Journal*. DOI: 10.2139/ssrn.3175792

Criado, J. I., & de Zarate-Alcarazo, L. O. (2022). Technological frames, CIOs, and Artificial Intelligence in public administration: A socio-cognitive exploratory study in Spanish local governments. *Government Information Quarterly, 39*(3), 1–13. DOI: 10.1016/j.giq.2022.101688

Criado, J. I., & Gil-Garcia, J. R. (2019). Creating public value through smart technologies and strategies: From digital services to artificial intelligence and beyond. *International Journal of Public Sector Management, 32*(5), 438–450. DOI: 10.1108/IJPSM-07-2019-0178

Curti, F., Ivanov, I. T., Macchiavelli, M., & Zimmermann, T. (2024). Exposure to Cyber Risk and Inadequate Cybersecurity Regulations: Evidence from Municipalities. *Chicago Fed Letter, 501.*

Cybernetica. (2023). Cybernetica signs contract to develop cryptographically secure artificial intelligence with US Office of Naval Research. https://cyber.ee/resources/news/ONR- 2024/

Dahl, R. A. (2018). The science of public administration: Three problems. In *Democracy, bureaucracy, and the study of administration* (pp. 60–76). Routledge. DOI: 10.4324/9780429501036-6

Damar, M., Aydın, Ö., Nihal Cagle, M., Özoğuz, E., Ömer Köse, H., & Özen, A. (2024). Navigating the digital frontier: Transformative technologies reshaping public administration. *EDPACS, 69*(9), 41–69. DOI: 10.1080/07366981.2024.2376792

Danaher, J., Hogan, M. J., Noone, C., Kennedy, R., Behan, A., de Paor, A., Felzmann, H., Haklay, M., Khoo, S.-M., Morison, J., Murphy, M. H., O'Brolchain, N., Schafer, B., & Shankar, K. (2017). Algorithmic governance: Developing a research agenda through the power of collective intelligence. *Big Data & Society*, *4*(2), 1–21. DOI: 10.1177/2053951717726554

Danks, D., & London, A. (2017). Algorithmic Bias in Autonomous Systems., 4691-4697. .DOI: 10.24963/ijcai.2017/654

Dastin, J. (2018). "Amazon scraps secret AI recruiting tool that showed bias against women." *Reuters*. https://www.reuters.com/article/us-amazon-com-jobs-automation-insight-idUSKCN1MK08G

Datta, A., Tschantz, M. C., & Datta, A. (2015). Automated experiments on ad privacy settings: A tale of opacity, choice, and discrimination. *Proceedings on Privacy Enhancing Technologies. Privacy Enhancing Technologies Symposium, 2015*(1), 92–112. DOI: 10.1515/popets-2015-0007

Datta, P., Walker, L., & Amarilli, F. (2020). Digital transformation: Learning from Italy's public administration. *Journal of Information Technology Teaching Cases, 10*(2), 54–71. DOI: 10.1177/2043886920910437

David, S., Zinica, D., Bărbu ă-Mi u, N., Savga, L., & Virlanuta, F. O. (2024). Public administration managers' and employees' perceptions of adaptability to change under "the future of work" paradigm. *Technological Forecasting and Social Change, 199,* 1–13. DOI: 10.1016/j.techfore.2023.123088

Demartini, C. G., Sciascia, L., Bosso, A., & Manuri, F. (2024). Artificial Intelligence Bringing Improvements to Adaptive Learning in Education: A Case Study. *Sustainability (Basel), 16*(3), 1347. DOI: 10.3390/su16031347

Demirtaş, İ. (2020). Baltık ülkelerinin AB'ye entegrasyon sürecinde Rusya faktörü, (Yayımlanmamış yüksek Lisans Tezi). İstanbul Üniversitesi Sosyal Bilimler Enstitüsü, İstanbul. https://tez.yok.gov.tr/UlusalTezMerkezi/tezDetay.jsp?id=H9xIDamkop_QRtFFgvWUWQ&no=NHS9eR0ybTNb68yfnJLcpQ

Denhardt, J. V., & Denhardt, R. B. (2000). The New Public Service: Serving rather than steering. *Public Administration Review, 60*(6), 549–559. DOI: 10.1111/0033-3352.00117

Deni, S., Husain, T., & Deni, A. (2020). Bureaucracy and Challenges in Digital Era: A New Concept of Information Technology Integration in the Archipelagic Country. *Journal of Public Policy and Administration, 4*(4), 71. DOI: 10.11648/j.jppa.20200404.12

Desouza, K. C., Dawson, G. S., & Chenok, D. (2020). AI practices and digital transformation strategies. *Public Administration Review, 80*(4), 547–553. DOI: 10.1111/puar.13218

Desouza, K. C., & Jacob, B. (2017). Big Data in the Public Sector: Lessons for Practitioners and Scholars. *Administration & Society, 49*(7), 1043–1064. DOI: 10.1177/0095399714555751

Di Giulio, M., & Vecchi, G. (2023). Implementing digitalization in the public sector. Technologies, agency, and governance. *Public Policy and Administration, 38*(2), 133–158. DOI: 10.1177/09520767211023283

Donthu, N., Kumar, S., Mukherjee, D., Pandey, N., & Lim, W. M. (2021). How to conduct a bibliometric analysis: An overview and guidelines. *Journal of Business Research, 133*, 285–296. DOI: 10.1016/j.jbusres.2021.04.070

Dressel, J., & Farid, H. (2018). The Accuracy, Fairness, and Limits of Predicting Recidivism. *Science Advances, 4*(1), eaao5580. Advance online publication. DOI: 10.1126/sciadv.aao5580 PMID: 29376122

Dreyling, R. M., Koppel, T., Tammet, T., & Pappel, I. (2024). Challenges of generative AI chatbots in public services – An integrative review. Available at *SSRN*: https://ssrn.com/abstract=4850714 or DOI: 10.2139/ssrn.4850714

Dreyling, R., Tammet, T., Pappel, I., & McBride, K. (June 01, 2024). Navigating the AI Maze: Lessons from Estonia's Bürokratt on public sector aı digital transformation. DOI: 10.2139/ssrn.4850696

Dube, I. (2024). Chatbots: A tool to improve public service delivery and create public value. Journal of Public Administration and Development Affairs, 1(1), Article. .DOI: 10.55190/JPADA.2024.341

Duberry, J. (2022). Artificial intelligence and democracy: risks and promises of AI-mediated citizen–government relations. In *Artificial Intelligence and Democracy*. Edward Elgar Publishing. DOI: 10.4337/9781788977319

Ducatel, K., Michlmayr, T., Merle, P., Baskovc, D., & Mestre, F. (2020). The European Commission goes 'cloud first': A roadmap towards trusted cloud adoption to seize the opportunities of digital transformation for EU institutions and agencies. *Cyber Security: A Peer-Reviewed Journal, 3*(3), 220. DOI: 10.69554/YDMP5350

Duffy, D. (2000). The internet as a research and dissemination resource. *Health Promotion International, 15*(4), 349–353. DOI: 10.1093/heapro/15.4.349

Duman, H. (2024). Use of Digital Technologies in Migration and Asylum Management. In *Media representation of migrants and refugees* (pp. 169–188). IGI Global. DOI: 10.4018/979-8-3693-3459-1.ch011

Dunleavy, P. (2020). *Digital-Era Governance: IT Corporations, the State, and E-government.* Oxford University Press.

Dunleavy, P., & Margetts, H. (2015). *Digital Era Governance: IT Corporations, the State, and E-Government.* Oxford University Press.

Dunleavy, P., Margetts, H., Bastow, S., & Tinkler, J. (2006). New public management is dead—Long live digital-era governance. *Journal of Public Administration: Research and Theory, 16*(3), 467–494. DOI: 10.1093/jopart/mui057

Durukal, O., & Öztürk, N. K. (2019). Blockchain Technology in the Provision of Public Services. *Ege Academic Review, 23*(77), 449–456.

Ecas. (2017). Estonia brings digital focus to EU presidency. https://ecas.org/estonia-eu-presidency/

ECRI. (European Commission against Racism and Intolerance). (2024). Ecri conclusions on the implementation of the recommendations in respect of Estonia subject to interim follow-up. https://rm.coe.int/ecri-conclusions-on-the-implementation-of-the-recommendation-in-respec/1680b1e954

Education Estonia. (2021). ProgeTiger-Estonian way to create interest in technology. https://www.educationestonia.org/progetiger/

e-Estonia. (2025). Estonia and automated decision-making: Challenges for public administration. https://e-estonia.com/estonia-and-automated-decision-making-challenges-for-public-administration/

e-Estonia. (2025). Estonia's groundbreaking national initiative: AI Leap programme to bring AI tools to all schools. https://e-estonia.com/estonia-announces-a-groundbreaking-national-initiative-ai-leap-programme-to-bring-ai-tools-to-all-schools/

e-Estonia. (2025). Factsheet ai strategy. https://e-estonia.com/wp-content/uploads/factsheet-ai-strategy.pdf

Ekarini, M. I., & Wibowo, L. A. (2022). *The Implementation of Digital Transformation on Improving Public Services. Advances in Economics*. Business and Management Research/Advances in Economics, Business and Management Research., DOI: 10.2991/aebmr.k.220701.096

ELIZA. (1966). ELIZA: a very basic Rogerian psychotherapist chatbot. Retrieved from: https://web.njit.edu/~ronkowit/eliza.html, June 2025.

Elliott, K., Price, R., Shaw, P., Spiliotopoulos, T., Ng, M., Coopamootoo, K., & van Moorsel, A. (2021). Towards an Equitable Digital Society: Artificial Intelligence (AI) and Corporate Digital Responsibility (CDR). *Society*, *58*(3), 179–188. DOI: 10.1007/s12115-021-00594-8 PMID: 34149122

Empowering Estonia, A. I. (2025). AI use cases. https://www.kratid.ee/ai-use-cases

ENISA. (2023). *European Cybersecurity Threat Landscape 2023*. European Union Agency for Cybersecurity.

Ensign, D., Friedler, S. A., Neville, S., Scheidegger, C., & Venkatasubramanian, S. (2018). Runaway feedback loops in predictive policing. *Proceedings of the 1st Conference on Fairness, Accountability and Transparency (FAT*)*, 160–171.

Enterprise Estonia. (2018). Estonia invites new cyber security startups - a unique cyber security and AI accelerator to be opened. https://investinestonia.com/estonia-invites-new-cyber-security-startups-a-unique-cyber-security-and-ai-accelerator-to-be-opened/

Eom, S.-J., & Lee, J. (2022). Digital government transformation in turbulent times: Responses, challenges, and future direction. *Government Information Quarterly, 39*(2), 101690. DOI: 10.1016/j.giq.2022.101690 PMID: 35291492

Equality and Human Rights Commission. (2021). Artificial intelligence case studies: Good practice by local authorities. https://www.equalityhumanrights.com/en/publication-download/artificial-intelligence-case-studies-good-practice-local-authorities

Eravcı, A. (2020). Estonya tarihinin güncel Eston dış politikasına etkisi. *Academic Social Resources Journal, 5*(19), 710–724. DOI: 10.31569/ASRJOURNAL.127

Eren, V., & Duman, H. (2025). Artificial intelligence support in disaster management. *Kamu Yönetimi ve Teknoloji Dergisi, 7*(1), 13–36. DOI: 10.58307/kaytek.1580460

e-Residency. (2024). e-Residency annual report 2024. https://e-resident.gov.ee/annual-report

Erhueh, O. V., Nwakile, C., Akano, O. A., Esiri, A. E., & Hanson, E. (2024). Digital transformation in energy asset management: Lessons for building the future of energy infrastructure. *Global Journal of Research in Science and Technology, 2*(2), 010–037. DOI: 10.58175/gjrst.2024.2.2.0071

Estonian Librarians Association. (2024). *Public access infrastructure in Estonia: 2024 assessment*. https://www.ell.ee/en/publications

Etscheid, J. (2019). AI governance and policy issues. *IEEE Transactions on Technology and Society, 1*(1), 30–37. DOI: 10.1109/TTS.2019.2946204

EU. (2024). *Artificial Intelligence Act*. Official Journal of the European Union.

Eubanks, V. (2018). *Automating Inequality*. St. Martin's Press.

Eubanks, V. (2018). *Automating inequality: How high-tech tools profile, police, and punish the poor*. St. Martin's Press.

Eubanks, V. (2018). *Automating Inequality: How High-Tech Tools Profile, Police, and Punish the Poor*. St. Martin's Press.

European Commission, Joint Research Centre. (2021). *Italy: Public Sector Dimension of AI Strategy. AI Watch Report.* https://ai-watch.ec.europa.eu/topics/public-sector/public-sector-dimension-ai-national-strategies/italy-public-sector-dimension-ai-strategy_en (Accessed: May 9, 2025).

European Commission. (2018). Artificial intelligence for Europe. https://eur-lex.europa.eu/legal-content/EN/TXT/?uri=COM%3A2018%3A237%3AFIN

European Commission. (2020). *Ethics Guidelines for Trustworthy AI.* High-Level Expert Group on Artificial Intelligence.

European Commission. (2021). Proposal for a Regulation on Artificial Intelligence.

European Commission. (2022). Digital Public Administration factsheet 2022, European Commission. (2022). eGovernment Benchmark 2022: Trust and User-Centric Services.

European Commission. (2023). 2023 Country report ESTONIA. https://economy-finance.ec.europa.eu/publications/2023-country-report-estonia_en

European Commission. (2024). Cohesive Estonia strategy 2030. https://commission.europa.eu/system/files/202210/1_2_cohesive_estonia_strategy_2030_en.pdf

Eurostat. (2023). *Digital economy and society statistics - households and individuals.* https://ec.europa.eu/eurostat/databrowser/view/isoc_ci_in_h

Fabbrini, F. (2022). Italy's national recovery and resilience plan: Context, content and challenges. *Journal of Modern Italian Studies*, *27*(5), 658–676. DOI: 10.1080/1354571X.2022.2124672

Fatima, S., Desouza, K. C., & Dawson, G. S. (2020). Maximizing public value with AI. *Government Information Quarterly*, *37*(4), 101579. DOI: 10.1016/j.giq.2020.101579

Fazelpour, S., & Danks, D. (2021). Algorithmic bias: Senses, sources, solutions. *Philosophy Compass*, *16*(8), e12760. Advance online publication. DOI: 10.1111/phc3.12760

Febiandini, V. V., & Sony, M. S. (2023). Analysis of public administration challenges in the development of artificial intelligence industry 4.0. *IAIC Transactions on Sustainable Digital Innovation*, *4*(2), 164–168. DOI: 10.34306/itsdi.v4i2.586

Filgueiras, F. (2022). New Pythias of public administration: Ambiguity and choice in AI systems as challenges for governance. *AI & Society*, *37*(4), 1473–1486. DOI: 10.1007/s00146-021-01201-4

Floridi, L. (2021). AI and Its New Regulatory Framework in Europe. *Philosophy & Technology*, *34*, 1–7. PMID: 33717860

Flowerman, C. (2023). (Some) algorithmic bias as institutional bias. *Ethics and Information Technology*, *25*(2), 1–10. DOI: 10.1007/s10676-023-09698-7

Følstad, A., & Bjerkreim-Hanssen, N. (2023). User interactions with a municipality chatbot—Lessons learnt from dialogue analysis. *International Journal of Human-Computer Interaction*, *40*(18), 4973–4986. DOI: 10.1080/10447318.2023.2238355

Foucault, M., & Papadopoulos, D. (2021). Artificial Intelligence, Surveillance and the Politics of Visibility. *Information Communication and Society*, *24*(1), 1–17.

Fratini, S., Hine, E., Novelli, C., Roberts, H., & Floridi, L. (2024). Digital Sovereignty: A Descriptive Analysis and a Critical Evaluation of Existing Models. *Digital Society : Ethics, Socio-Legal and Governance of Digital Technology*, *3*(3), 59. Advance online publication. DOI: 10.1007/s44206-024-00146-7

Fredriksson, C., Mubarak, F., Tuohimaa, M., & Zhan, M. (2017). Big data in the public sector: A systematic literature review. *Scandinavian Journal of Public Administration*, *21*(3), 39–61. DOI: 10.58235/sjpa.v21i3.11563

Frey, C. B., & Osborne, M. A. (2017). The Future of Employment: How Susceptible are Jobs to Computerisation? *Technological Forecasting and Social Change*, *114*, 254–280. DOI: 10.1016/j.techfore.2016.08.019

Fu, R., Huang, Y., & Singh, P. (2020). AI and Algorithmic Bias: Source, Detection, Mitigation and Implications. *InfoSciRN: Machine Learning (Sub-Topic)*. DOI: 10.2139/ssrn.3681517

Galetta, D.-U. (2018). Access to Administrative Documents and to Public Sector Information in Italy. In *The Right of Access to Public Information* (pp. 343–367). Springer Berlin Heidelberg., DOI: 10.1007/978-3-662-55554-5_8

Gasser, U., & Almeida, V. A. F. (2017). A Layered Model for AI Governance. *IEEE Internet Computing*, *21*(6), 58–62. DOI: 10.1109/MIC.2017.4180835

Gentelet, K., & Mizrahi, S. K. (2024). A Human-Centered Approach to AI Governance: Operationalizing Human Rights Through Citizen Participation. In Human-Centered AI (pp. 215-230). Chapman and Hall/CRC.

Gerontas, A., Zeginis, D., Promikyridis, R., Androš, M., Tambouris, E., Cipan, V., & Tarabanis, K. (2022). Enhancing core public service vocabulary to enable public service personalization. *Information (Basel)*, *13*(5), 225. DOI: 10.3390/info13050225

Gesk, T. S., & Leyer, M. (2022). Artificial intelligence in public services: When and why citizens accept its usage. *Government Information Quarterly*, *39*(3), 101704. DOI: 10.1016/j.giq.2022.101704

Ghani, A. S. (2024). Revolutionizing Supply Chains: A Comprehensive Study of Industry 4.0 Technologies (IoT, Big Data, AI, etc.). *International Journal of Scientific Research in Engineering and Management*, *08*(04), 1–5. DOI: 10.55041/IJSREM30037

Gil-García, J. R., & Flores-Zúñiga, M. Á. (2020). Towards a comprehensive understanding of digital government success: Integrating implementation and adoption factors. *Government Information Quarterly*, *37*(4), 101518. DOI: 10.1016/j.giq.2020.101518

Gladkov, M. Yu. (2024). Features of the Cloud Governance as Part of the Digital Transformation of the Public Administration SECTOR. *Science and Art of Management / Bulletin of the Institute of Economics. Management and Law of the Russian State University for the Humanities*, *3*(3), 10–23. DOI: 10.28995/2782-2222-2024-3-10-23

Gómez, E. A. R. (2017). Perceptions about the concept and benefits of open government in local governments in Spain. *ACM International Conference Proceeding Series, Part F1280*, 594–597. DOI: 10.1145/3047273.3047338

Government of Estonia. (2021). *Digital agenda 2030*. https://www.riigikantselei.ee/en/digital-agenda-2030

Government of Estonia. 2023, (2023). Estonia's European Union policy priorities 2023–2025. https://www.riigikantselei.ee/sites/default/files/documents/2023-07/Estonia's EU policy priorities for 2023-2025.pdf

Government of Singapore. (2022). Smart Nation: What is it? Hood, C. (1991). A public management for all seasons? *Public Administration*, *69*(1), 3–19.

Govlaunch. (n.d.). Ten local government chatbots that are making a difference. Retrieved from https://govlaunch.com/stories/ten-local-government-chatbots-that-are-making-a-difference

Green, B. (2022). The flaws of policies requiring human oversight of government algorithms. *Computer Law & Security Review*, *45*, 105681. DOI: 10.1016/j.clsr.2022.105681

Greenway, A., Terrett, B., Bracken, M., & Loosemore, T. (2021). *Digital transformation at scale: Why the strategy is delivery*. London Publishing Partnership.

Grimmelikhuijsen, S., & Tangi, L. (2024). What factors influence perceived artificial intelligence adoption by public managers? Publications Office of the European Union. JRC138684.

Grimmelikhuijsen, S. G., & Feeney, M. K. (2017). Developing and Testing an Integrative Framework for Open Government Adoption in Local Governments. *Public Administration Review*, *77*(4), 579–590. DOI: 10.1111/puar.12689

Guo, Y. (2024). *Digital Government and Public Interaction: Platforms, Chatbots, and Public Satisfaction: Platforms, Chatbots, and Public Satisfaction*. IGI Global. DOI: 10.4018/979-8-3693-3665-6

Hadjidemetriou, G. M., Herrera, M., & Parlikad, A. K. (2021). Condition and criticality-based predictive maintenance prioritisation for networks of bridges. *Structure and Infrastructure Engineering*, *18*(8), 1207–1221. DOI: 10.1080/15732479.2021.1897146

Hadjiefthymiades, S. (2020). Internet of Things in E-Government: Applications and Challenges. https://www.igi-global.com/gateway/article/257274

Hakimi, M., Hamidi, M. S., Miskinyar, M. S., & Sazish, B. (2023). Integrating artificial intelligence into e-government: Navigating challenges, opportunities, and policy implications. *International Journal of Academic and Practical Research*, *2*(2), 11–21. DOI: 10.5281/zenodo.13142637

Halchin, L. E. (2004). Electronic government: Government capability and terrorist resource. *Government Information Quarterly*, *21*(4), 406–419. DOI: 10.1016/j.giq.2004.08.002

Hamid, S., & Huda, M. N. (2025). Mapping the landscape of government data breaches: A bibliometric analysis of literature from 2006 to 2023. *Social Sciences & Humanities Open*, *11*, 101234. DOI: 10.1016/j.ssaho.2024.101234

Hansson, K., Belkacem, K., & Ekenberg, L. (2015). Open Government and Democracy: A Research Review. *Social Science Computer Review*, *33*(5), 540–555. DOI: 10.1177/0894439314560847

Hardt, M., Price, E., & Srebro, N. (2016). "Equality of Opportunity in Supervised Learning." *Advances in Neural Information Processing Systems (NeurIPS)*, 29.

Hardy, K., & Maurushat, A. (2017). Opening up government data for Big Data analysis and public benefit. *Computer Law & Security Review*, *33*(1), 30–37. DOI: 10.1016/j.clsr.2016.11.003

Harfouche, A., & Robbin, A. (2015). E-Government. In book: Wiley Encyclopedia of Management. DOI:DOI: 10.1002/9781118785317.weom070001

Headrick, G., Ruth, A., White, S., Ellison, C., Seligman, H. K., Bleich, S. N., & Moran, A. J. (2022). Integration and coordination across public benefit programs: Insights from state and local government leaders in the United States. *Preventive Medicine Reports, 31*, 102077. DOI: 10.1016/j.pmedr.2022.102077 PMID: 36483579

Heeks, R. (2022). Digital inequality beyond the digital divide: Conceptualizing adverse digital incorporation in the global South. *Information Technology for Development, 28*(4), 688–704. DOI: 10.1080/02681102.2022.2068492

Henman, P. (2020). Improving public services using artificial intelligence: Possibilities, pitfalls, governance. *Asia Pacific Journal of Public Administration, 42*(4), 209–221. DOI: 10.1080/23276665.2020.1816188

Hermanto, A., Solimun, S., Fernandes, A. A. R., Wahyono, W., & Zulkarnain, Z. (2018). The importance of open government data for the private sector and NGOs in Indonesia. *Digital Policy. Regulation & Governance, 20*(4), 293–309. DOI: 10.1108/DPRG-09-2017-0047

Hickman, T., ... (2024). Long Awaited EU AI Act Becomes Law After Publication in the EU's Official Journal. *White & Case LLP.* https://www.whitecase.com/insight-alert/long-awaited-eu-ai-act-becomes-law-after-publication-eus-official-journal (Accessed: May 9, 2025).

Hildreth, W. B. (2021). *Handbook of public administration* (Hildreth, W. B., Miller, G., & Rabin, J., Eds.). Routledge. DOI: 10.4324/9780429270680

Hjaltalin, I. T., & Sigurdarson, H. T. (2024). The strategic use of AI in the public sector: A public values analysis of national AI strategies. *Government Information Quarterly, 41*(1), 1–16. DOI: 10.1016/j.giq.2024.101914

Ho, A. T. K. (2002). Reinventing Local Governments and the E-Government Initiative. *Public Administration Review, 62*(4), 434–444. DOI: 10.1111/0033-3352.00197

Hofeditz, L., Jung, A.-K., Mirbabaie, M., & Stieglitz, S. (2025). Ethical Guidelines for the Application of Generative AI in German Journalism. *Digital Society : Ethics, Socio-Legal and Governance of Digital Technology, 4*(1), 4. Advance online publication. DOI: 10.1007/s44206-024-00151-w

Holmes, L., Cresswell, K., Williams, S., Parsons, S., Keane, A., Wilson, C., Islam, S., Joseph, O., Miah, J., Robinson, E., & Starling, B. (2019). Innovating public engagement and patient involvement through strategic collaboration and practice. *Research Involvement and Engagement, 5*(1), 1–12. DOI: 10.1186/s40900-019-0160-4 PMID: 31646001

Hossain, S. T., Yiğitcanlar, T., Nguyen, K., & Xu, Y. (2025). Cybersecurity in Local Governments: A Systematic Review and Framework of Key Challenges [Review of Cybersecurity in Local Governments: A Systematic Review and Framework of Key Challenges]. Urban Governance. Elsevier BV. DOI: 10.1016/j.ugj.2024.12.010

Huang, C., & Gan, K. (2023). Enhancing citizen engagement in smart cities with chatbot. *International Journal of Smart Systems*, *1*(1), 34–39. https://ijss.etunas.com/index.php/ijss/article/view/6. DOI: 10.63876/ijss.v1i1.6

Huang, J. (2021). Leveraging Big Data and Machine Learning for Digital Transformation. *Journal of Integrated Design & Process Science*, *23*(3), 1–3. DOI: 10.3233/JID190020

Hurley, M., & Adebayo, J. (2016). Credit Scoring in the Era of Big Data. *Yale Journal of Law and Technology*, *18*(1), 148–216.

IAPP. (2025). AI Governance Profession Report 2025. https://iapp.org/resources/article/ai-governance-profession-report/

Ibrahimy, M. M., Norta, A., & Normak, P. (2022). *Achieving Corruption-Transparency in Service Governance Processes with Blockchain-Technology Based e-Participation.*, DOI: 10.1007/978-3-031-09917-5_29

Ibrus, I., Tamm, M., & Tiidenberg, K. (January 4, 2022). Estonia's digital culture manifesto. DOI: 10.2139/ssrn.4000959

IMDA. (2019). *Model AI Governance Framework*. Infocomm Media Development Authority.

Imran, A. (2023). Why addressing digital inequality should be a priority. *The Electronic Journal on Information Systems in Developing Countries*, *89*(3), e12255. DOI: 10.1002/isd2.12255

iMUGS (The Integrated Modular Unmanned Ground System), (2025). https://imugs.eu/

INPS. (2023). *Use of artificial intelligence for certified e-mail classification.* Italian National Social Security Institute Project Report.

Irani, Z., Abril, R. M., Weerakkody, V., Omar, A., & Sivarajah, U. (2023). The impact of legacy systems on digital transformation in European public administration: Lesson learned from a multi case analysis. *Government Information Quarterly*, *40*(1), 1–14. DOI: 10.1016/j.giq.2022.101784

ITU. (2022). *Measuring digital development: Facts and figures*. International Telecommunication Union.

Izdebski, W., Zwirowicz-Rutkowska, A., & Nowak da Costa, J. (2021). Open data in spatial data infrastructure: The practices and experiences of Poland. *International Journal of Digital Earth, 14*(11), 1547–1560. DOI: 10.1080/17538947.2021.1952323

Jalakas, P. (2018). *Blockchain from public administration perspective: Case of Estonia*. Tallinn University of Technology.

Janssen, M., Charalabidis, Y., & Zuiderwijk, A. (2012). Benefits, adoption barriers and myths of open data and open government. *Information Systems Management, 29*(4), 258–268. DOI: 10.1080/10580530.2012.716740

Janssen, M., & Kuk, G. (2016). The Challenges and Limits of Big Data Algorithms in Technocratic Governance. *Government Information Quarterly, 33*(3), 371–377. DOI: 10.1016/j.giq.2016.08.011

Janssen, M., & van der Voort, H. (2020). Agile and adaptive governance in crisis response: Lessons from the COVID-19 pandemic. *International Journal of Information Management, 55*, 102180. DOI: 10.1016/j.ijinfomgt.2020.102180 PMID: 32836637

Janssen, M., van der Voort, H., & Wahyudi, A. (2020). Factors influencing big data decision-making quality. *Journal of Business Research, 70*, 338–345. DOI: 10.1016/j.jbusres.2016.08.007

Jeganathan, S., Raj, L. A., Parthasarathy, S., Khan, A. A. A., & Sathick, K. J. (2024). OptCatB: Optuna Hyperparameter Optimization Model to Forecast the Educational Proficiency of Immigrant Students based on CatBoost Regression. *Journal of Internet Services and Information Security, 14*(3), 111–132. DOI: 10.58346/JISIS.2024.I2.008

Jermalavičius, T. (2024). Caught Between Today and Tomorrow: Defence AI in Estonia. In Borchert, H., Schütz, T., & Verbovszky, J. (Eds.), *The Very Long Game. Contributions to Security and Defence Studies*. Springer., DOI: 10.1007/978-3-031-58649-1_7

Jha, M., & Jha, R. K. (2024). Exploring the Influence of Cloud Computing on Workflow Efficiency in Public Administration. *Recent Research Reviews Journal, 3*(1), 148–168. DOI: 10.36548/rrrj.2024.1.011

Jha, R. K., & Jha, M. (2024). Optimizing E-Government Cybersecurity through Artificial Intelligence Integration. *Journal of Trends in Computer Science and Smart Technology, 6*(1), 67–87. DOI: 10.36548/jtcsst.2024.1.005

Jiang, L., Wu, Z., Xu, X., Zhan, Y., Jin, X., Wang, L., & Qiu, Y. (2021). Opportunities and challenges of artificial intelligence in the medical field: Current application, emerging problems, and problem-solving strategies. *The Journal of International Medical Research, 49*(3), 03000605211000157. DOI: 10.1177/03000605211000157 PMID: 33771068

Jobin, A., Ienca, M., & Vayena, E. (2019). The Global Landscape of AI Ethics Guidelines. *Nature Machine Intelligence, 1*(9), 389–399. DOI: 10.1038/s42256-019-0088-2

Johnson, G. (2020). Algorithmic bias: On the implicit biases of social technology. *Synthese, 198*(10), 9941–9961. DOI: 10.1007/s11229-020-02696-y

Kaivo-oja, J., Santonen, T., Lauraëus, T., & Knudsen, M. S. (2022). *Google Big Data Trend Index Analysis of Industry 4.0 Technologies: Technology and Key Concept Trends of Global Landscape in 2004–2021* (pp. 193–206). DOI: 10.1007/978-3-031-07920-7_15

Kalvet, T. (2012). Innovation: a factor explaining e-government success in Estonia. *Electronic Government, an International Journal, 9*(2), 142. DOI: 10.1504/EG.2012.046266

Kamukapa, T. D., Lubinga, S., Masiya, T., & Sono, L. (2024). Assessing the integration of AI competencies in undergraduate public administration curricula in selected South African higher education institutions. *Teaching Public Administration, Ahead-of-print*, 1–18. DOI: 10.1177/01447394241266443

Kane, G. C., Palmer, D., Phillips, A. N., Kiron, D., & Buckley, N. (2017). Achieving digital maturity. *MIT Sloan Management Review, 59*(1), 1–29.

Kankanhalli, A., Charalabidis, Y., & Mellouli, S. (2019). AI in government: Opportunities and challenges. *Public Management Review, 21*(2), 122–140. DOI: 10.1080/14719037.2018.1524352

Karpa, M., Kitsak, T., Domsha, O., Zhuk, O., Akimova, L., & Akimov, O. (2023). Artificial Intelligence as a Tool of Public Management of Socio-Economic Development: Economic Systems, Smart Infrastructure, Digital Systems of Business Analytics and Transfers. *Ad Alta: Journal of Interdisciplinary Research, 13*(1), 13–20. DOI: 10.33543/1301341320

Kaska, K., Rebane, L., & Vask, T. (2021). Lessons from Estonia's national cybersecurity strategy: How to succeed or fail in delivering value. In Rõigas, H., & Jermalavičius, T. (Eds.), *So far, yet so close: Japanese and Estonian cybersecurity policy perspectives and cooperation* (pp. 12–21). International Centre for Defence and Security., https://icds.ee/wp-content/uploads/2021/05/ICDS_Report_So_Far_Yet_So_Close_Roigas_Jermalavicius_May_2021.pdf

Kaun, A., & Männiste, M. (2025). Public sector chatbots: AI frictions and data infrastructures at the interface of the digital welfare state. *New Media & Society*, *27*(4), 1962–1985. DOI: 10.1177/14614448251314394

Kawabata, M. K., & Camargo, A. S.Jr. (2023). E-Government Innovation Initiatives in Public Administration: A Systematic Literature Review and a Research Agenda. *Administration & Society*, *55*(9), 1758–1790. DOI: 10.1177/00953997231185847

Kayyali, M. (2025). Digital Transformation in Public Sector Management: An Overview. Enhancing Public Sector Accountability and Services Through Digital Innovation, 289-324.

Kayyali, M. (2026). Digital Transformation in Public Administration: Global Case Studies. In Sustainable Innovation in the Middle East and North Africa (MENA) Region (pp. 1-26). IGI Global Scientific Publishing.

Kellerhals, A. (2018). Open Government Data – ein Beitrag zur Digitalisierung von Demokratie und öffentlicher Verwaltung. *Yearbook of Swiss Administrative Sciences*, *9*(1), 66. DOI: 10.5334/ssas.120

Kem, D. (2022). Personalised and adaptive learning: Emerging learning platforms in the era of digital and smart learning. *International Journal of Social Science and Human Research*, *5*(2), 385–391. DOI: 10.47191/ijsshr/v5-i2-02

Kemp, A. (2024). Competitive advantage through artificial intelligence: Toward a theory of situated AI. *Academy of Management Review*, *49*(3), 618–635. DOI: 10.5465/amr.2020.0205

Khalid, H., Khan, M. F., & Qureshi, S. (2024). Technological Leapfrogging: Estonia's E-Governance Odyssey by using Emerging Technologies and Lesson for Developing States. *Pakistan Languages and Humanities Review*, *8*(2), 406–414. DOI: 10.47205/plhr.2024(8-II-S)40 PMID: 38256300

Kim, J., & Cho, S. (2022). An information theoretic approach to reducing algorithmic bias for machine learning. *Neurocomputing*, *500*, 26–38. DOI: 10.1016/j.neucom.2021.09.081

King, J. L. (1982). Local government use of information technology: A survey of recent research. *Public Administration Review*, *42*(1), 25–36. DOI: 10.2307/976089

Kirkpatrick, K. (2016). Battling algorithmic bias. *Communications of the ACM*, *59*(10), 16–17. DOI: 10.1145/2983270

Kitchin, R. (2014). *The Data Revolution: Big Data, Open Data, Data Infrastructures and Their Consequences*. SAGE Publications.

Kiviaho, A., & Einolander, J. (2023). Digital transformation, well-being and shrinking communities: Narrowing the divides between urban and rural. *Heliyon*, *9*(8), e18801. Advance online publication. DOI: 10.1016/j.heliyon.2023.e18801 PMID: 37600410

KOÇ, H. (2021). Dijital Dünyada Yeni Vatandaşlık Konsepti: Estonya'da E-Vatandaşlık Örneği. *OPUS Uluslararası Toplum Araştırmaları Dergisi, 17*(35), 2254–2289. DOI: 10.26466/opus.869773

Kocaoğlu, M., & Şahnagil, S. (2022). *Veriye Dayalı Kamu Politikası - Yerel Düzeydeki Yansımaları; Kuram, Kavram & Ülke Örnekleri*. Necmettin Erbakan Üniversitesi Yayınları.

Kocharian, M. (2023). TRENDS OF THE DIGITAL TECHNOLOGIES APPLICATION IN PUBLIC ADMINISTRATION. *Modern Scientific Journal*, 91–96. DOI: 10.36994/2786-9008-2023-1-12

König-Kersting, C., Pollmann, M., Potters, J., & Trautmann, S. (2020). Good decision vs. good results: Outcome bias in the evaluation of financial agents. *Theory and Decision*, *90*(1), 31–61. DOI: 10.1007/s11238-020-09773-1

Kordzadeh, N., & Ghasemaghaei, M. (2021). Algorithmic bias: Review, synthesis, and future research directions. *European Journal of Information Systems*, *31*(3), 388–409. DOI: 10.1080/0960085X.2021.1927212

Kornberger, M., Meyer, R. E., Brandtner, C., & Höllerer, M. A. (2017). When Bureaucracy Meets the Crowd: Studying "Open Government" in the Vienna City Administration. *Organization Studies*, *38*(2), 179–200. DOI: 10.1177/0170840616655496

Körner-Wyrtki, K., Buck, C., Krombacher, A., & Röglinger, M. (2024). Exploring success factors for developing citizen-centric digital public services-insights from a case study. *Electronic Government, an International Journal, 20*(5), 591–620. DOI: 10.1504/EG.2024.140777

Köseoğlu, Ö., & Sobacı, M. Z. (2015). Kamu yönetimi kuramının geleceği: yeni kamu işletmeciliğinden hibritleşmeye doğru. In Köseoğlu, Ö., & Sobacı, M. Z. (Eds.), *Kamu Yönetiminde Paradigma Arayışları: Yeni Kamu İşletmeciliği ve Ötesi* (pp. 297–314). Dora Yayıncılık.

Kotter, J. P. (1996). *Leading Change*. Harvard Business Press.

Krizhevsky, A., Sutskever, I., & Hinton, G. E. (2012). ImageNet Classification with Deep Convolutional Neural Networks. *Advances in Neural Information Processing Systems (NeurIPS)*, 25.

Kučera, J., Chlapek, D., & Nečaský, M. (2013). Open government data catalogs: Current approaches and quality perspective. *Lecture Notes in Computer Science (Including Subseries Lecture Notes in Artificial Intelligence and Lecture Notes in Bioinformatics), 8061 LNCS*, 152–166. DOI: 10.1007/978-3-642-40160-2_13

Kulal, A., Rahiman, H. U., Suvarna, H., Abhishek, N., & Dinesh, S. (2024). Enhancing public service delivery efficiency: Exploring the impact of AI. *Journal of Open Innovation*, *10*(3), 1–16. DOI: 10.1016/j.joitmc.2024.100329

Kumar, D. (2024). AI-driven automation in administrative processes: Enhancing efficiency and accuracy. *International Journal of Engineering Science and Humanities*, *14*(1), 256–265. DOI: 10.62904/qg004437

Kunze, A., Summerskill, S. J., Marshall, R., & Filtness, A. J. (2019). Automation transparency: Implications of uncertainty communication for human-automation interaction and interfaces. *Ergonomics*, *62*(3), 345–360. DOI: 10.1080/00140139.2018.1547842 PMID: 30501566

Kuziemski, M., & Misuraca, G. (2020). AI governance in the public sector: Three tales from the frontiers of automated decision-making in democratic settings. *Telecommunications Policy*, *44*(6), 101976. DOI: 10.1016/j.telpol.2020.101976 PMID: 32313360

Kyodo News. (2023). Yokosuka becomes 1st local gov't in Japan to begin ChatGPT trial use. Retrieved From: https://english.kyodonews.net/articles/-/40065

Kyrychenko, O., & Kyrychenko, M. (2025). THE IMPACT OF DIGITALISATION ON THE EFFICIENCY OF BUSINESS PROCESSES IN THE MODERN ECONOMY. *Економіка Розвитку Систем*, *6*(2), 117–122. DOI: 10.32782/2707-8019/2024-2-16

Larsen, A. G., & Følstad, A. (2024). The impact of chatbots on public service provision: A qualitative interview study with citizens and public service providers. *Government Information Quarterly*, *41*(2), 101927. DOI: 10.1016/j.giq.2024.101927

Layne, K., & Lee, J. (2001). Developing fully functional e-government: A four stage model. *Government Information Quarterly*, *18*(2), 122–136. DOI: 10.1016/S0740-624X(01)00066-1

Lazuashvili, N., Norta, A., & Draheim, D. (2019). *Integration of Blockchain Technology into a Land Registration System for Immutable Traceability: A Casestudy of Georgia.*, DOI: 10.1007/978-3-030-30429-4_15

Lee, L.-W., & Chu, P.-Y. (2018). A user approach to open government data impact assessment. In R. A.C. & B.-L. R. (Eds.), *Proceedings of the European Conference on e-Government, ECEG* (Vols. 2018-Octob, pp. 111–118). Academic Conferences Limited.

Lee, C., & Lim, W. (2020). Governing Smart Nation: Policy, politics and digital innovation in Singapore. *Policy and Society*, *39*(3), 335–351. PMID: 35039726

Lee, H.. (2022). Health disparities and bias in machine learning models for medical imaging. *Radiology. Artificial Intelligence*, *4*(2), e210179.

Lee, J. (2022). Algorithmic bias and the New Chicago School. *Law, Innovation and Technology*, *14*(1), 95–112. DOI: 10.1080/17579961.2022.2047520

Lee, S. Y., Díaz-Puente, J. M., & Martin, S. (2019). The Contribution of Open Government to Prosperity of Society. *International Journal of Public Administration*, *42*(2), 144–157. DOI: 10.1080/01900692.2017.1405446

Leiser, M., & Murray, A. (2016). Non-state actors in AI governance. Technology and Regulation Journal, 2016, 1–14. https://doi.org/DOI: 10.26116/techreg.2016.001

Lewis, K. (2023). Colonising the narrative space: Unliveable lives, unseeable struggles and the necropolitical governance of digital populations. *Information Communication and Society*, *26*(12), 2398–2418. DOI: 10.1080/1369118X.2023.2230260

Lexology. (2024). Innovation Law insights. https://www.lexology.com/library/detail.aspx?g=0e955715-4e58-450d-8ffe-d6dccd4117d5 (Accessed: May 9, 2025).

Linders, D. (2012). From e-government to we-government: Defining a typology for citizen coproduction in the age of social media. *Government Information Quarterly*, *29*(4), 446–454. DOI: 10.1016/j.giq.2012.06.003

Lin, P., Abney, K., & Bekey, G. A. (2012). *Robot Ethics: The Ethical and Social Implications of Robotics*. MIT Press.

Li, X., & Wang, J. (2024). Should government chatbots behave like civil servants? The effect of chatbot identity characteristics on citizen experience. *Government Information Quarterly*, *41*(3), 101957. Advance online publication. DOI: 10.1016/j.giq.2024.101957

Li, Y., & Liu, Q. (2021). A comprehensive review study of cyber-attacks and cyber security; Emerging trends and recent developments. *Energy Reports*, *7*, 8176–8186. DOI: 10.1016/j.egyr.2021.08.126

London, A. J. (2019). Artificial Intelligence and Black-Box Medical Decisions: Accuracy versus Explainability. *The Hastings Center Report*, *49*(1), 15–21. DOI: 10.1002/hast.973 PMID: 30790315

Longo, J. (2022). When artificial intelligence meets real public administration. *Canadian Public Administration*, *65*(2), 384–388. DOI: 10.1111/capa.12465

Looks, H., Fangmann, J., Thomaschewski, J., Escalona, M. J., & Schön, E. M. (2024). Towards improving agility in Public Administration. *Software Quality Journal*, *32*(1), 283–311. DOI: 10.1007/s11219-023-09657-x

Loukis, E. N., Maragoudakis, M., & Kyriakou, N. (2020). Artificial intelligence-based public sector data analytics for economic crisis policymaking. *Transforming Government: People. Transforming Government*, *14*(4), 639–662. DOI: 10.1108/TG-11-2019-0113

Loukis, E., Maragoudakis, M., & Kyriakou, N. (2019). *Economic Crisis Policy Analytics Based on Artificial Intelligence*., DOI: 10.1007/978-3-030-27325-5_20

Luckin, R., Holmes, W., Griffiths, M., & Forcier, L. B. (2016). *Intelligence Unleashed: An Argument for AI in education*. Pearson.

Lum, K., & Isaac, W. (2016). To predict and serve? *Significance*, *13*(5), 14–19. DOI: 10.1111/j.1740-9713.2016.00960.x

Luo, J., Liu, P., Xu, W., Zhao, T., & Biljecki, F. (2024). A perception-powered urban digital twin to support human-centered urban planning and sustainable city development. *Cities (London, England)*, *156*, 105473. DOI: 10.1016/j.cities.2024.105473

Lutsenko, K. (2024). Digitalisation of public administration: Challenges and prospects. *Health Leadership and Quality of Life*, *3*. Advance online publication. DOI: 10.56294/hl2024.434

Ma'rup, M., & Rokhman, A. (2024). Utilization of Artificial Intelligence (AI) Chatbots in Improving Public Services: A Meta-Analysis Study. *Open Access Indonesia Journal of Social Sciences*, *7*(4), 1610–1618. DOI: 10.37275/oaijss.v7i4.255

Maciejewski, M. (2017). To do more, better, faster and more cheaply: Using big data in public administration. *International Review of Administrative Sciences*, *83*(1, suppl), 120–135. DOI: 10.1177/0020852316640058

Madan, R., & Ashok, M. (2023). AI adoption and diffusion in public administration: A systematic literature review and future research agenda. *Government Information Quarterly*, *40*(1), 1–18. DOI: 10.1016/j.giq.2022.101774

Madise, Ü., & Martens, T. (2006). E-voting in Estonia 2005. The first practice of country-wide binding Internet voting in the world. *Electronic Voting*, *86*(3), 15–26.

Makasi, T., Nili, A., Desouza, K., & Tate, M. (2020). Chatbot-mediated public service delivery: A public service value-based framework. *First Monday*, *25*(12). Advance online publication. DOI: 10.5210/fm.v25i12.10598

Makasi, T., Nili, A., Desouza, K., & Tate, M. (2022, January). Public service values and chatbots in the public sector: Reconciling designer efforts and user expectations. In *Proceedings of the 55th Hawaii International Conference on System Sciences*. DOI: 10.24251/HICSS.2022.292

Manny, L., Duygan, M., Fischer, M., & Rieckermann, J. (2021). Barriers to the digital transformation of infrastructure sectors. *Policy Sciences*, *54*(4), 943–983. DOI: 10.1007/s11077-021-09438-y PMID: 34751195

Manoharan, A., Melitski, J., & Holzer, M. (2022). Digital Governance: An Assessment of Performance and Best Practices. *Public Organization Review*, *23*(1), 265–283. DOI: 10.1007/s11115-021-00584-8

Mansoor, M. A., Ali, M., Mateen, A., Kaleem, M., & Nazir, S. (2023). Blockchain Technology for Land Registry Management in Developing Countries. *2023 2nd International Conference on Emerging Trends in Electrical, Control, and Telecommunication Engineering (ETECTE)*, 1–6. DOI: 10.1109/ETECTE59617.2023.10396736

Mansour, T., & Bick, M. (2024). How can physicians adopt AI-based applications in the United Arab Emirates to improve patient outcomes? *Digital Health*, *10*, 20552076241284936. Advance online publication. DOI: 10.1177/20552076241284936 PMID: 39351313

Mao, Z., Zhang, W., Zou, Q., & Deng, W. (2024). E-katılımın söz hakkı ve hesap verebilirlik Mao, Z., Zhang, W., Zou, Q., & Deng, W. (2024). The effects of e-participation on voice and accountability: Are there differences between countries? *Information Technology for Development*, *31*(2), 473–498. DOI: 10.1080/02681102.2024.2373745

Maragno, G., Tangi, L., Gastaldi, L., & Benedetti, M. (2023). AI as an organizational agent to nurture effectively introducing chatbots in public entities. *Public Management Review, 25*(11), 2135–2165. DOI: 10.1080/14719037.2022.2063935

Maramieri, J. (2014). Open Government Data: A citizen's right or a concession of public authorities? *Journal of E-Learning and Knowledge Society, 10*(2). https://doi.org/https://doi.org/10.20368/1971-8829/928

Marcus, G. (2022). Artificial Intelligence: The Challenges of Trustworthy AI. *Daedalus, 151*(2), 130–144.

Margetts, H., & Dunleavy, P. (2013). The Second Wave of Digital-Era Governance. *Philosophical Transactions of the Royal Society A: Mathematical, Physical and Engineering Sciences*, 371(1987), 20120382.

Margetts, H., & Dunleavy, P. (2013). The second wave of digital-era governance: A quasi-paradigm for government on the Web. *Philosophical Transactions of the Royal Society A: Mathematical, Physical and Engineering Sciences, 371*(1987), 20120382.

Margetts, H., & Dorobantu, C. (2019). Rethink government with AI. *Nature Human Behaviour, 3*, 14–16. PMID: 30967667

Margetts, H., & Dorobantu, C. (2024). Rethinking public policy in the age of AI: A socio-technical perspective. *Policy and Internet, 16*(1), 5–20. DOI: 10.1002/poi3.234

Marini, F. (1971). *Toward a new public administration: The Minnowbrook perspective*. Chandler Publishing.

Martinson, P. (2019). *Estonia – the Digital Republic Secured by Blockchain.*

Matheus, R., & Janssen, M. (2020). A Systematic Literature Study to Unravel Transparency Enabled by Open Government Data: The Window Theory. *Public Performance & Management Review, 43*(3), 503–534. DOI: 10.1080/15309576.2019.1691025

Matnenko, N. N. (2020). Digital Transformation of the Public Sector off the Economy. *Scientific Journal Economic Systems, 13*(3), 32–44. DOI: 10.29030/2309-2076-2020-13-3-32-44

Mavrogiorgos, K., Kiourtis, A., Mavrogiorgou, A., Menychtas, A., & Kyriazis, D. (2024). Bias in Machine Learning: A Literature Review. *Applied Sciences (Basel, Switzerland), 14*(19), 8860. Advance online publication. DOI: 10.3390/app14198860

Mayer, R. C., Davis, J. H., & Schoorman, F. D. (1995). An Integrative Model of Organizational Trust. *Academy of Management Review, 20*(3), 709–734. DOI: 10.2307/258792

McCarthy, J., Minsky, M., Rochester, N., & Shannon, C. E. (1956). *A Proposal for the Dartmouth Summer Research Project on Artificial Intelligence*. Dartmouth College.

McQuiston, J., & Manoharan, A. P. (2021). E-government and information technology coursework in public administration programs in Asia. *Teaching Public Administration, 39*(2), 210–226. DOI: 10.1177/0144739420978249

Medaglia, R., Mikalef, P., & Tangi, L. (2024). Competences and governance practices for artificial intelligence in the public sector. Publications Office of the European Union. JRC138702.

Medaglia, R., Gil-García, J. R., & Pardo, T. A. (2023). Artificial intelligence in government: Taking stock and moving forward. *Social Science Computer Review, 41*(1), 123–140. DOI: 10.1177/08944393211034087

Megahed, N. A., & Abdel-Kader, R. F. (2022). Smart Cities after COVID-19: Building a conceptual framework through a multidisciplinary perspective. *Scientific African, 17*, e01374. Advance online publication. DOI: 10.1016/j.sciaf.2022.e01374 PMID: 36128003

Meijer, A. (2015). E-governance innovation: Barriers and strategies. *Government Information Quarterly, 32*(2), 198–206. DOI: 10.1016/j.giq.2015.01.001

Meijer, A., Curtin, D., & Hillebrandt, M. (2019). Open government: Connecting vision and voice. *International Review of Administrative Sciences, 85*(2), 311–316. DOI: 10.1177/0020852311429533

Mergel, I. (2015). Opening Government: Designing Open Innovation Processes to Collaborate With External Problem Solvers. *Social Science Computer Review, 33*(5), 599–612. DOI: 10.1177/0894439314560851

Mergel, I. (2019). Digital service teams in government. *Government Information Quarterly, 36*(4), 101389. DOI: 10.1016/j.giq.2019.07.001

Mergel, I., Edelmann, N., & Haug, N. (2020). Defining digital transformation: Results from expert interviews. *Government Information Quarterly, 37*(4), 101385. DOI: 10.1016/j.giq.2019.06.002

Mergel, I., Kleibrink, A., & Sörvik, J. (2018). Open data outcomes: U.S. cities between product and process innovation. *Government Information Quarterly, 35*(4), 622–632. DOI: 10.1016/j.giq.2018.09.004

Mexhid Ferati, F. D. (2020). *Z. K.* Open Government Data Through the Lens of Universal Design. In Universal Access in Human-Computer Interaction. Applications and Practice., DOI: 10.1007/978-3-030-49108-6_24

Mezquita, Y., Parra, J., Perez, E., Prieto, J., & Corchado, J. M. (2021). *Blockchain-Based Systems in Land Registry, A Survey of Their Use and Economic Implications* (pp. 13–22). DOI: 10.1007/978-3-030-57805-3_2

Mihus, I., Zahorskyi, V., & Lipentsev, A. (2024). Navigation in e-government: The role of artificial intelligence in the formation of the legal framework for the protection of intellectual property rights. *Public Administration and Law Review, 3*(19), 17–34. DOI: 10.36690/2674-5216-2024-3-17-34

Mijwil, M., Youssef Filali, , Mohammad Aljanabi, , Mariem Bounabi, , & Humam Al-Shahwani, . (2023). The Purpose of Cybersecurity Governance in the Digital Transformation of Public Services and Protecting the Digital Environment. *Mesopotamian Journal of CyberSecurity, 2023*, 1–6. DOI: 10.58496/MJCS/2023/001

Mikalef, P., Lemmer, K., Schaefer, C., Ylinen, M., Fjørtoft, S. O., Torvatn, H. Y., Gupta, M., & Niehaves, B. (2022). Enabling AI capabilities in government agencies: A study of determinants for European municipalities. *Government Information Quarterly, 39*(4), 1–14. DOI: 10.1016/j.giq.2021.101596

Ministry of Economic Affairs and Communications. (2021). *Estonian rural broadband initiative: Final implementation report.* https://www.mkm.ee/en/reports

Ministry of Economic Affairs and Communications. (2023). *Multilingual accessibility framework for digital public services.* https://www.mkm.ee/en/reports

Ministry of Finance. (2020). *Tax policy for digital inclusion.* https://www.rahandusministeerium.ee/en/publications

Ministry of Industry and Technology. (2021). *National Artificial Intelligence Strategy (2021–2025).*

Mishra, A. K., Tyagi, A. K., Dananjayan, S., Rajavat, A., Rawat, H., & Rawat, A. (2024). Revolutionizing government operations: The impact of artificial intelligence in public administration. *Conversational Artificial Intelligence*, 607-634.

Mishra, A. K., Tyagi, A. K., Dananjayan, S., Rajavat, A., Rawat, H., & Rawat, A. (2024). Revolutionizing government operations: The impact of artificial intelligence in public administration. In Rawat, R., Chakrawarti, R. K., Sarangi, S. K., Rajavat, A., Alamanda, M. S., Srividya, K., & Sankaran, K. S. (Eds.), *Conversational Artificial Intelligence* (pp. 607–634). John Wiley & Sons., DOI: 10.1002/9781394200801.ch34

Misuraca, G., & Van Noordt, C. (2020). AI Watch - Artificial Intelligence in public services, EUR 30255 EN, Publications Office of the European Union, Luxembourg. ISBN 978-92-76-19540-5, , JRC120399.DOI: 10.2760/039619

Misuraca, G., & van Noordt, C. (2020). *AI Watch – Artificial Intelligence in Public Services: Overview of the use and impact of AI in public services in the EU*. Publications Office of the European Union.

Mitchell, T. M. (1997). *Machine Learning*. McGraw-Hill.

Mittelstadt, B. D., Allo, P., Taddeo, M., Wachter, S., & Floridi, L. (2016). The Ethics of Algorithms: Mapping the Debate. *Big Data & Society*, *3*(2), 2053951716679679. Advance online publication. DOI: 10.1177/2053951716679679

Mkrtchyan, T., & Melkumyan, N. (2023). The Foundations of Digital Transformation of the Public Administration System. *Alternative*, •••, 118–127. DOI: 10.55528/18292828-2023.2-118

Moe, N. B., & Mikalsen, M. (2020). Large-Scale Agile Transformation: A Case Study of Transforming Business, Development and Operations. In Lecture notes in business information processing (p. 115). Springer Science+Business Media. DOI: 10.1007/978-3-030-49392-9_8

Monteiro, P., & Adler, P. S. (2022). Bureaucracy for the 21st century: Clarifying and expanding our view of bureaucratic organization. *The Academy of Management Annals*, *16*(2), 427–475. DOI: 10.5465/annals.2019.0059

Moon, M. J. (2002). The evolution of e-government among municipalities: Rhetoric or reality? *Public Administration Review*, *62*(4), 424–433. DOI: 10.1111/0033-3352.00196

Moore, M. H. (1995). *Creating Public Value: Strategic Management in Government*. Harvard University Press.

Moreira, J., & Naranjo-Zolotov, M. (2023). Exploring potential drivers of citizen's acceptance of artificial intelligence use in e-government. In *Proceedings of the 16th International Conference on Theory and Practice of Electronic Governance* (pp. 336–345). Springer. DOI: 10.1007/978-3-031-45648-0_33

Mountasser, T., & Abdellatif, M. (2023). Digital Transformation in Public Administration: A Systematic Literature Review. *International Journal of Professional Business Review*, *8*(10), e02372. DOI: 10.26668/businessreview/2023.v8i10.2372

Muiderman, K., Vervoort, J., Gupta, A., Norbert-Munns, R. P., Veeger, M., Muzammil, M., & Driessen, P. (2023). Is anticipatory governance opening up or closing down future possibilities? Findings from diverse contexts in the Global South. *Global Environmental Change*, *81*, 102694. DOI: 10.1016/j.gloenvcha.2023.102694

Mukherjee, D., Lim, W. M., Kumar, S., & Donthu, N. (2022). Guidelines for advancing theory and practice through bibliometric research. *Journal of Business Research, 148*(May), 101–115. DOI: 10.1016/j.jbusres.2022.04.042

Naik, K., Goyal, R. K., Foschini, L., Chak, C. M., Thielscher, C., Zhu, H., Lu, J., Lehár, J., Pacanoswki, M. A., Terranova, N., Mehta, N., Korsbo, N., Fakhouri, T., Liu, Q., & Gobburu, J. (2023). Current Status and Future Directions: The Application of Artificial Intelligence/Machine Learning for Precision Medicine. *Clinical Pharmacology and Therapeutics, 115*(4), 673–686. DOI: 10.1002/cpt.3152 PMID: 38103204

Nandini, N., Indora, P., & Singh, R.R K Singh. (2024). Artificial Intelligence in Journalism: An Overview of its Applications and Uses. *Journal of Communication Management (London), 3*(3), 237–242. DOI: 10.58966/JCM2024337

Nanos, I., Manthou, V., & Androutsou, E. (2019). *Cloud Computing Adoption Decision in E-government.*, DOI: 10.1007/978-3-319-95666-4_9

Nascimento Silva, P., & Nascimento Silva, S. (2025). Open government data in health sector: A systematic literature review open government data in health sector. *BMC Public Health, 25*(1), 47. Advance online publication. DOI: 10.1186/s12889-024-21149-6 PMID: 39762782

Network360. (2025). Smart City: Comune di Milano with Cyclomedia for Mapping the City into a Digital Twin. https://www.zerounoweb.it/iot/smart-city-comune-di-milano-con-cyclomedia-per-mappare-il-capoluogo-in-un-digital-twin/ (Accessed: August 18, 2025).

Neumann, O., Guirguis, K., & Steiner, R. (2024). Exploring artificial intelligence adoption in public organizations: A comparative case study. *Public Management Review, 26*(1), 114–141. DOI: 10.1080/14719037.2022.2048685

Newman, J., Mintrom, M., & O'Neill, D. (2022). Digital technologies, artificial intelligence, and bureaucratic transformation. *Futures, 136*, 102886. DOI: 10.1016/j.futures.2021.102886

Nielsen, M. M. (2017). eGovernance and Online Service Delivery in Estonia. *Proceedings of the 18th Annual International Conference on Digital Government Research*, 300–309. DOI: 10.1145/3085228.3085284

Nikiforova, A. (2020). Timeliness of Open Data in Open Government Data Portals through Pandemic-related Data: A long data way from the publisher to the user. *2020 4th International Conference on Multimedia Computing, Networking and Applications, MCNA 2020*, 131–138. DOI: 10.1109/MCNA50957.2020.9264298

Nikiforova, A., & McBride, K. (2021). Open government data portal usability: A user-centred usability analysis of 41 open government data portals. *Telematics and Informatics, 58*(December 2020), 101539. DOI: 10.1016/j.tele.2020.101539

Nikiforova, A., Rizun, N., Ciesielska, M., Alexopoulos, C., & Miletić, A. (2023). Towards High-Value Datasets Determination for Data-Driven Development: A Systematic Literature Review. In L. I., C. C., K. E., T. E., J. M., Z. A., V. P. G., & V. S. (Eds.), *Lecture Notes in Computer Science (including subseries Lecture Notes in Artificial Intelligence and Lecture Notes in Bioinformatics): Vol. 14130 LNCS* (pp. 211–229). Springer Science and Business Media Deutschland GmbH. DOI: 10.1007/978-3-031-41138-0_14

Nikiforova, A., & Lnenicka, M. (2021). A multi-perspective knowledge-driven approach for analysis of the demand side of the Open Government Data portal. *Government Information Quarterly, 38*(4), 101622. DOI: 10.1016/j.giq.2021.101622

Nirala, K. K., Singh, N. K., & Purani, V. S. (2022). A survey on providing customer and public administration based services using AI-chatbot. *Multimedia Tools and Applications, 81*(16), 22215–22246. DOI: 10.1007/s11042-021-11458-y PMID: 35002470

Nirala, K. K., Singh, N. K., & Purani, V. S. (2022). AI-Chatbot to determine citizen centric solution of Aadhaar Card services in Public Administration: Aadhaarbot. *Bengal, Past & Present, 140*(VII), 37–48.

Nishant, R., Schneckenberg, D., & Ravishankar, M. (2023). The formal rationality of artificial intelligence-based algorithms and the problem of bias. *Journal of Information Technology, 39*(1), 19–40. DOI: 10.1177/02683962231176842

NIST. (2020). *Zero Trust Architecture*. National Institute of Standards and Technology, Special Publication 800–207.

Noble, S. U. (2018). *Algorithms of Oppression: How Search Engines Reinforce Racism*. NYU Press. DOI: 10.18574/nyu/9781479833641.001.0001

Nogueira, V. B., Teixeira, D. G., de Lima, I. A. C. N., Moreira, M. V. C., de Oliveira, B. S. C., Pedrosa, I. M. B., Queiroz, J. W., & Jerônimo, S. M. B. (2021). Towards an inclusive digital literacy: An experimental intervention study in a rural area of Brazil. *Education and Information Technologies, 27*(2), 2807–2834. DOI: 10.1007/s10639-021-10711-z PMID: 34493924

Norris, D. F., & Kraemer, K. L. (1996). Mainframe and PC Computing in American Local Governments: Myths and Realities. *Public Administration Review, 56*(6), 568–576. DOI: 10.2307/977255

Norris, P. (2001). *Digital divide: Civic engagement, information poverty, and the Internet worldwide*. Cambridge University Press. DOI: 10.1017/CBO9781139164887

Nzobonimpa, S. (2023). Artificial intelligence, task complexity and uncertainty: Analyzing the advantages and disadvantages of using algorithms in public service delivery under public administration theories. *Digital Transformation and Society*, 2(3), 219–234. DOI: 10.1108/DTS-03-2023-0018

O'Neil, C. (2016). *Weapons of Math Destruction: How Big Data Increases Inequality and Threatens Democracy*. Crown Publishing Group.

Obermeyer, Z., & Emanuel, E. J. (2016). Predicting the future—Big data, machine learning, and clinical medicine. *The New England Journal of Medicine*, *375*(13), 1216–1219. DOI: 10.1056/NEJMp1606181 PMID: 27682033

Obermeyer, Z., Powers, B., Vogeli, C., & Mullainathan, S. (2019). Dissecting racial bias in an algorithm used to manage the health of populations. *Science*, *366*(6464), 447–453. DOI: 10.1126/science.aax2342 PMID: 31649194

Obolonsky, Y. V. (2022). Digital Transformation of Public Administration. *Ekonomika I Upravlenie: Problemy, Resheniya, 10/1*(130), 103–109. DOI: 10.36871/ek.up.p.r.2022.10.01.014

OECD. (2003). *The e-government imperative*. Organisation for Economic Co-operation and Development.

OECD. (2019). *Artificial Intelligence in Society*. OECD Publishing.

OECD. (2019). *The Path to Becoming a Data-Driven Public Sector*. OECD Digital Government Studies.

OECD. (2020). *AI and the Future of Skills*. OECD Publishing.

OECD. (2020). *Digital Government in Chile: Digital Transformation and Public Sector Innovation*. OECD Digital Government Studies.

OECD. (2020). Digital Government Index: 2019 Results. OECD Public Governance Policy Papers, No. 03.

OECD. (2020). The Ethical Use of Artificial Intelligence in the Public Sector.

OECD. (2020). The OECD Digital Government Policy Framework.

OECD. (2020). The OECD Digital Government Policy Framework: Six dimensions of a Digital Government. In *OECD Public Governance Policy Papers, No. 02*. OECD Publishing., DOI: 10.1787/f64fed2a-

OECD. (2020). The OECD Digital Government Policy Framework: Six Dimensions of a Digitally-Enabled Public Sector.

OECD. (2021). *Bridging the Digital Divide.* OECD Publishing.

OECD. (2021). Principles on Artificial Intelligence.

OECD. (2021). Recommendation of the Council on the Governance of Critical Risks.

OECD. (2021). *Recommendation on Artificial Intelligence in the Public Sector.* OECD Publishing.

OECD. (2025). AI in Estonia. https://oecd.ai/en/dashboards/countries/Estonia

Olanipekun, S. O.Samson Olufemi Olanipekun. (2025). Ethical frameworks for AI in journalism: Balancing technological innovation and journalistic integrity. *World Journal of Advanced Research and Reviews, 25*(1), 1342–1351. DOI: 10.30574/wjarr.2025.25.1.0187

Olivi, G. (2025). Seeds and Sparks: Italy's Journey to AI. *Dentons.* https://www.dentons.com/en/insights/articles/2025/march/27/seeds-and-sparks-italys-journey-to-ai (Accessed: May 9, 2025).

Ömürgönülşen, U. (2014). Kamu sektörünün yönetimi sorununa yeni bir yaklaşım: Yeni kamu işletmeciliği. In Acar, M., & Özgür, H. (Eds.), *Çağdaş kamu yönetimi I: Konular, kuramlar, kavramlar* (pp. 1–35). Nobel Yayıncılık.

Onabanjo A., E. (2024). Digital Transformation: The impact of AI on Cloud Transformation. *Journal of Artificial Intelligence General Science (JAIGS) ISSN:3006-4023, 5*(1), 174–183. DOI: 10.60087/jaigs.v5i1.188

Ongaro, E. (2006). The dynamics of devolution processes in legalistic countries: Organizational change in the Italian public sector. *Public Administration, 84*(3), 737–770. DOI: 10.1111/j.1467-9299.2006.00610.x

Orhan, G., & Yalçın, S. (2015). Yönetişim ve kamu yönetimi. *Kamu Yönetimi Dergisi, 47*(1), 175–190.

Origlia, C., Cersosimo, D., Bianchi, T., & Fortunato, A. (2016). Assessing an Open Government Data Initiative. The Case of OpenCoesione. *2016 Conference for E-Democracy and Open Government (CeDEM)*, 164–171. DOI: 10.1109/CeDEM.2016.26

OSTP. (2019). *Guidance for Regulation of Artificial Intelligence Applications.* Office of Science and Technology Policy.

Owens, M. A., Ravi, V., & Hunter, E. J. (2023). Digital Inclusion as a Lens for Equitable Parent Engagement. *TechTrends*. Advance online publication. DOI: 10.1007/s11528-023-00859-5 PMID: 37362590

Özgür, H. (2014). Yeni Kamu Yönetimi Hareketi. Çağdaş Kamu Yönetimi 1. Nobel yayınları, Ankara.

Ozmen Garibay, O., Winslow, B., Andolina, S., Antona, M., Bodenschatz, A., Coursaris, C., Falco, G., Fiore, S. M., Garibay, I., Grieman, K., Havens, J. C., Jirotka, M., Kacorri, H., Karwowski, W., Kider, J., Konstan, J., Koon, S., Lopez-Gonzalez, M., Maifeld-Carucci, I., & Xu, W. (2023). Six human-centered artificial intelligence grand challenges. *International Journal of Human-Computer Interaction, 39*(3), 391–437. DOI: 10.1080/10447318.2022.2153320

Pakhnenko, O., & Kuan, Z. (2023). Ethics of digital innovation in public administration. *Business Ethics and Leadership*, *7*(1), 113–121. DOI: 10.21272/bel.7(1).113-121.2023

Palmirani, M., Martoni, M., & Girardi, D. (2014). Open Government Data Beyond Transparency. *Electronic Government and the Information Systems Perspective (EGOVIS 2014)*, 275–291. DOI: 10.1007/978-3-319-10178-1_22

Panagiotopoulos, P., Klievink, B., & Cordella, A. (2019). Public value creation in digital government. *Government Information Quarterly*, *36*(4), 101421. DOI: 10.1016/j.giq.2019.101421

Parasuraman, R., & Riley, V. (1997). Humans and Automation: Use, Misuse, Disuse, Abuse. *Human Factors*, *39*(2), 230–253. DOI: 10.1518/001872097778543886

Pariser, E. (2011). *The Filter Bubble: What the Internet Is Hiding from You*. Penguin Press.

Pasquale, F. (2015). *The Black Box Society: The Secret Algorithms That Control Money and Information*. Harvard University Press. DOI: 10.4159/harvard.9780674736061

Patwari, S., Ashish, S. S., Vashisht, A., Rajpurohit, E., & K, V. (2024). Digital Transformation in Various Sectors of the Indian Economy. *2024 8th International Conference on Computational System and Information Technology for Sustainable Solutions (CSITSS)*, 1–6. DOI: 10.1109/CSITSS64042.2024.10816887

Pedreschi, D., Giannotti, F., Guidotti, R., Monreale, A., Ruggieri, S., & Turini, F. (2019, July). Meaningful explanations of black box AI decision systems. *Proceedings of the AAAI Conference on Artificial Intelligence*, *33*(01), 9780–9784. DOI: 10.1609/aaai.v33i01.33019780

Pedwell, C. (2024). Speculative machines and us: More-than-human intuition and the algorithmic condition. *Cultural Studies*, *38*(2), 188–218. DOI: 10.1080/09502386.2022.2142805

Pencheva, I., Esteve, M., & Mikhaylov, S. J. (2020). Big data and AI–transformational shift for government: So, what next for research? *Public Policy and Administration*, *35*(1), 24–44. DOI: 10.1177/0952076718780537

Phillips, P. J., Hahn, C. A., Fontana, P. C., Broniatowski, D. A., & Przybocki, M. A. (2021). *Four principles of explainable artificial intelligence* (NIST Interagency/Internal Report No. 8312). National Institute of Standards and Technology.

Phuangthuean, P., & Nuansang, J. (2024). The transforming public administration: The role of AI in shaping the future. *Journal of Social Science and Multidisciplinary Research*, *1*(3), 21–41.

Pica-Alfano, L. (n.d.). Ten local government chatbots that are making a difference. Retrieved from: https://govlaunch.com/stories/ten-local-government-chatbots-that-are-making-a-difference, June 2025.

Pilving, I., & Mikiver, M. (2020). A Kratt as an administrative body: Algorithmic decisions and principles of administrative law. *Juridica International*, *29*, 47–61. DOI: 10.12697/JI.2020.29.05

Plantinga, P. (2024). Digital discretion and public administration in Africa: Implications for the use of artificial intelligence. *Information Development*, *40*(2), 332–352. DOI: 10.1177/02666669221117526

Polkowski, Z., & Jozwiak, M. (2021). Internet of things in public administration. In *2021 Fourth International Conference on Computational Intelligence and Communication Technologies (CCICT)* (pp. 343-349). IEEE.

Pollina, E. (2025, May 19). Italy's Data Watchdog Fines AI Company Replika's Developer €5.6 million. *Reuters*. https://www.reuters.com/sustainability/boards-policy-regulation/italys-data-watchdog-fines-ai-company-replikas-developer-56-million-2025-05-19 (Accessed: May 20, 2025).

Pollina, E., & Armellini, A. (2025, January 28). Italy Regulator Seeks Information from DeepSeek on Data Protection. *Reuters*. https://www.reuters.com/technology/artificial-intelligence/italy-regulator-seeks-info-deepseek-data-protection-2025-01-28 (Accessed: May 9, 2025).

Pollitt, C., & Bouckaert, G. (2017). *Public management reform: A comparative analysis-into the age of austerity*. Oxford university press.

Pozgar, G. D. (2023). *Legal and Ethical Issues for Health Professionals with Navigate Advantage Access*. Jones & Bartlett Learning.

Radziwill, N. (2018). *Quality 4.0: Let's Get Digital - The many ways the fourth industrial revolution is reshaping the way we think about quality*.

Raji, I. D., & Buolamwini, J. (2019). "Actionable Auditing: Investigating the Impact of Publicly Naming Biased Performance Results of Commercial AI Products." *AAAI/ACM Conference on AI, Ethics, and Society*, 429–435. DOI: 10.1145/3306618.3314244

Rane, N., Choudhary, S. P., & Rane, J. (2024). Acceptance of artificial intelligence: Key factors, challenges, and implementation strategies. *Journal of Applied Artificial Intelligence*, *5*(2), 50–70. DOI: 10.48185/jaai.v5i2.1017

Rathnayake, A. S., Nguyen, T. D. H. N., & Ahn, Y. (2025). Factors Influencing AI Chatbot Adoption in Government Administration: A Case Study of Sri Lanka's Digital Government. *Administrative Sciences*, *15*(5), 157. DOI: 10.3390/admsci15050157

Reginato, E., Fadda, I., & Paglietti, P. (2016). The influence of resistance to change on public-sector reform implementation: The case of Italian municipalities' internal control system. *International Journal of Public Administration*, *39*(12), 989–999. DOI: 10.1080/01900692.2015.1068325

Republic of Estonia Information System Authority. (2025). The Vision of Bürokratt. https://www.ria.ee/en/state-information-system/personal-services/burokratt (Accessed: August 18, 2025).

Reuters. (2024). *California DMV puts 42 million car titles on blockchain to fight fraud*. https://www.reuters.com/technology/california-dmv-puts-42-million-car-titles-blockchain-fight-fraud-2024-07-30/

Ricart, G., Gonzalez, J., Papanikolaou, V., Santer, H., Clari, F., Sarris, N., Van Daele, P., & Tavernier, W. (2020). The Next Generation Internet Initiative. In *ICT Policy, Research, and Innovation* (pp. 217–253). Wiley. DOI: 10.1002/9781119632481.ch9

Rice, N. F. (2019). Estonia's digital embassies and the concept of sovereignty. https://georgetownsecuritystudiesreview.org/2019/10/10/estonias-digital-embassies-and-the-concept-of-sovereignty/

Richardson, R., Schultz, J. M., & Crawford, K. (2019). Dirty Data, Bad Predictions: How Civil Rights Violations Impact Police Data, Predictive Policing Systems, and Justice. *New York University Law Review*, *94*(1), 192–233.

Riigi Teataja. (2025). Consolidated texts of English translations of Estonian legislation. https://www.riigiteataja.ee/en/

Riisalo, T. (2023, October 18). Artificial Intelligence is part of the next chapter in Estonia's Digital Story. PublicTechnology. https://www.publictechnology.net/2023/10/18/government-and-politics/artificial-intelligence-is-part-of-the-next-chapter-in-estonias-digital-story/

Rizal Batubara, F., Ubacht, J., & Janssen, M. (2019). Unraveling Transparency and Accountability in Blockchain. *Proceedings of the 20th Annual International Conference on Digital Government Research*, 204–213. DOI: 10.1145/3325112.3325262

Roa, H. N., Loza-Aguirre, E., & Flores, P. (2019). A survey on the problems affecting the development of open government data initiatives. *2019 6th International Conference on EDemocracy and EGovernment, ICEDEG 2019*, 157–163. DOI: 10.1109/ICEDEG.2019.8734452

Robinson, N., Hardy, A., & Ertan, A. (2022). Estonia: A Curious and Cautious Approach to Artificial Intelligence and National Security (2021). *SSRN, 2021*. Advance online publication. DOI: 10.2139/ssrn.4105328

Rohoza, A. (2024). Directions of digital transformation of analytical activities in public administration. *Actual Problems of Innovative Economy and Law*, *2024*(1), 41–45. DOI: 10.36887/2524-0455-2024-1-9

Roonemaa, M. (2017). Global lessons from Estonia's tech-savvy government. *UNESCO Courier*. https://courier.unesco.org/en/articles/global-lessons-estonias-tech-savvy-government

Rossi, A., & Lenzini, G. (2020). Transparency by design in data-informed research: A collection of information design patterns. *Computer Law & Security Review, 37*, 105402. DOI: 10.1016/j.clsr.2020.105402

Ruijer, E., & Meijer, A. (2020). Open Government Data as an Innovation Process: Lessons from a Living Lab Experiment. *Public Performance & Management Review*, *43*(3), 613–635. DOI: 10.1080/15309576.2019.1568884

Russell, S., & Norvig, P. (2021). *Artificial Intelligence: A Modern Approach* (4th ed.). Pearson.

Sabbagh, P. (2019). The Public Value of E-Government: A Blockchain-Based Approach. *European Integration Studies and International Conference Proceedings*, University of Verona.

Safarov, I. (2020). Institutional Dimensions of Open Government Data Implementation: Evidence from Transition Countries. *Public Performance & Management Review*, *43*(6), 1359–1389. DOI: 10.1080/15309576.2020.1805336

Saha, A. K., & Khan, I. (2025). Disaggregating air, water and renewable energy disclosures in developing economies: The role of regulatory impact and board characteristics. *Journal of Applied Accounting Research, 26*(2), 498–530. DOI: 10.1108/JAAR-08-2023-0233

Sah, C. K., & Chandavarkar, B. R. (2023). Adoption of Blockchain Technology in Land Registry Systems. *2023 Third International Conference on Secure Cyber Computing and Communication (ICSCCC)*, 548–553. DOI: 10.1109/ICSCCC58608.2023.10176550

Salah, M., Abdelfattah, F., & Al Halbusi, H. (2023). Generative artificial intelligence (ChatGPT & bard) in public administration research: A double-edged sword for street-level bureaucracy studies. *International Journal of Public Administration, Ahead-of-print*, 1–7. DOI: 10.1080/01900692.2023.2274801

Sandhu, K. (2021). *Advancing Cybersecurity for Digital Transformation.*, DOI: 10.4018/978-1-7998-6975-7.ch001

Saprudin, S. (2024). Artificial Intelligence Function Management in Supporting the Process of Government Implementation and Public Services in Indonesia. *Journal of Management and Administration Provision, 4*(1), 88–96. DOI: 10.55885/jmap.v4i1.352

Sarker, M. N. I., Wu, M., & Hossin, M. A. (2018). Smart governance through bigdata: Digital transformation of public agencies. In *2018 international conference on artificial intelligence and big data (ICAIBD)* (pp. 62-70). IEEE.

Sartor, G., & Lagioia, F. (2020). The impact of the General Data Protection Regulation (GDPR) on artificial intelligence.

Satkunanandan, S. (2019). Bureaucratic passions. *Law, Culture and the Humanities, 15*(1), 14–29. DOI: 10.1177/1743872115614801

Saura, J. R., Ribeiro-Soriano, D., & Palacios-Marqués, D. (2022). Assessing behavioral data science privacy issues in government artificial intelligence deployment. *Government Information Quarterly, 39*(4), 101679. DOI: 10.1016/j.giq.2022.101679

Sayogo, D. S., & Yuli, S. B. C. (2018). Critical success factors of open government and open data at local government level in Indonesia. *International Journal of Electronic Government Research, 14*(2), 28–43. DOI: 10.4018/IJEGR.2018040103

Scantamburlo, T., Cortés, A., Foffano, F., Barrué, C., Distefano, V., Pham, L., & Fabris, A. (2024). Artificial intelligence across europe: A study on awareness, attitude and trust. *IEEE Transactions on Artificial Intelligence*, •••, 1–14. DOI: 10.1109/TAI.2024.3461633

Schiff, D., Rakova, B., Ayesh, A., Fanti, A., & Lennon, M. (2020). Principles to practices for responsible AI: Closing the gap. *AI and Ethics Journal*, *1*(1), 1–17. DOI: 10.1007/s43681-020-00007-2

Schmager, S., Pappas, I., & Vasilakopoulou, P. (2024). Citizens-Focused Design Principles for Human-Centered AI in Public Services. AMCIS 2024 Proceedings.

Scholta, H., Mertens, W., Kowalkiewicz, M., & Becker, J. (2019). From one-stop shop to no-stop shop: An e-government stage model. *Government Information Quarterly*, *36*(1), 11–26. DOI: 10.1016/j.giq.2018.11.010

Schwab, K. (2023). *Dördüncü Sanayi Devrimi* (Çev. Zülfü Dicleli). Dünya Ekonomik Forumu. İstanbul: Optimist Yayınları.

Schwarz, G., Christensen, T., & Zhu, X. (2022). Bounded rationality, satisficing, artificial intelligence, and decision-making in public organizations: The contributions of Herbert Simon. *Public Administration Review, Ahead-of-print*, 1–9. DOI: 10.1111/puar.13540

Serac, C. A. (2023). Digital Transformation Vulnerabilities: Assessing The Risks and Strengthening Cyber Security. *The Annals of The University of Oradea. Economic Sciences, 3*(1), 771–781. Https://Doi.Org/10.47535/1991auoes32(1)059

Shaikh, F. K., Karim, S., Zeadally, S., & Nebhen, J. (2022). Recent Trends in Internet-of-Things-Enabled Sensor Technologies for Smart Agriculture. *IEEE Internet of Things Journal*, *9*(23), 23583–23598. DOI: 10.1109/JIOT.2022.3210154

Shao, D., Ishengoma, F. R., Alexopoulos, C., Saxena, S., Nikiforova, A., & Matheus, R. (2023). Integration of IoT into e-government. *Foresight*, *25*(5), 734–750. DOI: 10.1108/FS-04-2022-0048

Sharma, M., Paliwal, T., & Baniwal, P. (2024). Challenges in Digital Transformation and Automation for Industry 4.0. In AI-Driven IoT Systems for Industry 4.0 (pp. 143-163). CRC Press.

Shen, X., & Haldane, M. (2023). Blockchain-managed IDs arrive in China with new government-backed scheme aiming to reduce data leaks. *South China Morning Post*. https://www.scmp.com/tech/policy/article/3245028/blockchain-managed-ids-arrive-china-new-government-backed-scheme-aiming-reduce-data-leaks

Shevchenko, D., & Mihaylov, V. (2021). Digital Transformation of the Service Sector. *Scientific Research and Development. Economics of the Firm*, *10*(3), 41–54. DOI: 10.12737/2306-627X-2021-10-3-41-54

Shin, D. H. (2009). Ubiquitous city: Urban technologies, urban infrastructure and urban informatics. *Journal of Information Science*, *35*(5), 515–526. DOI: 10.1177/0165551509100832

Shi, Y., & Sun, L. (2024). How Generative AI Is Transforming Journalism: Development, Application and Ethics. *Journalism and Media*, *5*(2), 582–594. DOI: 10.3390/journalmedia5020039

Sholola, Y. A., Banjo, Y. O., Saliu-Yusuf, M. J., Ogundeyi, T. S., & Ayantunji, K. A.-A. (2024). Perceived effect of Artificial Intelligence on Ethical Journalism among Journalists in Kwara State. *International Journal of Research and Innovation in Social Science*, *2051*(II), 2051–2063. Advance online publication. DOI: 10.47772/IJRISS.2024.802145

Showkat Ahmad Dar. (2024). Unleashing the Power of Artificial Intelligence and Automation in Public Administration. *Journal of Public Administration Research*, *1*(1), 01–13. DOI: 10.32996/jpar.2024.1.1.1

Sienkiewicz-Małyjurek, K. (2023). Whether AI adoption challenges matter for public managers? The case of Polish cities. *Government Information Quarterly*, *40*(3), 1–19. DOI: 10.1016/j.giq.2023.101828

Sigfrids, A., Nieminen, M., Leikas, J., & Pikkuaho, P. (2022). How should public administrations foster the ethical development and use of artificial intelligence? A review of proposals for developing governance of AI. *Frontiers in Human Dynamics*, *4*, 1–19. DOI: 10.3389/fhumd.2022.858108

Singh, N., Misra, R., Quan, W., Radić, A., Lee, S.-M., & Han, H. (2024). An analysis of consumer's trusting beliefs towards the use of e-commerce platforms. *Humanities & Social Sciences Communications*, *11*(1), 899. Advance online publication. DOI: 10.1057/s41599-024-03395-6

Slade, S., & Prinsloo, P. (2013). Learning analytics: Ethical issues and dilemmas. *The American Behavioral Scientist*, *57*(10), 1510–1529. DOI: 10.1177/0002764213479366

Smith, J., & Marx, L. (2020). *Does technology drive history? The dilemma of technological determinism*. MIT Press., DOI: 10.7551/mitpress/9780262691673.001.0001

Sobacı, M. Z. (2012). E-devlet: Kuramsal bir bakış. In Sobacı, M. Z., & Yıldız, M. (Eds.), *E-Devlet: Kamu Yönetimi ve Teknoloji İlişkisinde Güncel Gelişmeler* (pp. 3–37). Nobel Yayınları.

Söker, B. (2024). Leveraging Artificial Intelligence for Public Sector Decision-Making: Balancing Accountability and Efficiency in Digital Public Services. *Human-Computer Interaction*, *8*(1), 105. DOI: 10.62802/ejr09s21

Sompie, S. R. U. A., Sambul, A. M., & Rumpesak, I. C. A. (2024). IoT-Based Monitoring and Control of a Hybrid Renewable Energy System Utilizing Solar and Microhydro Sources. *Journal of Sustainable Engineering Proceedings Series*, *2*(1), 23–28. DOI: 10.35793/joseps.v2i1.3942

Song, J. (2022). The implications of providing voice-based chatbots in public service for digital inclusion and public communication. OMNES. *The Journal of Multicultural Society*, *12*(2), 26–68. DOI: 10.14431/omnes.2022.07.12.2.26

Statistics Estonia. (2023). *Information society yearbook 2023*. https://www.stat.ee/publication-2023

Stempeck, M. (2024). How Italy's Government is Using AI. *Innovation in Politics Institute – Democracy Technologies*. https://democracy-technologies.org/ai-data/how-italys-government-uses-ai-data/ (Accessed: May 9, 2025).

Stoker, G. (2006). Public value management: A new narrative for networked governance? *American Review of Public Administration*, *36*(1), 41–57. DOI: 10.1177/0275074005282583

Storozhenko, L. (2023). Using Artificial Intelligence in Public Management: Aspects of Integration. *Krakowskie Studia Małopolskie*, *40*(4), 37–49. DOI: 10.15804/ksm20230403

Sund, T., Lööf, C., Nadjm-Tehrani, S., & Asplund, M. (2020). Blockchain-based event processing in supply chains—A case study at IKEA. *Robotics and Computer-integrated Manufacturing*, *65*, 101971. DOI: 10.1016/j.rcim.2020.101971

Sun, T. Q., & Medaglia, R. (2019). Mapping the Challenges of Artificial Intelligence in the Public Sector: Evidence from Public Healthcare. *Government Information Quarterly*, *36*(2), 368–383. DOI: 10.1016/j.giq.2018.09.008

Sun, W., Nasraoui, O., & Shafto, P. (2020). Evolution and impact of bias in human and machine learning algorithm interaction. *PLoS One*, *15*(8), e0235502. Advance online publication. DOI: 10.1371/journal.pone.0235502 PMID: 32790666

T.C. Sanayi ve Teknoloji Bakanlığı. (2021). National Artificial Intelligence Strategy (2021-2025).

Tai, K. T. (2021). Open government research over a decade: A systematic review. *Government Information Quarterly*, *38*(2), 101566. DOI: 10.1016/j.giq.2021.101566

TalTech. (2024). *Public understanding of algorithmic governance in Estonia*. https://www.taltech.ee/publications

Tamer, H. Y. (2025). AI-Based Chatbots as Civil Servants: A Utopia or a Dystopia? In Sevinç Çubuk, E. (Ed.), *Digital Competency Development for Public Officials: Adapting New Technologies in Public Services* (pp. 121–152). IGI Global Scientific Publishing., DOI: 10.4018/979-8-3693-6547-2.ch006

Tangi, L., Janssen, M., Benedetti, M., & Noci, G. (2021). Digital government transformation: A structural equation modelling analysis of driving and impeding factors. *International Journal of Information Management, 60*, 102356. DOI: 10.1016/j.ijinfomgt.2021.102356

Temel, Y., & Coşkun, B. (2024). A Review on Artificial Intelligence Applications in Education in Some Countries and Türkiye. *International Technology and Education Journal, 8*(1), 9–23.

Terzi, S., ... (2019). Blockchain 3.0 Smart Contracts in E-Government 3.0 Applications. arXiv preprint arXiv:1910.06092. https://arxiv.org/abs/1910.06092

Thais, S., Shumway, H., & Saragih, A. (2023). *Algorithmic bias: Looking beyond data bias to ensure algorithmic accountability and equity*. MIT Science Policy Review., DOI: 10.38105/spr.5lwvw66ssy

Thierer, A., Castillo O'Sullivan, A., & Russell, R. (2017). AI policy and regulatory issues. Mercatus Center Working Paper. https://www.mercatus.org/publications/technology-and-innovation/artificial-intelligence-policy-and-regulatory-issues

Tiger Leap Foundation. (2025). *Digital champions initiative: Impact evaluation.* https://www.tiigrihype.ee/reports

Topol, E. (2019). *Deep Medicine: How Artificial Intelligence can Make Healthcare Human Again*. Basic Books.

Torabi, Z.-A., Rezvani, M. R., Hall, C. M., & Allam, Z. (2023). On the post-pandemic travel boom: How capacity building and smart tourism technologies in rural areas can help - evidence from Iran. *Technological Forecasting and Social Change, 193*, 122633. DOI: 10.1016/j.techfore.2023.122633 PMID: 37223653

Totonchi, A. (2025). Artificial intelligence in e-government: Identifying and addressing key challenges. *Malaysian Journal of Information and Communication Technology, 10*, 10–24. https://myjict.utm.my/index.php/myjict/article/view/1234

Toufaily, É., Zalan, T., & Dhaou, S. B. (2021). A framework of blockchain technology adoption: An investigation of challenges and expected value. *Information & Management, 58*(3), 103444. DOI: 10.1016/j.im.2021.103444

Trist, E., & Emery, F. (2022). The socio-technical systems perspective. In *Organizational Change and Innovation Processes* (pp. 123–150). Springer., DOI: 10.1007/978-3-030-12345-6_6

Tuebou, B. F. (2024). The Digitization of Public Services and Its Contribution to the Quality of Service in Relation to User Satisfaction. *Open Journal of Applied Sciences, 14*(9), 2697–2716. DOI: 10.4236/ojapps.2024.149177

Turing, A. M. (1950). Computing Machinery and Intelligence. *Mind, 59*(236), 433–460. DOI: 10.1093/mind/LIX.236.433

Twizeyimana, J. D., & Andersson, A. (2019). The public value of E-Government – A literature review. *Government Information Quarterly, 36*(2), 167–178. DOI: 10.1016/j.giq.2019.01.001

Ugwu Jovita Nnenna, Ugwuanyi Ifeoma Perpetua, Asuma Mariita Nchaga, Tushabe Hadijah, E. M. and T. O. N. (2024). Challenges and Opportunities in Implementing Open Government Data Initiatives in East Africa. *International Academic Association Journal, 10(2):1-11.*

UN. (2022). *United Nations E-government Survey 2022: The Future of Digital Government.* United Nations Publishing.

UNESCO. (2021). Digital Inclusion: Connecting the Unconnected. .

UNESCO. (2021). Re-Shaping Policies for Creativity: Addressing Culture as a Global Public Good.

UNICEF. (2022). *Bridging the digital divide in Ida-Viru County.* https://www.unicef .org/estonia/reports

UNIDIR. (2018). *The Weaponization of Increasingly Autonomous Technologies.* United Nations Institute for Disarmament Research.

United Nations Department of Economic and Social Affairs. (2024). E-Government survey 2024: A digital government model framework for sustainable development. *UN Publications.* https://desapublications.un.org/sites/default/files/publications/2024-09/E-Government_Survey_2024.pdfDESA Publications

United Nations. (2020). E-Government Survey 2020 Digital Government in the Decade of Action for Sustainable Development With addendum on COVID-19 Response. https://publicadministration.un.org/egovkb/Portals/egovkb/Documents/un/2020-Survey/2020 UN E-Government Survey (Full Report).pdf

United Nations. (2020). *E-Government Survey 2020: Digital Government in the Decade of Action for Sustainable Development.* United Nations.

United Nations. (2022). E-Government Development Index: Trends and Analysis.

United Nations. (2022). E-Government Survey 2022 The Future of Digital Government. https://desapublications.un.org/sites/default/files/publications/2022-09/Web version E-Government 2022.pdf

United Nations. (2024). E-Government Survey 2024 Department of Economic and Social Affairs Accelerating Digital Transformation for Sustainable Development. https://www.unsdsn.org/resources/the-sustainable-development-report-2024/?gad_source=1&gad_campaignid=13253704546&gbraid=0AAAABdu6wyw9vKRJNI8dFZR-maQbMFcW&gclid=CjwKCAiA55rJBhByEiwAFkY1QLudyWMeUkXsVieJ_eKGesxIV8PJCQ0NPaj7ogiwIhDYWfuKJS-n8hoCdaMQAvD_BwE

United Nations. (2024). E-Government Survey 2024: Accelerating Digital Transformation for Sustainable Development with the addendum on Artificial Intelligence

Üstüner, M. (1995). Kamu Yönetiminde Kimlik Arayışı ve Yeni Kamu Yönetimi Hareketi. *Ankara Üniversitesi Siyasal Bilgiler Fakültesi Dergisi*, *50*(3), 89–103.

Valentine, S. (2019). Impoverished algorithms: Misguided governments, flawed technologies, and social control. *The Fordham Urban Law Journal*, *46*, 364.

Valle-Cruz, D., Alejandro Ruvalcaba-Gomez, E., Sandoval-Almazan, R., & Ignacio Criado, J. (2019). A review of artificial intelligence in government and its potential from a public policy perspective. In *Proceedings of the 20th annual international conference on digital government research* (pp. 91-99). DOI: 10.1145/3325112.3325242

Valle-Cruz, D., Criado, J. I., Sandoval-Almazán, R., & Ruvalcaba-Gomez, E. A. (2020). Assessing the public policy-cycle framework in the age of artificial intelligence: From agenda-setting to policy evaluation. *Government Information Quarterly*, *37*(4), 1–12. DOI: 10.1016/j.giq.2020.101509

van Eck, M., & Leurs, K. (2020). Data justice and the welfare state: Lessons from the Dutch SyRI case. *Internet Policy Review*, *9*(4).

Van Noordt, C., & Misuraca, G. (2019). New wine in old bottles: Chatbots in government – Exploring the transformative impact of chatbots in public service delivery Proceedings of the 11th IFIP WG 8.5 international conference on electronic participation, Springer, pp. 49-59.

Van Noordt, C., & Misuraca, G. (2022). Artificial intelligence for the public sector: Results of landscaping the use of AI in government across the European Union. *Government Information Quarterly*, *39*(3), 101714. DOI: 10.1016/j.giq.2022.101714 van Noordt, C., & Tangi, L. (2023). The dynamics of AI capability and its influence on public value creation of AI within public administration. *Government Information Quarterly*, *40*(4), 1–14. DOI: 10.1016/j.giq.2023.101860

Veale, M., & Brass, I. (2019). Administration by algorithm? Public management meets algorithmic governance. *Public Administration Review*, *79*(4), 567–581.

Veale, M., & Brass, I. (2019). Administration by algorithm? Public management meets public sector machine learning. In Lodge, M., & Wegrich, K. (Eds.), *The problem-solving capacity of the modern state* (pp. 413–432). Oxford University Press. DOI: 10.31235/osf.io/mwhnb

Veale, M., & Brass, I. (2019). Administration by Algorithm? Public Management Meets Public Sector Machine Learning. *Public Administration Review*, *79*(6), 811–825.

Veebel, V. (2009). Estonia's Involvment in eu Policy-Making. In Lisonova, Z. (Ed.), *Preference Formation in the New eu Member States* (pp. 53–73). Comenius University.

Velsberg, O., Westergren, U. H., & Jonsson, K. (2020). Exploring smartness in public sector innovation-creating smart public services with the Internet of Things. *European Journal of Information Systems*, *29*(4), 350–368. DOI: 10.1080/0960085X.2020.1761272

Verma, S., Kumar Pathak, S., Chaudhary, P., Yadav, P., & Yousuf, S. (2024). Land Registry System Using Blockchain Technology. *2024 International Conference on Emerging Innovations and Advanced Computing (INNOCOMP)*, 170–177. DOI: 10.1109/INNOCOMP63224.2024.00035

Vesnic-Alujevic, L., Nascimento, S., & Polvora, A. (2020). Societal and ethical impacts of artificial intelligence: Critical notes on European policy frameworks. *Telecommunications Policy*, *44*(6), 1–14. DOI: 10.1016/j.telpol.2020.101961

Vial, G. (2019). Understanding digital transformation: A review and a research agenda. *The Journal of Strategic Information Systems*, *28*(2), 118–144. DOI: 10.1016/j.jsis.2019.01.003

Viana, A. C. A. (2021). Digital transformation in public administration: from e-Government to digital government. *International Journal of digital law, 1*(1), 29-44.

Villegas Tovar, R., & Marcos Recio, J. C. (2019). Information intermediaries within the open government model. *Ibersid*, *13*(1), 37–42.

Virtanen, P., & Jalonen, H. (2023). Public value creation mechanisms in the context of public service logic: An integrated conceptual framework. *Public Management Review*, *26*(8), 2331–2354. DOI: 10.1080/14719037.2023.2268111

Viscusi, G., Spahiu, B., Maurino, A., & Batini, C. (2014). Compliance with open government data policies: An empirical assessment of Italian local public administrations. *Information Polity*, *19*(3–4), 263–275. DOI: 10.3233/IP-140338

Vrabie, C. (2023). E-Government 3.0: An AI model to use for enhanced local democracies. *Sustainability (Basel)*, *15*(12), 9572. DOI: 10.3390/su15129572

Vujković, P., Ravšelj, D., Umek, L., & Aristovnik, A. (2022). Bibliometric Analysis of Smart Public Governance Research: Smart City and Smart Government in Comparative Perspective. *Social Sciences (Basel, Switzerland)*, *11*(7), 293. Advance online publication. DOI: 10.3390/socsci11070293

Vuorikari, R., Kluzer, S., & Punie, Y. (2022). *European Digital Competence Framework for the Public Sector: DigCompOrg*. Publications Office of the European Union.

Waldo, D. (1948). *The administrative state: A study of the political theory of American public administration*. Ronald Press.

Wang, C. W., Hsu, B. Y., & Chen, D. Y. (2024). Chatbot applications in government frontline services: Leveraging artificial intelligence and data governance to reduce problems and increase effectiveness. *Asia Pacific Journal of Public Administration*, *46*(4), 488–511. DOI: 10.1080/23276665.2024.2397677

Wang, X., Liu, Y., Zhang, H., Ma, Q., & Cao, Z. (2018). Public Health Emergency Management and Multi-Source Data Technology in China. *Intelligent Automation & Soft Computing*, *24*(1), 89–96. DOI: 10.1080/10798587.2016.1267246

Wang, Y., Zhang, N., & Zhao, X. (2022). Understanding the determinants in the different government AI adoption stages: Evidence of local government chatbots in China. *Social Science Computer Review*, *40*(2), 534–554. DOI: 10.1177/0894439320980132

Warschauer, M. (2004). *Technology and social inclusion: Rethinking the digital divide*. MIT press.

Wattoo, M. U., Du, J., Shahzad, F., & Kousar, S. (2025). Shaping E-commerce Experiences: Unraveling the Impact of Service Quality on Youth Customer Behavior in a Developing Nation. *SAGE Open*, *15*(1), 21582440241311786. Advance online publication. DOI: 10.1177/21582440241311786

Weigl, L., Roth, T., Amard, A., & Zavolokina, L. (2024). When public values and user-centricity in e-government collide – A systematic review [Review of When public values and user-centricity in e-government collide – A systematic review]. Government Information Quarterly, 41(3), 101956. Elsevier BV. DOI: 10.1016/j.giq.2024.101956

Weingärtner, T., Batista, D., Köchli, S., & Voutat, G. (2021). Prototyping a Smart Contract Based Public Procurement to Fight Corruption. *Computers*, *10*(7), 85. DOI: 10.3390/computers10070085

West, S. M., Whittaker, M., & Crawford, K. (2019). *Discriminating Systems: Gender, Race, and Power in AI*. AI Now Institute.

WHO. (2021). *Ethics and Governance of Artificial Intelligence for Health: WHO Guidance*. World Health Organization.

Wibowo, H. A. (2025). An Explication Of How Website Design Actually Shapes Online Customer Loyalty: Incorporating Sem And Person-Items Map Analysis. *International Journal of Social Service and Research*, *5*(1), 123–135. DOI: 10.46799/ijssr.v5i1.1190

Wiethölter, J., Kühl, L., & Feldmann, C. (2024). AI-based chatbots as enabler for efficient external knowledge management in public administration. In Proceedings of the 7th Conference on Legal and Administrative Informatics (RVI 2024): New Approaches to Collaboration and Networking for Digital Transformation and Administrative Modernization (pp. 149–160). Gesellschaft für Informatik e.V. DOI: 10.18420/rvi2024-12

Wilner, A., & Roy, M. (2020). Canada's emerging foresight landscape: Observations and lessons. *Foresight*, *22*(5/6), 551–562. DOI: 10.1108/FS-03-2020-0027

Wirtz, B. W., & Birkmeyer, S. (2015). Open Government: Origin, Development, and Conceptual Perspectives. *International Journal of Public Administration*, *38*(5), 381–396. DOI: 10.1080/01900692.2014.942735

Wirtz, B. W., Daiser, P., & Mermann, M. (2018). Social Media as a Leverage Strategy for Open Government: An Exploratory Study. *International Journal of Public Administration*, *41*(8), 590–603. DOI: 10.1080/01900692.2017.1289388

Wirtz, B. W., & Müller, W. M. (2019). An integrated artificial intelligence framework for public management. *Public Management Review*, *21*(7), 1076–1100. DOI: 10.1080/14719037.2018.1549268

Wirtz, B. W., Müller, W. M., Weyerer, J. C., & Geyer, C. (2020). Public Administration in the Age of Artificial Intelligence. *Public Management Review*, *22*(5), 733–751.

Wirtz, B. W., Weyerer, J. C., Becker, M., & Müller, W. M. (2022). Open government data: A systematic literature review of empirical research. *Electronic Markets*, *32*(4), 2381–2404. DOI: 10.1007/s12525-022-00582-8 PMID: 36158525

Wirtz, B. W., Weyerer, J. C., & Geyer, C. (2019). Artificial Intelligence and the Public Sector—Applications and Challenges. *International Journal of Public Administration*, *42*(7), 596–615. DOI: 10.1080/01900692.2018.1498103

Wirtz, B. W., Weyerer, J. C., & Geyer, C. (2020). Artificial Intelligence and the Public Sector Applications and Challenges. *International Journal of Public Administration*, *43*(9), 816–830.

Wirtz, B. W., Weyerer, J. C., & Sturm, B. J. (2019). AI in e-governance: A review. *Government Information Quarterly*, *36*(2), 201–209.

Wirtz, B. W., Weyerer, J. C., & Sturm, B. J. (2020). The dark sides of artificial intelligence: An integrated AI governance framework for public administration. *International Journal of Public Administration*, *43*(9), 818–829. DOI: 10.1080/01900692.2020.1749851

Wolniak, R., & Stecuła, K. (2024). Artificial intelligence in smart cities—applications, barriers, and future directions: A review. *Smart Cities*, *7*(3), 1346–1389. DOI: 10.3390/smartcities7030057

Wong, S. L., Liu, H. T., & Cheng, L. J. (2011). Elucidating the relationship between satisfaction and citizen involvement in public administration. *Public Management Review*, *13*(4), 595–618. DOI: 10.1080/14719037.2010.525032

World Bank. (2024). Digital Progress and Trends Report 2023. Washington, DC: World Bank. . https://openknowledge.worldbank.org/server/api/core/bitstreams/95fe55e9-f110-4ba8-933f-e65572e05395/contentDOI: 10.1596/978-1-4648-2049-6

Wyatt, S. (2021). Technological determinism is dead; long live technological determinism. In *The Handbook of Science and Technology Studies* (pp. 165–180). MIT Press., DOI: 10.7551/mitpress/9780262539487.003.0009

Xu, J., Xiao, Y., Wang, W., Ning, Y., Shenkman, E., Bian, J., & Wang, F. (2022). Algorithmic fairness in computational medicine. *EBioMedicine*, *84*, 104250. Advance online publication. DOI: 10.1016/j.ebiom.2022.104250 PMID: 36084616

Xu, Y., Gao, W., Wang, Y., Shan, X., & Lin, Y. (2024). Enhancing user experience and trust in advanced LLM-based conversational agents. *Computers and Artificial Intelligence*, 2(2), 1467. DOI: 10.59400/cai.v2i2.1467

Yadav, M., & Banerji, P. (2024). Systematic literature review on Digital Financial Literacy. *SN Business & Economics*, *4*(11), 142. Advance online publication. DOI: 10.1007/s43546-024-00738-y

Yang, L. (2017). Exploring the factors influencing agencies' engagement in open data: A case study of Taichung city government. *Journal of Educational Media and Library Science*, *54*(2), 185. DOI: 10.6120/JoEMLS.2017.542/0026.RS.BM

Yan, Z. (2018). Big data and government governance. In *2018 International Conference on Information Management and Processing (ICIMP)* (pp. 111-114). IEEE. DOI: 10.1109/ICIMP1.2018.8325850

Yavuz, N. (2015). Dijital çağda kamu yönetimi ve e-devlet. *Kamu Yönetimi Dergisi*, *50*(2), 270–285.

Yeung, K. (2019). Regulation by blockchain: The emerging battle for supremacy between the code of law and code as law. *The Modern Law Review*, *82*(2), 207–239. DOI: 10.1111/1468-2230.12399

Yıldız, M. (2014). E-devlet teorisi ve pratiğinin genel bir değerlendirmesi. M. Acar ve H. Özgür (Ed.), Çağdaş Kamu Yönetimi-1 (s. 305-328). İstanbul: Nobel Yayınları.

Yıldız, M. (2007). E-government research: Reviewing the literature, limitations, and ways forward. *Government Information Quarterly*, *24*(3), 646–665. DOI: 10.1016/j.giq.2007.01.002

Yin, R. K. (2009). *Case Study Research: Design and methods*. Sage Publishing.

Young, M., et al. (2019). Artificial intelligence and public standards: A review by the UK Committee on Standards in Public Life.

Young, M. M., Bullock, J. B., & Lecy, J. D. (2019). Artificial discretion as a tool of governance: A framework for understanding the impact of artificial intelligence on public administration. *Perspectives on Public Management and Governance*, *2*(4), 301–313. DOI: 10.1093/ppmgov/gvz014

Yu, M., Yang, C., & Li, Y. (2018). Big data in natural disaster management: A review. *Geosciences*, *8*(5), 165. DOI: 10.3390/geosciences8050165

Yun, C. (2020). Early innovation adoption: Effects of performance-based motivation and organizational characteristics. *Public Performance & Management Review*, *43*(4), 790–817. DOI: 10.1080/15309576.2019.1666725

Zerilli, J., Knott, A., Maclaurin, J., & Gavaghan, C. (2019). Algorithmic Decision-Making and the Control Problem. *Minds and Machines*, *29*(4), 555–578. DOI: 10.1007/s11023-019-09513-7

Zhou, M., Liu, L., & Feng, Y. (2025). Building citizen trust to enhance satisfaction in digital public services: The role of empathetic chatbot communication. *Behaviour & Information Technology*, •••, 1–20. DOI: 10.1080/0144929X.2025.2585328

Zouridis, S., van Eck, M., & Bovens, M. (2020). Automated Discretion. In Evans, T., & Hupe, P. (Eds.), *Discretion and the Quest for Controlled Freedom*. Palgrave Macmillan., DOI: 10.1007/978-3-030-19566-3_20

Zuboff, S. (2019). *The Age of Surveillance Capitalism: The Fight for a Human Future at the New Frontier of Power*. PublicAffairs.

Zuiderwijk, A., Chen, Y. C., & Salem, F. (2021). Implications of the use of artificial intelligence in public governance: A systematic literature review and a research agenda. *Government Information Quarterly*, *38*(3), 101577. DOI: 10.1016/j.giq.2021.101577

About the Contributors

Elvettin Akman graduated from Suleyman Demirel University Faculty of Economics and Administrative Sciences Department of Public Administration in 2007 and completed his Master's degree in Sakarya University Social Sciences Institute Department of Public Administration in 2009. He received his PhD in Suleyman Demirel University Institute of Social Sciences Department of Public Administration in 2015. Akman has been working as a faculty member since 2010, received the title of professor in 2025. His main areas of interest include management, public policy, e-government, governance, local governments and digitalization. Email: elvettinakman@sdu.edu.tr.

Çiğdem Akman graduated from Suleyman Demirel University, Department of Public Administration. She completed her master's degree at Sakarya University at the Institute of Social Sciences, Program of Public Administration. She completed her doctorate at Suleyman Demirel University Institute of Social Sciences Program of Public Finance 2015. She worked as a Lecturer at the Egirdir Vocational School between 2010-2015. In 2016, she was appointed as an assistant professor at the Department of Public Administration at Suleyman Demirel University. Since 2020, she has worked as a professor at Suleyman Demirel University, Department of Political Science and Public Administration. The author has books, many book chapters, and articles on Local Governments, Local Government Finance, E-government, Artificial Intelligence, Government Systems, Policy Boards, Twinning City, and Cittaslow.

***

Andi Asrifan is an accomplished educator and academic leader with a Doctorate in Education, specializing in English Language Education from Universitas Negeri Makassar. With a strong academic foundation, he holds a Master's degree in the same field and a Bachelor's degree in Secondary Education. His dissertation focused on developing bilingual educational materials, reflecting his commitment to enhancing language education. Dr. Asrifan has extensive experience in various educational roles, including serving as the Head of the International Affairs Office at Politeknik Negeri Nunukan and as the Head of the Institute for Student Development and Alumni at Universitas Muhammadiyah Sidenreng Rappang. He is also an active member of several professional organizations, including the Linguistics Society of Indonesia and TEFLIN. In addition to his administrative roles, Dr. Asrifan is a passionate advocate for educational innovation and has participated in numerous international conferences and webinars, sharing his insights on language teaching and curriculum development. His dedication to professional development is evident through his participation in various training programs.

Filomena Buonocore is Full Professor of Organization studies at the University of Naples "Parthenope" and Professor at the Italian National School of Public Administration (SNA). She also serves as a member of the University's Board of Directors and as Vice-Director of the Department of Law. Her research focuses on organizational behavior, human resource management in public administration, job crafting, diversity management, and digital innovation in organizational processes. She has held numerous academic and institutional positions, coordinating and actively participating in nationally and internationally significant research projects. Member of editorial boards of top-tier academic journals and prestigious scholarly associations (AOM, EGOS, ASSIOA), she is committed to promoting inclusion, organizational sustainability, and the dissemination of managerial culture, with strong engagement in both the national and international scientific community.

Davide de Gennaro is an Assistant Professor in Organization Studies at the University of Naples "Parthenope," where he earned his Ph.D. and currently teaches and conducts research on organizational theory and behavior. He is currently collaborating with Formez PA and the Italian Ministry of Justice, and has previously worked with the National School of Administration (SNA) and SDA Bocconi School of Management. His research interests include job crafting, motivation, organizational sustainability, the adoption of artificial intelligence in the public sector, and the ethical management of human resources. He serves as Associate Editor of the Baltic Journal of Management and is actively involved in national and international academic networks. Alongside his scientific work, he is strongly committed to educational innovation and the promotion of organizational transformation within public administration.

Ludovica Del Barone is a PhD candidate in Regulation, Management, and Law of Public Sector Organizations at the University of Salento, with an affiliation to the University of Naples "Parthenope." She holds a Bachelor's degree in Management and a Master's degree in Business Administration. Her research interests primarily concern public administration, performance management, and human resource management practices in public sector organizations.

Hasret Duman completed her undergraduate studies in Political Science and Public Administration at Gazi University. She earned her master's degree in Public Administration at Hacettepe University with a thesis titled "Comparative Analysis of Vaccination-Related Public Policies Around the World: The Case of COVID-19." She is currently pursuing her PhD in Public Administration at Hacettepe University, working on a dissertation titled "The Export of Digital Government Applications in Terms of Public Diplomacy and the Use of Soft Power: Country Case Studies and a Model Proposal for Turkey." She also works as a research assistant at Hatay Mustafa Kemal University. Her research interests include public administration, public policy, and digital technologies in public administration.

Sebiha Düz is a Research Assistant in the Department of Political Science and Public Administration at the Faculty of Economics and Administrative Sciences, Süleyman Demirel University. She has completed her undergraduate education at Ankara University, Department of Political Science and Public Administration on July 20, 2017, and her master's degree with a thesis in Administrative Sciences at Ankara University on June 30, 2021. She is currently continuing her PhD at Süleyman Demirel University, Department of Political Science and Public Administration, where she currently works. Her research interests include digitalization, artificial intelligence strategies, local governments, and public policies.

Veysel Eren completed his undergraduate studies in Public Administration at Selçuk University. He began his academic career in 1995 as a Research Assistant at Niğde University. He earned his MA in 1996 from Selçuk University with a thesis on democracy and participation in local governments, and completed his PhD in 2001 at Sakarya University with a dissertation on New Public Management and municipalities. He became Assistant Professor in 2002 and Associate Professor in 2008 at Niğde University. In 2009, he joined Hatay Mustafa Kemal University as Associate Professor and was promoted to Full Professor in Administrative Sciences in 2014. He has held key administrative roles, including Department Head, Division Chair, Vice Dean, Vice Rector, and University Senate Member. On December 9, 2022, he was appointed Rector of Hatay Mustafa Kemal University. He also served as the President of the 42nd Term of the Interuniversity Board (ÜAK).

Beyza Güdek completed her undergraduate studies in Management Information Systems at Necmettin Erbakan University. She earned her master's degree in the same field at Karadeniz Technical University and is currently pursuing her Ph.D. in Management Information Systems at İzmir Bakırçay University. Her academic interests focus on digital transformation, data science, and the integration of information technologies into business processes.

Yakup Karaca holds a Ph.D. in Public Administration from Muğla Sıtkı Koçman University (2024), an M.A. in Political Science and Public Administration from Aydın Adnan Menderes University (2013), and a B.A. in Public Administration from the Faculty of Economics and Administrative Sciences at the same university (2011). His research interests lie in the fields of public administration, public policy, bureaucracy, governance, constitutional law, local governments, and systems of government. He currently works as a Lecturer at Aydın Adnan Menderes University, Çine Vocational School. He continues his academic activities with a focus on interdisciplinary approaches to governance and policy studies.

Mustafa Kayyali is an ardent advocate for excellence in higher education, driven by a relentless pursuit of quality, recognition, and innovation. Their journey in academia started with a Master's in Quality Management and Evaluation in Higher Education from Universitat Oberta de Catalunya, followed by a Ph.D. in Quality Management from Azteca University. These academic pursuits have laid a strong foundation for their expertise in Accreditation, Quality Assurance, and Higher Education Rankings. As an entrepreneur, researcher, translator, and publisher, they are deeply involved in various facets of the academic world. Their diverse interests encompass Management, Translation, Interpretation, and Academic consulting, contributing to a well-rounded understanding of the industry. Throughout their career, they have made significant contributions to academic literature, with more than 40 published papers and 30 book chapters to my name. Additionally, they take pride in having translated 6 books, bridging language gaps, and promoting knowledge exchange on a global scale. They are committed to fostering positive change in higher education and contributing to its continuous improvement.

Ahmad Luthfi is a Lecturer in the Public Administration Study Program at Universitas Merdeka Malang, Indonesia. He earned both his Bachelor's and Master's degrees in Public Administration from Universitas Hasanuddin, Indonesia. His research interests include governance, public service, public administration, and public sector innovation. In addition to his academic role, he also serves as the Managing Editor of Publisia: Jurnal Ilmu Administrasi Publik, a reputable journal in Indonesia. Beyond teaching and research, he actively participates in various academic forums and community engagement initiatives that focus on improving the quality of public services and promoting adaptive and responsive governance in the face of evolving societal challenges

Namik Kemal Öztürk completed his primary and secondary education in this province. He completed his undergraduate education at Istanbul University Faculty of Political Sciences between 1984-1988. He completed his master's and doctorate education at Dokuz Eylül University, Institute of Social Sciences, Department of Public Administration between 1988-1994. In 1999, he became an Associate Professor in Public Administration and in 2006 he was appointed as a professor in the field of Public Administration “management sciences” at Muğla Sıtkı Koçman University. Öztürk, who has written many books, articles, researches and theses on public administration, bureaucracy, governance, constitution, local governments, performance management, government systems, merit etc., has been continuing his education and training activities at Muğla Sıtkı Koçman University Public Administration Department since 1996.

Çiğdem Pank Yildirim started working as a Research Assistant at Muğla Sıtkı Koçman University in 2011. She completed her master's degree at Muğla Sıtkı Koçman University, Institute of Social Sciences in 2012. She started her doctorate education at Muğla Sıtkı Koçman University, Institute of Social Sciences, Department of Public Administration in September 2012. She completed her doctorate education at Muğla Sıtkı Koçman University, Institute of Social Sciences, Department of Public Administration in 2024. She currently works as a Research Assistant Doctor in the Department of Public Administration, Faculty of Economics and Administrative Sciences, Muğla Sıtkı Koçman University. She has numerous academic studies published on management sciences, local governments, constitutional institutions, and environmental management.

Azaria Eda Pradana, S.AP., M.AP., is a lecturer in the Public Administration Study Program Universitas Diponegoro with a research area in the field of Public Sector Human Resource Management, Environtmental Issues, and Digital Governance. The focus of my studies and research includes His research focuses on how strengthening human resource capacity can drive the effectiveness of environmental policies and how the application of digital technology can improve transparency and accountability in public governance. I'm actively publishes my research results in various national and international journals, and is involved in community service activities that integrate the principles of sustainability and technological innovation in public services.

Rismawati is a distinguished academic and consultant with a robust focus on sustainability reporting. She currently holds the position of lecturer and Head of the Quality Assurance Institute at Universitas Muhammadiyah Palopo, where she has been pivotal in ensuring the quality of university processes and outputs since February 2020. Additionally, she serves as an Assurer for Sustainability Reporting at the National Center for Sustainability Reporting in Jakarta, specializing in the evaluation of sustainability reports for mining companies across Indonesia. Her academic qualifications are extensive, comprising a Bachelor's degree in Economics and Accounting, a Master's degree in Accounting Science, and a Doctorate in Accounting from Universitas Brawijaya, Malang. Rismawati is also a certified specialist in sustainability reporting, risk management, and tax planning, holding several prestigious certifications including Certified Sustainability Reporting Specialist (CSRS), Certified Risk Management Practitioner (CRMP), Certified Management Accountant (CMA) and Certified Enterprise Risk Analysis (CERA). In her professional capacity, she has provided consultancy services in financial management and tax compliance for companies such as PT. Reski Barito Timur and PT. Helay Raya. Furthermore, she has authored multiple publications on Social Accounting, Sustainability Accounting, Management Accounting and CSR, contributing significantly to the academic community. Her interests in reading, writing, and travel reflect her commitment to lifelong learning and professional growth in her field.

Ali Roziqin is a Lecturer in the Department of Government Studies, Universitas Muhammadiyah Malang, Indonesia. He obtained his bachelor's degree from the Department of Public Administration at Universitas Diponegoro, Indonesia. He holds a Master of Public Administration from the Universitas Gadjah Mada, Indonesia. His research interests are in bureaucracy, public policy and administration, and public sector innovation. He has published papers in the reputable international journals like Sustainability (MDPI), Local Environment (Taylor and Francis), Tourism Critiques, Journal of Science and Technology Policy Management, Journal of the Knowledge Economy, Frontiers in Communication and Public Administration and Policy: An Asia-Pacific Journal, as well as in the IGI Global

M. Ihwan Salsabila is research assistant the Department of Government Studies, Universitas Muhammadiyah Malang. He has several experiences in research. He has also published articles in some national journals.

M. Husni Tamrin is a scholar and public administration expert currently serving as the Dean of the Faculty of Social and Political Sciences at Hang Tuah University, Surabaya. His academic interests span public policy, governance, community empowerment, and sustainable marine ecotourism. Known for his collaborative leadership, he bridges academic research with practical solutions for public issues. He earned his Bachelor's degree in Public Administration from Hang Tuah University, continued with a Master's in Public Policy at Airlangga University, and is now completing his Doctoral studies in Administrative Sciences at Padjadjaran University, focusing on intergovernmental management and policies for protecting Indonesian migrant workers abroad. In his role as educator and researcher, Husni has led various initiatives including training programs for local entrepreneurs, student organization development, and multi-sectoral policy discussions. His work is grounded in the Penta Helix and Collaborative Governance frameworks, emphasizing education as a driver of inclusive and impactful public transformation.

Tangguh Okta Wibowo earned his Master's and Doctoral degrees from the Cultural and Media Studies at Universitas Gadjah Mada (UGM), Yogyakarta. His research interests include cyber culture, critical advertising studies, and prosumerism. He is currently pursuing a career as a lecturer at Universitas Multimedia Nusantara, Tangerang, in the Communication Science.

Index

A

AI Chatbots 230, 291
Algorithmic Bias 54, 65, 72, 75, 76, 81, 92, 136, 181, 182, 183, 184, 185, 186, 188, 190, 191, 192, 193, 194, 195, 196, 198, 200, 201, 202, 203, 204, 205, 235, 237, 257, 259, 261, 270, 275, 276, 311, 317
Algorithmic Decision-Making 77, 82, 136, 144, 162, 164, 165, 182, 185, 189, 206, 248, 270
Algorithmic Neutrality 220, 225, 234
Artificial Intelligence 1, 2, 3, 5, 7, 14, 19, 20, 21, 22, 23, 24, 25, 27, 28, 29, 30, 31, 32, 35, 36, 43, 46, 50, 52, 53, 54, 56, 59, 60, 61, 62, 65, 66, 67, 68, 72, 75, 77, 79, 80, 81, 83, 84, 85, 86, 88, 89, 90, 96, 105, 106, 110, 112, 113, 119, 120, 123, 124, 127, 128, 129, 139, 140, 141, 142, 144, 145, 147, 148, 149, 150, 151, 153, 154, 155, 158, 165, 168, 169, 172, 174, 176, 177, 178, 179, 180, 181, 182, 183, 191, 193, 201, 202, 203, 204, 206, 207, 209, 224, 230, 231, 232, 233, 235, 236, 243, 245, 247, 250, 257, 259, 262, 263, 264, 265, 266, 267, 269, 270, 291, 292, 293, 294, 295, 296, 297, 298, 299, 301, 302, 303, 304, 305, 306, 307, 308, 309, 310, 311, 312, 313, 314, 315, 316, 317, 318, 320, 321, 322, 323, 324, 325, 326, 327, 328
Artificial Intelligence Adoption 148, 231, 296
Artificial Intelligence and Big Data 61, 67, 72, 113, 129, 139, 142, 145
Artificial Intelligence Strategy 141, 151, 243, 245, 301, 302, 303, 304, 306, 307, 308, 325

B

Bibliometric Analysis 2, 12, 13, 19, 22, 28, 59, 93, 98, 118, 121
Big Data 1, 2, 3, 5, 7, 8, 9, 14, 24, 25, 28, 29, 35, 36, 39, 50, 51, 53, 54, 58, 59, 60, 61, 62, 63, 66, 67, 68, 72, 81, 93, 113, 116, 117, 118, 123, 124, 127, 128, 129, 130, 136, 139, 142, 143, 145, 149, 202, 203, 204, 205, 248, 294, 296, 297, 305, 313, 319, 324
Blockchain 1, 2, 3, 5, 6, 9, 12, 14, 24, 27, 29, 30, 31, 32, 33, 35, 36, 50, 52, 56, 58, 59, 61, 65, 66, 73, 74, 79, 81, 83, 84, 89, 91, 92, 112, 127, 128, 144, 151, 241, 299, 319, 324

C

Case Study 85, 87, 89, 121, 208, 220, 232, 269, 272, 274, 280, 281, 285, 288, 289, 295, 296, 299
Citizen Engagement 36, 52, 68, 94, 97, 107, 108, 140, 144, 231, 236, 237, 240, 259, 269, 270, 271, 272, 274, 277, 278, 283, 284, 289, 313
Citizen Participation 1, 2, 25, 35, 37, 40, 49, 51, 52, 53, 56, 94, 107, 108, 109, 110, 126, 129, 130, 131, 146, 177, 199, 211, 212, 217, 227, 230, 250, 259, 289, 293, 319

D

Data-Based Decision 2, 4, 24, 145, 207
Data-Driven Decision-Making 3, 51, 53, 114, 126, 128, 132, 139, 183, 220, 224, 269, 271
Digital Governance 9, 16, 36, 54, 67, 74, 75, 77, 78, 79, 80, 81, 87, 107, 108, 123, 125, 126, 127, 134, 136, 137, 157, 235, 236, 241, 243, 244, 247, 248, 256, 257, 259, 260, 261, 274, 289
Digital Government 9, 19, 31, 35, 36, 42, 43, 44, 45, 48, 55, 56, 57, 58, 61, 62, 65, 66, 72, 74, 75, 76, 77, 78, 79, 81, 82, 83, 85, 89, 90, 91, 92, 106, 127,

131, 133, 138, 144, 150, 151, 230, 232, 244, 267, 286, 294, 326
Digital Inclusion 70, 88, 115, 129, 133, 135, 146, 151, 174, 180, 232, 249, 258, 265
Digital Transformation 1, 2, 3, 4, 5, 7, 8, 9, 12, 13, 14, 15, 16, 17, 18, 19, 20, 21, 22, 23, 24, 25, 26, 27, 28, 29, 30, 31, 32, 35, 36, 37, 38, 39, 41, 42, 43, 46, 48, 49, 50, 54, 55, 56, 57, 61, 62, 65, 67, 68, 69, 76, 77, 78, 79, 81, 82, 84, 85, 86, 87, 105, 106, 117, 123, 125, 129, 131, 132, 133, 134, 135, 136, 137, 138, 139, 141, 142, 144, 146, 147, 150, 178, 179, 200, 207, 208, 209, 210, 212, 222, 224, 227, 228, 233, 236, 242, 244, 250, 256, 257, 259, 260, 261, 262, 263, 267, 270, 271, 272, 273, 281, 283, 284, 285, 286, 287, 288, 291, 294, 295, 297, 299

E

E-Government 1, 2, 4, 8, 19, 20, 21, 22, 23, 24, 25, 27, 29, 31, 32, 35, 36, 39, 40, 41, 42, 43, 44, 45, 46, 48, 55, 56, 58, 59, 60, 61, 62, 63, 65, 66, 67, 70, 75, 76, 78, 81, 86, 90, 91, 94, 105, 110, 118, 119, 127, 128, 138, 141, 148, 149, 151, 212, 224, 230, 232, 242, 249, 250, 262, 264, 265, 267, 288, 291, 293, 296, 298, 314, 324, 326
Ethical Governance 26, 72, 78, 124, 129, 135, 136, 141, 145, 146, 166, 168, 236, 285

G

Governance 2, 3, 4, 6, 7, 8, 9, 10, 16, 19, 20, 21, 23, 24, 25, 26, 27, 28, 29, 31, 35, 36, 37, 38, 39, 40, 43, 44, 45, 49, 51, 53, 54, 56, 57, 58, 59, 60, 61, 62, 65, 66, 67, 68, 69, 70, 71, 72, 73, 74, 75, 76, 77, 78, 79, 80, 81, 82, 85, 86, 87, 88, 89, 91, 92, 94, 95, 97, 101, 104, 107, 108, 112, 113, 115, 118, 121, 123, 124, 125, 126, 127, 128, 129, 130, 131, 132, 133, 134, 135, 136, 137, 139, 140, 141, 142, 143, 144, 145, 146, 148, 149, 150, 151, 153, 154, 155, 156, 157, 164, 165, 166, 168, 169, 170, 171, 172, 173, 174, 175, 176, 177, 178, 179, 180, 181, 194, 195, 197, 198, 200, 205, 207, 208, 210, 211, 214, 215, 216, 217, 218, 220, 222, 227, 228, 229, 232, 234, 235, 236, 237, 238, 239, 240, 241, 242, 243, 244, 245, 246, 247, 248, 250, 255, 256, 257, 258, 259, 260, 261, 262, 264, 265, 266, 267, 269, 270, 271, 272, 273, 274, 275, 276, 278, 279, 280, 281, 283, 284, 285, 286, 287, 288, 289, 290, 291, 294, 295, 298, 299, 304, 308, 312, 318, 319, 322, 324, 325, 327
Governance Ethics 140, 144
Governance Innovation 60, 66, 74

H

Human-Centric AI 243

I

Institutional Capacity 8, 96, 108, 125, 131, 133, 141, 195, 199, 207, 211, 212, 218, 220, 223, 227, 234

K

Knowledge Management 233

L

Local Innovation 66

O

Open Government Data 41, 44, 56, 93, 94, 95, 97, 98, 99, 100, 101, 103, 104, 105, 106, 107, 109, 110, 111, 113, 114, 116, 117, 118, 119, 120, 121, 131, 230, 293
Organizational Dynamics 269, 280, 285

P

Public Administration 1, 2, 3, 4, 5, 6, 7, 8, 9, 12, 13, 14, 15, 16, 17, 18, 19, 20, 21, 22, 23, 24, 25, 26, 27, 28, 29, 30, 31, 32, 35, 36, 37, 38, 39, 40, 41, 42, 43, 45, 49, 51, 52, 53, 54, 55, 56, 57, 58, 59, 60, 61, 62, 65, 66, 67, 68, 69, 70, 73, 74, 77, 83, 84, 86, 91, 92, 93, 94, 95, 98, 100, 101, 103, 104, 105, 106, 107, 108, 109, 112, 113, 114, 115, 116, 118, 119, 121, 124, 125, 126, 127, 128, 129, 130, 132, 133, 134, 135, 136, 137, 138, 139, 140, 141, 142, 143, 144, 145, 146, 148, 149, 151, 153, 154, 155, 156, 157, 162, 165, 166, 167, 168, 169, 170, 171, 172, 173, 174, 175, 176, 177, 178, 179, 180, 181, 182, 183, 191, 194, 195, 196, 198, 199, 200, 202, 205, 207, 208, 209, 210, 211, 215, 216, 217, 218, 220, 222, 228, 230, 232, 233, 235, 236, 238, 240, 257, 259, 261, 262, 263, 265, 267, 269, 270, 271, 272, 273, 274, 275, 276, 277, 278, 279, 280, 281, 283, 284, 285, 286, 287, 288, 289, 290, 291, 292, 293, 294, 295, 296, 297, 298, 299, 302, 303, 307, 308, 312, 313, 314, 316, 318, 319, 327

Public Sector Innovation 16, 52, 62, 67, 68, 94, 131, 150, 273, 287

Public Services 2, 4, 5, 6, 7, 9, 19, 20, 22, 23, 24, 26, 29, 31, 32, 35, 36, 38, 39, 40, 41, 42, 43, 45, 46, 48, 51, 52, 53, 54, 55, 56, 62, 66, 67, 68, 70, 73, 76, 77, 85, 86, 90, 94, 97, 98, 112, 113, 118, 123, 124, 126, 127, 128, 129, 130, 131, 132, 135, 136, 137, 138, 139, 141, 142, 143, 145, 147, 150, 153, 158, 159, 160, 161, 162, 165, 168, 172, 174, 175, 179, 181, 195, 198, 200, 207, 208, 209, 210, 211, 212, 215, 216, 217, 220, 225, 226, 227, 230, 231, 232, 233, 234, 236, 237, 241, 242, 247, 249, 255, 258, 259, 262, 265, 274, 275, 277, 278, 279, 286, 291, 292, 294, 295, 301, 302, 303, 304, 307, 308, 313, 316, 317, 318, 320, 321, 324, 327

Public Value 2, 4, 9, 23, 38, 52, 58, 65, 73, 76, 79, 80, 81, 90, 91, 92, 123, 124, 125, 126, 127, 128, 129, 130, 131, 132, 133, 134, 135, 137, 138, 139, 140, 141, 142, 144, 145, 146, 147, 148, 150, 151, 207, 208, 210, 212, 215, 217, 219, 220, 225, 226, 227, 228, 229, 230, 232, 233, 234, 237, 264, 293, 298

S

Smart Government 27, 113, 121

Social Justice 37, 80, 82, 123, 124, 129, 136, 137, 144, 181

T

Transparency 2, 3, 4, 6, 12, 24, 26, 29, 31, 35, 36, 37, 38, 39, 40, 43, 45, 48, 49, 51, 52, 53, 54, 56, 65, 66, 67, 68, 71, 72, 73, 74, 76, 77, 78, 79, 81, 82, 88, 92, 93, 94, 95, 96, 97, 98, 104, 106, 107, 108, 109, 110, 112, 113, 114, 116, 119, 120, 123, 124, 126, 128, 129, 130, 132, 133, 136, 137, 140, 141, 144, 146, 148, 153, 154, 157, 164, 165, 166, 167, 168, 170, 171, 174, 175, 177, 178, 180, 182, 190, 192, 193, 194, 195, 197, 198, 199, 200, 202, 203, 209, 210, 212, 217, 218, 222, 223, 225, 226, 228, 229, 234, 238, 244, 245, 250, 257, 260, 270, 273, 274, 275, 276, 277, 278, 279, 281, 283, 284, 285, 286, 287, 288, 290, 317, 323

www.ingramcontent.com/pod-product-compliance
Lightning Source LLC
LaVergne TN
LVHW081544300926
849161LV00006B/1515